Visual Word Recognition

Word recognition is the component of reading which involves the identification of individual words. Together the two volumes of *Visual Word Recognition* offer a state-of-the-art overview of contemporary research from leading figures in the field.

This second volume examines how research on word recognition has been linked to the study of concepts and meaning, such as how morphemes affect word recognition, how the meaning of words affects their processing and the effect of priming on the processing of words.

The book also discusses eye-movement research, the reading of whole sentences and passages, how bilinguals recognize words in different languages, individual differences in visual word recognition, and the development of visual word recognition and difficulties in developmental dyslexia.

The two volumes serve as a state-of-the-art, comprehensive overview of the field. They are essential reading for researchers of visual word recognition, and students on undergraduate and postgraduate courses in cognition and cognitive psychology, specifically the psychology of language and reading. They will also be of use to those working in education and speech-language therapy.

James S. Adelman first became involved in visual word recognition research whilst reading for a degree in Mathematics and Psychology at the University of Liverpool. From there, he went on to complete a PhD and various externally funded research projects at the University of Warwick, where he has been an Assistant Professor since 2010.

Current Issues in the Psychology of Language
Series Editor: Trevor A. Harley

Current Issues in the Psychology of Language is a series of edited books that will reflect the state-of-the-art in areas of current and emerging interest in the psychological study of language.

Each volume is tightly focused on a particular topic and consists of seven to ten chapters contributed by international experts. The editors of individual volumes are leading figures in their areas and provide an introductory overview.

Example topics include: language development, bilingualism and second language acquisition, word recognition, word meaning, text processing, the neuroscience of language, and language production, as well as the inter-relations between these topics.

Visual Word Recognition Volume 1
Edited by James S. Adelman

Visual Word Recognition Volume 2
Edited by James S. Adelman

Forthcoming Titles:

Sentence Processing
Edited by Roger van Gompel

Visual Word Recognition

Volume 2

Meaning and context, individuals
and development

**Edited by
James S. Adelman**

 Psychology Press
Taylor & Francis Group

LONDON AND NEW YORK

First edition published 2012
27 Church Road, Hove, East Sussex, BN3 2FA

Simultaneously published in the USA and Canada
by Psychology Press
711 Third Avenue, New York, NY 10017

Psychology Press is an imprint of the Taylor & Francis Group, an informa business

© 2012 Psychology Press

British Library Cataloguing in Publication Data
A catalogue record for this book is available from the British Library

Library of Congress Cataloging-in-Publication Data
Visual word recognition: Models and methods, orthography and phonology /
    Edited by James S. Adelman, University of Warwick.
        pages cm
    Includes bibliographical references and index.
    ISBN 978-1-84872-058-9 (hb)
    1. Word recognition. I. Adelman, James S.
    LB1050.44.V57   2012
    372.46'2—dc23   2012000617

ISBN13: 978-1-84872-059-6 (hbk)
ISBN13: 978-0-20310-697-6 (ebk)

Typeset in Times New Roman
by Cenveo Publisher Services

MIX
Paper from
responsible sources
FSC
www.fsc.org   FSC® C004839

Printed and bound in Great Britain by
CPI Group (UK) Ltd, Croydon, CR0 4YY

Contents

List of Figures

List of Tables

List of Contributors

James S. Adelman, Department of Psychology, University of Warwick, Gibbet Hill Road, Coventry CV4 7AL, UK

Yusra Ahmed, Florida State University, Department of Psychology, 1107 W. Call Street, Tallahassee, FL 32306, USA

Sally Andrews, School of Psychology, Brennan MacCallum Building (A18), The University of Sydney, NSW 2006, Australia

Anne E. Cunningham, Graduate School of Education, Tolman Hall, University of California, Berkeley, Berkeley, CA 94720-1670, USA

Zachary Estes, Department of Psychology, University of Warwick, Gibbet Hill Road, COVENTRY, CV4 7AL, UK

Laurie Beth Feldman, Haskins Laboratories, 300 George Street, New Haven, CT 06511, USA

Julian Hester, Department of Psychology, University of Potsdam, Karl-Liebknecht-Str. 24–25, 14476 Potsdam, Germany

Lara L. Jones, Department of Psychology, Wayne State University, 5057 Woodward Ave., Detroit, MI 48202, USA

Patricia Thatcher Kantor, Florida State University, Department of Psychology, 1107 W. Call Street, Tallahassee, FL 32306, USA

Reinhold Kliegl, Department of Psychology, University of Potsdam, Karl-Liebknecht-Str. 24–25, 14476 Potsdam, Germany

Nicola A. McClung, Graduate School of Education, Tolman Hall, University of California, Berkeley, Berkeley, CA 94720-1670, USA

Colleen R. O'Donnell, Graduate School of Education, Tolman Hall, University of California, Berkeley, Berkeley, CA 94720-1670, USA

Penny Pexman, Department of Psychology, University of Calgary, 2500 University Dr. NW, Calgary, Alberta, T2N 1N4, Canada

Keith Rayner, Department of Psychology, University of California, San Diego, 9500 Gilman Drive, La Jolla, CA 92093, USA

Elizabeth R. Schotter, Department of Psychology, University of California, San Diego, 9500 Gilman Drive, La Jolla, CA 92093, USA

Ana I. Schwartz, Department of Psychology, University of Texas at El Paso, 500 W. University Ave., El Paso, TX 79902, USA

John F. Stein, Department of Physiology, Anatomy and Genetics, Le Gros Clark Building, South Parks Road, Oxford OX1 3QX, UK

Janet G. van Hell, Department of Psychology, Pennsylvania State University, 619 Moore Building, University Park, PA 16802, USA

Richard K. Wagner, Florida State University, Department of Psychology, 1107 W. Call Street, Tallahassee, FL 32306, USA

Katherine Weber, Haskins Laboratories, 300 George Street, New Haven, CT 06511, USA

Kay-Michael Würzner, Department of Psychology, University of Potsdam, Karl-Liebknecht-Str. 24–25, 14476 Potsdam, Germany

Acknowledgments

I thank the contributors for their efforts, Suzanne Marquis for her aid in reminding contributors of their promises and Julia Carroll for additional comments on some chapters. Preparation of this book was supported in part by Economic and Social Research Council (UK) grant RES-062-23-0545. Figures 7.1 and 7.2 are adapted from Andrews S. and Hersch, J. (2010). Lexical precision in skilled readers: Individual differences in masked neighbor priming. Adapted with permission from *Journal of Experimental Psychology: General, 139*, 299–318, published by American Psychological Association.

Introduction

James S. Adelman

Words are the building blocks of language, and are the interface between written and spoken language. Recognition of the printed word is both essential to the important skill of reading and among the easiest routes for the experimenter to access higher cognition. In this light, it is little surprise that the identification and pronunciation of written (or more often, printed) words are among the earliest studied (Cattell, 1886) and most studied aspects of cognition.

Visual word recognition is studied both in its own right, in terms of the processes of recognizing a word and the performance of word-based tasks, but also more broadly in context as a link to semantics and concepts, cognitive individual differences, reading prose and learning to read. This volume concentrates on the latter, broader, form of study of visual word recognition, whilst its companion concentrates on the former, narrower form of study.

The first three chapters consider how written words link to their meanings, and how those meanings affect the recognition of those words. In Chapter 1, Feldman and Weber argue that morphological processing is best characterized within a single graded mechanism that incorporates both meaning and form from the earliest stages. In Chapter 2, Pexman discusses a variety of meaning-based variables that are known to affect word recognition, and what they mean for the processing of words. In Chapter 3, Jones and Estes review lexical priming effects, where word recognition is influenced by a preceding, related, word context, and what this means for the organization of concepts.

Chapters 4 and 5 consider how words are recognized within sentences, as evidenced by eye movements. In Chapter 4, Schotter and Rayner review the experimental evidence, and argue it is consistent with the idea that the reading system operates on a serial, word-by-word basis. In Chapter 5, Kliegl and colleagues consider the analysis of large databases of eye-movement data, and argue that parafoveal effects are evidence for concurrent processing of words.

The remaining chapters consider a variety of issues surrounding how individuals differ and how reading develops. In Chapter 6, Schwartz and van Hell consider how knowing more than one language affects word recognition in sentence context. In Chapter 7, Andrews considers individual differences among skilled readers, and argues that they may be interpreted in terms of lexical quality: how precisely words are represented. In Chapter 8, Cunningham and colleagues argue that orthographic learning, improving the orthographic dimension lexical quality, is a major (and often overlooked) aspect of reading development. In Chapter 9, Wagner and colleagues discuss developmental dyslexia from a cognitive perspective that emphasizes the role phonological processing has in reading development and impairment. In Chapter 10, Stein considers the biological bases of developmental dyslexia and argues that visual-orthographic processes are impaired and phonological impairments are markers not causes of impaired reading.

In sum, these chapters cover the key issues involved in understanding the processing of the written word in the context of reading and its development.

Visual word recognizers come in sizes big and small.

References

Cattell, J. M. (1886). The time taken up by cerebral operations. *Mind, 11*, 377–92. Retrieved from http://psychclassics.yorku.ca

1 Morphological processing

A comparison of graded and categorical accounts

Laurie Beth Feldman and Katherine Weber

Debate between single- and dual-route accounts of language processing plays out in the morphological domain as it does in the phonological domain (cf. Coltheart, accompanying volume, Chapter 1). For this reason, morphological processing has gained attention in recent years. At issue is whether there are two distinct and independent mechanisms for recognizing a word or whether lexical and sublexical contributions work cooperatively and interdependently and comprise a single mechanism. Cast in phonological terms, words can be either regular, in that they respect a mapping between orthographic and phonological units that can be characterized by correspondence rule or they can be irregular, in which case they do not and must be learned by association among whole-word orthographic and phonological forms. By a dual mechanism account, either the sublexical (rule based) or the lexical (associative) alternative can apply to regular words. This is not the case for irregular words where the sole option is lexical. In essence, by a dual mechanism account, the choice of mechanism depends on whether a word belongs to the *regular* or *irregular category* and, importantly, the options cannot operate cooperatively. Cast in morphological terms, the dual mechanism debate focuses on the efficacy of relying on rules to capture regular morphological processes such as past tense formation (add ED), with an associative mechanism between present and irregular past tense forms that functions as the backup. The single mechanism alternative contrasts sharply in that it eschews categories like regular and irregular. It emphasizes, instead, systematic correspondences between orthographic and phonological or between orthographic-phonological and semantic dimensions of similarity as the basis of recognizing a word in the phonological and morphological domains respectively. In this chapter, we argue that because many effects are graded, some within a category, morphological processing can be better captured by a single mechanism graded account than by a dual mechanism account determined by category.

Variation among morphologically related words

Morphemes are the meaningful elements that comprise the internal or sublexical structure of words. For example, the words PAINT and TOAST are composed of a single morpheme and cannot be broken down into smaller elements that contribute to the meaning of the word as a whole. By contrast, the words PAINTED and PAINTER are morphologically complex because they are composed of multiple morphemes and thus can be broken down further. In the case of PAINTED, the stem is PAINT and the affix, ED, is *inflectional* in that it serves a grammatical function. In the case of PAINTER, the stem is also PAINT but here the affix, ER, is *derivational* in that it serves to form a new word whose meaning and word class can differ from that of the stem in isolation. These meanings may differ in ways that are not always totally predictable by rule. For example, based on knowledge about the ways in which morphemes combine to form PAINTER, it could be difficult to arrive at an accurate interpretation for TOASTER. The PAINTER-TOASTER comparison shows one aspect of *semantic transparency* or predictability; that is, how a stem contributes to the meaning of a complex word form. Attenuated transparency is not exclusively a property of a particular affix, in this case ER. Analogously, attenuated transparency is not an exclusive property of a particular stem. Therefore, it is difficult to classify a word as semantically 'transparent' or 'opaque' on the basis of either its stem or its affix in isolation. In effect, transparency is more of a relative than an absolute property. For example, although both are formed from the stem ALLOW, ALLOWABLE is semantically more transparent than ALLOWANCE. Note that the meaning of ALLOWANCE is related to ALLOW, albeit in a more idiosyncratic manner.

Transparency and opacity can be defined in an analogous manner at the level of language form. For example, both DIVIDEND and DIVISOR are derivations formed from the stem DIVIDE. In this instance, the former is more transparent than the latter with respect to *orthographic* and *phonological form*. Because semantic and orthographic transparency each varies in a continuous manner and because they vary independently of each other it is difficult to classify words as categorically transparent or opaque.

The recognition and the production of complex forms pose slightly different challenges to a rule-based account. The comparison of ALLOWANCE, DIVISION and AMENDMENT demonstrates that there are many affixes (e.g., ANCE, SION, MENT) with which one may form nouns from verbs. Likewise, the comparison of APOLOGIZE, STRENGTHEN and VACCINATE demonstrates that there are many affixes (e.g., IZE, EN, ATE) with which one may form verbs from nouns. Collectively, neither the meaning nor the form of all words composed of more than one morpheme within a language can be described easily in terms of rules for combining morphological segments (or morphemes). At best, linguistically analytic recognition processes based on rules for segmenting words into morphemes can succeed to the extent that morphologically complex words within a language are transparent. While the production of morphologically complex forms can be described reliably in terms of rules for combining morphemes overall, selection within the class of affixes as well as the full word meaning can be more complex. When words cannot be recognized or produced with reference to rules that account for the segmentation or combination of sublexical constituents, it is generally postulated that they are treated as wholes.

The rules for forming morphologically complex words can vary across languages and some have claimed that models of morphological processing emphasize word form more in languages such as Hebrew than in others (Frost, Kugler, Deutsch, & Forster, 2005). In English, the sublexical structure of morphologically complex words can consist of a stem or base morpheme such as PAINT and an affix, either a prefix as in RE+ PAINT or a suffix such as PAINT +ABLE. In some cases it is possible to append multiple affixes as in the English word RE+ PAINT +ABL(E) +ITY. Sequencing of affixes is more characteristic of some languages than of others. For example in Turkish, an agglutinative language, multiple inflectional affixes followed by multiple derivational affixes can be appended to a stem (EV meaning 'house') to form a single word such as EVINIZDEYIM (meaning 'I am in your house'). Languages differ one from another not only with respect to the prevalence of multiply affixed word forms but also with respect to the patterns for combining morphemes. Some languages (e.g., Chinese) tend not to combine morphemes to form new words. Others do form new words that way, and, among those, some (e.g., Turkish) change the form of the affix depending on the stem to which it is appended. Further, many morphemes, even many inflectional affixes can combine within a single word. Fusional languages like Serbian tend to change the inflectional affix as grammatical function (number, gender and case) changes rather than by appending more separate affixes. The nature of the constraints on forming morphologically complex words can differ across languages as well. In French or English as well as Serbian and Turkish, for example, morphemes are connected linearly (e.g., RE+ PAINT +AB(I)L(E) +ITY). In Hebrew, by contrast, morphemes can be *infixed* one within another (e.g., -a-a- is infixed into the root pattern N-F-L to form NaFaL meaning 'he fell' and -o-e- is infixed o form NoFeL meaning 'he falls') so that morphemes are not composed of contiguous letters (phonemes).

Words formed from a shared morpheme (e.g., PAINT, PAINT+ ABLE, PAINT +ER, PAINT+ER+LY, PAINT +ING, PAINT +WORK) are *morphologically related*. Because they share a morpheme, morphological relatives tend to be similar along dimensions of meaning as well as form. Inflectionally related forms share a stem but differ with respect to an inflectional affix (e.g., S, ED, ING in English). As a rule, regularly inflected forms (e.g., DIVIDED-DIVIDE, PAINTED-PAINT) tend to share greater form similarity with their stems than do irregularly inflected forms such as those whose past tense does not end in ED or D (e.g., SANG-SING). Exceptions to the claim that irregulars tend to share less form overlap with their morphological relatives than do regulars are those irregulars in English formed by affixing an N to the stem (e.g., SHOWN-SHOW). Here, the stem (SHOW) is preserved so shared form between stem and past participle is as high as for regulars. It is irregular, however, because the past form does not end in ED. Similar processes occur in other languages as well. In general, however, gradations of form similarity when degree of shared meaning is constant are characteristic of irregularly inflected morphological forms.

Complementarily, gradations of meaning similarity or semantic transparency when degree of shared form is constant are characteristic of many derivationally related forms. Transparent derived forms (e.g., ALLOWABLE-ALLOW) tend to share greater meaning similarity than do opaque derived forms (e.g., ALLOWANCE-ALLOW). In the ALLOW example, degree of shared form (orthographic transparency) based on the stem is constant but in other pairs of derived words such as DIVISIVE-DIVIDE degree of shared form as well as meaning can vary.

The study of the morphology of a language allows researchers to ask questions about the nature of the cognitive mechanism(s) at the word and sublexical levels by which words are recognized and produced. Current investigation is often framed in terms of one of two issues:

(1) Are there categories of words (e.g., irregular/regular, derivation/ inflection) under which morphologically complex words are treated only as wholes and others where they are decomposed by rule into constituent morphemes? Inherent in the categorical versus graded debate are conflicting assumptions about whether morphological structure is represented explicitly in the lexicon so that different rules apply to different categories of morphological structures. Graded effects of similarity within a category are not easily compatible with two mechanisms that are independent and cannot work in parallel or sequentially.

(2) Is there an initial phase of morphological processing based exclusively on form that is blind to semantics? That is, does recognition of regular and decomposable morphologically complex words rely initially on decomposition into orthographically defined morphemes and only subsequently on analysis for meaning? Inherent in this debate are conflicting assumptions about the potential separation between linguistic levels and about the locus of semantic effects. For example, many more words are formed from the ACT stem (e.g., ACTION, ACTIVE, ACTIVATE, ACTOR) than from the stem YELL. Successive exposures to a word permit orthographic codes to get restructured by semantic as well as phonological systematicity (see e.g., Rueckl, 2010). Thus, the form-meaning mapping will be stronger for ACT than for YELL. Degree of covariation among morphological relatives in conjunction with degree of form similarity in the absence of similar meaning provides a way to characterize variation in morphological processing within as well as across languages (Feldman, Basnight-Brown, & Pastizzo, 2006). By this account, semantic properties of words or morphemes cannot be separated from form-based properties, even early in the course of word recognition. Further, word pairs that share form and meaning tend to behave differently than pairs that share only form or only meaning.

In the remaining sections we review categorical and graded accounts of regularity, inflections vs derivations, and semantic influences on morphological processing.

Regularity and morphological processing

Differences in how speakers of a language recognize and produce regularly (PAINTED-PAINT) and irregularly (SANG-SING) inflected words serve as the focus of heated debate. On one side are those who advocate a dual mechanism account, with computation based on rules as one option and association among whole word forms as the other. Here, the interaction of the grammar of morphological (specifically, inflectional) rules and lexical-semantic knowledge is assumed to be highly constrained and some theorists use this to argue that qualitatively different mechanisms apply to regular and irregular categories of morphological structures (Clahsen, 1999; Pinker, 1999; Ullman, 2004). On the other are those who advocate a single mechanism account based on graded similarity (Joanisse & Seidenberg, 1999).

Regular past-tense formations in English generally follow an ED-affixation-to-the-stem rule and plurals generally follow an-affix-S-to-the-stem rule. For regularly inflected forms, language users can treat morphologically complex words as wholes but the consensus is that more typically they decompose them into constituent morphemes. Inflected forms of irregular words such as SANG and CHILDREN are not easily characterized in terms of rules, however. For irregulars, changes to the stem are more idiosyncratic than rule-governed and thus they invite a whole word characterization of processing and lexical representation. At the same time, however, clusters of irregulars can follow the same pattern of change to the stem. Consider, for example, RING-RUNG, SING-SUNG, STING-STUNG. These present tense-past tense pairs have similar phonological structure (phonological neighbors) and tend to undergo similar changes between present and past (Bybee, 1995).

Proponents of *dual mechanism accounts* of morphological processing often characterize the processing of irregulars as holistic, nondecompositional, and noncombinatorial, and point to effects that reflect principles of organization among stored forms within the lexicon. Evidence of whole word processing derives from differences in recognition latencies that covary with frequency of the whole word form, imageability or similarity to other words based on alternation patterns between present and irregular past tense such as SING-SANG, RING-RANG (Alegre & Gordon, 1999; Clahsen, 1999; Huang & Pinker, 2010; Prado & Ullman, 2009; Pinker, 1999; Pinker & Prince, 1994; Pinker & Ullman, 2002a; Ullman, 2004). Dual mechanism proponents interpret effects of frequency for irregulars but not regulars as evidence that irregulars must be stored and retrieved from lexical memory by a mechanism of association between whole word forms (Prasada & Pinker, 1993; Silva & Clahsen, 2008). When frequency effects also arise for regularly inflected forms, the dual mechanism explanation is that regulars can be processed as (noncombinatorial) wholes so that frequency effects can emerge but, importantly, they also can be processed in with reference to morphological formation rules that entail segmenting a suffix from the stem (decomposition) for recognition or affixing a suffix by rule to the stem for production. Therefore smaller effects of a lexical variable in decision latencies in word recognition tasks for regularly inflected forms than for irregularly inflected words also are compatible with variants of the dual mechanism account.

Different response patterns for regulars and irregulars are termed *regularity effects*. Effects of regularity in single word recognition include not only interactions of inflectional regularity with lexical variables like frequency, but also differences in magnitude of facilitation. In a priming task, the response to a target word varies systematically as a function of the preceding linguistic context or prime (see Jones and Estes, this volume). In variants of the priming paradigm where participants decide whether the target is a word (lexical decision), regularity also can interact with facilitation. Specifically, differences are greater between target decision latencies after unrelated and regularly inflected prime target pairs (PAINTED-PAINT vs. STARTED-PAINT) than between unrelated and irregularly inflected prime target pairs (SANG-SING vs. WROTE-SING). In single word and primed word recognition tasks, when they arise, interactions such as these are also interpreted as evidence of different processing mechanisms for inflectionally regular and irregular forms. One variant of dual-mechanism morphology is the words-and-rules model of Pinker (Pinker, 1991, 1999; Pinker & Ullman, 2002b). Roughly stated, morphologically related regularly inflected pairs like PAINTED-PAINT can benefit not only from a mechanism of decomposition into morphemes where the same stem is activated in prime and in target but also from activation that spreads between various inflected full forms of PAINT. Related irregular pairs benefit only from a mechanism of activation that spreads between forms of SING. Thus, nondecomposable irregular forms such as SANG can prime by association but not by repeated activation of the morpheme SING. Less orthodox variants of the dual route account interpret regularity effects in terms of which route has priority (e.g., Chialant & Caramazza, 1995) and whether routes can work in parallel with the option that outcomes combine (Schreuder & Baayen, 1995).

The leading contenders to the dual mechanism accounts are *single mechanism accounts*. This class of models often assumes 'distributed' lexical representations. In distributed representations, morphological structure of an inflected or derived word is not explicitly represented but emerges from systematic activation patterns that map between form and meaning. That is PAINT, PAINTABLE, PAINTER, PAINTERLY, PAINTING, PAINTWORK share aspects of meaning as well as aspects of form and the patterns that reflect lexical knowledge reflect this similarity. Here, differences in processing can be characterized in terms of stronger or more systematic mappings between form and meaning for the stems of regulars than of stems like SING, that have regular (e.g., SINGS) as well as irregular (e.g., SANG, SUNG) variants (Gonnerman, Seidenberg, & Andersen, 2007; Rueckl & Raveh, 1999; Seidenberg & Elman, 1999; Seidenberg & Gonnerman, 2000). In this framework, the representations for regulars and irregulars differ quantitatively but not qualitatively. In addition to semantic, phonological and orthographic transparency, number of words formed from a stem (morphological family size), as well as the relative frequency of each, can play a role in determining the strength of a mapping. Proponents of the single mechanism account claim that the same mechanism is responsible for the processing of regularly and irregularly inflected forms and that differences reflect the relative strength of the mapping between form and meaning rather than the existence of two mechanisms that operate by either a decomposition or an association principle (Feldman, Rueckl, Pastizzo, Diliberto, & Vellutino, 2002a; Kielar et al., 2008; Pastizzo & Feldman, 2002a,b, Rueckl, Mikolinski, Raveh, Miner, & Mars, 1997; Rueckl & Raveh, 1999; Woollams, Joanisse, & Patterson, 2009). Accordingly, whole word frequency effects should arise for both regular and irregular forms.

When differences between regulars and irregular inflections do arise, rather than invoke different mechanisms, proponents of the single mechanism framework look for differences in the degree of similarity along one or more dimensions. Form contributions can be greater for regulars than for irregulars because stems are orthographically transparent across all inflectional variants. Complementarily, meaning contributions can be greater for irregulars because of greater semantic density. Semantic density measures include the number and interconnectivity among semantic associates of the stem (e.g., semantic resonance, connectivity, number of synonyms) (Baayen & Moscoso del Prado Martin, 2005). Collectively, stems of regularly and irregularly inflected verbs tend to differ not only on form overlap but also along a variety of semantic dimensions that reflect contextual usage and the number and interconnectivity among semantic associates of the stem (Baayen & Moscoso del Prado Martin, 2005). They also differ on measures based on the number and form frequency of various words formed from a morphological stem (family size, derivational entropy) and the number of words that are similar in form (orthographic neighborhood density, phonological neighborhood density). Differences between regulars and irregulars such as these have been documented to influence performance in the lexical decision and naming tasks not only in English (Baayen, Feldman, & Schreuder, 2006) but also in Finnish, German, Hebrew, and Serbian. As a rule, variables such as these are not well controlled in word recognition studies with factorial designs that purport to find differences between regulars and irregulars (but see Prado & Ullman, 2009).

In fact, in experiments that rely on multiple regression analytic techniques to predict single word response times from word properties such as those delineated above, effects of whole word frequency have been documented for regulars as well as irregulars. For example, Baayen, Wurm, & Aycock, (2007) failed to find a significant interaction between whole word (surface) frequency and regularity in their lexical decision and verb naming tasks with visual presentation. There also was no interaction between whole word (surface) and stem (or root) morpheme frequency. Generally, variation in the surface frequency influences recognition latencies more than did variation in stem frequency. In contrast to studies where regularity effects were reported but confounding variables were not controlled, Baayen et al. (2007) failed to find any difference in the role of whole word frequency for regularly and irregularly inflected verbs. The strong implication is that whole word frequency effects may not be a reliable measure of lexical storage as currently defined.

Perhaps more relevant, irregulars and regulars tend to differ on the distribution of frequencies of the various inflected forms, and differential weightings on these forms could produce apparent differences between irregulars and regulars. Of recent interest is inflectional entropy – a measure that captures the average amount of information in a set of inflected forms for a word when information is expressed in bits. The entropy of a word is higher when the probabilities of the inflectional variants are distributed uniformly. Its entropy decreases as the probabilities of occurrence (frequency) of the inflected forms differ. Similarly, relative entropy captures the extent to which the probability distribution of a particular noun (or verb) diverges from the probability distribution of its word class (nouns or verbs). As a rule, decision latencies become longer when the inflectional probability distribution for a particular noun deviates from that of its inflectional class (Baayen, Milin, Filipovi Durdevi, Hendrix, & Marelli, 2011). When left uncontrolled, differences between the frequencies for past and other inflected forms for many verbs can differ more for irregular than for regular verbs so that the entropy is less for irregular than for regular forms. A related frequency measure of particular relevance for the typical priming study is variation in the extent to which the frequency of the present form exceeds the frequency of the past form. Also relevant is that effects derived from stem frequency can interact with affix length. When stem frequency is low, affix length gains importance (Kuperman, Bertram, & Baayen, 2010).

Priming experiments investigate inflectional regularity by presenting words in pairs and looking at the effect of the context or prime word on recognition of the target. As delineated above, facilitation purportedly reflects the savings incurred by lexical activation of a same base morpheme in related primes and targets. In this framework, facilitation for regulars such as PAINTED-PAINT reflects activation of the same base morpheme in prime and target, and facilitation for irregulars such as SANG-SING, reflects activation based on association among irregular and regular morphologically related forms. Experiments in the dual route framework have been conducted with various tasks in German (Sonnenstuhl, Eisenbeiss, & Clahsen, (1999), Hebrew (Berent, Pinker, & Shimron, 1999), and Italian (Say & Clahsen, 2002) among other languages. As previously described, however, regular and irregular verbs tend to vary on many characteristics in addition to decomposability (Baayen & Moscoco del Prado Martin, 2005) and these factors are not always well controlled in studies that compare regular and irregular inflectional morphology and purport to find effects of regularity. With respect to baseline latencies, word frequency, orthographic neighborhood size, semantic richness, and morphological family size all influence recognition (Baayen et al., 2006). This makes pinpointing a uniquely morphological source for any observed difference after related and unrelated primes nearly impossible especially when different target words enter into different priming comparisons. Unfortunately, this is typically the case in studies of regularity (e.g., Clahsen, Felser, Neubauer, Sato, & Silva, 2010; Silva & Clahsen, 2008). The implication of failing to control for differences along these measures is that the purported regularity effects may be capturing properties of the verb stems themselves, rather than the operation of different processing mechanisms.

It is worth noting again that facilitation for regulars as well as irregulars that covaries with degree of similarity among (both presented and nonpresented) related forms is not only tolerated but anticipated by a single mechanism account where degree of facilitation reflects degree of similarity within a morphologically related prime-target pair (e.g., Gonnerman et al., 2007; Keilar, Joanisse, & Hare, 2008; Kielar & Joanisse, 2011; Rueckl & Raveh, 1999; Seidenberg & Gonnerman, 2000). By comparison, it is not anticipated by an account where category determines mechanism and graded effects can only reflect averaging over trials. At least two studies, one in English (Basnight-Brown, Chen, Shu, Kosti, & Feldman, 2007) and one in German (Smolka, Zwitserlood, & Rosler, 2007) have compared irregular verbs that preserve the stem in a past tense form, such as SHOWN (N forms an irregular past form in English), with regular verbs. German participle formation differs from English in that one morpheme is concatenated to another for both regular and irregular verbs. Stated alternatively, regular and irregular German verb forms differ on whether regular or irregular suffixes attach to a stem, as well as on whether or not the stem undergoes change. In each case, patterns of facilitation are not reliably different when form similarity is matched across regular and irregular verb types. Gradations of form affect regulars and irregulars similarly.

Inflections versus derivations

Linguists distinguish between two categories of morphological formation, inflections and derivations but it has been difficult to use the outcome of priming tasks to establish unequivocally that inflections and derivations are processed by different mechanisms. When different response patterns to inflections and derivations do arise, dual mechanism proponents interpret this difference as evidence that processing of inflections and derivations require different mechanisms, rules and associations respectively. A central problem, however, is that pairs related by inflectional morphology such as RUNS-RUN tend to differ less with respect to the degree of shared meaning and of shared form than do pairs related by derivation such as RUNNER-RUN. This is the case both because stems undergo less dramatic semantic changes and because affixes tend to be shorter so that whole word forms share a larger proportion of letters with the stem. When dimensions of similarity are equated, single route but not dual route accounts anticipate that magnitudes of facilitation will not differ for pairs related by inflection and pairs related by derivation. To make a compelling argument for differences between inflections and derivations, both types of prime-target pairs should be matched on semantic and form similarity. Another possible option is to present relatives with several intervening items, so that semantic effects are experimentally attenuated. Under these conditions, researchers seldom report statistically reliable differences in patterns of facilitation between inflectionally and derivationally related prime-target pairs (e.g., Fowler, Napps, & Feldman, 1985; Rueckl & Raveh, 1999).

In conclusion, contrasting outcomes with inflections and derivations also are recruited in support of the dual mechanism claim with a rule-based process of mental computation (decomposition) for inflection and a second whole word process that applies to derivation (e.g., Pinker & Ullman, 2002b). The absence of morphological facilitation by inflected primes in conjunction with the presence of facilitation by derivations in second language speakers of a language is also offered in support of the dual mechanism claim. A problem here is that statistically reliable interactions of (inflected vs. derived) word type by prime type (related vs. unrelated) are rarely reported in this literature (see e.g., Clahsen et al., 2010). Other complications arise because results vary depending on modality of the prime and on whether visual primes are forward masked (Basnight-Brown et al., 2007; Feldman, Kostić, Basnight-Brown, Djurdjevi, & Pastizzo, 2009). Without statistical documentation of an interaction, it is unwarranted to conclude that inflections and derivations are processed in qualitatively different ways.

In summary, inflectionally and derivationally related pairs in English tend to differ on shared meaning as well as shared form. Shared form can be better equated in languages other than English, like in Serbian, where morphology plays a more prominent role (e.g., Feldman, Barac-Cikoja, & Kostić, 2002b). One consequence, however, is that families of morphologically related words will tend to be larger and increases in family size can attenuate the magnitude of morphological facilitation. In conclusion, incontrovertible evidence that morphological processing differs across languages is sparse and purported evidence may derive from uncontrolled aspects of the patterning of form or of meaning or of their nonlinear combination. Differences along these dimensions make it difficult to argue that the processing of regular versus irregular or inflectional versus derivational categories is qualitatively different either within or across languages.

Semantic versus morphological processing

Morphological relatives generally share a stem and stems generally retain aspects of meaning as well as form. To the extent that stems behave consistently, morphological relatives tend to be similar in form and similar in meaning. Researchers have contrasted pairs related by morphology (e.g., VOWED-VOW) with morphologically unrelated pairs related by form (e.g., VOWEL-VOW) or by meaning (e.g., PLEDGE-VOW) in an attempt to determine whether morphological relatedness among whole word forms can be equated with either form similarity among whole word forms or with semantic similarity among whole word forms (for reviews, see Feldman, 2000; Rastle et al., 2000). Complementarily, in order to track the interaction of semantic with morphological form, researchers examine the effect of semantic transparency on morphological processing as revealed by magnitudes of facilitation in variants of the primed lexical decision task.

Comparing morphological relatedness with shared meaning and shared form

One strategy to determine experimentally whether morphology is explicitly represented entails comparing priming effects of shared morphology with the combined effects of shared meaning and shared form (Feldman, 2000;

Rastle, 2000). Ideally, in these investigations, the same target is paired with a semantic, a morphological and an orthographic prime and patterns of facilitation are examined across tasks or across stimulus onset asynchronies (SOAs) within a task (see Feldman, 2000). The underlying logic of repeated target designs in which the same target appears in different prime conditions is to control maximally for differences between targets that can influence recognition latency such as their frequency, number of neighbors and length and then to compare morphological, orthographic/ phonological and semantic dimensions of similarity.

Typically, facilitation is greater for morphologically (e.g., VOWED-VOW) than for semantically related (e.g., PLEDGE-VOW) pairs and the magnitude of each increases with SOA when primes and targets follow each other in succession. When primes are masked and presented for durations less than about 50 ms, so that primes are unavailable for conscious report, or when primes and targets are separated by about ten intervening items, morphologically related but not semantically related pairs produce facilitation. Sometimes, the effect of a dimension of similarity changes direction with duration and visibility of the prime. For example, orthographic similarity (e.g., VOWEL-VOW) facilitates at short SOAs (e.g., 34 ms) when prime processing is allegedly incomplete and becomes inhibitory at longer SOAs (e.g., 230 ms). Similar effects emerge when primes are presented auditorily and targets are visual (Plaut & Gonnerman, 2000).

Studies show that the effects of morphological relatedness cannot be predicted from linearly combining the separate effects of form similarity and of semantic similarity within prime-target pairs. More precisely, even when ratings of semantic similarity for morphologically related pairs are equated to those for semantic pairs (e.g., VOWED-VOW to PLEDGE-VOW) and are equated for form-based similarity (letter overlap) to those of form pairs (e.g., VOWED-VOW and to VOWEL-VOW), magnitudes of morphological facilitation for a target could not be predicted reliably by summing priming effects of similar form and similar meaning for that same target. Throughout, the outcome depends on task and on SOA. This includes conditions in which primes are forward masked and presented at very brief SOAs (less than 60 ms), when primes precede targets by an average of ten intervening items, and when prime and target occur in succession with no mask (Feldman, 2000). Collectively, the variation over SOA is important because it demonstrates that facilitation based on morphological similarity (VOWED-VOW) is most similar to form similarity in the absence of semantics (VOWEL-VOW) at very short SOAs, and most similar to semantic similarity when processing time for the prime is temporally more extended. Morphological facilitation differed significantly from the combined effects orthographic and semantic facilitation when SOAs were pooled but not at individual SOAs. One interpretation of the priming pattern whereby shared morphology is distinct from shared form or shared meaning is that morphology is explicitly represented and priming allows repeated activation of the stem morpheme (Rastle, Davis, Marslen-Wilson, & Tyler, 2000). An alternative is that a more complex (less linear, more dynamic) interaction of form and meaning underlies morphological processing. Crucially, when interactions between the form and meaning dimensions of similarity that are graded displace the idea that there are different types of linguistic representations, dimensions need not combine in an additive manner (Plaut & Gonnerman, 2000; Rueckl et al., 1997). If contributions of form and meaning can combine nonlinearly then evidence that facilitation from morphological relatives (e.g., VOWED-VOW) differs from that for pairs that share only meaning (e.g., PROMISE-VOW) and from pairs that share only form (e.g., VOWEL-VOW) is of minimal relevance to the issue of whether or not morphological structure is explicitly represented (e.g., Drews & Zwitserlood, 1995; Feldman 2000; Rastle, et al., 2000).

   In summary, patterns of facilitation that vary over task and SOA highly constrain a purely structural interpretation of facilitation based on repeated activation of the same morpheme by prime and target. The implication of patterns of morphological facilitation that resemble form effects when processing time for the prime is restricted and semantic effects when processing time is less restricted is that activation of the same morphemic unit by prime and then in target may not be the most parsimonious description of morphological processing as revealed by facilitation in the lexical decision task. We return to this point in the next section.

   Further, the claim that form similarity produces facilitation most similar to morphological relatedness early in processing and semantic similarity is more similar to morphological relatedness later in processing is not meant to imply that semantic effects are always absent early in the time course of processing. When primes are forward masked, Crepaldi, Rastle, Coltheart, and Nickels, (2010) observed facilitation for FELL-FALL relative to FILL-FALL pairs but not for orthographically similar but morphologically unrelated pairs such as TELL-TALL relative to TOLL-TALL type pairs. To elaborate, when style of form change was equated, facilitation arose for pairs that were morphologically related and thus were semantically similar, but not for pairs that shared only the same style of form change. The Crepaldi et al. (2010) results demonstrate early effects of semantic similarity between prime and target on patterns of morphological facilitation when primes are forward masked. Crepaldi and colleagues accounted for the pattern of facilitation in terms of activation among lemmas at a lexical level. It is important to point out that their solution violates the adequacy of accounts of early facilitation based on morpho-orthographic segmentation as a prelexical process.

   Comparisons of morphological and orthographic forward masked primes with and without transposed letters also have been used to study letter coding within morphological units. Typically, target recognition latencies continue to benefit from a prime where contiguous letters are transposed (WOKR-WORK) relative to an orthographically similar prime that differs from the target by letter substitutions such as WOLF-WORK (e.g., Perea & Lupker, 2004). Results indicate that transposition is less detrimental than letter substitution and that morphological primes with and without a transposition do not differ reliably. Morphological facilitation, despite a transposition of letters within the prime, is consistent with models of orthographic encoding where coding of letter positions is imprecise at early stages of word processing (Gómez, Ratcliff, & Perea, 2008). When primes are affixed, some claim that the benefit is greater when the transposition occurs within a morpheme (WO**KR**ER-WORK) than between two morphemes (WO**RE**KR-WORK). Transpositional effects that are less detrimental (i.e., greater facilitation) when letter position is disturbed within a morpheme than across a morpheme boundary are taken as evidence of the primacy of morpheme units in early visual processing (Duñabeitia, Perea, & Carreiras, 2007). However, recent reports of equivalent facilitation with transposition within a morpheme and across morphemic boundaries challenge this claim (Rueckl & Rimzhim, 2011) and have been interpreted by some as evidence that the transposition effect is not isolated from whole word semantic influences (Diependaele Sandra, & Grainger, 2009).

Effects of semantic transparency

Among morphologically complex words, those whose meaning is similar to that of the base morpheme are semantically transparent and those whose meanings tend to be more remotely related (dissimilar) to that of the base are opaque or partially opaque forms. As a rule, pairs of inflectionally related forms (RUNNING-RUNS) tend to semantically more similar than are two derived relatives (RUNNER-RUNNY) or a derived with an inflected relative (RUNNY-RUNS). In addition, as delineated in the ALLOWANCE-ALLOW discussion above, semantic similarity can be greater between some pairs of words related by morphological derivation than between others. This can be assessed by a rating task but also by patterns of usage based on co-occurrence measures such as Latent Semantic Analysis (Landauer, Foltz, & Laham, 1998). Note that other forms (e.g., DOLL+AR, EARN+EST, FAIR+Y) appear to be morphologically complex in that they are exhaustively decomposable into stem and affix even though the stem (viz., DOLL, EARN, FAIR) does not function as a morpheme in the longer virtually complex form. Words such as DOLLAR are *pseudocomplex*, as there is no true affix. Although DOLLAR-DOLL type pairs are sometimes described as 'semantically opaque', and this term typically applies to morphological relatives, pairs such as DOLLAR-DOLL are not, in fact, morphologically related. Nonetheless, because they appear exhaustively decomposable, pairs such as DOLLAR-DOLL are often compared to semantically transparent pairs in studies to probe effects of semantic transparency on morphological processing.

In priming tasks, when semantically transparent and opaque related word primes have different effects on a target, it is sometimes argued that morphologically complex words may not all be lexically represented in the same manner. In particular, facilitation for visual targets after transparent (DEPARTURE-DEPART) but not opaque (DEPARTMENT-DEPART) auditory primes led Marslen-Wilson, Tyler, Waksler, & Older, (1994) to claim that in English, only those derivations that are semantically transparent with respect to their constituents are decomposed in the lexicon. By this account, opaque forms do not benefit from facilitation because they are not represented in a decomposed manner. This means that activation cannot spread from prime to target. Importantly, however, sometimes opaque pairs do produce facilitation. In early work (Feldman &

Soltano, 1999; Rastle et al., 2000), morphological facilitation was equivalent for transparent and opaque pairs at an SOA of about 40 ms and pairs differed by transparency only at an SOA of 250 ms. When presentations are visual and SOAs are longer than 250 ms, effects of transparency have been reported in many languages including Serbian (Feldman et al., 2002b) and Dutch (Diependaele, Sandra, & Grainger, 2005, 2009) as well as English (Feldman & Soltano, 1999; Feldman, Soltano, Pastizzo, & Francis, 2004; Rastle et al., 2000; Rueckl & Aicher, 2008). Even in Hebrew, effects of transparency arise at long SOAs. To elaborate, primes as well as targets are presented visually, and participants make a lexical decision to primes as well as targets each of which appears for 1000 ms, semantically dissimilar morphologically related prime-target pairs such as (e.g., NUMBER-LIBRARY in Hebrew) produce less facilitation than do semantically similar pairs such as LIBRARIAN-LIBRARY (Bentin & Feldman, 1990).

The main controversy about the role of semantics in morphological processing centers on data from the masked priming task at SOAs shorter than 60 ms, where the focus is on the earliest phase of word recognition (Forster & Davis, 1984). The debate centers on whether morphologically complex words are first segmented based on orthographically defined morphemes, such that semantic properties of morphemes play a role only at a later stage, after lexical access (Longtin, Segui, & Halle, 2003; Rastle & Davis, 2008; Rastle, Davis, & New, 2004). Conflicting results come from Feldman, O'Connor, & Moscoso del Prado Martín, (2009), who compared patterns of facilitation between semantically transparent (e.g., COOLANT-COOL) and opaque (e.g., RAMPANT-RAMP) prime-target pairs and found significantly greater facilitation among pairs that were semantically transparent even at a 48 ms SOA. Further, in a repeated target design with different materials, they observed greater facilitation to targets (RAT) that follow primes that are similar in form and meaning (RATTY-RAT) as compared to prime that are similar in form but not in meaning (RATIFY-RAT) as early as 34 ms (Feldman, Moscoso del Prado Martín, & O'Connor, 2010b). Effects of semantic transparency under forward masked priming conditions are important because they undermine claims for an initial stage of morphological processing that is exclusively orthographic and independent from semantics. Although the early semantic effect is small, it has been documented in meta-analyses by both camps (Davis & Rastle, 2010; Feldman et al., 2009).

Models of early morphological processing

Accounts of morphological processing differ as to how early in the course of recognition semantic effects can emerge. In large part, accounts diverge on whether semantic effects in priming tasks can arise because of covarying ortho-graphic and semantic similarity due to a shared morpheme or whether they arise only lexically at the level of whole words. If one assumes that semantic effects originate from whole word representations, this question can be rephrased as when in the course of recognition of a morphologically complex word, whole word semantic and morphemic form (morpho-orthographic or morph-phonological) representations are activated and how they can interact.

According to the *obligatory prelexical decomposition account*, there is an analysis of morphologically complex words into morphemes that precedes and guides lexical access (Taft, 1994, 2003; Taft & Forster, 1975). Crucially, this decomposition process treats morpheme as units of form devoid of meaning. Thus, because AR (like ANCE) can be an affix, DOLLAR is processed in the same way as it ALLOWANCE. It is decomposed into the stem DOLL and the affix AR and the absence of a semantic relation between DOLLAR and DOLL is inconsequential at the decomposition stage. Transparency effects arise later and reflect the links between lemmas (Taft & Nguyen-Hoan, 2010). This account differs from the *supralexical account*, which posits initial access based on the whole word (Giraudo & Grainger, 2001, 2003). Accordingly, decomposition of a letter string into morphemes occurs only after the lexicon has been accessed from a whole word unit and only at the whole word level are semantic representations activated (Giraudo & Grainger, 2001, 2003). Further, activation can spread from supralexical to sublexical levels for PUNISHMENT-PUNISH type pairs but not for DEPARTMENT-DEPART or DOLLAR-DOLL type pairs. In addition to these two accounts there is a third variant of the prelexical decomposition approach where initially morphological decomposition is based only on a word's orthographic form (*morpho-orthographic segmentation*) and a word's semantics contributes to recognition only at a later point (morpho-semantic processes). By the morpho-orthographic account, the early stage of morphological processing is decompositional but semantically blind so that AMENDMENT-AMEND, DEPARTMENT-DEPART and DOLLAR-DOLL all activate their targets equivalently. However, later in the course of visual word recognition it is possible for activation based on morpho-orthographic segmentation to cascade with another independent process that includes semantic aspects of morphological processing (Davis & Rastle, 2010; Longtin & Meunier, 2005; Rastle et al., 2004).

These three accounts differ with respect to the units with which one accesses the lexicon (whole words or morphemes) although all of them can be classified as form-then-meaning accounts in that semantics is not activated until linguistic analysis of form (viz., morpho-orthographic segmentation, Rastle & Davis, 2008) is under way. They contrast critically with a fourth class of models, those that assert that morpho-orthographic and morpho-semantic processes are not independent even very early in the course of word recognition. *Form-with-meaning accounts* differ with respect to whether semantic effects necessarily arise at the word level and feed back to a form level so that there are separate semantic and form based morphological priming effects (Diependaele, Duñabeitia, Morris, & Keuleers, 2011) or whether morphemes function concurrently as units of meaning and as units of form from the outset (Feldman et al., 2009). By form-with-meaning accounts, form and meaning are interdependent processes and early semantic transparency effects attest to the influence of semantics on a purportedly pure orthographic stage.

All agree that effects of semantic similarity between a forward masked prime and its target tend to come and go depending on particulars of the experiment such as the proportion of related pairs and on other aspects of list composition (Bodner & Masson, 2003; Feldman & Basnight-Brown, 2008). Transient effects are difficult to reconcile with accounts of facilitation that presuppose activation of a lexical structure (morpheme) shared by prime and target. Not everyone believes that patterns of facilitation when primes are forward masked are most usefully interpreted as revealing about the all or none activation of morphological and whole representations in lexical memory, however (Baayen et al., 2011; Norris & Kinoshita, 2008). With respect to semantic transparency among morphological relatives, the interaction of semantic transparency with SOAs in the 34 ms to 100 ms range demonstrates the need for a more dynamic characterization of morphological processing, as revealed by graded patterns of facilitation. Specifically, when primes are masked but SOAs remain shorter than 100 ms, there is a tendency for facilitation with semantically transparent morphologically related pairs to increase significantly while facilitation with opaque pairs stays statistically constant (Feldman et al., 2010b). This pattern is reminiscent of diverging patterns for morphologically and orthographically related pairs as SOA increases (Feldman, 2000). Different temporal dynamics for facilitation with transparent morphological and opaque pairs, whereby effects of semantic similarity increase in the 34–100-ms time frame while effects of form similarity change more slowly, are revealing about the style of interaction for form and meaning early in the course of word recognition.

- The study of morphological processing deals with ways in which whole word and sublexical word structure influence recognition and production.
- Dual route accounts assume categories or qualitatively different structures for regularly and irregularly inflected word forms, for inflectional and derivational formations, or for semantically transparent and opaque derived forms.
- Single route accounts see graded quantitative rather than qualitative differences as underlying each of these contrasts.
- All models of morphological processing include both form-based and meaning-based contributions. Accounts differ as to whether form-based early processing, based on the forward masked priming task, reveals processing that is independent of meaning-based processing or whether semantics structures orthographic patterning so that the two have the potential to interact in a complex, dynamic and nonadditive manner.

Acknowledgments

The research reported here was supported by National Institute of Child Health and Development Grant HD-01994 to Haskins Laboratories.

References

Alegre, M. & Gordon, P. (1999). Frequency effects and the representational status of regular inflections. *Journal of Memory and Language, 40*, 41–61.

Baayen, R. H., Feldman, L. B., & Schreuder, R. (2006). Morphological influences on the recognition of monosyllabic monomorphemic words. *Journal of Memory and Language, 55*, 290–313.

Baayen, R. H. & Moscoso del Prado Martín, F. (2005). Semantic density and past-tense formation in three Germanic languages. *Language, 81*, 1–27.

Baayen, R. H., Wurm, L. H., & Aycock, J. (2007). Lexical dynamics for low-frequency complex words: A regression study across tasks and modalities. *The Mental Lexicon, 2*, 419–463.

Baayen, R. H., Milin, P., Filipović Durdević, D., Hendrix, P., & Marelli, M. (2011). An amorphous model for morphological processing in visual comprehension based on naive discriminative learning. *Psychological Review, 118*, 438–481.

Basnight-Brown, D. M. Chen, L., Shu, H., Kostić, A., & Feldman, L. B. (2007). Monolingual and bilingual recognition of regular and irregular English verbs: Sensitivity to form similarity varies with first language experience. *Journal of Memory and Language, 57*, 65–80.

Bentin, S. & Feldman, L. B. (1990). The contribution of morphological and semantic relatedness to repetition priming at short and long lags: Evidence from Hebrew. *The Quarterly Journal of Experimental Psychology A: Human Experimental Psychology, 42A*, 693–711.

Berent, I., Pinker, S., & Shimron, J. (1999). Default nominal inflection in Hebrew: Evidence for mental variables. *Cognition, 72*, 1–44.

Bodner, G. E., & Masson, M. E. J. (2003). Beyond spreading activation: An influence of relatedness proportion on masked semantic priming. *Psychonomic Bulletin & Review, 10*, 645–652.

Bybee, J. (1995). Regular morphology and the lexicon. *Language and Cognitive Processes, 10*, 425–455.

Chialant, D. & Caramazza, A. (1995). Where is morphology and how is it processed? The case of written word recognition. In L. B. Feldman (Ed.), *Morphological aspects of language processing* (pp. 55–76). Hillsdale, NJ: Erlbaum Press.

Clahsen, H. (1999). Lexical entries and rules of language: A multidisciplinary study of German inflection. *Behavioral and Brain Sciences, 22*, 991–1060.

Clahsen, H., Felser, C., Neubauer, K., Sato, M., & Silva, R. (2010). Morphological structure in native and nonnative language processing. *Language Learning, 60*, 21–43.

Crepaldi, D., Rastle, K., Coltheart, M., & Nickels, L. (2010). 'Fell' primes 'fall', but does 'bell' prime 'ball'? Masked priming with irregularly-inflected primes. *Journal of Memory and Language, 63*, 83–99.

Davis, M. H. & Rastle, K. R. (2010). Form and meaning in early morphological processing: Comment on Feldman, O'Connor, and Moscoso del Prado Martin. *Psychonomic Bulletin & Review, 17*, 749–55.

Diependaele, K., Sandra, D., & Grainger, J. (2005). Masked cross-modal morphological priming: Unraveling morpho-orthographic and morpho-semantic influences in early word recognition. *Language and Cognitive Processes, 20*, 75–114.

Diependaele, K., Sandra, D., & Grainger, J. (2009). Semantic transparency and masked morphological priming: The case of prefixed words. *Memory and Cognition, 37*, 895–908.

Diependaele, K., Duñabeitia, J. A. Morris, J., & Keuleers, E. (2011). Fast morphological effects in first and second language word recognition. *Journal of Memory and Language,64*(4), 344–58.

Duñabeitia, J. A., Perea, M., & Carreiras, M. (2007). Do transposed-letter similarity effects occur at a morpheme level? Evidence for morpho-orthographic decomposition? *Cognition, 105*, 691–703.

Drews, E. & Zwitserlood, P. (1995). Morphological and orthographic similarity in visual word recognition. *Journal of Experimental Psychology: Human Perception and Performance, 21*, 1098–1116.

Feldman, L. B. (2000). Are morphological effects distinguishable from the effects of shared meaning and shared form? *Journal of Experimental Psychology: Learning, Memory and Cognition, 26*, 1431–1444.

Feldman, L. B. & Basnight-Brown, D. (2008). List context fosters semantic processing: Parallels between semantic and morphological facilitation when primes are forward masked. *Journal of Experimental Psychology: Learning, Memory and Cognition, 34*, 680–687.

Feldman, L. B. & Soltano, E. G. (1999). Morphological priming: The role of prime duration, semantic transparency and affix position. *Brain and Language, 68*, 33–39. doi:10.1006/brln.1999.2077.

Feldman, L. B., Rueckl, J., Pastizzo, M., Diliberto, K., & Vellutino, F. (2002a). Morphological analysis in beginning readers as revealed by the fragment completion task. *Psychological Bulletin and Review, 77*, 529–535.

Feldman, L. B., Barac-Cikoja, D., & Kostić, A. (2002b). Semantic aspects of morphological processing: Transparency effects in Serbian. *Memory & Cognition, 30*, 629–636.

Feldman, L. B., Soltano, E.G., Pastizzo, M., & Francis, S. E. (2004). Semantic transparency influences morphological processing. *Brain and Language, 90*, 17–30. doi:10.1016/S0093-934(03)00416-4.

Feldman, L. B., Basnight-Brown, D. M., & Pastizzo, M. J. (2006). Semantic influences on morphological facilitation: Concreteness and family size. *The Mental Lexicon, 1*, 61–84.

Feldman, L. B., O'Connor, P. A., & Moscoso del Prado Martín, F. (2009). Early morphological processing is morpho-semantic and not simply morpho-orthographic: A violation of form-then-meaning accounts of word recognition. *Psychological Bulletin and Review, 16*, 684–691. doi:10.3758/PBR.16.4.684

Feldman, L. B., Kostić, A., Basnight-Brown, D., Djurdjević, D. & Pastizzo, M. J. (2010a). Morphological facilitation for regular and irregular verb formations in native and non-native speakers: Little evidence for two distinct mechanisms. *Bilingualism, Language and Cognition, 13*, 119–135. doi:10.1017/S1366728909990459

Feldman, L. B., Moscoso del Prado Martín, F & O'Connor, P. A. (2010b). Must analysis of meaning follow analysis of form? A time course analysis. Manuscript submitted for publication.

Forster, K. I. & Davis, C. (1984). Repetition priming and frequency attenuation in lexical access. *Journal of Experimental Psychology: Learning, Memory, and Cognition, 10*, 680–698.

Fowler, C. A., Napps, S. E., & Feldman, L. B. (1985). Relations among regular and irregular morphologically-related words in the lexicon as revealed by repetition priming. *Memory and Cognition, 13*, 241–255.

Frost, R., Kugler, T., Deutsch, A., & Forster, K.I. (2005). Orthographic structure versus morphological structure: Principles of lexical organization in a given language. *Journal of Experimental Psychology: Learning, Memory & Cognition, 31*, 1293–1326.

Giraudo, H. & Grainger, J. (2001). Priming complex words: Evidence for supralexical representation of morphology. *Psychonomic Bulletin and Review, 8*, 127–131.

Giraudo, H. & Grainger, J. (2003). A supralexical model for French derivational morphology. In D. Sandra and H. Assink (Eds), *Reading complex words* (pp. 139–157). Amsterdam: Kluwer.

Gomez, P., Ratcliff, R., & Perea, M. (2008). The Overlap Model: A model of letter position coding. *Psychological Review, 115*, 577–601.

Gonnerman, L. M., Seidenberg, M. S., & Andersen, E. S. (2007). Graded semantic and phonological similarity effects in priming: Evidence for a distributed connectionist approach to morphology. *Journal of Experimental Psychology: General, 136*, 323–345.

Huang, Y. T. & Pinker, S. (2010). Lexical semantics and irregular inflection. *Language and Cognitive Processes.* doi: 10.1080/01690961003589476

Joanisse, M. F., & Seidenberg, M. S. (1999). Impairments in verb morphology following brain injury: A connectionist model. *Proceedings of the National Academy of Science of the United States of America, 96*, 7592–7597.

Kielar, A. & Joanisse, A. F. (2008). Graded effects of regularity in language revealed by N400 indices of morphological priming. *Journal of Cognitive Neuroscience, 22*, 1373–1398.

Kielar, A. & Joanisse, M. F. (2011). The role of semantic and phonological factors in word recognition: An ERP cross-modal priming study of derivational morphology. *Neuropsychologia, 49*, 161–177.

Kielar, A., Joanisse, A. F., & Hare, M. L. (2008). Priming English past tense verbs: Rules or statistics? *Journal of Memory and Language, 58*, 327–346.

Kuperman, V., Bertram, R., & Baayen, R.H. (2010). Processing trade-offs in the reading of Dutch derived words. *Journal of Memory and Language, 62*, 83–97.

Landauer, T. K., Foltz, P. W., & Laham, D. (1998). Introduction to latent semantic analysis. *Discourse Processes, 25*, 259–284. http://lsa.colorado.edu/.

Longtin, C. M. & Meunier, F. (2005). Morphological decomposition in early visual word processing. *Journal of Memory and Language, 53*, 26–41.

Longtin, C. M., Segui, J., & Halle, P. A. (2003). Morphological priming without morphological relationship. *Language and Cognitive Processes, 18*, 313–334.

Marslen-Wilson, W., Tyler, L. K., Waksler, R., & Older, L. (1994). Morphology and meaning in the English mental lexicon. *Psychological Review, 101*, 3–33.

Norris, D. & Kinoshita, S. (2008). Perception as evidence accumulation and bayesian inference: Insights from masked priming. *Journal of Experimental Psychology: General, 137*, 434–455.

Pastizzo, M. J. & Feldman, L. B. (2002a). Discrepancies between orthographic and unrelated baselines in masked priming undermine a decompositional account of morphological facilitation. *Journal of Experimental Psychology: Learning, Memory and Cognition, 28*, 244–249.

Pastizzo, M. J. & Feldman, L. B. (2002b). Does prime modality influence morphological processing? *Brain and Language, 81*, 28–41. doi: 10.1006/brln.2001.2504

Perea, M. & Lupker, S. J. (2004). Can CANISO activate CASINO! Transposed-letter similarity effects with nonadjacent letter positions. *Journal of Memory and Language, 51*, 231–246.

Pinker, S. (1991). Rules of language. *Science, 253,* 530–535.

Pinker, S. (1999). *Words and rules: The ingredients of language.* New York: Basic Books.

Pinker, S. & Prince, A. (1994). Regular and irregular morphology and the psychological status of rules of grammar. In S. D. Lima, R. L. Corrigan, and G. K. Iverson (Eds), *The reality of linguistic rules* (pp. 321–354). Philadelphia, PA: John Benjamins.

Pinker, S. & Ullman, M. T. (2002a). The past and future of the past tense. *Trends in Cognitive Sciences, 6,* 456–463.

Pinker, S. & Ullman, M. T. (2002b). Combination and structure, not gradedness, is the issue. *Trends in Cognitive Sciences, 6,* 472–474.

Plaut, D. C. & Gonnerman, L.M. (2000). Are non-semantic morphological effects incompatible with a distributed connectionist approach to lexical processing? *Language and Cognitive Processes, 15,* 445–485.

Prado, E. L. & Ullman, M. (2009). Can imageability help us draw the line between storage and composition? *Journal of Experimental Psychology: Learning, Memory, and Cognition, 35,* 849–866.

Prasada, S. & Pinker, S. (1993). Generalizations of regular and irregular morphological patterns. *Language and Cognitive Processes, 8,* 1–5. doi:10.1080/0169096930 8406948

Rastle, K. & Davis, M. H. (2008). Morphological decomposition based on the analysis of orthography. *Language and Cognitive Processes, 23,* 942–971.

Rastle, K., Davis, M. H., Marslen-Wilson, W. D., & Tyler, L. K. (2000). Morphological and semantic effects in visual word recognition: A time-course study. *Language and Cognitive Processes, 15,* 507–537.

Rastle, K., Davis, M. H., & New, B. (2004). The broth in my brother's brothel: Morphoorthographic segmentation in visual word recognition. *Psychonomic Bulletin & Review, 11,* 1090–1098.

Rueckl, J. G. (2010). Connectionism and the role of morphology in visual word recognition. *The Mental Lexicon, 3,* 371–400.

Rueckl, J. G. & Aicher, K.A. (2008). Are CORNER and BROTHER morphologically complex? Not in the long term. *Language and Cognitive Processes, 23,* 972–1001.

Rueckl, J. G. & Raveh, M. (1999). The influence of morphological regularities on the dynamics of a connectionist network. *Brain and Language, 68,* 110–117.

Rueckl, J. G. & Rimzhim, A. (2011). On the interaction of letter transpositions and morphemic boundaries. *Language and Cognitive Processes, 26,* 482–508. 10.1080/01690965.2010.500020

Rueckl, J. G., Mikolinski, M., Raveh, M., Miner, C. S., & Mars, F. (1997). Morphological priming, connectionist networks, and masked fragment completion. *Journal of Memory and Language, 36,* 382–405.

Say, T. & Clahsen, H. (2002). Words, rules and stems in the Italian mental lexicon. In: S. Nooteboom, F. Weerman, & F. Wijnen (Eds). *Storage and computation in the language faculty* (pp. 93–129). Dordrecht: Kluwer.

Schreuder, R. & Baayen, R. H. (1995). Modeling morphological processing. In: L. B. Feldman (Ed). *Morphological aspects of language processing.* Hillsdale, NJ: Erlbaum Press. 131–154.

Seidenberg, M. S. & Elman, J. L. (1999). Networks are not 'hidden rules'. *Trends in Cognitive Sciences, 3,* 288–289.

Seidenberg, M. S. & Gonnerman, L. M. (2000). Explaining derivational morphology as the convergence of codes. *Trends in Cognitive Sciences, 4,* 353–361.

Silva, R. & Clahsen, H. (2008). Morphologically complex words in L1 and L2 processing: Evidence from masked priming experiments in English. *Bilingualism: Language & Cognition, 11*, 245–260.

Smolka, E., Zwitserlood, P., & Rosler, F., (2007). Stem access in regular and irregular inflection: Evidence from German participles. *Journal of Memory and Language, 57*, 325–347.

Sonnenstuhl, I., Eisenbeiss, S., & Clahsen, H. (1999). Morphological priming in the German mental lexicon. *Cognition, 72*, 203–236.

Taft, M. (1994). Interactive-activation as a framework for understanding morphological processing. *Language and Cognitive Processes, 9*, 271–294.

Taft, M. (2003). Morphological representation as a correlation between form and meaning. In: E. Assink & D. Sandra (Eds). *Reading complex words* (pp. 113–137). Amsterdam: Kluwer.

Taft, M. & Forster, K. I. (1975). Lexical storage and retrieval of prefixed words. *Journal of Verbal Learning and Verbal Behavior, 14*, 638–647.

Taft, M. & Nguyen-Hoan, M. (2010). A sticky stick: The locus of morphological representation in the lexicon. *Language and Cognitive Processes, 25*, 277–296.

Ullman, M. T. (2004). Contributions of memory circuits to language: The declarative/procedural model. *Cognition, 92*, 231–270.

Woollams, A. M., Joanisse, M. F., & Patterson, K. (2009). Past-tense generation from form and meaning: Behavioural data and simulation evidence. *Journal of Memory and Language. 61*, 55–77.

2 Meaning-based influences on visual word recognition

Penny M. Pexman

When we read, the usual goal is to generate meaning from the words on a page. Reading connected text involves a number of component processes, one of which is assumed to be visual word recognition. That is, recognition of isolated words is assumed to be a component skill of reading. As such, one might assume that activation of word meaning would be an integral part of all models of the visual word recognition process. In fact, the influence of meaning or semantic information in word recognition has been controversial.

This chapter has two aims. The first is to demonstrate that meaning influences visual word recognition. The second is to provide a synthesis of the ways in which meaning influences the process of word recognition in order that we might have a better understanding of the dimensions of meaning that are accessed in lexical processing.

The role of meaning in theories of word recognition

The visual lexical decision task (LDT), in which participants are asked to judge whether a printed letter string is a word or nonword, is the standard paradigm for assessing word recognition behaviour (models of the task are reviewed in Gomez, accompanying volume, Chapter 4). It has sometimes been argued that lexical decision can be performed before semantic access (e.g., Forster, 1976; Morton, 1969). Indeed, "theories of word recognition typically give a miniscule role, if any, to the meaning of words in determining word recognition speed" (Larsen, Mercer, Balota, & Strube, 2008, p. 449). In contrast, other theories have given semantic activation a central role in word recognition. Balota and Chumbley (1984) argued that lexical decisions are performed on the basis of a familiarity/meaningfulness dimension. That is, for each stimulus, the first stage of processing involves a familiarity/meaningfulness assessment. The second stage of processing is performed when the first assessment is not sufficient to provide categorization of the stimulus as a word or a nonword. In these cases, an additional spelling check may be required. According to this model, semantic processing is a critical aspect of lexical decision performance. Similarly, Balota, Ferraro, and Connor (1991) proposed that the Interactive Activation model (McClelland & Rumelhart, 1981) could be modified to include representation of meaning-level units, which could provide feedback activation to word-level units. As such, meaning information would be activated in the process of word recognition. By this account, lexical decisions are based on word-level activation, and so meaning information would influence lexical decisions via semantic feedback activation. Further, Balota et al. suggested that for semantic activation in lexical decision, "more means better" (p. 214), since more semantic activation will support a word decision via feedback.

Although many current models of word recognition assume that semantic processing is an important aspect of lexical access (e.g., Norris, 2006; Wagenmakers, Steyvers, Raaijmakers, Shiffrin, van Rijn, & Zeelenberg, 2004), the semantic component of these models has rarely been implemented. For instance, Ratcliff, Gomez, and McKoon (2004) assumed that semantic information is simply one source of information about "wordness" of a stimulus (along with phonological and orthographic information) that feeds into the diffusion model of lexical decision. Thus, semantic information is given a role in the process but is not specified. On the other hand, Harm and Seidenberg (2004) implemented a semantic component in their model of word recognition, and so specified one scenario for semantic representation, but did not offer a detailed account of how lexical decisions are made. Plaut (1997) suggested that lexical decisions could be performed as a function of a familiarity measure applied to semantics, but also assumed that lexical decision did not *require* semantic information. That is, there are circumstances under which orthographic information alone is sufficient and semantic information is not necessary in order for a lexical decision to be made.

In the present chapter I will provide an overview of the various semantic dimensions that have been shown to influence visual word recognition. I will focus on recognition of single words; semantic influences in priming paradigms are reviewed in Jones and Estes (this volume, Chapter 3). I will further focus on studies involving the lexical decision task, because this task has been the most widely used to study semantic influences. Admittedly, the focus on LDT does strengthen my case for semantic influences; where meaning-based influences have been examined in word naming tasks the results have tended to show smaller effects than in lexical decision (for a review see Balota, Cortese, Sergent-Marshall, Spieler, & Yap, 2004). I will further emphasize lexical decision studies in which the foils are pronounceable nonwords. In this "standard" version of the LDT the nonwords are orthographically legal but not pseudohomophones (they do not sound like real words when pronounced). It is well known that the LDT is made more difficult when pseudohomophones (e.g., BRANE), rather than standard nonwords (e.g., PRANE) are used as foils, and that this difficulty manipulation modulates effects observed on the word trials (e.g., Pexman, Lupker, & Jared, 2001; Stone & Van Orden, 1993). By emphasizing data collected in the standard (non-pseudohomophone) version of the LDT, I can more readily make comparisons between studies and across different semantic dimensions. Most of the data reviewed come from behavioural studies, but where available, I will also review results of neuroimaging studies. As I believe this review will illustrate, it is now quite clear that semantic information is activated in the process of word recognition. Furthermore, the effects that have been observed for each of these semantic dimensions provide us with important clues about how word meaning is represented.

Imageability

The imageability dimension characterizes the extent to which a word evokes mental imagery of things or events, and is usually established with subjective ratings (Cortese & Fugett, 2004). There exists a continuum of imageability, ranging from words rated to be highly imageable (e.g., truck) to more abstract words that are rated to be less imageable (e.g., truth). A related (indeed, highly correlated, Toglia & Battig, 1978) dimension is concreteness. Imageability was one of the first semantic dimensions examined in the context of visual word recognition. When lexical decisions for high imageability (concrete) words were compared to those for low imageability (abstract) words, results of early studies generally showed that LDT response latencies were faster for concrete words than for abstract words (Day, 1977; James, 1975). These results, however, were among those criticized by Gernsbacher (1984), who pointed out that subjective familiarity had been confounded with concreteness or imageability in a number of the previous studies, such that high imageability words also tended to be rated as more familiar. Thus, it was not clear whether the observed imageability effects were actually effects of familiarity (for related discussion, see Adelman, accompanying volume, Chapter 6). Resolution to this problem was presented by Balota et al. (2004), who examined effects of imageability in a large set of words and reported that lexical decisions were faster and more accurate for high imageability words than for low imageability words, even when a number of other lexical characteristics (including both subjective and objective frequency) were statistically controlled.

One of the early accounts of imageability effects was provided by Paivio's Dual-Code Theory (Paivio, 1971, 1991). According to dual-code theory, high imageability (concrete) words are represented by both verbal and visual codes, whereas low imageability (abstract) words are represented by only verbal codes. As a consequence, high imageability words are more quickly recognized. In contrast, the context-availability theory suggests that high imageability words are more easily recognized because more contextual information is available in memory for highly imageable concepts (Schwanenflugel, 1991). This contextual information includes the situations and settings in which concepts are encountered. For low imageability concepts, associated contextual information is less readily available.

Several researchers have attempted to distinguish these two accounts with neuroimaging data. That is, it has been argued that the dual-code theory predicts that the processing of high imageability words will be associated with activation both in left-lateralized language regions and in image-processing regions that are typically in the right hemisphere (although see, for instance, Fiebach & Friederici, 2003, for arguments that right hemisphere activation is not necessary to support the dual-code theory). Processing of low imageability words will be associated predominantly with activation in left hemisphere language-processing regions, without recruitment of regions in the right hemisphere. In contrast, the predictions derived from context availability theory involve greater activation in the left hemisphere for high imageability words. The efforts to determine the neural correlates of the imageability effect and resolve the theoretical debate between dual-code and context-availability theories have produced remarkably inconsistent results. If the discussion is limited to neuroimaging studies that have used the LDT, there is one that appears to be consistent with the dual-code theory and inconsistent with context-availability theory: Binder, Westbury, McKiernan, Possing, and Medler (2005) reported that a left-lateralized network of brain regions (including left inferior frontal and superior temporal gyri) was associated with processing of abstract concepts, whereas a bilateral network (including right hemisphere regions such as middle temporal and angular gyri) was associated with processing of concrete concepts. The results of other studies have been taken as support for both dual-code and context-availability theories. Fiebach and Friederici (2003) reported that concrete words generated more activation in the left basal temporal lobe than did abstract words. They argued that this region has been associated with mental imagery (e.g., Farah, 2000), and thus, activation here supports the dual-code theory. Further, Fiebach and Friederici reported that abstract words generated more activation in the left inferior frontal gyrus, an area associated with selection of semantic knowledge (e.g., Thompson-Schill, D'Esposito, Aguirre, & Farah, 1997). This finding was taken as support for the context-availability theory. Finally, the results of other studies involve a pattern whereby no neural regions showed greater activation for concrete than for abstract words (e.g., Kiehl, Liddle, Smith, Mendrek, Forster, & Hare, 1999). Instead, abstract words were associated with greater activation in left inferior frontal gyrus. These results are not consistent with either dual-coding or context-availability theories because neither predicts that abstract words should be associated with greater activation than concrete words. Despite inconsistent imaging results, the behavioural results across these studies were consistent: concrete words were processed faster than abstract words in LDT. The inconsistent imaging results may, in part, be attributable to the fact that while some authors controlled for reaction time differences between concrete and abstract words in their imaging analyses (e.g., Binder et al., 2005), others did not (e.g., Kiehl et al., 1999).

As such, there is still disagreement as to the best explanation for behavioral effects of imageability in LDTs. At minimum, however, the demonstration that lexical decisions are faster for concrete, highly imageable words than for abstract, less imageable words suggests that the dimension of imageability is activated in the process of visual word recognition. Neither dual-coding theory nor context availability theory offer an explanation that fully accounts for the observed effects of imagery in word recognition. It seems, however, that by virtue of being associated with relatively more perceptual information, the lexicality of a letter string can more readily be judged. Balota et al. (1991) proposed that semantic feedback activation would be greater for concrete words (their imaginal representations provide additional semantic activation) than for abstract words, providing extra feedback activation to the word level. Plaut and Shallice (1993) argued that imageability or concreteness effects could be explained in a distributed attractor network model, in which meaning was represented by activation of semantic feature units (units representing attributes or features of a concept's meaning). Concrete words were assumed to have richer semantic representations and as such to activate more semantic feature units than abstract words. Plaut and Shallice's simulations showed that the semantic units settle more quickly into a stable pattern of activation for concepts with more semantic features. As such, this framework seems capable of explaining the visual word recognition advantage for concrete or highly imageable words. This facilitory effect of additional semantic information is also demonstrated by the next effect discussed: the number of semantic features effect.

Number of semantic features

One of the tools used by researchers who study semantic processing is the feature listing task. In this task, participants are asked to list the attributes or semantic features that describe different concepts. The features listed for different concepts are considered "verbal proxies for packets of knowledge" (McRae, 2005, p. 42), rather than veridical descriptions of semantic memory. As they generate features, participants access representations derived from their experience with the concepts. McRae and colleagues (McRae, Cree, Seidenberg, & McNorgan, 2005) published feature norms for 541 concrete concepts (for additional norms see Vinson & Vigliocco, 2008). For instance, the normative features for the concept *cow* include perceptual characteristics like *has four legs*, *has an udder*, and *is smelly*. Other features describe behaviors, like *eats grass*, and *moos*. Some of the features describe the concept's function, like *produces milk*, or its context, as in *lives on farms*. The normative data show that for some concepts participants tend to list many features (e.g., 20 for couch, 23 for cougar) and for other concepts participants list fewer features (e.g., 11 for table, nine for leopard). The effect of this variability in number of semantic features was first explored in a 2002 study: High number of features (NoF) words elicited faster and more accurate LDT responses than low NoF words, even when printed frequency and subjective familiarity were controlled (Pexman, Lupker, & Hino, 2002). Replication of this effect was provided by Grondin, Lupker, and McRae (2009). Grondin et al. controlled even more lexical and semantic dimensions (e.g., frequency, familiarity, orthographic N, semantic category) for the high NoF and low NoF words sets, and again found that lexical decisions were faster and more accurate for high NoF words than for low NoF words (see also Pexman, Holyk, & Monfils, 2003; Pexman, Hargreaves, Siakaluk, Bodner, & Pope, 2008; Yap, Tan, Pexman, & Hargreaves, 2011).

My colleagues and I have argued that, consistent with the simulation results of Plaut and Shallice (1993), words with high NoF generate more semantic activation than words with low NoF (Pexman et al., 2002, 2003, 2008). We adopt the assumption that semantic activation influences lexical decision performance through feedback from the semantic units to the orthographic units (Hino & Lupker, 1996; Pexman & Lupker, 1999; Pexman et al., 2001). The additional semantic activation for high NoF words will provide stronger feedback activation from the semantic units to the orthographic units. As such, the result will be faster responding for high NoF words than for low NoF words in LDTs.

NoF effects are further demonstration that semantic information influences visual word recognition. NoF effects also suggest that feature listing data tap into, or are related to, some dimension that is important to semantic processing. Certainly, the features that participants list in a feature listing task do not reflect the entirety of their knowledge of the concepts; there is much they know that is not listed. Further, there is plenty of data to suggest that semantic knowledge is more sophisticated than that which could be conveyed by feature lists. Yet the amount of information participants list for each concept is related to their visual word recognition behaviour, even when the other lexical and semantic dimensions that we know to be influential are controlled. As such, it is possible that the feature listing task provides an approximation of some of the semantic information that is activated in the LDT.

Number of associates

The notion that LDT performance will be facilitated for words that are associated with more semantic information has also been examined in terms of effects of words' number of associates. Thanks to the work undertaken by Nelson, McEvoy, and Schreiber (1998) there are now free association norms for over 5000 English concepts. These list the most frequent first associate for each concept in the norms, as well as all of the associates of those concepts that were produced by at least two participants. As such, for a given concept, one can readily establish a number of associates (NoA, sometimes also referred to as semantic set size): the number of different free association responses generated for a given concept. For instance, the concept LAMP has just seven associates (light, shade, bulb, post, desk, table, burn), while the concept LACE has 24 (shoe, dress, frill, pretty, white, gown, clothes, etc.).

The effect of NoA on lexical decision was first examined by Buchanan, McEvoy, and Schreiber, (2001). Buchanan et al. reported modest facilitory effects of NoA: Faster lexical decisions for high NoA words than for low NoA words. In a subsequent large-scale study, Balota et al. (2004) reported that lexical decision responses were related to NoA, such that high NoA words tended to produce faster lexical decision responses than low NoA words, even when subjective and objective frequencies were equated. Similarly, Pexman, Hargreaves, Edwards, Henry, and Goodyear (2007) compared lexical decision performance for high NoA and low NoA words, matched for a number of lexical and semantic characteristics (e.g., frequency, length, orthographic N, number of meanings, number of senses, concreteness) and reported that lexical decisions were faster for high NoA words. Facilitory NoA effects have also been reported in LDT for Spanish stimuli (Duñabeitia, Avilés, & Carreiras, 2008).

It has been argued that when a word is processed there is implicit activation of the word's interconnected set of associates (Nelson, Bennett, Gee, Schreiber, & McKinney, 1993). This claim would seem to be supported by the observation of NoA effects in visual word recognition. Again, the explanation is that "more is better" (Buchanan et al., 2001). Activation of relatively more associates provides relatively more evidence to support a "word" response in the LDT, likely via semantic feedback activation.

Semantic neighbourhoods

The principle that more semantic activation facilitates visual word recognition has also been tested by examining effects of semantic neighbourhood size (SN) on lexical decision performance. Buchanan et al. (2001) proposed that an important dimension of lexical semantics is characterized by the way words are used in language. That is, words that co-occur or are used in similar lexical contexts are semantic neighbours. As such, words' semantic neighbourhoods can be extracted from corpora of text (e.g., Burgess & Lund, 2000). Large SN words share lexical contexts with many other words (e.g., 28 semantic neighbours for bed, 24 for celery), whereas small SN words share lexical contexts with few other words (e.g., three semantic neighbours for door, two for carrot). Buchanan et al. found that large SN words generated faster responses than small SN words in LDTs, and they attributed this advantage to stronger semantic activation.

Similarly, Mirman and Magnuson (2008) reported facilitory SN size effects in LDT. Pexman et al. (2008) also reported that lexical decision responses were related to SN size, such that words with larger SN were associated with faster lexical decision response times, even when words' frequency, imageability, orthographic N, and length were statistically controlled. Pexman et al. also examined whether the SN size variable might be measuring the same construct as the NoF variable. In other words, are these just different labels for the same dimension? As such, Pexman et al. first examined the correlation between SN and NoF for a set of 479 items. The relationship between SN and NoF for these items was positive, but modest, r (478) = 0.15, $p < 0.01$, suggesting that the variables were not measuring exactly the same construct. More importantly, analysis of lexical decision data showed that both SN and NoF had significant, unique relationships with lexical decision performance. Thus, both SN and NoF tap dimensions that seem to be important to semantic processing.

The reported SN effects demonstrate that visual word recognition is facilitated for words that are used in the context of many other words (vs few other words). These effects provide support for models of lexical semantics that are structured by lexical co-occurrence. For instance, Burgess and Lund's Hyperspace Analogue to Language (HAL) model assumes that semantic representation involves a high-dimensional semantic space. The model has been improved on in recent years in order to correct problems with frequency confounds and to more readily generate semantic neighbourhood information (e.g., Shaoul & Westbury, 2006). The result is a framework for semantics that assumes words' meanings are stored in a way that reflects the way the words are used, and captures the contexts in which words occur.

Body-object interaction

In a recent set of studies, researchers have examined a new semantic dimension called body-object interaction, which captures the extent to which a human body can physically interact with a word's referent (Siakaluk, Pexman, Aguilera, Owen, & Sears, 2008a; Siakaluk, Pexman, Sears, Wilson, Locheed, & Owen, 2008b; Tillotson, Siakaluk, & Pexman, 2008). This dimension is assumed to measure the extent to which a word evokes sensorimotor information, but is argued to be independent of imageability. That is, while the referents of the words CAVE and CHAIR may be equally imageable, it is probable that you have had more opportunities to physically interact with a CHAIR than you have with a CAVE. Thus, CHAIR would likely receive higher ratings of body-object interaction. Siakaluk and colleagues have collected body-object interaction ratings for a large set of words (Tillotson et al. 2008), and have established that words with high BOI are associated with faster and more accurate lexical decision responses than are words with low BOI, even when a number of other lexical and semantic characteristics (e.g., imageability, length, frequency, orthographic N, phonological N) are controlled.

The fact that bodily experience with a word's referent influences visual word recognition provides support for the embodied cognition framework. By this framework, many different modalities are involved in the acquisition and processing of conceptual knowledge (e.g., Anderson, 2003; Barsalou, 1999, 2003, 2008; Pecher & Zwaan, 2005; Wilson, 2002). In addition to cognitive systems (e.g., attention and language processing) and sensory systems (e.g., vision and olfaction), the theory suggests that motor, kinesthetic, and proprioceptive systems (e.g., grasping, manual manipulation, and internal feedback from muscles and joints) and emotional systems (e.g., fear and pleasure), are fundamental to semantic processing. Accessing conceptual knowledge involves partial activation or simulation of the varied systems that were involved in the original encoding of the object or event. According to this perspective, sensory and motor knowledge gained via bodily experience with the environment is an important part of what is learned about concepts, and is accessible to the linguistic system. Indeed, the lexicon is distributed throughout the same brain systems as the conceptual system. Further, the amount of sensorimotor knowledge activated for particular concepts can influence visual word recognition behavior. As such, lexical decisions are facilitated for words that evoke relatively more sensorimotor knowledge (high BOI words) than for words that evoke less sensorimotor knowledge (low BOI words).

For each of the semantic dimensions discussed thus far, the nature of the effects has been similar. That is, higher values on a semantic dimension (imageability, NoF, NoA, SN, BOI) are associated with faster and more accurate visual word recognition. I would refer to all of these as *semantic richness effects*: When a word is associated with relatively more semantic information, it can be assumed to have a richer semantic representation, and recognition is facilitated. In the following two sections, however, I will examine the influence of two semantic dimensions that are not entirely consistent with this trend: the effects of semantic ambiguity and the effects of valence.

Semantic ambiguity

Most English words have more than one meaning, and are thus referred to as semantically ambiguous (e.g., bank). For these words, the visual information (letter string) maps onto multiple referents (meanings). For a number of years, researchers have been interested in how these words are processed in the visual word recognition system. In early studies researchers had reported that lexical decision latencies were faster for ambiguous words (e.g., bank) than for unambiguous words (e.g., tent, Jastrzembski, 1981; Jastrzembski & Stanners, 1975; Rubenstein, Garfield, & Millikan, 1970; Rubenstein, Lewis, & Rubenstein, 1971). However, these studies were, again, among those criticized for confounds involving familiarity (Gernsbacher, 1984). Subsequent studies, involving more stringent control of potential confounds, have typically shown that lexical decision response latencies are faster for ambiguous words than for unambiguous words (e.g., Borowsky & Masson, 1996; Ferraro & Hansen, 2002; Hargreaves, Pexman, Pittman, & Goodyear, 2011; Hino Z& Lupker, 1996; Hino, Lupker, & Pexman, 2002; Hino, Pexman, & Lupker, 2006; Kellas, Ferraro, & Simpson, 1988; Millis & Button, 1989; Pexman & Lupker, 1999). For instance, Hino and Lupker (1996) investigated the effects of semantic ambiguity, and used participant ratings to index words' number of meanings (see also Kellas et al., 1988). Hino and Lupker then compared lexical decision performance for a set of words rated to have multiple meanings and a set of words rated to have single meanings. The two word sets were matched for a number of factors including frequency, familiarity, length, and orthographic *N*. Hino and Lupker's results showed that lexical decision latencies were faster and more accurate for ambiguous words than for unambiguous words. Similarly, with Japanese stimuli, Hino et al. (2006) compared lexical decision performance for ambiguous and unambiguous word sets matched for frequency, familiarity, length, and orthographic N, and reported that lexical decisions were faster for ambiguous words than for unambiguous words. These ambiguity effects have typically been explained in terms of semantic feedback: for ambiguous words, more semantic activation is generated (than for unambiguous words), which provides stronger feedback to the orthographic units and facilitates lexical decision performance (e.g., Hino & Lupker, 1996; Pexman & Lupker, 1999).

A different index of ambiguity was developed by Rodd and colleagues (Rodd, Gaskell, & Marslen-Wilson, 2002). Rodd et al. argued that there is an important difference between ambiguous words like BANK, that have multiple *unrelated* meanings, and polysemous words like TWIST, that have multiple *related* meanings. Rodd et al. distinguished these two word types on the basis of dictionary entries: words with multiple meanings (ambiguous words) have multiple dictionary entries while words with multiple senses (polysemous words) have a single dictionary entry. Rodd et al. examined effects of these word categories on lexical decision performance. With statistical control for a number of lexical variables, including familiarity and concreteness, Rodd et al. reported that ambiguous words were responded to more slowly than unambiguous words. At the same time, ambiguous words with multiple related meanings (polysemous words) were responded to more quickly than ambiguous words with multiple unrelated meanings. Thus, Rodd et al. concluded that the ambiguity advantage in LDTs is restricted to ambiguous words with related meanings (see also Klepousniotou & Baum, 2007), and that ambiguous words with unrelated meanings should actually produce an ambiguity disadvantage.

In a follow up study, Beretta, Fiorentino, and Poeppel (2005) presented Rodd et al.'s stimuli in a magnetoencephalography (MEG) experiment. Behavioral results showed, as in the Rodd et al. study, faster lexical decision latencies for polysemous words (with multiple related meanings) than for nonpolysemous words, and slower lexical decision latencies for ambiguous words (with multiple unrelated meanings) than for unambiguous words. The MEG results showed an earlier peak latency (M350 component) for polysemous words than for nonpolysemous words, and a later peak latency for ambiguous words than for unambiguous words. Others, however, have reported that the extent to which an ambiguous word's meanings are related does not influence lexical decision performance (Hino et al., 2006).

There is an aspect of semantic ambiguity effects that is different than each of the other semantic effects (imageability, NoF, NoA, SN, BOI) discussed above. That is, each of the other semantic effects tends to be consistent across lexical decision and other semantic tasks: for instance, the effect of NoF is facilitory in LDT and also in semantic categorization tasks (Pexman et al., 2003, 2008), and connected reading (Pexman et al., 2003). Similarly, the effect of NoA is facilitory in lexical decision and also in semantic categorization (Duñabeitia et al., 2008) and connected reading (Duñabeitia et al., 2008). Ambiguity effects, however, present a wrinkle in this otherwise consistent picture. The ambiguity advantage (when it is observed) is limited to LDTs. In contrast, in semantic tasks, the effects of ambiguity are quite different.

Using the same set of items that produce an ambiguity advantage in LDT, Piercey and Joordens (2000) reported an ambiguity disadvantage for words presented on the "yes" trials in a semantic relatedness decision task (i.e., are these two words related?). They interpreted this result within a connectionist framework, assuming that ambiguous words activated a blend state in the semantic units, which is a pattern of activation that represents multiple learned meanings but is not fully settled on any one meaning. They assumed that the blend state is sufficient to support LDT performance, arguing that lexical decision requires only that semantic activation reaches some threshold level, but does not require full semantic settling. Ambiguous words are likely to meet this threshold earlier than unambiguous words, producing the semantic ambiguity advantage they observed in lexical decision. Piercey and Joordens also assumed, however, that although a blend state might be sufficient for LDT performance, it would be insufficient in tasks requiring more complete semantic processing (e.g., their semantic relatedness decision task). In order to perform a semantic task, the system would need to escape the blend state, and thus processing would be more difficult for ambiguous words than for unambiguous words. Piercey and Joordens dubbed this the "efficient then inefficient" explanation, and argued that it explained the fact that an ambiguity advantage is observed in LDTs and an ambiguity disadvantage is observed in semantic tasks.

Consistent with the "efficient then inefficient account", Hino et al. (2002) observed an ambiguity advantage in LDT and, with the same words, an ambiguity disadvantage in a semantic categorization task where the decision category was "living thing". Although Hino et al.'s findings with the "living thing" category were consistent with the efficient then inefficient explanation, their findings from other versions of the semantic categorization task were not. Hino et al. demonstrated that, while the ambiguity disadvantage is observed with semantic categorization tasks involving broad categories like "living thing", it is not observed in semantic categorization tasks with easier, narrower decision categories (e.g., "vegetable"). With more narrow, less analytic decision categories null effects of ambiguity were observed (see also Siakaluk, Pexman, Sears, & Owen, 2007). Similarly, using a semantic relatedness decision task, Pexman, Hino, and Lupker (2004) reported that while there was a clear ambiguity disadvantage when the ambiguous words were presented on "yes" trials (e.g., money-bank), replicating Piercey and Joordens (2000), there was no effect of ambiguity when the ambiguous words were presented on "no" trials (e.g., horse-bank).

A possible explanation for this varied pattern of results is based on the assumption that performance in most semantic tasks (semantic categorization, relatedness decision) is a function of both the meaning activation process and a decision making process. These two processes probably overlap in time, but they could be sufficiently distinct so that they provide separate sources for behavioral effects (see also Balota & Paul, 1996). When ambiguous words are presented on the "yes" trials in semantic relatedness decision tasks, there is inevitably a response conflict due to there being two meanings of the ambiguous word. That is, one meaning is consistent with a "yes" response (i.e., the meaning that is related to the paired word) and the other is consistent with a "no" response (i.e., unrelated to the meaning of the paired word). The ambiguity disadvantage observed on "yes" trials of relatedness decision tasks could, therefore, be the result of response competition and not because of the meaning activation process per se. In contrast, on "no" trials, both meanings of the ambiguous words are consistent with a "no" response, so the ambiguity does not create response competition. The fact that the disadvantage disappears on "no" trials (as Pexman et al., 2004, observed) is consistent with the response competition explanation for ambiguity effects in semantic tasks, and suggests that activation of multiple meanings will not necessarily slow semantic processing. Similarly, the fact that the ambiguity disadvantage in semantic categorization tasks is limited to certain decision categories (Hino et al., 2006) suggests that this effect can also be attributed to decision-phase processes rather than meaning activation processes.

The suggestion, then, is that the multiple meanings activated for ambiguous words will facilitate lexical decision performance (via semantic feedback to the orthographic units) but will not necessarily affect semantic processing, or performance in tasks like semantic categorization or relatedness decision, where semantic activation is the primary basis for responding. In other words, if ambiguous words activate a blend state in the semantic units, the blend state is in some sense tolerated; it does not delay semantic processing per se. The problem with this account, however, is that it predicts a null effect of ambiguity in semantic tasks (in the absence of response competition), and if there is a null behavioral effect, how can one be certain that multiple meanings have actually been activated for ambiguous words? Recently, my colleagues and I investigated whether there might be neural evidence for activation of multiple meanings for ambiguous words, even in the absence of a behavioral effect (Hargreaves et al., 2011). We used a set of items that produced the standard ambiguity advantage in LDT, and then presented them to participants in a semantic categorization task with a narrow decision category ("consumable"). The behavioral results showed, as expected, a null effect of ambiguity in the semantic categorization task. The functional Magnetic Resonance Imaging (fMRI) results showed, however, that the ambiguous words were associated with greater activation in the left inferior frontal gyrus (LIFG) than were the unambiguous words. The LIFG has been implicated in semantic processing and in modulation of noisy activity. As such, we took this activation as evidence that multiple meanings were activated for ambiguous words, despite the null behavioral effect of ambiguity.

As such, the effects of semantic ambiguity seem to be distinct from those of other semantic dimensions. As mentioned, a number of studies have shown that words with higher richness produce faster lexical decision and semantic categorization latencies (Duñabeitia et al., 2008; Grondin et al., 2009; Pexman et al., 2003, 2008). While semantic ambiguity might, at first glance, appear to be another form of richness, the behavioural data suggest a different pattern: faster lexical decision responses but null effects in semantic categorization. The imaging results for ambiguity show that ambiguous words are associated with greater cortical activation than are unambiguous words (Hargreaves et al., 2011). In contrast, my colleagues and I have shown that in semantic categorization, again with the "consumable" decision category, words with high numbers of associates were associated with *less* cortical activation in a number of regions (e.g., LIFG, left inferior temporal gyrus) compared to words with low numbers of associates (Pexman et al., 2007). These results suggest very different consequences for richer semantic representations, if one conceived of ambiguity as a form of richness. What should be noted, however, is that richness effects like those of NoA examined in the Pexman et al. (2007) study have only been examined for unambiguous words that refer to concrete concepts (e.g., tiger, potato). For that class of items, the more efficiently processed (richer) words produce less cortical activation than do the less efficiently processed (less rich) words. A key difference is that such richness is associated with a single meaning and a single referent, whereas the ambiguous words used in the Hargreaves et al. study generate semantic information for multiple referents. It seems probable that there are different neural consequences for unambiguous richness and ambiguous richness, and that these different consequences would also be modulated by task demands. Certainly, much remains to be worked out in future research.

Despite the complexity involved in the nature of semantic ambiguity effects, the more important point, for present purposes, is the simple fact that effects of semantic ambiguity are observed in LDTs. The presence of such effects (regardless of their direction, or their extension to semantic tasks) is further evidence that meaning-based variables influence visual word recognition performance.

Valence

A number of studies have examined the effect of emotional valence on visual word recognition. Typically, emotional valence is established by collecting ratings of an affective dimension like "pleasantness". The results from research exploring effects of affective dimensions have been mixed. Kuchinke, Vo, Hofmann, and Jacobs (2007) investigated effects of frequency and valence (positive, neutral, and negative) on visual word recognition. The authors selected stimuli to ensure good control of a number of other lexical factors (imageability, orthographic N, length, part of speech) and presented words in a LDT. For high frequency words, participants were faster and more accurate for positive items (e.g., love) than for neutral (e.g., shadow) or negative items (e.g., burn). For low frequency words, the response pattern was somewhat different, with faster and more accurate responses for both positive (e.g., conjure) and negative items (e.g., corpse) than for neutral items (e.g., parking). The authors also measured pupillary responses in the LDT and found that while frequency modulated pupillary responses, valence did not. They thus argued that valence may influence word recognition behaviour by a different mechanism than does frequency. Specifically, Kuchinke et al. suggested that valence facilitates lexical access, whereas frequency influences the sense of familiarity associated with a word.

Similar behavioural results were obtained by Scott, O'Donnell, Leuthold, and Sereno (2009). In LDT, Scott et al. reported in their behavioural results the same interaction as was observed by Kuchinke et al. (2007): for high frequency words, positive items were responded to more quickly than negative or neutral items, whereas for low frequency words both positive and negative items were responded to more quickly than neutral items. Event-related potential (ERP) data for the Scott et al. study showed that both frequency and emotional valence influenced an early stage of processing (the N1 component, 135–180 ms). As such, the ERP results point to a somewhat different conclusion than that drawn by Kuchinke et al.; Scott et al. concluded that emotional quality and frequency both influence early lexical processing. That is, emotionally valenced words have stronger, more salient representations which facilitate visual word recognition.

In contrast, other studies have reported that valence does not interact with frequency. Nakic, Smith, Busis, Vythilingam, and Blair (2006) examined lexical decision responses to six types of words, created by the factorial manipulation of frequency (high and low) and emotion (high negative, mild negative, and neutral). Word types were matched on length and concreteness. Behavioural results showed that for both high and low frequency words, lexical decision latencies were faster to high negative words than to mild negative or neutral words. fMRI results showed that the high negative words were also associated with greater activation in the bilateral amygdala, middle temporal cortex, and rostral anterior and posterior cingulate cortex. The authors concluded that the faster lexical decision latencies to high negative words could be attributed to augmentation of semantic representations for emotion words due to reciprocal connections from the amygdala to temporal and occipital cortices.

In another study, Estes and Adelman (2008a) argued that words of positive and negative valence have very different effects on visual word recognition, and that in many of the previous investigations researchers may have confounded effects of valence with effects of arousal. Estes and Adelman analyzed Elexicon lexical decision data (Balota, Yap, Cortese, Hutchison, Kessler, Loftis, et al., 2007) for a large set of items (1011 words). With this large data set, the authors were able to covary effects of several other lexical factors, including length, frequency, orthographic N, contextual diversity, and, importantly, arousal. Results showed that lexical decision latencies were faster for positively valenced words than for negatively valenced words. Further, the authors concluded that the effect of valence was categorical, not linear. Estes and Adelman attributed the observed valence effects to automatic vigilance, which involves a rapid affective evaluation (categorization) of perceptual stimuli. If the stimulus is categorized as negative, then it receives preferential attention but processing of other (e.g., lexical) aspects of the stimulus is slowed. If the stimulus is categorized as positive, then processing of other aspects of the stimulus proceeds relatively quickly.

Other authors (Larsen et al., 2008) have taken issue with Estes and Adelman's (2008a) conclusion that the effect of word negativity is categorical (for additional discussion of this issue see Estes & Adelman, 2008b; Kousta, Vinson, & Vigliocco, 2009). Larsen et al. argued that not all negative words slow processing to the same degree, and demonstrated that negativity interacts with arousal. That is, lexical decision latencies are slower for low arousal negative words than for high arousal negative words. Thus, Larsen et al. argued that negativity and arousal are both linear semantic dimensions that influence visual word recognition behaviour.

The relationship between negativity and arousal was addressed further by Hofmann, Kuchinke, Tamm, Vo, and Jacobs (2009). These authors noted that negative words tend to have higher arousal values than positive words, and so determined that a factorial manipulation of valence and arousal was not feasible. Instead, they constructed four word groups, three of which were matched for arousal level (positive, neutral, and low-arousal negative) and two of which were matched for valence (low-arousal negative and high-arousal negative). All four word groups were well matched on lexical dimensions, including frequency (all items were low-frequency words), imageability, length, and orthographic N. Behavioural results from the LDT showed fastest and most accurate responses for positive and high-arousal negative items. Further, responses for high-arousal negative items were faster and more accurate than responses for low-arousal negative items. That is, responses for positive words were facilitated despite their lower arousal level, but responses for negative words were modulated by arousal level. ERP data showed increased negativity for positive and high-arousal negative words at an early time window (80–120 ms), suggesting that valence and arousal influenced early phases of lexical processing. Hofmann et al. argued that since emotional words have more associations than neutral words their semantic representations are more cohesive, and that this contributes to the processing advantage for emotion words.

Finally, a somewhat different characterization of these valence and arousal dimensions has been proposed by Lee Wurm and colleagues (e.g., Wurm, 2007; Wurm, Vakoch, Seaman, & Buchanan, 2004). These authors have examined effects of the rated dimensions of "danger to human survival" and "usefulness to human survival". Even though a number of lexical dimensions (frequency, familiarity, length, concreteness, meaningfulness, etc.) were statistically controlled, Wurm et al. observed an interaction of danger and usefulness in lexical decision. That is, for words rated low on usefulness, lexical decisions were faster to high danger words (e.g., thief) than to low danger words (e.g., magazine). In contrast, for words rated high on usefulness, lexical decisions were faster to low danger words (e.g., lemon) than to high danger words (e.g., sword). Wurm argued that these effects arise from a two-pass system. The first pass involves a rapid decision about whether an approach or avoid orientation should be adopted for the stimulus. The second pass involves more extensive semantic analysis. The interaction is produced because there is conflict between approach response tendencies (engaged by highly useful items) and avoid response tendencies (engaged by highly dangerous items).

Given the varied findings reported here, there is clearly much work to be done to resolve the nature of affective or approach-avoidance effects in visual word recognition. The important point, for present purposes, is that in a number of experiments using standard lexical decision procedures, the semantic dimensions of valence and arousal have been shown to influence responses. The implication is that these are aspects of lexical semantics, and should be incorporated in theories of visual word recognition.

Conclusions

Given the literature reviewed here, showing a broad range of semantic effects in standard LDTs, I suggest that meaning-based influences are robust in visual word recognition. Similar conclusions were drawn by Balota et al. (2004), based on their examination of the effects of a number of semantic variables on visual word recognition performance. Balota et al. argued that their results were "… most consistent with a view in which meaning becomes activated very early on, in a cascadic manner, during lexical processing and contributes to the processes involved in reaching a sufficient level of information to drive a lexical decision" (p. 312).

The results reviewed here suggest that a number of different semantic dimensions are activated in lexical processing: these include the extent to which words evoke imagery, featural information, associated concepts, co-occurring concepts, bodily experience, multiple meanings, and affect. In the few cases where the effects of different dimensions of semantic richness have been directly compared (e.g., Mirman & Magnuson, 2008; Pexman et al., 2008; Yap et al., 2011) the dimensions have each had independent relationships with word recognition behaviour. In fact, there is little evidence that these dimensions have substantial overlap. As such, one must assume that any model of semantics that is structured on the basis of only one dimension will have very limited success explaining the range of semantic richness effects in visual word recognition. Thus, the best approach, at present, would seem to be a model that incorporates multiple dimensions of semantic information. To my knowledge, this does not yet exist, and its design would certainly be challenging. Yet given what has been reviewed here, about the range of semantic effects in visual word recognition, this will, in the long term, be the most successful strategy.

- As reviewed here, visual word recognition is influenced by a number of different semantic dimensions: imageability, number of features, number of associates, semantic neighbourhoods, body–object interaction, semantic ambiguity, and valence.
- To a large degree, these different dimensions seem to have independent influences on lexical decision behaviour and this suggests that any model of lexical–semantic knowledge will need to incorporate many different types of semantic information.

References

Anderson, M. L. (2003). Embodied cognition: A field guide. *Artificial Intelligence, 149*, 91–130.

Balota, D. A. & Chumbley, J. I. (1984). Are lexical decisions a good measure of lexical access? The role of word frequency in the neglected decision stage. *Journal of Experimental Psychology: Human Perception and Performance, 10*, 340–357.

Balota, D. A. & Paul, S. T. (1996). Summation of activation: Evidence from multiple primes that converge and diverge within semantic memory. *Journal of Experimental Psychology: Learning, Memory, and Cognition, 22*, 827–845.

Balota, D. A., Ferraro, F. R., & Connor, L. T. (1991). On the early influence of meaning in word recognition: A review of the literature. In P. J. Schwanenflugel (Ed.), *The Psychology of word meanings* (pp. 187–222). Hillsdale, NJ: Erlbaum.

Balota, D. A., Cortese, M. J., Sergent-Marshall, S. D., Spieler, D. H., & Yap, M. J. (2004). Visual word recognition of single-syllable words. *Journal of Experimental Psychology: General, 133*, 283–316.

Balota, D. A., Yap, M. J., Cortese, M. J., Hutchison, K. A., Kessler, B., Loftis, B., Neely, J. H., Nelson, D. L., Simpson, G. B., and Treiman, R. (2007). The English lexicon project. *Behavior Research Methods, 39*, 445–459.

Barsalou, L. W. (1999). Perceptual symbol systems. *Behavioral and Brain Sciences, 22*, 577–660.

Barsalou, L. W. (2003). Abstraction in perceptual symbol systems. *Philosophical Transactions of the Royal Society of London: Biological Sciences, 358*, 1177–1187.

Barsalou, L. W. (2008). Cognitive and neural contributions to understanding the conceptual system. *Current Directions in Psychological Science, 17*, 91–95.

Beretta, A., Fiorentino, R., & Poeppel, D. (2005). The effects of homonymy and polysemy on lexical access: An MEG study. *Cognitive Brain Research, 24*, 57–65.

Binder, J. R., Westbury, C. F., McKiernan, K. A., Possing, E. T., & Medler, D. A. (2005). Distinct brain systems for processing concrete and abstract concepts. *Journal of Cognitive Neuroscience, 17*, 1–13.

Borowsky, R. & Masson, M. E. J. (1996). Semantic ambiguity effects in word identification. *Journal of Experimental Psychology: Learning, Memory, and Cognition, 22*, 63–85.

Buchanan, L., Westbury, C., & Burgess, C. (2001). Characterizing semantic space: Neighborhood effects in word recognition. *Psychonomic Bulletin & Review, 8*, 531–544.

Burgess, C. & Lund, K. (2000). The dynamics of meaning in memory. In E. Dietrich & A. B. Markman (Eds), *Cognitive dynamics: Conceptual and representational change in humans and machines* (pp. 117–156). Mahwah, NJ: Erlbaum.

Cortese, M. J. & Fugett, A. (2004). Imageability ratings for 3,000 monosyllabic words. *Behavior Research Methods, Instruments, & Computers, 36*, 384–387.

Day, J. (1977). Right-hemisphere language processing in normal right-handers. *Journal of Experimental Psychology: Human Perception and Performance, 3*, 518–528.

Duñabeitia, J. A., Avilés, A., & Carreiras, M. (2008). NoA's ark: Influence of the number of associates in visual word recognition. *Psychonomic Bulletin & Review, 15*, 1072–1077.

Estes, Z. & Adelman, J. S. (2008a). Automatic vigilance for negative words in lexical decision and naming: Comment on Larsen, Mercer, and Balota (2006). *Emotion, 8*, 441–444.

Estes, Z. & Adelman, J. S. (2008b). Automatic vigilance for negative words is categorical and general. *Emotion, 8*, 453–457.

Farah, M. J. (2000). The neural bases of mental imagery. In M. S. Gazzaniga (Ed.), *The new cognitive neurosciences* (2nd edn, pp. 965–974). Cambridge, MA: MIT Press.

Ferraro, F. R. & Hansen, C. L. (2002). Orthographic neighborhood size, number of word meanings, and number of higher frequency neighbors. *Brain and Language, 82*, 200–205.

Fiebach, C. J. & Friederici, A. D. (2003). Processing concrete words: fMRI evidence against a specific right-hemisphere involvement. *Neuropsychologia, 42*, 62–70.

Forster, K. I. (1976). Accessing the mental lexicon. In R. J. Wales & E. Walker (Eds), *New approaches to language mechanisms* (pp. 257–287). Amsterdam: North-Holland.

Gernsbacher, M. A. (1984). Resolving 20 years of inconsistent interactions between lexical familiarity and orthography, concreteness, and polysemy. *Journal of Experimental Psychology: General, 113*, 256–281.

Grondin, R., Lupker, S. J., & McRae, K. (2009). Shared features dominate semantic richness effects for concrete concepts. *Journal of Memory and Language, 60*, 1–19. doi: 10.1016/j.jml.2008.09.001

Hargreaves, I. S., Pexman, P. M., Pittman, D. J., & Goodyear, B. G. (2011). Tolerating ambiguity: Ambiguous words recruit the left inferior frontal gyrus in absence of a behavioral effect. *Experimental Psychology, 58*, 19–30.

Harm, M. W. & Seidenberg, M. S. (2004). Computing the meanings of words in reading: Cooperative division of labor between visual and phonological processes. *Psychological Review, 111*, 662–720.

Hino, Y. & Lupker, S. J. (1996). Effects of polysemy in lexical decision and naming: An alternative to lexical access accounts. *Journal of Experimental Psychology: Human Perception and Performance, 22*, 1331–1356.

Hino, Y., Lupker, S. J. & Pexman, P. M. (2002). Ambiguity and synonymy effects in lexical decision, naming and semantic categorization tasks: Interactions between orthography, phonology and semantics. *Journal of Experimental Psychology: Learning, Memory, and Cognition, 28*, 686–713.

Hino, Y., Pexman, P. M., & Lupker, S. J. (2006). Ambiguity and relatedness effects in semantic tasks: Are they due to semantic coding? *Journal of Memory and Language, 55*, 247–473.

Hofmann, M. J., Kuchinke, L., Tamm, S., Vo, M. L.-H., & Jacobs, A. M. (2009). Affective processing within 1/10th of a second: High arousal is necessary for early facilitative processing of negative but not positive words. *Cognitive, Affective, & Behavioral Neuroscience, 9*, 389–397.

James, C. T. (1975). The role of semantic information in lexical decisions. *Journal of Experimental Psychology: Human Perception and Performance, 1*, 130–136.

Jastrzembski, J. E. (1981). Multiple meanings, number of related meanings, frequency of occurrence, and the lexicon. *Cognitive Psychology, 13*, 278–305.

Jastrzembski, J. E. & Stanners, R. F. (1975). Multiple word meanings and lexical search speed. *Journal of Verbal Learning and Verbal Behavior, 14*, 534–537.

Kellas, G., Ferraro, F. R., & Simpson, G. B. (1988). Lexical ambiguity and the timecourse of attentional allocation in word recognition. *Journal of Experimental Psychology: Human Perception and Performance, 14*, 601–609.

Kiehl, K. A., Liddle, P. F., Smith, A. M., Mendrek, A., Forster, B. B., & Hare, R. D. (1999). Neural pathways involved in the processing of concrete and abstract words. *Human Brain Mapping, 7*, 225–233.

Klepousniotou, E. & Baum, S. R. (2007). Disambiguating the ambiguity advantage effect in word recognition: An advantage for polysemous but not homonymous words. *Journal of Neurolinguistics, 20*, 1–24.

Kousta, S-T., Vinson, D. P., & Vigliocco, G. (2009). Emotion words, regardless of polarity, have a processing advantage over neutral words. *Cognition, 112*, 473–481.

Kuchinke, L., Vo, M. L.-H., Hofmann, M., & Jacobs, A. M. (2007). Pupillary responses during lexical decisions vary with word frequency but not emotional valence. *International Journal of Psychophysiology, 65*, 132–140.

Larsen, R. J., Mercer, K. A., Balota, D. A., & Strube, M. J. (2008). Not all negative words slow down lexical decision and naming speed: Importance of word arousal. *Emotion, 8*, 445–452.

McClelland, J. L. & Rumelhart, D. E. (1981). An interactive activation model of context effects in letter perception: Part 1. An account of basic findings. *Psychological Review, 88*, 375–407.

McRae, K. (2005). Semantic memory: Some insights from feature-based connectionist attractor networks. In B. H. Ross (Ed.), *The psychology of learning and motivation: Advances in research and theory, 45* (pp. 41–86). San Diego, CA: Elsevier Academic Press.

McRae, K., Cree, G. S., Seidenberg, M. S., & McNorgan, C. (2005). Semantic feature production norms for a large set of living and nonliving things. *Behavior Research Methods, 37*, 547–559.

Millis, M. L. & Button, S. B. (1989). The effect of polysemy on lexical decision time: Now you see it, now you don't. *Memory & Cognition, 17*, 141–147.

Mirman, D. & Magnuson, J. S. (2008). Attractor dynamics and semantic neighbourhood density: Processing is slowed by near neighbours and speeded by distant neighbours. *Journal of Experimental Psychology: Learning, Memory, & Cognition, 34*, 65–79.

Morton, J. (1969). The interaction of information in word recognition. *Psychological Review, 76*, 165–178.

Nakic, M., Smith, B. W., Busis, S., Vythilingam, M., & Blair, R. J. R. (2006). The impact of affect and frequency on lexical decision: The role of the amygdale and inferior frontal cortex. *NeuroImage, 31*, 1752–1761.

Nelson, D. L., Bennett, D. J., Gee, N. R., Schreiber, T. A., & McKinney, V. M. (1993). Implicit memory: effects of network size and interconnectivity on cued recall. *Journal of Experimental Psychology: Learning, Memory, & Cognition, 19*, 747–764.

Nelson, D. L., McEvoy, C. L., & Schreiber, T. A. (1998). The University of South Florida word association, rhyme, and word fragment norms. Retieved from: http://w3.usf.edu/FreeAssociation/.

Norris, D. (2006). The Bayesian reader: explaining word recognition as an optimal Bayesian decision process. *Psychological Review, 113*, 327–357.

Paivio, A. (1971). *Imagery and verbal processes.* New York: Holt, Rinehart, & Winston.

Paivio, A. (1991). Dual coding theory: Retrospect and current status. *Canadian Journal of Psychology, 45*, 255–287.

Pecher, D. & Zwaan, R. A. (2005). Introduction to grounding cognition. In D. Pecher & R. A. Zwaan (Eds), *Grounding cognition: The role of perception and action in memory, language, and thinking* (pp. 1–7). Cambridge, UK: Cambridge University Press.

Pexman, P. M. & Lupker, S. J. (1999). Ambiguity and visual word recognition: Can feedback explain both homophone and polysemy effects? *Canadian Journal of Experimental Psychology, 53*, 323–334.

Pexman, P. M., Lupker, S. J., & Jared, D. (2001). Homophone effects in lexical decision. *Journal of Experimental Psychology: Learning, Memory, and Cognition, 27*, 139–156.

Pexman, P. M., Lupker, S. J., & Hino, Y. (2002). The impact of feedback semantics in visual word recognition: Number-of-features effects in lexical decision and naming tasks. *Psychonomic Bulletin & Review, 9*, 542–549.

Pexman, P. M., Holyk, G. G., & Monfils, M.-H. (2003). Number-of-features effects and semantic processing. *Memory & Cognition, 31*, 842–855.

Pexman, P. M., Hino, Y., & Lupker, S. J. (2004). Semantic ambiguity and the process of generating meaning from print. *Journal of Experimental Psychology: Learning, Memory, and Cognition, 30*, 1252–1270.

Pexman, P. M., Hargreaves, I. S., Edwards, J. D., Henry, L. C., & Goodyear, B. G. (2007). The neural consequences of semantic richness: When more comes to mind, less activation is observed. *Psychological Science, 18*, 401–406.

Pexman, P. M., Hargreaves, I. S., Siakaluk, P. D., Bodner, G. E., & Pope, J. (2008). There are many ways to be rich: Effects of three measures of semantic richness on visual word recognition. *Psychonomic Bulletin & Review, 15*, 161–167.

Piercey, C. D. & Joordens, S. (2000). Turning an advantage into a disadvantage: Ambiguity effects in lexical decision versus reading tasks. *Memory & Cognition, 28*, 657–666.

Plaut, D. C. (1997). Structure and function in the lexical system: Insights from distributed models of word reading and lexical decision. *Language and Cognitive Processes, 12*, 765–805.

Plaut, D. C. & Shallice, T. (1993). Deep dyslexia: A case study of connectionist neuropsychology. *Cognitive Neuropsychology, 10*, 377–500.

Ratcliff, R., Gomez, P., & McKoon, G. (2004). A diffusion model account of the lexical decision task. *Psychological Review, 111*, 159–182.

Rodd, J., Gaskell, G., & Marslen-Wilson, W. (2002). Making sense of semantic ambiguity: Semantic competition in lexical access. *Journal of Memory and Language, 46*, 245–266.

Rubenstein, H., Garfield, L., & Millikan, J. A. (1970). Homographic entries in the internal lexicon. *Journal of Verbal Learning and Verbal Behavior, 9*, 487–494.

Rubenstein, H., Lewis, S. S., & Rubenstein, M. A. (1971). Evidence for phonemic recoding in visual word recognition. *Journal of Verbal Learning and Verbal Behavior, 10*, 645–657.

Schwanenflugel, P. J. (1991). Why are abstract concepts hard to understand? In P. J. Schwanenflugel (Ed.), *The psychology of word meanings* (pp. 223–250). Hillside, NJ: Erlbaum.

Scott, G. G., O'Donnell, P. J., Leuthold, H., & Sereno, S. C. (2009). Early emotion word processing: Evidence from event-related potentials. *Biological Psychology, 80*, 95–104.

Shaoul, C. & Westbury, C. (2006). Word frequency effects in high-dimensional co-occurrence models: A new approach. *Behavior Research Methods, 38*, 190–195.

Siakaluk, P., Pexman, P., Sears, C., & Owen, W. (2007). Multiple meanings are not necessarily a disadvantage in semantic processing: Evidence from homophone effects in semantic categorisation. *Language and Cognitive Processes, 22*, 453–467.

Siakaluk, P. D., Pexman, P. M., Aguilera, L., Owen, W. J., & Sears, C. R. (2008a). Evidence for the activation of sensorimotor information during visual word recognition: The body-object interaction effect. *Cognition, 106*, 433–443.

Siakaluk, P. D., Pexman, P. M., Sears, C. R., Wilson, K., Locheed, K., & Owen, W. J. (2008b). The benefits of sensorimotor knowledge: Body-object interaction facilitates semantic processing. *Cognitive Science, 32*, 591–605.

Stone, G. O. & Van Orden, G. C. (1993). Strategic control of processing in word recognition. *Journal of Experimental Psychology: Human Perception and Performance, 19*, 744–774.

Thompson-Schill, S. L., D'Esposito, M., Aguirre, G. K., & Farah, M. J. (1997). Role of left inferior prefrontal cortex in retrieval of semantic knowledge: A reevaluation. *Proceedings of the National Academy of Sciences, U.S.A., 94*, 14792–14797.

Tillotson, S. M., Siakaluk, P. D., & Pexman, P. M. (2008). Body-Object interaction ratings for 1,618 monosyllabic nouns. *Behavior Research Methods, 40*, 1075–1078.

Toglia, M. P. & Battig, W. F. (1978). *Handbook of semantic word norms.* Hillsdale, NJ: Erlbaum.

Vinson, D. P. & Vigliocco, G. (2008). Semantic feature production norms for a large set of objects and events. *Behavior Research Methods, 40*, 183–190.

Wagenmakers, E.-J., Steyvers, M., Raaijmakers, J. G. W., Shiffrin, R. M., van Rijn, H., & Zeelenberg, R. (2004). A model for evidence accumulation in the lexical decision task. *Cognitive Psychology, 48*, 332–367.

Wilson, M. (2002). Six views of embodied cognition. *Psychonomic Bulletin & Review, 9*, 625–636.

Wurm, L. H. (2007). Danger and usefulness: An alternative framework for understanding rapid evaluation effects in perception? *Psychonomic Bulletin & Review, 14*, 1218–1225.

Wurm, L. H., Vakoch, D. A., Seaman, S. R., & Buchanan, L. (2004). Semantic effects in auditory word recognition. *Mental Lexicon Working Papers, 1*, 47–62.

Yap, M. J., Tan, S. E., Pexman, P. M., & Hargreaves, I. S. (2011). Is more always better? Effects of semantic richness on lexical decision, speeded pronunciation, and semantic classification. *Psychonomic Bulletin & Review, 18*, 742–750.

3 Lexical priming

Associative, semantic, and thematic influences on word recognition

Lara L. Jones and Zachary Estes

Lexical priming occurs when the response to a target word varies systematically as a function of the preceding linguistic context. Typically, the target word elicits a faster response after a context that is related than after an unrelated context. For example, following the related prime word "cat", the target word "mouse" tends to elicit faster and/or more accurate responses. Although much of the research has employed single word primes (e.g., Meyer & Schvaneveldt, 1971), as in this example, more complex contexts such as sentence frames and discourse contexts can also induce lexical priming (e.g., Camblin, Gordon, & Swaab, 2007; Hess, Foss, & Carroll, 1995). This chapter provides an overview of the many measures, models, and types of lexical priming. It also summarizes individual differences in lexical priming across the lifespan and among healthy and cognitively impaired populations.

Lexical priming is an extremely pervasive phenomenon in visual word recognition. Because words rarely occur in isolation, they are nearly always subject to the many potential influences of preceding words. Understanding lexical priming is thus paramount for understanding word recognition. Lexical priming can also be used to discriminate between models of cognition more generally. For example, the connectionist (e.g., Rogers Foss, D. J., and Carroll, McClelland, 2004), rational (e.g., Anderson Foss, D. J., and Carroll, Lebiere, 1998), and embodied (e.g., Barsalou, 2008) approaches to cognition all attempt to explain lexical priming in different ways. Research on lexical priming therefore can impact psychology beyond word recognition.

In addition to its theoretical implications, lexical priming also has important implications for many practical areas of study, such as the development of reading skill (e.g., Andrews, 2008; Michael, 2009; Nation & Snowling, 1999) and conceptual organization (Perraudin & Mounoud, 2009), and the understanding of disorders such as schizophrenia (e.g., Kostova, Passerieux, Laurent, & Hardy-Baylé, 2005; Lecardeur, Foltz, & Laham, 2007) and Alzheimer's disease (e.g., Giffard, Laisney, Eustache, & Desgranges, 2009). Knowledge of the recent developments in lexical priming may also enable researchers to further investigate topics of interest in education, gerontology, and other related fields. Hence, we present an overview of the methods and models of lexical priming, and we discuss some of the prevailing questions within the field. In doing so, we will emphasize recent research and newer methods that have addressed some of the fundamental questions raised in prior reviews of lexical priming (e.g., Hutchison, 2003; Lucas, 2000; McNamara, 2005; Neely, 1991).

Measures of lexical priming

In this section we briefly describe several measures of lexical priming, including the lexical decision, word naming, perceptual identification, and semantic decision tasks, as well as more recent eye-tracking and neuroimaging methods. First, however, we consider the most appropriate control or *baseline condition* against which lexical priming should be compared. This choice of a baseline has proven somewhat problematic regardless of which task one employs, as unfortunately there is no consensus about what baseline is most appropriate. Researchers have used a number of different baseline primes, including a string of neutral symbols such as asterisks or Xs, a word like "blank" or "ready", a blank pause, a nonword like "brid", and a prime word that is unrelated to the target. One problem in using a repeated baseline is that participants may become habituated to these repeated primes during the course of the experiment and consequently may attend less to both the repeated neutral primes and the related primes (Jonides & Mack, 1984; McNamara, 2005). McNamara suggests using pronounceable nonwords (e.g., "brid"), though he cautions that the increased latencies for processing these nonword primes may carry over to artificially longer target latencies. Alternatively, Bodner, Masson, and Richard (2006) found that a 45-ms blank pause baseline eliminated the tendency for slower responses on baseline trials than on unrelated-prime trials. Several behavioral studies have demonstrated that lexical priming is robust across the various baseline measures (e.g., Bodner et al., 2006; Bodner & Masson, 2001; Estes & Jones, 2009; Jones, 2010) up to 1000 ms. However, at longer SOAs (> 1000 ms), nonword repetitive baselines have been found to artificially inflate priming effects (de Groot, Thomassen, & Hudson, 1982; Jones, 2012a, 2012b; Jonides & Mack, 1984), and thus should be avoided or supplemented with other baseline primes. The choice of baseline prime may be even more important in ERP studies. Unrelated word primes tend to maximize the N400 effect (described below), whereas a repeated neutral word like "blank" may produce an N400 that is similar to a related prime (Dien, Franklin, & May, 2006). Overall, the consensus is that there is no truly neutral prime (Bodner et al., 2006; Jonides & Mack, 1984; McNamara, 2005; Neely, 1991). The best option for purposes of convergent validity is to use more than one type of baseline prime, either within or across experiments.

Lexical decision

The most common measure of lexical priming is the lexical decision task (LDT), whereby participants decide whether a given letter string is a real word (e.g., "bird") or a nonword (e.g., "brid"). There are several variations of the LDT. In the *continuous LDT* (a.k.a. *sequential* or *single LDT*), participants respond to each individually presented prime and target letter string. In the *standard LDT*, primes and targets are presented individually, and participants respond only to the target. In the *double LDT*, prime and target strings are displayed simultaneously, and participants indicate by a single response whether both are real words. Priming is observed as a difference in response times or error rates following a related prime relative to a baseline prime. For example, in their seminal study, Meyer and Schvaneveldt (1971) found that responses in a double LDT were 80 ms faster for related pairs such as "NURSE – DOCTOR" than for unrelated pairs such as "BREAD – DOCTOR". The primary advantages of the LDT are its minimal technical requirements and its ease of administration.

To administer a LDT, the researcher must specify a number of procedural parameters. First, one must choose the prime duration and the *stimulus onset asynchrony* (SOA), which is the delay between prime and target onset. The prime duration is important because it determines whether the prime can be processed consciously (i.e., generally at durations longer than 30 ms), or only unconsciously (i.e., generally 30 ms or less, followed by a visual mask such as "#######"). The SOA is important because it determines the extent to which the prime may be processed prior to target presentation (i.e., prospectively), with longer SOAs allowing more prospective processing. The researcher must also specify a number of properties of the nonword trials. One must determine the percentage of trials for which the target is a nonword. Although this is typically 50%, this can be manipulated to bias participants toward either "word" responses (e.g., only 25% nonword targets) or nonword responses (e.g., 75% nonword targets). The researcher must also determine whether the nonwords are pronounceable (e.g., "brid") or unpronounceable (e.g., "bdri"), which affects how deeply the targets are processed. One must additionally determine the *relatedness proportion* (RP), which is the proportion of trials on which the prime and target are related (for a review, see Hutchison, 2007). This factor is often used to test whether an effect is strategic or automatic. If an effect is under participants' strategic control, then presumably it should occur under conditions in which the prime and target are likely to be related (i.e., high RP) but should be attenuated when the prime and target are unlikely to be related (i.e., low RP). Thus, the observation of an RP effect provides evidence of strategic processing. A potentially more important but often overlooked factor is the *nonword ratio* (NR), which is the probability that the target is a nonword given that it is unrelated to the prime (Neely & Keefe, 1989). Although RP and NR are conceptually related and often confounded, they can differentially affect lexical decisions (Neely, Keefe, & Ross, 1989).

Word naming (reading aloud)

In the word naming task, participants simply read aloud as quickly as possible the given word. The onset and accuracy of the vocal response typically serve as the dependent measures, though a number of other measures are also available (e.g., duration, pitch, jitter, shimmer; see Kent & Read, 2002). As in the LDT, lexical priming is observed as a difference in response times or error rates following a related prime relative to a baseline prime. Word naming is higher than the LDT in ecological validity (because the task only entails reading), it is more efficient (because nonword trials are unnecessary), it is less likely to exhibit a speed–accuracy tradeoff (because errors are less common), and it is simpler to administer (because the RP and NR factors do not apply). The primary disadvantage of the word naming task is that analysis of participants' sound files may be cumbersome. The word naming task is less susceptible than the LDT to strategic processing, so word naming provides a stronger test of automaticity, whereas the LDT may be necessary to observe strategic effects (Balota & Chumbley, 1984). Similarly, because semantic effects tend to be smaller in word naming than in lexical decisions, the LDT may be more effective for comparing different types of priming.

Perceptual identification

The perceptual identification task entails very brief presentation of target words, which participants attempt to identify. For example, the target word "mouse" might appear for only 30 ms. Several response types are possible. For instance, participants could be asked to report the presented word, to indicate whether the presented letter string is a word or a nonword, or to choose the presented word from several options (e.g., "mouse or house?"). The dependent measure here is accuracy, and lexical priming is observed as a difference in accuracy following a related prime relative to a baseline prime. As in the LDT and word naming, the duration of the prime word and the SOA must be determined by the researcher, but note that the prime is typically presented for a longer duration (e.g., 500 ms). The target duration is typically between 15 and 45 ms, so as to avoid floor and ceiling accuracy rates. Moreover, perception of the target is further controlled by overlaying a visual mask (e.g., #####), which prevents continued inspection of the perceptual representation of the target in iconic memory (Masson & MacLeod, 1992; for a review see Van den Bussche, Van den Noortgate, & Reynvoet, 2009). Target accuracies in this perceptual identification paradigm typically are in the 60–80% range, with reliably higher accuracies for related than unrelated prime-target pairs.

Semantic decision

In a semantic decision task, participants make some semantic judgment of a target word. For example, participants may be asked to indicate the semantic category of the target (e.g., "animal or object?", Spuryt, De Houwer, & Hermans, 2009), or to verify a particular semantic feature (e.g., "Does the word refer to something that is alive?", Hare, Jones, Thomson, Kelly, & McRae, 2009). Affirmative "yes" responses are faster for targets following primes that share the semantic feature of interest (e.g., animals). This task can take the form of a continuous procedure (in which decisions are made for both prime and target), a naming procedure (in which the participant verbally responds with the correct semantic decision; "animal" or "object"; Spuryt et al., 2009), or a standard procedure (in which only the targets are evaluated; Hare et al., 2009). Semantic decision tasks offer a couple of advantages over the LDT. First, a semantic decision task requires participants to more closely attend to a particular semantic dimension (e.g., animacy, valence, concreteness), which increases the activation of the concept's semantic representation. In turn, this heightened activation of the concept's semantic representation may facilitate priming across long SOAs and intervening items between prime and target (Becker, Moscovitch, Behrmann, & Joordens, 1997). Indeed, long-term priming across 0, 4, and 8 intervening items was found for highly similar pairs in a semantic decision task but not in a LDT (Becker et al., 1997). Second, the filler items can be related but still require a "no" response (e.g., TABLE → CHAIR for "Does the word refer to something that is alive?"). Consequently, prime-target relatedness does not become a cue for a "yes" or "no" response, thereby hindering a relatedness checking strategy (Hare et al., 2009).

Eye tracking

Eye tracking, whereby participants' eye movements and fixations are recorded in relation to visual stimuli, is a rich alternative for assessing lexical priming (Ledoux, Camblin, Swaab, & Gordon, 2006; Odekar, Hallowell, Kruse, Moates, & Lee, 2009). It offers a number of methodological advantages, including high ecological validity and continuous measurement without disruptive behavioral responses such as button presses or vocal responses. Eye tracking also provides a wealth of data, including multiple measures of the latency, location, and duration of fixations, as well as the trajectory and speed of eye movements. One paradigm for measuring lexical priming via eye tracking is to follow a prime word with an array of target words, one of which is semantically related to the prime. For instance, "king" might be followed by "monkey", "candle", "bicycle", and "queen", and lexical priming would be manifest as an earlier and/or longer fixation on the semantically related word "queen" (e.g., Meyer & Federmeier, 2008). Another paradigm is to present a target word in the presence of a context, such as a sentence or prime word, and to observe eye movements to and fixations on the context and/or target words (e.g., Camblin et al., 2007; Morris, 1994; Rayner, Warren, Juhasz, & Liversedge, 2004). Such eye tracking measures of lexical priming correlate with standard behavioral measures of priming (Folk & Morris, 1995; Odekar et al., 2009).

Neuroimaging

The rapid growth of cognitive neuroscience has provided researchers with a valuable tool for studying the temporal and spatial patterns of brain activity during lexical priming. These neural measures have the potential to reveal effects of lexical priming that may not be detected via standard behavioral methods. For instance, such measures can provide additional information regarding the time course of lexical priming and/or the underlying neural regions involved in lexical priming (e.g., Rossell, Price, & Nobre, 2003). Moreover, lexical priming may involve some observable neural processes that ultimately produce no observable behavioral effects. Event-related potential (ERP) priming studies provide information on the valence (positive or negative) and timing of neural voltages recorded as wave amplitudes by an electroencephalogram (EEG). Functional magnetic resonance imaging (fMRI) indirectly measures cerebral blood flow via the BOLD (blood-oxygen level dependent) response and provides better spatial resolution than ERP. Of these methods, the N400 ERP component has been the most studied. The N400 refers to larger negative amplitudes approximately 400 ms following stimulus onset for items that are semantically incongruent with the previous context than for items that are semantically congruent (Chwilla, Hagoort, & Brown, 1998, 2000). Though the N400 is thought to reflect controlled processes (e.g., semantic matching, lexical integration), some have argued that it may also reflect uncontrolled processes such as automatic spreading activation (see Franklin, Dien, Neely, Huber, & Waterson, 2007). Studies using fMRI may also differentiate between various mechanisms of priming (e.g., Franklin et al., 2007; Sass, Krach, Sachs, & Kircher, 2009) and representational codes (e.g., conceptual versus perceptual; Giesbrecht, Camblin, & Swaab, 2004).

Models of lexical priming

Models of lexical priming traditionally are distinguished along two main theoretical dimensions: Priming may occur prospectively or retrospectively, and it may be controllable (a.k.a. strategic) or automatic. *Prospective* models claim that the prime word pre-activates the target word, thereby speeding its recognition. *Retrospective* models posit that the prime and target words are considered together, and if they are congruent in any way (e.g., associated, similar, familiar), then the target elicits a fast response. For example, the prime "cat" could pre-activate the target "mouse" before the target is even presented (i.e., prospectively), or "cat" and "mouse" could be considered together after the target is presented (i.e., retrospectively). *Strategic* models assert that individuals can strategically control how the target word is processed. For example, one can opt to compare "cat" and "mouse" or not, depending on one's current goals and the task conditions. *Automatic* models, in contrast, suppose that individuals are unable to intentionally modulate processing of the target word. That is, "cat" and "mouse" are compared regardless of one's intention.

These two theoretical dimensions – direction (prospective or retrospective) and controllability (automatic or strategic) of priming – are orthogonal, thus yielding four basic classes of models (see Table 3.1). To illustrate, the spreading activation model (described below) posits that priming occurs prospectively and automatically, whereas the semantic matching model claims that priming acts retrospectively and strategically (Hutchison, 2002; Jones, 2010). Several other computational and mathematical models of word recognition are addressed in detail in Volume 1 (Forster; Gomez; Sibley and Kello), and therefore we will present only briefly some of the major models as they relate to the various types of lexical priming.

Table 3.1 Theoretical dimensions and major models of lexical priming

Direction	Control	
	Automatic	*Strategic*
Prospective	Spreading activation ACT* Thematic integration	Expectancy
Retrospective	ACT*	Semantic matching Compound cue Episodic retrieval

Spreading activation

According to the spreading activation model, concepts are represented as nodes in a semantic network. Perception or memory of a target word activates its semantic representation, and that activation spreads very quickly ($\approx$1 ms per link) to neighboring nodes representing related concepts. Activation decays with the distance it travels in the semantic network, and when attention to a source node (e.g., the prime) ceases, the pattern of activation emanating from that node rapidly decays. Alternative models of spreading activation explain lexical priming in different ways. Collins and Loftus (1975) attribute lexical priming to the prime word causing a spread of activation to the target concept, thereby pre-activating the target word. Anderson's (1983) ACT* model describes lexical priming in terms of *reverberation*, in which activation can spread back from a target node to its source node and then back from the source node to the target until an asymptotic level of activation is reached. Thus, the ACT* model predicts that "asymptotic target activation is determined by associations in the forward and backward directions" (McNamara, 1992a, p. 1177). This model thus accommodates retrospective, in addition to prospective, explanations of lexical priming (see Table 3.1). Priming effects occurring in tasks that do not permit an awareness of prime-target pairing (e.g., naming, continuous LDT) are generally considered to indicate automatic spreading activation.

Expectancy

During a lexical priming task people may form predictions about what words will follow a given prime. This "expectancy set" can vary in size based in large part on the consistency of relations used within a list. That is, if just one type of relation (e.g., antonyms) is used within the list, participants should be better able to predict the related word that will follow a prime. Moreover, primes (e.g., DAY) that have only one or two strongly associated targets (e.g., NIGHT) should yield a smaller expectancy set. The generation of an expectancy set appears to be a controlled process, as it is subject to the RP effect (Bodner & Masson, 2003; Hutchison, 2002). Thus, the generation of an expectancy set is prospective, meaning that target activation increases *prior to* its actual presentation (see

Table 3.1). The formation of an expectancy set is thought to take approximately 300 ms to fully develop (Becker, 1980; den Heyer, Briand, & Smith, 1985; Hutchison, Neely, & Johnson, 2001; Neely, 1991; Perea & Rosa, 2002). Expectancy generation may account for lexical priming found at intermediate and longer SOAs (up to 2000 ms) for highly associated items. However, it may be difficult to maintain the generated expectancy set in working memory over very long SOAs (>2000 ms). Further research is needed to test the influence of working memory in the maintenance of an expectancy set across a long SOA and/or intervening items.

Semantic matching

Semantic matching refers to a search for a meaningful relation between prime and target (Jones, 2010; Neely, 1977; Neely et al., 1989). In a LDT, for instance, participants may check for a relation between prime and target words following presentation of the target. If the prime and target are indeed related, then the target must be a word, since words are rarely related to nonwords. So participants are biased to respond that the stimulus is a word if a semantic relation is present and to respond that it is a nonword if a relation is not present. Thus, as characterized in Table 3.1, semantic matching is a retrospective process that can occur only after target presentation. It is also a controlled process that varies across RP manipulations (Estes & Jones, 2009).

Episodic retrieval

In lexical priming studies, a target word may elicit retrieval of the prime. If the target is in any way related to or consistent with the prime, then its recognition will be facilitated (Bodner & Masson, 2001, 2003). Thus, episodic retrieval is conceptually similar to semantic matching. It is also similar to the compound cue model (McKoon & Ratcliff, 1992; Ratcliff & McKoon, 1988), which attributes lexical priming to the retrieval of the prime-target compound from long-term memory. All three of these processes (i.e., semantic matching, episodic retrieval, and compound cue) act retrospectively to interpret the target in the context of the prime and assume priming to be controllable.

Thematic integration

Thematic integration entails the inference of a plausible thematic relation and the assignment of concepts to complementary functional roles in that theme (Coolen, van Jaarsveld, & Schreuder, 1991; Estes, Golonka, & Jones, 2011a; Estes & Jones, 2008, 2009; Wisniewski, 1997). For example, a "winter holiday" is a holiday *during* the winter, and a "chocolate bar" is a bar *composed of* chocolate. By a thematic integration model, lexical priming occurs when the target word is thematically integrated with the prime. That is, if the target word (e.g., "holiday") can perform a different functional role in the same theme (e.g., X *during* Y) as the prime word (e.g., "winter"), then target recognition is facilitated.

Although the thematic integration model of lexical priming has not yet been thoroughly researched, some evidence indicates that thematic integration is beyond strategic control, as integrative priming is insensitive to manipulations of RP (Estes & Jones, 2009). That is, thematic integration occurs even among lists in which few of the words can plausibly be integrated. Other recent work in our laboratories suggests that thematic integration also occurs prospectively. In particular, we have found recently that integrative priming is obtained in the masked perceptual identification task in which target words were presented for only 20 ms. This very brief target presentation precludes retrospective processing, yet targets were identified more accurately when they could be easily integrated with the prime word than when they could not be integrated with the prime (Estes, Jones, & Mather, 2011b). Thus, preliminary evidence suggests that thematic integration occurs prospectively and automatically (see Table 3.1).

Types of lexical priming

Traditionally studies on lexical priming classified their stimuli as either associative or semantic (for reviews see Lucas, 2000, McNamara, 2005, and Hutchison, 2003). Semantic relations generally refer to any feature-based relationship between two concepts such as a category and exemplar (e.g., FRUIT and PEAR), category co-members (e.g., CAT and DOG), or instrument and object (e.g., BROOM and FLOOR). In contrast, associative relations are defined by the free-association task (described below) and are therefore assumed to reflect word use more than word meaning (Thompson-Schill, Kurtz, & Gabriele, 1998). In addition to associative and semantic priming, much recent research has examined thematic priming. Below we review the evidence concerning all three of these main sources of priming, as well as mediated priming.

Associative priming

Lexical association has been defined most frequently as the proportion of participants in a free association task who produce a specific target word (e.g., DOG) in response to a given cue word (e.g., CAT). The creation of online databases such as the University of South Florida Free Association Norms (Nelson, McEvoy, & Schreiber, 1998), which are based on samples of approximately 100 participants per cue word, have enabled researchers to easily control or manipulate association strengths for their stimuli. Many recent studies have adopted Nelson and colleagues' (1998) descriptive categories of association strengths: strong (>0.20), moderate (between 0.10 and 0.20), weak (between 0.01 and 0.10), and unassociated (< 0.01).

More recently, a number of other valid indicators of association have been found to produce reliable priming effects including whether the associate is the primary or non-primary response to a cue (Anaki & Henik, 2003), the number of associates produced for a given cue (Ron-Kaplan & Henik, 2007), and the connectivity among the associates (Nelson, Bennett, Gee, Schreiber, & McKinney,

1993; Wible, Han, Spencer, Kubicki, Niznikiewicz, et al., 2006). For example, the primary (most frequently provided) associate for a given cue may be strong (e.g., BROTH → SOUP, forward association strength = 0.806; values taken from Nelson et al., 1998) or weak (e.g., CHICKEN → SOUP, 0.092) in association strength. Anaki and Henik found that both strong and weak primary associates produce comparable priming effects that are larger than non-primary associates.

Moreover, co-occurrence of two items may also influence priming. Co-occurrence may be measured as the local co-occurrence of any two items as they appear together in a particular order in text. For instance, the number of Google hits for a word pair presented within quotation marks (e.g., "chicken soup") serves as a measure of local co-occurrence frequency in everyday language and is highly correlated with familiarity (Wisniewski & Murphy, 2005). Hence, Google can be used to assess this type of local co-occurrence (e.g., Estes & Jones, 2009; Jones, 2010). The British National Corpus and the American National Corpus are both searchable databases that can also be used for assessing local co-occurrence. Global co-occurrence is the frequency with which two words appear within the same or similar written text. For example, Latent Semantic Analysis cosines (*LSA*; Landauer et al., 1998) provide a very broad measure of global co-occurrence. However, LSA does not take word order into account (CHICKEN SOUP would have the same LSA value as SOUP CHICKEN). The BEAGLE model Jones & Mewhort, 2007) represents both global co-occurrence and word order. Other sources, such as the Usenet database (Lund & Burgess, 1996; see also Shaoul & Westbury, 2006) and the WordMine2 database (Durda & Buchanan, 2006), can provide both local and global measures of co-occurrence. Given the impact of co-occurrence in lexical priming, it is important to assess this factor when examining the differences in lexical priming across various relation types or task conditions.

In addition to association strength and frequency of co-occurrence, the type of relation may also influence lexical priming. Since the first lexical priming study (Meyer & Schvaneveldt, 1971), the last 40 years of research have demonstrated robust lexical priming between associated concepts sharing many different types of relations including antonyms (DAY NIGHT), synonyms (BOAT SHIP), attributes (ZEBRA STRIPES) and highly similar (APPLE PEAR) or less similar (GRAPE WATER-MELON) category coordinates, to name just a few. Among these, antonyms were the most frequently occurring relation in one set of norms for college-aged adults (see Hutchison, 2003, Table 1). Behavioral studies have found similar priming effects among antonyms, synonyms, and category coordinates that were either associated (e.g., HATE LOVE, HOUSE HOME, TABLE CHAIR) or unassociated (e.g., CRAZY SANE, SHOP STORE, SILK COTTON; Perea & Rosa, 2002; Williams, 1996). However, as we will discuss, ERP studies have found subtle differences among different types of associated items (see Franklin et al., 2007).

Recent research has expanded the investigation of lexical priming to several other types of relations including phrasal associates (WIND MILL) and locative (KITCHEN TABLE), compositional (GLASS TABLE), and event or script (PARTY MUSIC) relations. McRae and Boisvert (1998, p. 569) noted that "prime-target pairs often depict a number of types of relations and include primes from various grammatical and semantic categories." They noted that investigations of different types of relations with a broad category (e.g., unassociated semantically related items) would entail empirical work to norm the items to ensure that they exemplified the relation type. Hutchison (2003) further argued that more experimentation was needed to explore the priming effects of many of these less studied relations, such as phrasal associates and script relations.

Semantic priming

Several studies (e.g., Estes & Jones, 2009; Moss, Ostrin, Tyler, & Marslen-Wilson, 1995; Perea & Rosa, 2002) have found processing differences between associative and semantic priming, which suggests that different theoretical models may be required to explain these different processes.

Do associative and pure semantic priming reflect different processes?

The time course of activation (i.e., the extent of facilitation) differs between associative and semantic relations. At short (i.e., <300 ms) or medium (approximately 300–800 ms) SOAs, both associatively and semantically related primes facilitate target responses. But at longer SOAs (i.e., typically ≥1000 ms), semantic priming is reduced or eliminated, whereas associative priming remains stable or increases. For example, Estes and Jones (2009) found equivalent priming effects at a 500-ms SOA in a standard LDT between pure semantic relations (FOX → DOG) and associatively related items (BONE → DOG). For the semantic items, activation decreased only slightly at a 1500-ms SOA, but was eliminated at a 2500-ms SOA. In contrast, for the associative items, the priming effect increased at a 2000-ms SOA (see also den Heyer et al., 1985; Perea & Rosa, 2002).

Such behavioral studies suggest that pure semantic priming is a fast-acting process, which decays at longer SOAs (Van den Bussche et al., 2009). In contrast, associative priming is thought to reflect primarily spreading activation when occurring in standard LDTs at short SOAs (<300 ms) and in continuous LDTs, and expectancy when occurring at longer SOAs. The type of associative relation may determine the processing mechanism. For example, expectancy sets are smaller for antonyms than for category coordinates (Chwilla, Kolk, & Mulder, 2000), and thus antonyms may be processed via either spreading activation or expectancy.

ERP studies also suggest a difference between the processing involved in associative vs semantic relations (Rhodes & Donaldson, 2008; for review see Franklin et al., 2007). In a double LDT (Roehm, Bornkessel-Schlesewsky, Rösler, & Schlesewsky, 2007), antonyms (BLACK WHITE) had faster response times and lower N400 amplitudes than related category co-members (BLACK YELLOW), which in turn were faster and lower in N400 amplitudes than unrelated items (BLACK NICE). The difference may lie in the exact time window of the N400 amplitude. Semantically similar items (SOFA BED) exhibited an N400 effect at an earlier time-window (250–375 ms) but not in a later one (Koivisto & Revonsuo, 2001). In contrast, lexically associated compounds (WIND MILL) exhibited an N400 effect in both this earlier and a later time window (375–500 ms), which likely reflects a semantic matching or expectancy process rather than automatic spreading activation.

Is association required for semantic priming?

The answer to this question depends on several factors including the similarity of the prime and target and the type of task. Moss and colleagues (1995) found reliable priming for associated (DOG → CAT) but not for unassociated (PIG → HORSE) category coordinates (see also Shelton & Martin, 1992). Yet McRae and Boisvert (1998) noted that the stimuli used in Shelton and Martin (1992) and Moss et al. (1995) were lacking in similarity (e.g., DUCK → COW). To assess the importance of similarity in semantic priming, McRae and Boisvert tested whether highly similar (GOOSE → TURKEY) and less similar (ROBIN → TURKEY) category co-members would yield reliable priming effects at both short (250 ms) and long (750 ms) SOAs. Using a standard LDT, they found reliable priming at both SOAs for the highly similar items, but only at the long SOA for the less similar items. These studies, along with our findings of reliable priming for similar categorical coordinates at a short SOA of 100 ms (Estes & Jones, 2009, Experiment 2), suggest that similarity between prime and target is a critical factor in obtaining reliable priming at short SOAs (see also Bueno & Frenck-Mestre, 2008, for a similar result using a masked priming paradigm).

Thematic priming

In addition to the *featural similarity* and *taxonomic* information typically inves- tigated in studies of semantic priming, many other aspects of a concept's meaning are activated based on one's world knowledge about a concept (Estes & Jones, 2009; Hare et al., 2009; Moss et al., 1995) or even one's recent exposure to an incidental association (i.e., words that had appeared within a recently presented sentence; Prior & Bentin, 2008). Such world knowledge relations include: *locative* (BEACH HOUSE); *instrumental* (REALTOR HOUSE); *schematic* (a.k.a., *script* or *event-based*, RENTAL HOUSE); and *compositional* (BRICK HOUSE) among many others.

Theoretically, integration (either relational or situational) has been proposed to explain this type of priming and thus distinguishes it from the more traditional taxonomic/similarity-based semantic priming. For some of these relations (e.g., *locative*, *compositional*), integration occurs upon target presentation via the infer- ence of a relation (a BEACH HOUSE is a HOUSE that is *located* on a BEACH). Relational integration then entails the linking of prime and target into one plau- sible entity. To assess the extent of relational integration between prime and target, participants rate the extent to which the prime-target pairs "could be linked together to produce a sensible phrase" (Estes & Jones, 2009, p. 116). In contrast, for other relations (e.g., *script, instrumental*), the integration has occurred previously via the pairing of prime and target in one's experiences and/or vicariously by exposure to this pairing in text or other media. Unlike relational integration, thematic and instrumental priming do not necessarily entail the merging of two concepts into a single entity. Rather the concepts are connected via an action verb in the case of instrumental pairs (BROOM → FLOOR; a broom is used *to sweep* a floor). Indeed, such instrumental relations were found to have significantly lower integrative ratings than other thematic relations (Jones, 2010). Though we found no differences in priming magnitude between relationally integrative (e.g., TOMATO SOUP) and thematic (e.g., BOWL SOUP) pairs, target word recognition was differentially related to familiarity ratings and local co-occurrence measures (Google hits) for the integrative pairs and to more global co-occurrence measures (e.g., LSA) for the thematic pairs (Jones, Estes, & Golonka, 2011).

Like the more traditionally studied *taxonomic* and *similar* prime-target pairs, these thematic prime-target pairs may or may not also share a moderate to strong association. Moreover, some of these thematic relations produce equally robust priming effects in the presence or absence of an association. In a study using both ERP and behavioral measures, Chwilla and Kolk (2005) found a reliable 25-ms priming effect for unassociated thematic relations. They used a variant of a double LDT in which two primes (MOVE and PIANO) were presented immediately prior to the target (BACKACHE) in order to better create a story-like script in which none of the three words shared an association. These primes remained on the screen with the target, and participants judged whether all three items were real words. Moreover, the N400 priming effect differed from the scalp distribution found in the N400 for associative and semantic relations. In a subsequent experiment that increased thematic processing, participants judged whether the three words formed a plausible scenario. In comparison to the results in the LDT, the plausibility judgment task yielded larger priming effects and an N400 distribution that was more characteristic of that seen for semantic relations in its scalp distribution. Chwilla and Kolk concluded that a global integration process (see also Hess et al., 1995) accounted for their obtained thematic priming.

Two factors that affect thematic priming are the frequency and recency of the given relation. For instance, CHOCOLATE is integrated most frequently via a compositional relation (e.g., CHOCOLATE COIN), and is integrated only infrequently via a selling relation (e.g., CHOCOLATE SHOP). Words are integrated faster if they instantiate a frequent relation than an infrequent relation (Gagné & Shoben, 1997; Maguire, Maguire, & Cater, 2010; Storms & Wisniewski, 2005). Relations are also inferred on the basis of their recency, as evident from *relation priming*, whereby a target phrase is understood more quickly when preceded by a prime phrase that instantiates the same relation (e.g., WOOD CHAIR → CHOCOLATE COIN) than a prime with a different relation (e.g., WOOD SHOP → CHOCOLATE COIN; Estes, 2003; Estes & Jones, 2006; Raffray, Pickering, & Branigan, 2007). Thus, the frequency and recency of thematic relations both affect lexical priming.

Hare et al. (2009) found priming for both associated and unassociated event (script) relations using semantic rather than lexical decision tasks. They found robust priming for object targets following event primes (PICNIC → BLANKET), location primes (GARAGE → CAR), and instrument primes (OVEN → COOKIES), and for people/animal targets following event primes (REUNION → FRIENDS) and location primes (BARN → COW), but not for instrument-people primes (WRENCH → PLUMBER). Computational analyses with BEAGLE predicted the priming obtained for all but the instrumental-people pairs (i.e., higher cosines for the event than the unrelated pairs). As the authors noted, the instrument-people primes were not sufficiently constraining for the people targets (anyone can use a wrench). In a final experiment, however, priming was obtained for these items in the reverse people-instrument direction (PLUMBER → WRENCH). For each item type, priming effects for only the subset of weakly or unassociated items were equivalent to or higher than the overall priming effect. Hence, the obtained priming was not attributable to association strength. Rather this event-based knowledge forms an accessible part of a concept's meaning, which facilitates overall language comprehension upon encountering the word in context.

Together the Chwilla and Kolk (2005) and Hare et al. (2009) studies demonstrate that schematic knowledge is activated in a semantic decision task or in a highly strategic double LDT. However, in a continuous LDT (Moss et al., 1995), reliable priming did not obtain for either associated (GALLERY → ART) or unassociated (PARTY → MUSIC) script relations. This failure to find script priming in a continuous LDT suggests limits in the lexical activation of targets by schematically related primes. We (Estes & Jones, 2009) found lexical activation of relationally integrative unassociated prime-target pairs (OCEAN → FISH; *locative* relation) in a double LDT, and in a standard LDT with SOAs ranging from 100 to 2500 ms.

These studies (Chwilla & Kolk, 2005; Estes & Jones, 2009; Hare et al., 2009; Moss et al., 1995) illustrate that priming occurs as a result of the integration of two nouns based on a unifying relation (e.g., *locative*) or common theme. This thematic priming is similar to that previously found for transparent compounds (e.g., LIP → STICK) and phrasal associates (e.g., WIND → MILL; Hodgson, 1991; Koivisto & Revonsuo, 2001; Seidenberg, Waters, Sanders, & Langer, 1984). Thus, co-occurrence models (e.g., BEAGLE, Jones & Mewhort, 2007; LSA, Landauer et al., 1998) may explain thematic priming among items that also share a strong association (NEST → BIRD). Indeed, word recognition was faster for targets in integrative pairs that also shared a strong association from prime to target (e.g., FLANNEL → SHIRT) than for integrative pairs that were unassociated (e.g., SILK → SHIRT; Jones, 2012a). This associative boost in integrative priming occurred at a 500-ms SOA but not at a 200-ms SOA. Moreover, target response times were related to forward association strength as well as to familiarity. Thus, given sufficient time (>300 ms), relational integration may be facilitated or boosted by the formation of an expectancy set consisting of anticipated targets that are strongly associated with the prime (e.g., SHIRT, PAJAMAS, and NIGHTGOWN for the prime FLANNEL). Alternatively, a prime-target compound-cue may be formed and retrieved from LTM thereby bypassing the need for relation inference and role assignment – a process that is especially likely for highly familiar pairs (e.g., BRICK HOUSE, PUMPKIN PIE; Jones, 2012a).

However, thematic priming may also occur with little or no lexical co-occurrence or association (Estes & Jones, 2009; Estes et al., 2011b; Jones, 2012a). For
instance, "monkey" is unassociated with and rarely co-occurs with "foot", but
because "monkey foot" can be easily integrated, "monkey" facilitates recognition
of "foot". This integrative priming occurs with SOAs as short as 100 ms
(Estes & Jones, 2009; Jones et al., 2011) and with target presentation as brief as
20 ms (Estes et al., 2011b). Such integrative priming without lexical association,
semantic similarity, or compound familiarity cannot be explained by standard
mechanisms like spreading activation, expectancy generation or compound
retrieval, which are based on association and familiarity. At the same time, the
fact that such integrative priming occurs at short SOAs and with very brief target
durations also excludes retrospective mechanisms like semantic matching.
More work is needed to test this hypothesis, but it appears that thematic priming
is role-based (Estes & Jones, 2009; Hare et al., 2009). For example, hearing
or reading "jungle" activates the "habitat" role, thereby facilitating recognition
of subsequent words that denote typical "inhabitants" such as "bird", even though
"jungle" and "bird" might not co-occur frequently in language. Thus, priming of
more familiar thematic pairs (e.g., "flannel shirt") may be due to expectancy
generation or compound retrieval (Jones, 2011) but priming of more novel thematic
pairs (e.g., "monkey foot") appears to be due to thematic role activation.

Mediated priming

Mediated priming (a.k.a., two-step or indirect priming) is a facilitated response to
a target (e.g., MOUSE) following a prime (e.g., DOG) that is indirectly related to the
target via a connecting mediator (e.g., cat). Some researchers (McKoon &
Ratcliff, 1992; Ratcliff & McKoon, 1994) argued against the existence of mediated priming and stated that it was due to co-occurrence (albeit a weak one)
between the indirectly related prime and target (but see McNamara, 1994).
Indeed, some prior findings of mediated priming may have been attributable to
co-occurrence. Livesay & Burgess (2003) assessed the co-occurrence of the
mediated and control items originally used by Balota and Lorch (1986). They
found lower co-occurrence for the unrelated primes and targets than for the
mediated prime-target pairs. More recently, Jones and Mewhort (2007) also
found higher co-occurrence (BEAGLE cosines) for the mediated than the unrelated Balota and Lorch items. Chwilla and Kolk (2002) used LSA to assess
co-occurrence. Unfortunately, however, their mediated items were also much
higher in co-occurrence than were their unrelated control items.

However, most studies have argued that spreading activation from prime to
mediator and then from mediator to target underlies mediated priming (e.g.,
Bennet & McEvoy, 1999; McNamara, 1992a, b, 1994; McNamara & Altarriba,
1988; Shelton & Martin, 1992). Indeed, the occurrence of mediated priming has
been regarded as strong support for spreading activation models (Hutchison,
2003). However, the findings of mediated priming have been largely inconsistent,
with some studies showing robust priming effects (e.g., Bennet & McEvoy, 1999;

McNamara & Altarriba, 1988; Shelton & Martin, 1992), and other studies failing to find mediated priming in some lexical decision paradigms (e.g., Balota & Lorch, 1986; de Groot, 1983). One often cited reason for the failure to find mediated priming is a list effect produced by the inclusion of both directly and indirectly related (mediated) items within the same experimental list. This list effect is especially likely to occur in the more strategic lexical decision tasks, in which participants are aware of the prime-target pairings (Chwilla & Kolk, 2002; McNamara & Altarriba, 1988; Sass et al., 2009). The presence of directly related associates (DAY → NIGHT) may elicit a relatedness checking strategy in tasks allowing detection of prime-target pairs (McNamara & Altarriba, 1988). In a double LDT paradigm, mediated priming effects are heavily affected by the inclusion of more strongly related items (e.g., directly associated items). Chwilla and Kolk (2002) found priming in a mediated only list and no effect in the "mixed" (mediated plus direct) list.

This list effect (Chwilla & Kolk, 2002; McNamara & Altarriba, 1988) suggests that mediated priming may utilize strategic processes (e.g., noticing the stronger associative relation and using that relation to guide lexical decisions). Moreover, recent neuroscience studies (Chwilla et al., 2000; Sass et al., 2009) have suggested that post-lexical or semantic matching processes may partially explain mediated priming. For example, in an fMRI study, Sass et al. (2009) found greater activation in areas of the right hemisphere reflecting greater attentional demands indicative of a retrospective post-access search strategy.

These studies indicate that associative strength may not be a requirement for mediated priming. To test this hypothesis, Jones (2010) assessed mediated priming across a double LDT, a standard LDT, and a continuous LDT for items having no more than a weak association. Moreover, the primes shared an instrumental relation with their mediators (SPOON → SOUP) whereas the mediators and targets were connected by an integrative relation (SOUP → CAN; *contains*). Finally, co-occurrence was equated between the mediated and unrelated prime-target pairs. Mediated priming was strongest in the double LDT and was also reliable in the standard LDT. However, mediated priming did not obtain in the continuous LDT, thereby indicating a retrospective semantic matching and not a prospective process for pure mediated priming.

Though lexical association is not required for mediated priming, it does influence whether mediated priming can occur prospectively by spreading activation or expectancy at longer SOAs. Several studies found reliable mediated priming in more automatic tasks (e.g., Bennett & McEvoy, 1999; McNamara & Altarriba, 1988; both within a continuous LDT), whereas other studies have not (e.g., de Groot, 1983, Experiment 7, within a masked priming experiment; and Balota & Lorch, 1986, within a word naming task). An analysis of the items used in these experiments revealed a strong forward association (> 0.25) between mediator and target within the studies that exhibited mediated priming in a more automatic task, but only a weak mediator-target association in those studies that exhibited no mediated priming. Indeed, de Groot (1983) speculated that failure to obtain mediated priming may be due to a decay in spreading activation, with an insufficient amount of the activation that is needed for further spread from the mediator to the target. Jones (2012b) tested this hypothesis by systematically varying the mediator-target association strength (weak versus strong) while holding the prime-target association strength constant. Consistent with previous findings, mediated priming was reliable in tasks favoring a prospective process (i.e., continuous LDT and a standard LDT with a long 1800-ms SOA) for the items having a strong mediator-target association (e.g., CRATER → moon → SUN) but not for those with only a weak mediator-target association (e.g., RAIN → storm → SUN). Further item analyses demonstrated a reliable relationship between the forward mediator-target association strengths and the mediated target RTs within these tasks, which was suggestive of a spreading activation and expectancy hybrid process similar to the one proposed by Neely et al. (1989). That is, for the strongly associated mediator-target items, activation may spread from prime to mediator (e.g., CRATER → MOON), and then the target would be pre-activated by inclusion in an expectancy set of words related to the mediator (e.g., for MOON, the set would likely include the moderate and strong associates SUN, STAR, FULL, and NIGHT).

The above studies illuminate several methodological and theoretical implications. First, the presence of directly related prime target pairs within the same experimental list may overshadow the mediated pairs (McNamara & Altarriba, 1988). Co-occurrence needs to be equated between the experimental and unrelated control conditions and evaluated as a potential underlying factor. Mediated priming studies should use a variety of relations, association strengths, and tasks to determine which lexical priming model(s) may explain the obtained mediated priming. For example, double LDTs evoke more strategic processing than standard LDTs, and therefore permit more retrospective processing, whereas the more automatic continuous LDT favors prospective processing.

Individual differences in lexical priming

Lexical priming in healthy and cognitively impaired older adults

For healthy older adults, most studies have found few if any changes in the magnitude of lexical priming, despite longer overall response times (e.g., Bennett & McEvoy, 1999; Burke, White, & Diaz, 1987; Laver, 2009; for review see Laver & Burke, 1993). However, when RTs were standardized to control for this overall difference in response speed, younger adults exhibited greater lexical priming than did older adults (Hutchison, Balota, Cortese, & Watson, 2008). Hence, future research in lexical priming needs to compare the standardized RTs between younger and older adults to account for the overall longer RTs and the greater individual variation in older adults.

Lexical priming can serve as an effective mnemonic device among healthy older adults. Badham, Estes, & Maylor (2012) examined integrative priming among normal older adults (mean age = 73 years). They first demonstrated that older adults, like young adults (Estes & Jones, 2009), exhibit integrative priming.

They then tested older adults' and young adults' memory for integrative and semantically similar word pairs. For instance, participants studied either "monkey foot" (integrative), "paw foot" (semantic), or "campus foot" (unrelated baseline), and they were later given the first word of each pair (i.e., "monkey", "paw", or "campus") and were asked to recall the second word of the given pair. Among young adults, both integrative and semantic relations facilitated recall relative to unrelated pairs (see also Jones, Estes, & Marsh, 2008). Importantly, the same pattern occurred among healthy older adults (Badham et al., 2012). Thus, lexical priming continues to play an important role in cognition throughout adulthood (e.g., Old & Naveh-Benjamin, 2008).

Expectancy processing is particularly vulnerable to cognitive impairment. Both those with mild cognitive impairment and healthy older adults exhibited an expectancy bias in a high (0.80) RP condition, in which 80% of the stimuli were exemplar-category pairs (APPLE-FRUIT; Davie, Azuma, Goldinger, Connor, Sabbagh, & Silverberg, 2004). However, those with mild cognitive impairment exhibited even less priming for the unexpected category coordinate pairs (APPLE-PEAR).

Cognitive impairments may also lead to greater priming effects. For example, those in the early stages of Alzheimer's disease exhibit larger priming effects than control participants between category coordinates (e.g., increased activation of LION following TIGER). This *hyperpriming* is due to the loss during the earliest stages of semantic deterioration of a concept's attributes (e.g., stripes, mane) but not yet the categorical membership of the concept (i.e., both lions and tigers are still recognized as wild animals). Hence, these participants exhibit activation of the more general categorical representation wild animal for the prime concept TIGER, which in turn facilitates activation of the target concept, LION, which is also recognized as a wild animal. This repetition priming among Alzheimer's patients (wild animal → wild animal) is larger than the semantic priming exhibited between two category coordinates (TIGER → LION).

Lexical priming and conceptual organization in childhood

One avenue of developmental research compares the emergence of various conceptual organizations across the lifespan. Children demonstrate a conceptual shift from organization via thematic, functional, or instrumental relations to categorical relationships (Murphy, McKone, & Slee, 2003; Perraudin & Mounoud, 2009; for review see Estes et al., 2011a). In a naming task, Perraudin and Mounoud found that 5-year-old children exhibited a robust priming effect for instrumental word pairs (e.g., KNIFE → BREAD), but only a marginal effect for the taxonomic word pairs (e.g., CAKE → BREAD). In contrast, the 7-year-old and 9-year-old children and the young adults exhibited both instrumental and categorical priming. The finding of more robust instrumental priming for the 5-year-olds than for the other age groups further reflected this conceptual shift. Importantly, the association strengths were kept low in both conditions, thereby reflecting the influence of the relations themselves rather than association strength. Perraudin and Mounoud's results are consistent with Nation and Snowling's (1999) findings of reliable functional priming for good and poor 10-year-old readers and adults in the absence of a strong association, but categorical priming for poor 10-year-old readers only in the presence of a strong association.

Another avenue of research concerns the emergence of facilitation versus inhibition processes in lexical priming. Hence, the faster RTs for real word targets following related in comparison to unrelated primes may be due to either facilitation (related primes increasing target activation) or inhibition (unrelated primes decreasing target activation). Though the overall effect sizes of semantic priming do not differ between children and adults, inhibition effects are larger in children and facilitation effects are smaller, hence suggesting a greater ease in spreading activation as the individual's semantic network develops (Nakamura, Ohta, Okita, Ozaki, & Matsushima, 2006). Indeed, inhibitory processing emerges earlier in childhood than other components of executive functioning (*EF*, for review see Best, Miller, & Jones, 2009). Future research could incorporate a variety of tasks ranging from the more automatic (naming, continuous LDT) to the more strategic (double LDT, standard LDT with long SOAs and a high RP) to investigate the use of strategic versus automatic processing in lexical priming.

Executive functioning, attention, and other cognitive abilities

Even among young adults of the same age, recent research (e.g., Estes & Jones, 2009; Stolz, Besner, & Carr, 2005) has found individual variation in the prevalence and extent of lexical priming. Assuming that measures have been taken (e.g., standardization of RTs) to account for the greater individual variation occurring within the LDT than in naming tasks and within certain populations (e.g., older adults and children; Hutchison et al., 2008), then differences in EF may explain many of the obtained differences in lexical priming.

Executive functioning is typically conceptualized as three distinct yet correlated components: working memory, inhibition, and shifting (Miyake, Friedman, Emerson, Witzki, Howerter, & Wager, 2000). The combination of these three EF components has been characterized in the lexical priming literature as "attentional control" (Hutchison, 2007) or "executive control" (Kiefer, Ahlegian, & Spitzer, 2005). Hutchison (2007) found greater RP effects indicative of greater strategic (expectancy) processing for individuals scoring higher on a battery of EF measures, including measures of working memory and inhibition. In contrast, mediated priming occurred for individuals lower in working memory capacity but not for those high in working memory capacity (Kiefer et al., 2005). This finding is consistent with the greater mediated priming among those with thought-disorder schizophrenia (e.g., Spitzer, Braun, Maier, Hermle, & Maher, 1993). Hutchison (2007) and Kiefer et al. (2005) illustrate an underlying involvement of the prefrontal cortex in automatic tasks (indirect associative mediated priming) and in strategic tasks (expectancy processes in a RP manipulation). Notably, individuals with better EF exhibit greater priming in strategic tasks requiring effortful control, whereas those lower in EF exhibit greater priming in more automatic tasks. Indeed, individuals with higher working memory capacities are able to maintain focused attention on a target in the presence of distratctors over a longer period of time than those with lower working memory capacities (Poole & Kane, 2009).

Further research is needed to investigate the underlying role of EF in other forms of priming such as thematic/integrative priming. Prefrontal cortex activation is greater for maintaining integrated rather than non-integrated verbal and spatial information (Prabhakaran, Narayanan, Zhao, & Gabrieli, 2000), thereby demonstrating the role of increased working memory in integration. Moreover, integrative processing requires focused attention in order for binding elements of a proposition (e.g., Doumas, Hummel, & Sandhofer, 2008) and in integrative pairs (e.g., PAPER CUP) between relations (e.g., *compositional*) and roles (e.g., *material* and *object*; Estes & Jones, 2008, 2009). Thus, individual differences in executive control are likely to relate to the individual variation found in integrative priming (Estes & Jones, 2009).

In addition to examining individual differences between those with higher versus lower working memory capacities, the ability to maintain attentional control can also be experimentally manipulated in divided and selective attention tasks. Priming effects for semantically related pairs (CLOCK → TIME) in comparison to unrelated pairs (CIGAR → TIME) in a standard LDT were greater in a full attention condition than in a divided attention condition, in which participants had to determine whether a tone presented with the prime matched the tone presented with the fixation cross (Otsuka & Kawaguchi, 2007). The difficulty of the auditory attention task was also manipulated such that priming still occurred but to a lesser extent in the low divided attention condition in which two dissimilar tones were presented but disappeared in the high divided attention condition in which two very similar tones were presented.

Attention can also be increased by directing focus onto a particular stimulus dimension such as the semantic category of the prime. Following a semantically related prime word, Spruyt and colleagues (2009) cued participants to either (i) name the presented target or (ii) verbally evaluate the target by stating "animal" or "object". The targets exhibited priming only when evaluation responses were made to the remaining 75% of the trials; no priming occurred when only 25% of the trials were evaluated. Hence, in the 75% evaluation condition, directing attention to a relevant stimulus dimension (in this case the broad semantic category) increased attention to the categories of the prime-target pairs on the remaining trials. This result is similar to the RP effect (e.g., Hutchison, 2007), in that the focusing of attention onto a common stimulus dimension occurs without explicit instruction.

Other potential moderators of lexical priming include verbal ability (e.g., Nation & Snowling, 1999; Ron-Kaplan & Henik, 2007), creativity (Whitman, Holcombe, & Zanes, 2010), and convergent thinking. For example, mediated priming requires the ability to detect a relation between two seemingly unrelated concepts (e.g., WIND and STRING are related via the mediator kite). Likewise, the Remote Associates Task (RAT; Mednick, 1962) also requires participants to think of a word that can conceivably connect three other seemingly unrelated words (e.g., "card" relates to credit, report, and playing). Hence, individuals who score higher on the RAT are likely to exhibit greater mediated priming. Another often used measure of thinking and creativity, analogical reasoning ability, may underlie the individual variation in integrative priming. Like analogical reasoning, relational integration also requires the inference of a relation between two concepts (Estes & Jones, 2008; Leech, Mareschal, & Cooper, 2008). Thus, the general ability to detect a specific and plausible relation should predict larger integrative priming effects.

Future directions and conclusions

Research on lexical priming seems to gradually be shifting from broad categories of prime types (associative vs pure semantic vs integrative) towards more specific relations, such as antonyms versus synonyms (e.g., Perea & Rosa, 2002; Roehm et al., 2007) and event-related knowledge (e.g., location-thing vs location-object; Hare et al., 2009). Priming differences may also exist among various relation types within integrative priming (e.g., locative, ISLAND → HOUSE vs compositional relations, LOG → HOUSE). Prime-target relations likely vary in accessibility (Chwilla & Kolk, 2005). Furthermore, the type of relation may interact with various individual differences. For example, some individuals may find a locative relation to be more accessible whereas others may find a compositional relation to be more accessible. More research is needed to further illuminate differences in the accessibility of various relations across individuals and lexical priming paradigms.

In this chapter we have described several different types of lexical priming, along with several different mechanisms that have been proposed to explain lexical priming. Our general conclusion from this review is that no single

---

- Lexical priming occurs when the response to a target word varies systematically as a function of the preceding linguistic context.
- Lexical priming can be measured via a number of experimental paradigms, including lexical decisions (i.e., word/nonword judgments), word naming (i.e., reading aloud), perceptual identification of briefly presented words, semantic decisions (e.g., animacy judgments), eye tracking (i.e., optical fixations), and neuroimaging (e.g., the N400).
- Lexical priming may result from several mechanisms, including spreading activation (i.e., the prime word automatically activates associated and similar target words), expectancy (i.e., the participant generates a set of expected targets that typically follow the prime word), semantic matching (i.e., the participant checks whether the target is related to the prime), episodic retrieval (i.e., the participant

retrieves stored episodes of the prime and target), and thematic integration (i.e., the participant integrates the prime and target meanings).

- Lexical priming occurs among several types of primes and targets, including those that are linguistically associated (i.e., they frequently co-occur; e.g., DAY → NIGHT), semantically similar (i.e., they share many features; e.g., CAT → DOG), or easily integrated (i.e., they form a sensible phrase; e.g., HORSE → DOCTOR). Lexical priming can also occur among primes and targets that are related by a third, mediating concept (e.g., LION → tiger → STRIPES).
- Lexical priming emerges early in childhood, remains robust across adulthood, and is accentuated by some cognitive impairments (e.g., Alzheimer's Disease, thought-disordered schizophrenia). Lexical priming appears to be related to several components of executive functioning, such as working memory and attentional control.
- In sum, lexical priming capitalizes on context via multiple mechanisms to facilitate rapid and effective word recognition.

model is able to fully account for the varieties of lexical priming. Rather, because lexical priming has been observed across such a diverse range of methods, experimental conditions, and individual factors, it has become clear that lexical priming arises from multiple sources. In our opinion, this conclusion follows naturally from the extremely important role that lexical priming plays in language processing: Lexical priming occurs very frequently during normal discourse and reading, thereby facilitating rapid and effective communication. It therefore should come as little surprise that humans have adapted multiple mechanisms for capitalizing on context to facilitate word recognition under a great variety of conditions.

References

Anaki, D. & Henik, A. (2003). Is there a "strength effect" in automatic semantic priming? *Memory & Cognition, 31*, 262–272.

Anderson, J. R. (1983). A spreading activation theory of memory. *Journal of Verbal Learning and Verbal Behavior, 22*, 261–265.

Anderson, J. R. & Lebiere, C. (1998). *The Atomic Components of Thought.* Mahwah, NJ: Erlbaum.

Andrews, S. (2008). Lexical expertise and reading skill. In B. H. Ross (Ed.), *The psychology of learning and motivation: Advances in research and theory, Volume 49* (pp. 247–281). San Diego, CA: Elsevier Academic Press.

Badham, S. P., Estes, Z., & Maylor, E. A. (2012). Integrative and semantic relations equally alleviate age-related associative memory deficits. *Psychology and Aging, 27*, 141–52.

Balota, D. A. & Chumbley, J. I. (1984). Are lexical decisions a good measure of lexical access? The role of word frequency in the neglected decision stage. *Journal of Experimental Psychology: Human Perception and Performance*, *10*, 340–357.

Balota, D. A. & Lorch, R. F. (1986). Depth of automatic spreading activation: Mediated priming effects in pronunciation but not in lexical decision. *Journal of Experimental Psychology: Learning, Memory, and Cognition*, *12*, 336–345.

Barsalou, L. W. (2008). Grounded cognition. *Annual Review of Psychology*, *59*, 617–645.

Becker, C. A. (1980). Semantic context effects in visual word recognition: An analysis of semantic strategies. *Memory & Cognition*, *8*, 493–512.

Becker, S., Moscovitch, M., Behrmann, M., & Joordens, S. (1997). Long-term semantic priming: A computational account and empirical evidence. *Journal of Experimental Psychology: Learning, Memory, and Cognition*, *23*, 1059–1082.

Bennet, D. J. & McEvoy, C. L. (1999). Mediated priming in older and younger adults. *Experimental Aging Research*, *25*, 141–159.

Best, J. R., Miller, P. H., & Jones, L. L. (2009). Executive functioning after age 5: Changes and correlates. *Developmental Review*, *29*, 180–200.

Bodner, G. E. & Masson, M. E. J. (2001). Prime validity affects masked repetition priming: Evidence for an episodic resource account of priming. *Journal of Memory and Language*, *45*, 616–647.

Bodner, G. E. & Masson, M. E. J. (2003). Beyond spreading activation: An influence of relatedness proportion on masked semantic priming. *Psychonomic Bulletin & Review*, *10*, 645–652.

Bodner, G. E., Masson, M. E. J., & Richard, N. T. (2006). Repetition biases masked priming of lexical decisions. *Memory & Cognition*, *34*, 1298–1311.

Bueno, S. & Frenck-Mestre, C. (2008). The activation of semantic memory: Effects of prime exposure, prime-target relationship, and task demands. *Memory & Cognition*, *36*, 882–898.

Burke, D. M., White, H., & Diaz, D. L. (1987). Semantic priming in young and older adults: Evidence for age constancy in automatic and attentional processes. *Journal of Experimental Psychology: Human Perception and Performance*, *13*, 79–88.

Camblin, C. C., Gordon, P. C., & Swaab, T. Y. (2007). The interplay of discourse congruence and lexical association during sentence processing: Evidence from ERPs and eye tracking. *Journal of Memory and Language*, *56*, 103–128.

Chwilla, D. J. & Kolk, H. H. J. (2002). Three-step priming in lexical decision. *Memory & Cognition*, *30*, 217–225.

Chwilla, D. J. & Kolk, H. H. J. (2005). Accessing world knowledge: Evidence from N400 and reaction time priming. *Cognitive Brain Research*, *25*, 589–606.

Chwilla, D. J., Hagoort, P., & Brown, C. M. (1998). The mechanism underlying backward priming in a lexical decision task: Spreading activation versus semantic matching. *Quarterly Journal of Experimental Psychology*, *51A*, 531–560.

Chwilla, D. J., Kolk, H. H. J., & Mulder, G. (2000). Mediated priming in the lexical decision task: Evidence from event-related potentials and reaction time. *Journal of Memory and Language*, *42*, 314–341.

Collins, A. M. & Loftus, E. F. (1975). A spreading activation theory of semantic processing. *Psychological Review*, *82*, 407–428.

Coolen, R., van Jaarsveld, H. J., & Schreuder, R. (1991). The interpretation of isolated novel nominal compounds. *Memory & Cognition*, *19*, 341–352.

Davie, J. E., Azuma, T., Goldinger, S. D., Connor, D. J., Sabbagh, M., N., & Silverberg, N. B. (2004). Expectancy violations in healthy aging and mild cognitive impairment. *Neuropsychology, 18,* 269–275.

de Groot, A. M. B. (1983). The range of automatic spreading activation in word priming. *Journal of Verbal Learning and Verbal Behavior, 22,* 417–436.

de Groot, A. M. B., Thomassen, A. J. W. M., & Hudson, P. T. W. (1982). Associative facilitation of word recognition as measured from a neutral prime. *Memory & Cognition, 10,* 358–370.

den Heyer, K., Briand, K., & Smith, L. (1985). Automatic and strategic effects in semantic priming: An examination of Becker's verification model. *Memory & Cognition, 13,* 228–232.

Dien, J., Franklin, M. S., & May, C. J. (2006). Is "Blank" a suitable neutral prime for event-related potential experiments? *Brain and Language, 97,* 91–101.

Doumas, L. A. A., Hummel, J. E., & Sandhofer, C. M. (2008). A theory of the discovery and predication of relational concepts. *Psychological Review, 115,* 1–43.

Durda, K. & Buchanan, L. (2006). *WordMine2* [Online] Available: www.wordmine2. org.

Estes, Z. (2003). Attributive and relational processes in nominal combination. *Journal of Memory and Language, 48,* 304–319.

Estes, Z. & Jones, L. L. (2006). Priming via relational similarity: A copper horse is faster when seen through a glass eye. *Journal of Memory and Language, 55,* 89–101.

Estes, Z. & Jones, L. L. (2008). Relational processing in conceptual combination and analogy. *Behavioral and Brain Sciences, 31,* 385–386.

Estes, Z. & Jones, L. L. (2009). Integrative priming occurs rapidly and uncontrollably during lexical processing. *Journal of Experimental Psychology: General, 138,* 112–130.

Estes, Z., Golonka, S., & Jones, L. L. (2011a). Thematic thinking: The apprehension and consequences of thematic relations. In B. Ross (Ed.), *Psychology of Learning and Motivation* (Vol. 54, pp. 249–294). Burlington: Academic Press.

Estes, Z., Jones, L. L., & Mather, E. (2011b). *Lexical priming without similarity or association.* Poster presented at the 33rd Annual Meeting of the Cognitive Science Society. Boston, MA.

Folk, J. R. & Morris, R. K. (1995). Multiple lexical codes in reading: Evidence from eye movements, naming time, and oral reading. *Journal of Experimental Psychology: Learning, Memory, and Cognition, 21,* 1412–1429.

Franklin, M. S., Dien, J., Neely, J. H., Huber, E., & Waterson, L. D. (2007). Semantic priming modulates the N400, N300, and N400RP. *Clinical Neurophysiology, 118,* 1053–1068.

Gagné, C. L. & Shoben, E. (1997). The influence of thematic relations on the comprehension of modifier-noun combinations. *Journal of Experimental Psychology: Learning, Memory, and Cognition, 23,* 71–87.

Giesbrecht, B., Camblin, C. C., & Swaab, T. Y. (2004). Separable effects of semantic priming and imageability on word processing in human cortex. *Cerebral Cortex, 14,* 521–529.

Giffard, B., Laisney, M., Eustache, F., & Desgranges, B. (2009). Can the emotional connotation of concepts modulate the lexico-semantic deficits in Alzheimer's disease? *Neuropsychologia, 47,* 258–267.

Hare, M., Jones, M., Thomson, C., Kelly, S., & McRae, K. (2009). Activating event knowledge. *Cognition, 111,* 151–167.

Hess, D. J., Foss, D. J., & Carroll, P. (1995). Effects of global and local context on lexical processing during language comprehension. *Journal of Experimental Psychology: General, 124*, 62–82.

Hodgson, J. M. (1991). Information constraints on pre-lexical priming. *Language and Cognitive Processes, 6*, 169–205.

Hutchison, K. A. (2002). The effect of asymmetrical association on positive and negative semantic priming. *Memory & Cognition, 30*, 1263–1276.

Hutchison, K. A. (2003). Is semantic priming due to association strength or feature overlap? A microanalytic review. *Psychonomic Bulletin & Review, 10*, 785–813.

Hutchison, K. A. (2007). Attentional control and the relatedness proportion effect in semantic priming. *Journal of Experimental Psychology: Learning, Memory, and Cognition, 33*, 645–662.

Hutchison, K. A., Neely, J. H., & Johnson, J. D. (2001). With great expectations, can two "wrongs" prime a "right"? *Journal of Experimental Psychology: Learning, Memory, and Cognition, 27*, 1451–1463.

Hutchison, K. A., Balota, D. A., Cortese, M. J., & Watson, J. M. (2008). Predicting semantic priming at the item level. *The Quarterly Journal of Experimental Psychology, 61*, 1036–1066.

Jones, M. N. & Mewhort, D. J. K. (2007). Representing word meaning and order information in a composite holographic lexicon. *Psychological Review, 114*, 1–37.

Jones, L. L. (2010). Pure mediated priming: A retrospective semantic matching model. *Journal of Experimental Psychology: Learning, Memory, and Cognition, 36*, 135–146.

Jones, L. L. (2012a). *Association strength and familiarity boost integrative priming.* Manuscript submitted for publication.

Jones, L. L. (2012b). Prospective and retrospective processing in associative mediated priming. *Journal of Memory and Language, 66*, 52–67.

Jones, L. L., Estes, Z., & Marsh, R. L. (2008). An asymmetric effect of relational integration on recognition memory. *Quarterly Journal of Experimental Psychology, 61*, 1169–1176.

Jones, L. L., Estes, Z., & Golonka, S. (2011, July). *Dissociation of thematic, taxonomic, and integrative relations.* Poster presented at the 33rd Annual Meeting of the Cognitive Science Society. Boston, MA.

Jonides, J. & Mack, R. (1984). On the cost and benefit of cost and benefit. *Psychological Bulletin, 96*, 29–44.

Kent, R. D. & Read, C. (2002). *The acoustic analysis of speech* (2nd Edn). New York: Thompson.

Kiefer, M., Ahlegian, M., & Spitzer, M. (2005). Working memory capacity, indirect semantic priming, and Stroop interference: Pattern of interindividual prefrontal performance differences in healthy volunteers. *Neuropsychology, 19*, 332–344.

Koivisto, M. & Revonsuo, A. (2001). Cognitive representations underlying the N400 priming effect. *Cognitive Brain Research, 12*, 487–490.

Kostova, M., Passerieux, C., Laurent, J., & Hardy-Baylé, M. (2005). N400 anomalies in schizophrenia are correlated with the severity of formal thought disorder. *Schizophrenia Research, 78*, 285–291.

Landauer, T. K., Foltz, P. W., & Laham, D. (1998). Introduction to Latent Semantic Analysis. *Discourse Processes, 25*, 259–284.

Laver, G. D. (2009). Adult aging effects on semantic and episodic priming in word recognition. *Psychology and Aging, 24*, 28–39.

Laver, G. D. & Burke, D. M. (1993). Why do semantic priming effects increase in old age? A meta-analysis. *Psychology and Aging, 8*, 34–43.

Lecardeur, L., Giffard, B., Laisney, M., Brazo, P., Delamillieure, P., Eustache, F. Eustache, F., and Dollfus, S. (2007). Semantic hyperpriming in schizophrenic patients: Increased facilitation or impaired inhibition in semantic association processing? *Schizophrenia Research, 89*, 243–250.

Ledoux, K., Camblin, C. C., Swaab, T. Y., & Gordon, P. C. (2006). Reading words in discourse: The modulation of lexical priming effects by message-level context. *Behavioral and Cognitive Neuroscience Reviews, 5*, 107–127.

Leech, R., Mareschal, D., & Cooper, R. P. (2008). Analogy as relational priming: A developmental and computational perspective on the origins of a complex cognitive skill. *Behavioral and Brain Sciences, 31*, 357–378.

Livesay, K. & Burgess, C. (2003). Mediated priming in the cerebral hemispheres. *Brain and Cognition, 53*, 283–286.

Lucas, M. (2000). Semantic priming without association: A meta-analytic review. *Psychonomic Bulletin & Review, 7*, 618–630.

Lund, K. & Burgess, C. (1996). Producing high-dimensional semantic spaces from lexical co-occurrence. *Behavior Research Methods, Instruments & Computers, 28*, 203–208.

McKoon, G. & Ratcliff, R. (1992). Spreading activation versus compound cue accounts of priming: Mediated priming revisited. *Journal of Experimental Psychology: Learning, Memory, and Cognition, 18*, 1155–1172.

McNamara, T. P. (1992a). Theories of priming: I. Associative distance and lag. *Journal of Experimental Psychology: Learning, Memory, and Cognition, 18*, 1173–1190.

McNamara, T. P. (1992b). Priming and constraints it places on theories of memory and retrieval. *Psychological Review, 99*, 650–662.

McNamara, T. P. (1994). Theories of priming: II. Types of primes. *Journal of Experimental Psychology: Learning, Memory, and Cognition, 20*, 507–520.

McNamara, T. P. (2005). *Semantic priming: Perspectives from memory and word recognition.* New York: Psychology Press.

McNamara, T. P. & Altarriba, J. (1988). Depth of spreading activation revisited: Semantic mediated priming occurs in lexical decisions. *Journal of Memory and Language, 27*, 545–559.

McRae, K. & Boisvert, S. (1998). Automatic semantic similarity priming. *Journal of Experimental Psychology: Learning, Memory, and Cognition, 24*, 558–572.

Maguire, P., Maguire, R., & Cater, A. W. S. (2010). The influence of interactional semantic patterns on the interpretation of noun-noun compounds. *Journal of Experimental Psychology: Learning, Memory, and Cognition, 36*, 288–297.

Masson, M. E. J. & MacLeod, C. M. (1992). Reenacting the route to interpretation: Enhanced perceptual identification without prior perception. *Journal of Experimental Psychology: General, 121*, 145–176.

Mednick, S. A. (1962). The associative basis of the creative process. *Psychological Review, 69*, 220–232.

Meyer, A. M. & Federmeier, K. D. (2008). The divided visual world paradigm: Eye tracking reveals hemispheric asymmetries in lexical ambiguity resolution. *Brain Research, 1222*, 166–183.

Meyer, D. E. & Schvaneveldt, R. W. (1971). Facilitation in recognizing pairs of words: Evidence of a dependence between retrieval operations. *Journal of Experimental Psychology, 90*, 227–234.

Michael, M. (2009). Responses on a lateralized lexical decision task relate to both reading times and comprehension. *Brain and Cognition, 71*, 416–426.

Miyake, A., Friedman, N. P., Emerson, M. J., Witzki, A. H., Howerter, A., & Wager, T. D. (2000). The unity and diversity of executive functions and their contributions to complex "frontal lobe" tasks: A latent variable analysis. *Cognitive Psychology, 41*, 49–100.

Morris, R. K. (1994). Lexical and message-level sentence context effects on fixation times in reading. *Journal of Experimental Psychology: Learning, Memory, and Cognition, 20*, 92–103.

Moss, H. E., Ostrin, R. K., Tyler, L. K. & Marslen-Wilson, W. D. (1995). Accessing different types of lexical semantic information: Evidence from priming. *Journal of Experimental Psychology: Learning, Memory, and Cognition, 21*, 863–883.

Murphy, K., McKone, E. & Slee, J. (2003). Dissociations between implicit and explicit memory in children: The role of strategic processing and the knowledge base. *Journal of Experimental Child Psychology, 84*, 124–165.

Nakamura, E., Ohta, K., Okita, Y., Ozaki, J., & Matsushima, E. (2006). Increased inhibition and decreased facilitation effect during a lexical decision task in children. *Psychiatry and Clinical Neuroscience, 60*, 232–239.

Nation, K. & Snowling, M. J. (1999). Developmental differences in sensitivity to semantic relations among good and poor comprehenders: Evidence from semantic priming. *Cognition, 70*, B1–B13.

Neely, J. H. (1977). Semantic priming and retrieval from lexical memory: Roles of inhibitionless spreading activation and limited-capacity attention. *Journal of Experimental Psychology: General, 106*, 226–254.

Neely, J. H. (1991). Semantic priming effects in visual word recognition: A selective review of current findings and theories. In D. Besner & G. W. Humphreys (Eds), *Basic processes in reading: Visual word recognition* (pp. 264–336). Hillsdale, NJ: Erlbaum.

Neely, J. H. & Keefe, D. E. (1989). Semantic context effects on visual word processing: A hybrid prospective-retrospective processing theory. In G. H. Bower (Ed.), *The psychology of learning and motivation: Advances in research and theory* (Vol. 24, pp. 207–248). New York: Academic Press.

Neely, J. H., Keefe, D. E., & Ross, K. L. (1989). Semantic priming in the lexical decision task: Roles of prospective prime-generated expectancies and retrospective semantic matching. *Journal of Experimental Psychology: Learning, Memory, and Cognition, 15*, 1003–1019.

Nelson, D. L., Bennett, D. J., Gee, N. R., Schreiber, T. A., & McKinney, V. M. (1993). Implicit memory: Effects of network size and interconnectivity on cued recall. *Journal of Experimental Psychology: Learning, Memory, and Cognition, 19*, 747–764.

Nelson, D. L., McEvoy, C. L., & Schreiber, T. A. (1998). *The University of South Florida word association, rhyme, and word fragment norms.* http://w3.usf.edu/FreeAssociation/

Odekar, A., Hallowell, B., Kruse, H., Moates, D., & Lee, C-Y. (2009). Validity of eye movement methods and indices for capturing semantic (associative) priming effects. *Journal of Speech, Language, and Hearing Research, 52*, 31–48.

Old, S. R. & Naveh-Benjamin, M. (2008). Differential effects of age on item and associative measures of memory: A meta-analysis. *Psychology and Aging, 23*, 104–118.

Otsuka, S. & Kawaguchi, J. (2007). Divided attention modulates semantic activation: Evidence from a nonletter-level prime task. *Memory & Cognition, 35*, 2001–2011.

Perea, M. & Rosa, E. (2002). The effects of associative and semantic priming in the lexical decisión task. *Psychological Research*, *66*, 180–194.

Perraudin, S. & Mounoud, P. (2009). Contribution of the priming paradigm to the understanding of the coneptual developmental shift from 5 to 9 years of age. *Developmental Science*, *12*, 956–977.

Poole, B. J. & Kane, M. J. (2009). Working-memory capacity predicts the executive control of visual search among distracters: The influences of sustained and selective attention. *The Quarterly Journal of Experimental Psychology*, *62*, 1430–1454.

Prabhakaran, V., Narayanan, K., Zhao, Z., & Gabrieli, J. D. E. (2000). Integration of diverse information in working memory within the frontal lobe. *Nature Neuroscience*, *3*, 85–90.

Prior, A. & Bentin, S. (2008). Word associations are formed incidentally during sentential semantic integration. *Acta Psychologica*, *127*, 57–71.

Raffray, C. N., Pickering, M. J., & Branigan, H. P. (2007). Priming the interpretation of noun-noun combinations. *Journal of Memory and Language*, *57*, 380–395.

Ratcliff, R. & McKoon, G. (1988). A retrieval theory of priming in memory. *Psychological Review*, *95*, 385–408.

Ratcliff, R. & McKoon, G. (1994). Retrieving information from memory: Spreading activation theories versus compound-cue theories. *Psychological Review*, *101*, 177–184.

Rayner, K., Warren, T., Juhasz, B. J., & Liversedge, S. P. (2004). The effect of plausibility on eye movements in reading. *Journal of Experimental Psychology: Learning, Memory, and Cognition*, *30*, 1290–1301.

Rhodes, S. M. & Dondaldson, D. I. (2008). Association and not semantic relationships elicit the N400 effect: Electrophysiological evidence from an explicit language comprehension task. *Psychophysiology*, *45*, 50–59.

Roehm, D., Bornkessel-Schlesewsky, I., Rösler, F., & Schlesewsky, M. (2007). To predict or not to predict: Influences of task and strategy on the processing of semantic relations. *Journal of Cognitive Neuroscience*, *19*, 1259–1274.

Rogers, T. T. & McClelland, J. L. (2004). *Semantic cognition: A parallel distributed processing approach*. Cambridge, MA: MIT Press.

Ron-Kaplan, I. & Henik, A. (2007). Verbal ability modulates the associative neighbors effect. *Psychonomic Bulletin & Review*, *14*, 81–87.

Rossell, S. L., Price, C. J., & Nobre, A. C. (2003). The anatomy and time course of semantic priming investigated by fMRI and ERPs. *Neuropsychologia*, *41*, 550–564.

Sass, K., Krach, S., Sachs, O., & Kircher, T. (2009). Lion – tiger – stripes: Neural correlates of indirect semantic priming across processing modalities. *NeuroImage*, *45*, 224–236.

Seidenberg, M. S., Waters, G. S., Sanders, M., & Langer, P. (1984). Pre- and postlexical loci of contextual effects on word recognition. *Memory & Cognition*, *12*, 315–328.

Shaoul, C. & Westbury, C. (2006). Word frequency effects in high-dimensional co-occurrence models: A new approach. *Behavior Research Methods*, *38*, 190–195.

Shelton, J. R. & Martin, R. C. (1992). How semantic is automatic semantic priming? *Journal of Experimental Psychology: Learning, Memory, and Cognition*, *18*, 1191–1210.

Spitzer, M., Braun, U., Maier, S., Hermle, L., & Maher, B. A. (1993). Indirect semantic priming in schizophrenic patients. *Schizophrenic Research*, *11*, 71–80.

Spruyt, A., De Houwer, J., & Hermans, D. (2009). Modulation of automatic semantic priming by feature-specific attention allocation. *Journal of Memory and Language*, *61*, 37–54.

Stolz, J. A., Besner, D., & Carr, T. H. (2005). Implications of measures of reliability for theories of priming: Activity in semantic memory is inherently noisy and uncoordinated. *Visual Cognition, 12,* 284–336.

Storms, G. & Wisniewski, E. J. (2005). Does the order of head noun and modifier explain response times in conceptual combination? *Memory & Cognition, 33,* 852–861.

Thompson-Schill, S. L., Kurtz, K. J., & Gabriele, J. D. E. (1998). Effects of semantic and associative relatedness on automatic priming. *Journal of Memory and Language, 38,* 440–458.

Van den Bussche, E., Van den Noortgate, W., & Reynvoet, B. (2009). Mechanisms of masked priming: A meta-analysis. *Psychological Bulletin, 135,* 452–477.

Whitman, R. D., Holcombe, E., & Zanes, J. (2010). Hemispheric collaboration in creative subjects: Cross-hemisphere priming in a lexical decision task. *Creativity Research Journal, 22,* 109–118.

Wible, C. G., Han, S. D., Spencer, M. H., Kubicki, M., Niznikiewicz, M. H., Jolesz, F. A., McCarley, R. W., and Nestor, P. (2006). Connectivity among semantic associates: An fMRI study of semantic priming. *Brain and Language, 97,* 294–305.

Williams, J. N. (1996). Is automatic priming semantic? *European Journal of Cognitive Psychology, 8,* 113–161.

Wisniewski, E. J. (1997). When concepts combine. *Psychonomic Bulletin & Review, 4,* 167–83.

Wisniewski, E. J. & Murphy, G. L. (2005). Frequency of relation type as a determinant of conceptual combination: A reanalysis. *Journal of Experimental Psychology: Learning, Memory, and Cognition, 31,* 169–174.

4 Eye movements and word recognition during reading

Elizabeth R. Schotter and Keith Rayner

Skilled reading is a remarkable achievement for humans (Huey, 1908). The process of reading is extremely complex with many levels of representation; reading proceeds from 'low' levels to 'high' levels of representation. That is, first visual information is received through the eyes and the *orthographic*, *phonological*, and *morphological properties* (generally considered *sublexical* properties) of the word are analyzed. Finally the *semantic* and *syntactic* representations (generally considered *superlexical*) are accessed and integrated into the meaning of the sentence. Furthermore, the current sentence must be integrated with the discourse level representation of the entire text context (for a discussion of these various levels of representation, see Rayner & Pollatsek, 1989; Rayner et al., 2012). In this chapter, our goal is to provide an overview of research utilizing eye movement data to examine the relationship between word recognition and the oculomotor system in reading with our primary focus on recent models of eye movement control (discussed at the end of the chapter) that represent the identification of different words in the text in terms of either serial or parallel lexical processing.

One of the advantages that the word identification system has during natural reading as opposed to in other tasks commonly used in cognitive psychology (such as lexical decision and naming) is that the word is available to the reader before it is fixated because it is present in the parafovea when the eyes are on preceding words. This ability to do some preprocessing of the upcoming word – termed *parafoveal processing* – is part of the reason why eye fixations during reading are so short (i.e., not much longer than the time it takes to program and execute a saccade when little or no cognitive processing is required). For this reason, much of this chapter will address parafoveal processing during reading (see Schotter et al., 2012 for a review).

In this chapter, we will not address models of single word recognition as they are well represented elsewhere in this volume. It seems to be well established that letter identification occurs in parallel (Cattell, 1886; Reicher, 1969; Wheeler, 1970), but it is more controversial whether multiple words in a sentence are identified in parallel (Reichle, Liversedge, Pollatsek, & Rayner, 2009). It is our general position that lexical access in reading is serial, but we will review the evidence both for and against this claim. We will discuss this issue later in the chapter, but first we review some basic characteristics of eye movements and relevant terminology.

Basic characteristics of eye movements

We make eye movements in order to move the center of our retina (the *fovea*) – the region of highest acuity – to the location we wish to process. In reading the eyes can only be on one location at a time and the fovea only comprises about 2 degrees of visual angle. Thus, typically only one or two words (7–8 characters) lie within the word identification span (Rayner, 1998, 2009; Rayner, Well, Pollatsek, & Bertera, 1982). Outside the fovea, acuity drops off rapidly in the *parafovea* (out to 5 degrees of visual angle from fixation) and the *periphery* (everything beyond the parafovea). Eye movements per se (*saccades*) last approximately 25–35 ms, depending on the length of the saccade. Between saccades, the eyes are relatively stable (during *fixations*). Information is only obtained from words during fixations because vision is suppressed during saccades and we are essentially 'blind.' Therefore, reading is based on a series of snapshots of words. It is important to note, however, that just because no new visual information is obtained during saccades, cognitive processing based on information that had already been obtained during the previous fixation can, and does, occur (Rayner, 1998, 2009).

Reading rate, average saccade length, average fixation duration, and *percent regressions* are considered *global reading measures* (Rayner, 1998, 2009), and are generally considered to be measures of overall text difficulty. When the text is easier to read, the reading rate (words read per minute, wpm) is higher, saccade lengths (the distance the eyes travel between fixations) are longer, fixation durations are shorter, and regressions (instances in which a previous part of the text is returned to) are fewer. Skilled readers typically read between 200 and 350 wpm, their average saccade length is 7–9 letter spaces,[1] their average fixation duration is 225–250 ms, and they regress about 10–15% of the time. These values should not be taken as stable indices of eye movements since for any given reader there is considerable variability in a how far the eyes move and how long they remain fixated.

Although global measures are important indications of processing, more often in reading research local effects related to fixation time on a specific word in a sentence are reported. These measures include *first fixation duration* (the duration of the first fixation on a word), *single fixation duration* (duration of the fixation on a word in cases where the word was only fixated once, not including regressive fixations), and *gaze duration* (the sum of all fixations on a word before moving to another word). These measures are important because global measures would only be useful if readers fixated every word and each word only once, which is clearly not the case. Many words are *refixated* (fixated more than once before being left) and approximately a third of the words in the text are *skipped* (not fixated directly) during reading. Often times these skipped words are short, very common words (such as *the, of, in,* and *and*), although longer words that are highly predictable from prior text are also frequently skipped (Ehrlich & Rayner, 1981; Rayner, Yang, Castelhano, & Liversedge, 2011; Rayner & Well, 1996).

When words are skipped, there is good reason to believe that they were processed while the eyes were fixating the previous word. Whether that processing occurred in parallel with the foveal word, or during an attention shift to the parafoveal word while the eyes were on the foveal word is hotly debated. Conversely, the words that are refixated are more likely to be longer and less frequent, taking more time and more fixations to fully process for meaning. The aforementioned local measures are useful to estimate how long it takes to process a specific word in the context of the other words in the sentence or text (Rayner, 1998, 2009). As we document below, lexical properties of the fixated word (such as word frequency) very much influence how long readers look at that word (for a discussion of lexical parafoveal processing and parafoveal-on-foveal effects, see the section on models of eye movements during reading).

When words are not skipped, the eyes tend to land about halfway between the beginning of the word and the middle of the word, on what is referred to as the *preferred viewing location* (*PVL*, Rayner, 1979). It is generally believed that readers aim for the center of the word to the right of fixation (unless they skip it) at the *optimal viewing position* (*OVP*, O'Regan & Levy-Schoen, 1987), which is the location in a word where recognition time is fastest. Extensive research efforts examined the consequences of making fixations at locations other than the OVP. For words in isolation, two main effects emerged. First, there is a refixation effect: the further the eyes are from the OVP, the more likely it is that there will be a refixation on the word. Second, there is a processing cost effect: for every letter that the subject's eyes deviate from the OVP the cost is approximately 20 ms. However, when words are in text, while the refixation effect remains, the processing cost effect is greatly attenuated or absent (Rayner, Sereno, & Raney, 1996; Vitu, O'Regan, & Mittau, 1990).

With respect to the OVP effect, another interesting finding is that when readers make only one fixation on a word, if that fixation is at the center of the word (the OVP), then the fixation is longer than when a single fixation is at the end of the word. This effect, the *inverted optimal viewing position* (IOVP) effect, was first documented by Vitu, McConkie, Kerr, and O'Regan (2001) and a number of possible reasons for the effect have been examined by Vitu, Lancelin, and Marrier d' Unienville (2007). Nuthmann, Engbert, and Kliegl (2005) and Nuthmann, Engbert, & Kliegl (2007) suggested that mislocated fixations are the primary source of the effect. The basic argument is that many single fixations falling on the beginnings or ends of words are not on the targeted word (though the targeted word is being processed), but are due to overshoots (for fixations falling on the beginning of words) and undershoots (for fixations falling at the end of a word) of the eyes (and due to properties of the oculomotor system). Via clever modeling techniques, Nuthmann et al. were able to show how mislocated fixations could account for this effect. Perhaps more interestingly, however, it is the case that there are also word frequency effects independent of where the eyes land in a word when single fixations are made (Vitu et al., 2001; Rayner et al., 1996). Thus, although single fixations are longer when they fall in the middle of a word than at the ends, in both cases low frequency words receive longer fixations than high frequency words.

Although foveal processing in reading is very important, some processing can be done in the parafovea and much research has investigated the size of the perceptual span during a fixation in reading. Experiments using the gaze-contingent moving window paradigm introduced by McConkie and Rayner (1975;

see also Rayner & Bertera, 1979) have clearly demonstrated that readers have little or no access to information about the characters beyond a relatively small window (only a few words) around the character that they are fixating. In moving window experiments (see Rayner, 1998, 2009, for reviews and Rayner, Castelhano, & Yang, 2009 and 2010 for recent moving window experiments), the eyes are monitored and the text around the point of fixation is revealed (i.e., accurate information is provided within the window area), with the text outside that window replaced by other letters (typically with x's or random letters). Research using this paradigm has revealed that readers of English typically have a perceptual span comprising a region from 3–4 characters to the left of fixation to about 14–15 character spaces to the right of fixation.[2] If the presently fixated word and the following word are normal and the rest of the letters are replaced with other visually similar letters, readers are typically unaware that anything is strange about the text and reading is only about 10% slower than without a window. If two words to the right of the fixated word are revealed/available, reading is generally equivalent to normal, so clearly there is some information that is utilized from other words while the eyes are processing the foveal word.

Other research investigating how much information is obtained to the right of fixation involves another gaze-contingent display change paradigm called the *boundary paradigm* (Rayner, 1975). In the boundary paradigm, a preview word changes to a target word when the eyes cross an invisible boundary in the text. The boundary change paradigm has been used to compare fixation times on the target word between conditions in which the preview of the target word differs. For example, if the target word is *beach* the preview could be a random letter string (*hdien*), an unrelated word (*short*), an orthographically related word (*bench*), a homophone (*beech*), or a semantically related word (*ocean*), to name a few (various different manipulations will be discussed below). Any speeded processing with a related preview compared to an invalid or unrelated preview is termed *preview benefit*; there are clear benefits to having parafoveal preview of not-yet-fixated words. Whether this parafoveal processing is due to parallel processing of the two words or parafoveal preprocessing during an attention shift is a topic of considerable debate (see discussion of models and serial vs parallel lexical access below). Research using the boundary change paradigm has revealed that readers generally do not represent word information in a literal visual representation, but rather in an abstract form (McConkie & Zola, 1979; Rayner, McConkie, & Zola, 1980; Slattery, Angele, & Rayner, 2011). The exact underlying representation of the preview benefit is the focus of the present chapter and will be discussed below. First, however, we need to briefly mention something about the factors that influence the processing of the fixated word.

Properties of the fixated word influence how long the eyes remain on a word

There are a number of well-documented findings that relate to how long readers fixate on a word. We suspect that much of the variance in fixation time on a given word (generally measured by gaze duration, but also first fixation and single fixation duration) is due to the ease or difficulty associated with processing that word. However, there are spillover (or lag) effects – effects of the word before the currently fixated word – and effects associated with the nature of the word to the right of fixation (which we will discuss below). While there are undoubtedly effects due to higher level factors (such as syntactic and discourse processing), it is clear that lexical variables have a strong influence on how long readers look at a word. Here, we list some variables that have immediate effects on fixation time and list some of the original references for these effects (see Rayner, 1998, 2009 for reviews and further references). In all cases, the length of the target word is controlled since longer words yield longer gaze durations[3] (Rayner et al., 1996).

Word frequency

One extremely robust finding is that readers spend less time fixating on high frequency words than on low frequency words (Inhoff & Rayner, 1986; Rayner & Duffy, 1986). With word length controlled, readers are also more likely to skip high frequency words (Rayner et al., 1996), although the effect is rather small.

Word predictability

Word predictability is typically determined via a cloze task where a separate group of subjects from those used in the reading experiment have to guess the next word in the text given prior context. The proportion of those subjects who enter the word in the cloze task is used as the measure of predictability. When subjects then read sentences containing high- or low-predictable words, they reliably look longer at low-predictable words than high-predictable words (Ehrlich & Rayner, 1981; Rayner & Well, 1996). Readers are also much more likely to skip high predictable words including rather long predictable words (Rayner et al., 2011). An interesting issue is whether or not frequency and predictability exert interactive effects on fixation times in reading. While experiments using naming and lexical decision have typically found such an interaction, most eye movement studies have failed to find it (Rayner, Ashby, Pollatsek, & Reichle, 2004a).

Number of meanings

Lexical ambiguity (when a word has two or more, semantically unrelated meanings; for example, *bank* could mean a financial institution or the side of a river) has an interesting effect on fixation time on a word. Lexically ambiguous words come in two types: *balanced* (the two meanings of the word are equally frequent) and *biased* (one meaning is *dominant* – more frequent – and one is *subordinate* – less frequent). In a neutral context, readers look longer at a balanced ambiguous word than a control word, but they don't look longer at a *biased* ambiguous word than a control word (Rayner & Duffy, 1986). However, when a disambiguating context precedes the ambiguous word and the subordinate meaning is instantiated, the pattern of data is reversed and readers look longer at a biased word than its control word while there is no difference between the balanced word and its control (Duffy, Morris, & Rayner, 1988; Rayner, Cook, Juhasz, & Frazier, 2006a).

Age of acquisition

With word frequency controlled, readers look longer at late acquired words than early acquired words (Juhasz & Rayner, 2003, 2006).

Phonological properties of words

When a word is replaced by its homophone (e.g., hare), readers do not look at it longer (Daneman & Reingold, 1993) than if it is the correct word (e.g., hair), unless the context is highly constraining of the correct word (Jared, Levy, & Rayner, 1999; Rayner, Pollatsek, & Binder, 1998a).

Semantic relations between the fixated word and prior words

Words that are semantically related, and in close proximity to each other, produce priming effects (Carroll & Slowiaczek, 1986; Morris, 1994).

Word familiarity

Words that are relatively infrequent but more familiar to a reader yield shorter fixation times on words than less familiar words (Chaffin, Morris, & Seely, 2001).

Lexical variables, such as those listed here, thus have strong and immediate effects on how long readers look at a word.[4] While other linguistic variables (such as syntactic variables, discourse variables, and plausibility) can have an influence on fixation times, it is generally the case that these higher level linguistic variables yield somewhat later and more variable effects in terms of when they appear in the eye movement record (Clifton, Staub, & Rayner, 2007; Staub & Rayner, 2007). However, if a higher level variable more or less 'smacks you in the eye' there will also be an immediate effect. For example, when readers fixate on the disambiguating word in a syntactic garden path sentence there is increased fixation time on the word and/or a regression from the disambiguating word back to earlier parts of the sentence (Frazier & Rayner, 1982: Levy, Bicknell, Slattery, & Rayner, 2009). Readers also have longer fixations at the end of clauses and sentences where they presumably engage in higher level integration processes (Rayner, Kambe, & Duffy, 2000). And, when readers encounter an anomalous word that makes no sense in the text, they fixate on it longer, and the effect is quite immediate. However, when a word indicates an implausible but not truly anomalous event, the effect on readers' eye movements will typically be delayed (Rayner, Warren, Juhasz, & Liversedge, 2004b) showing up in later processing measures (such as *go-past* time, which is the time from first fixating a word or region until exiting forward in the text).

Parafoveal processing at the sub-lexical and super-lexical levels

One of the most pervasively studied phenomena in silent reading is the parafoveal *preview benefit*. In the majority of the following sections, we will review evidence for and against parafoveal preview benefits at different levels of linguistic analysis (though there will be some discussions of other phenomena, as well). Both a serial and parallel model can accommodate preview benefits of different natures (to be discussed in the section on the models themselves). In the following sections, we will merely state the findings and leave the discussion of how the models account for these data for later sections of the chapter.

Word length information

It is well established that the length of a parafoveal word is processed at the same time as the foveated word is being processed. In English, as well as in many other languages, words are separated by spaces in the text. It is the most intuitive way for a native English speaker to define a 'word' and normal spacing leads to the fastest processing of text. Fixation durations and saccade lengths are modulated by the spacing of the text – reading rate is fastest, mean fixation durations are shortest, and there are fewest regressions when the text contains spaces compared to when it has x's instead of spaces, has spaced words flanked by x's, or has the spaces removed (Rayner, Fischer, & Pollatsek, 1998b).

Further evidence for word length information being processed parafoveally comes from a boundary change experiment by Inhoff, Radach, Eiter, and Juhasz (2003) in which they manipulated the frequency of a target word (e.g., *subject*), whether the preview had the same word length (e.g., *subject* or *mivtirp*) or a different word length than the target (e.g., *sub ect* or *miv irp*), and whether the preview was orthographically similar to the target (e.g., *subtect* or *sub ect*) or not (e.g., *mivtirp* or *miv irp*). Inhoff et al. found that word length information is processed parafoveally: viewing times were shorter when word length preview was accurate. Furthermore, the effects of word length and word frequency did not interact. Therefore, they concluded that parafoveal word length information is used for saccade targeting (visual object selection), but is a functionally autonomous process from word recognition processes (i.e., lexical access).

In contrast to the claims of Inhoff et al. (2003), some data suggest that word length information obtained in the parafovea does interact with lexical access in that it facilitates the narrowing of lexical candidates (Juhasz, White, Liversedge, & Rayner, 2008; White, Rayner, & Liversedge, 2005). Juhasz et al. (2008) conducted a display change study in which a target could either be a one-word compound (*backhand*) or two words (*back and*). The previews were created by inserting or deleting a letter during the display change to alter the word length information. For example, the target word *backhand* could either have the correct length preview, *backhand*, or incorrect length preview, *back and*. The data suggested that word length information was obtained in the parafovea, so that if the word length changed when the eyes moved to foveate it, processing was slowed down. Importantly, the effect was only apparent when the preceding text was neutral to both target and preview; when the sentence biased the target the preview effect was eliminated. Juhasz et al. suggested that word length information helps to narrow the set of lexical candidates.

Orthographic information

As noted above, word length information is important for saccade planning and, to some extent, lexical processing. Beside this, though, orthographic information- letter identities- plays an important role in word identification. At least in alphabetic language, such as English, orthography supports phonological, lexical and semantic identification because it is the way spoken language is represented in text. Orthography is not only important for foveal identification, but a lot of what is processed from parafoveal words is orthographically based (Rayner, 1975; Rayner et al., 2010a). If the preview word shares word shape (e.g., ascenders like *l, k, h* are replaced with other ascenders or descenders like *p, g, q* are replaced with other descenders) with the target fixation times are faster on the target than when they don' (Rayner et al., 1980). Despite this, though, it seems that shape is really just a by-product of parafoveal orthographic processing. Specifically, preview benefit is obtained from identical letters, even if the word shape differs between preview and target for example when the case alternates between capital letters and lowercase letters (McConkie & Zola, 1979; Rayner et al., 1980; Slattery et al., 2011). Beyond an exact letter identity match, orthographically related previews provide strong preview benefit (Balota et al., 1985). Finally, preview benefit is also obtained when all the letters in the preview are correct, but some of them are in the wrong order (transposed letters, e.g., *jugde* as a preview for *judge*) and is larger than when letters are replaced instead of transposed (e.g., *jupbe*; Johnson et al., 2007).

Phonological information

Beyond word length information, there is evidence that some phonological processing of the parafoveal word occurs while the eyes are on the foveal word (Ashby & Rayner, 2004; Ashby, Treiman, Kessler, & Rayner, 2006; Chace, Rayner, & Well, 2005; Liu, Inhoff, Ye, & Wu, 2002; Miellet & Sparrow, 2004; Pollatsek, Lesch, Morris, & Rayner, 1992; Rayner, Sereno, Lesch, & Pollatsek, 1995; Tsai, Lee, Tzeng, Hung, & Yen, 2004). Specifically, a parafoveal preview of a phonologically related (homophone) word facilitates processing of the target word when it is ultimately fixated (Pollatsek et al., 1992). Chace et al. (2005) replicated this finding in skilled readers, but found that less skilled readers were not facilitated by homophone previews, indicating that they might not employ phonological information in the parafovea in the same way that skilled readers do. Chace et al. suggested this difference might be because less skilled readers need to devote more attention to processing the foveal word and might therefore have less attention to allocate to the parafoveal word.

Ashby and Rayner (2004) presented subjects with a parafoveal preview of a target word in which the first two or three initial letters of CV (consonant-vowel) or CVC (consonant-vowel-consonant) syllable initial words were manipulated. Therefore, the preview either preserved the first syllable's syllabic structure (i.e., *de_πxw* as a preview for *device*) or did not preserve the syllabic structure (i.e., *ba_πxwx* as a preview for *balcony*). First fixation durations were faster when the syllable structure of the preview was congruent with the target than when it was different, indicating that readers had obtained information about the syllabic structure of the upcoming word while they were still fixating the preceding word.

Other evidence that phonological information is processed parafoveally comes from the benefit of having a homophone or pseudohomophone parafoveal preview, demonstrated in Chinese (Liu et al., 2002; Tsai et al., 2004), French (Miellet & Sparrow, 2004) and English (Pollatsek et al., 1992). Ashby et al. (2006) conducted a boundary change experiment in which the target word (*flown*) could have a preview with a similarly pronounced vowel cluster (*floam*) or dissimilarly pronounced vowel cluster (*floim*). They found that parafoveal previews with similarly pronounced vowel clusters facilitated processing compared to previews with dissimilarly pronounced clusters. Furthermore, they found similar effects when nonword previews shared the same vowel cluster but the pronunciation differed depending on the consonants surrounding it (e.g., *foon* as a preview for the target word *fool* facilitated processing more than the preview *fook*).

Morphological information

There is mixed evidence for parafoveal preview benefit of morpholological information in alphabetic languages. While there is no evidence for parafoveal morphological processing in English (Kambe, 2004; Juhasz et al., 2008) and Finnish (Bertram & Hyönä, 2007), there is evidence that morphological information is processed parafoveally in Hebrew (Deutsch, Frost, Pollatsek, & Rayner, 2000; Deutsch, Frost, Peleg, Pollatsek, & Rayner, 2003; Deutsch, Frost, Pollatsek, & Rayner, 2005).

Kambe (2004) conducted a boundary change study in English in which the preview of a prefixed target word (*preview*) was a nonword that either contained the same prefix as the target (e.g., *preurcv*) or an illegal letter string (e.g., *qncurcv*). She found that a nonword preview that shared a prefix or stem with the target provided no preview benefit above and beyond a standard orthographic preview benefit, indicating that morphological information is not obtained in the parafovea (see also Lima, 1987).

Juhasz et al. (2008) also found a lack of parafoveal morphological processing in English; they manipulated word length preview of either a compound or long monomorphemic word and found no effect of the lexical status of the parafoveal preview. Juhasz et al. showed this by replacing a letter with a space in compound words and long monomorphemic words either in a place where the first letter string constituted a word (e.g., *pop orn* or *dip oma*) or did not (e.g., *popc rn* or *dipl ma*). In the compound words, the first word was a lexeme of the compound (i.e., morphologically related), but in the long monomorphemic condition the first word constituted a real word, but not a lexeme that was related to the whole word. Juhasz et al. found no difference between preview benefit when the initial letter string was a lexeme of a compound compared to when it was an unrelated but orthographically contained word, indicating that morphological information was not processed in the parafovea. Similarly, Bertram and Hyönä (2007) found no parafoveal processing of morphological information in Finnish. They manipulated preview of the first 3–4 letters of the compound word. They included words with either long or short first constituents so that the manipulated text either comprised the entire first constituent or just the first part of it. They found no benefit if the letters comprised a whole constituent over when they comprised only part of a constituent.

Although English and Finnish readers do not seem to process morphological information parafoveally, some studies found evidence for parafoveal morphological processing in Hebrew. For example, Deutsch et al. (2005) had native speakers of Hebrew read Hebrew sentences in which a target word had an identical, morphologically related, or orthographically related control word preview. Deutsch et al. found a larger preview benefit in the morphological preview condition compared to the orthographic preview condition. The reason for the discrepancy between the Hebrew and English/Finnish studies may be due to differences in the structure of the languages. In Hebrew, all words are marked semantically (by a word root, generally consisting of three consonants) and morphologically (by a word pattern, consisting of vowels or a mixture of vowels and consonants). The word root and the word pattern are interleaved instead of concatenated, so there is no spatial separation between them (i.e., it is not the case that the word root is the beginning of the word and the word pattern is the end, or vice versa). Furthermore, in this interleaved structure, the positions of the constituent letters of the root or the word pattern are not fixed, so the orthographic or phonological structure of the word does not transparently indicate morphology. For this reason, any preview benefit provided in the morphologically related preview condition above and beyond the orthographically related preview condition is due to morphological information being processed parafoveally, not due to a stronger relationship between the morphological preview and the target.

In contrast to Hebrew, multimorphemic Finnish and English words are concatenated instead of interleaved and words (especially compound words) are generally long (targets were 12.6 characters in the Bertram & Hyönä, 2007, study). From the aforementioned data it seems that a language where morphological constituents need to be separated and processed in order to identify the word may exhibit morphological parafoveal processing whereas languages where morphological constituents are spatially separated may not. The differences between the structures of the language may account for why there does not seem to be parafoveal processing of morphological information in Finnish and English, while there is evidence for it in Hebrew.

All of the above studies have addressed whether readers can process sublexical properties of the parafoveal word while processing the foveal word. The majority of the studies provide converging evidence that most sublexical properties *are* processed parafoveally, but this is compatible with both the parallel and serial models of eye movements during reading (see discussion below). As mentioned before, the crux of the issue is whether lexical access occurs in parallel. Before addressing that issue directly, we will briefly review what evidence there is for (or against) the parafoveal processing of superlexical properties of words – mainly, syntactic and semantic properties.

Syntactic information

Staub et al., (2007) had subjects read sentences with noun-noun compounds (like *cafeteria manager*) in which the first noun was either a plausible (*the new principal visited the cafeteria ...*) or implausible (*the new principal talked to the cafeteria ...*) continuation of the sentence before getting to the following word (*manager*). Before getting to *manager*, *cafeteria* is interpreted as the object of verbs *visited* or *talked*. If syntactic information were obtained from the parafoveal word, then reading times should not be longer in the implausible condition than the plausible condition, because the first noun would be disambiguated as the modifier in the noun-noun compound. This difference is called a *parafoveal-on-foveal* (PoF) effect (Rayner, White, Kambe, Miller, & Liversedge, 2003a), mainly the phenomenon in which the difficulty of processing the upcoming, parafoveal word affects the processing of the foveal word. PoF effects are very controversial and inconsistent in the literature (see discussion below).

Staub, Rayner, Pollatsek, Hyona, and Majewski (2007) found longer reading times in first pass measures on the modifier noun in the compound, indicating that there was no use of semantic or syntactic information from the parafoveal word. The fact that the parafoveal word was not identified, and therefore not used to disambiguate the first noun as the modifier suggests that there was no parallel processing occurring on the two words in the noun-noun compound. It is important to note, however, that the first noun in the compound was not a short word (mean length was over 6 characters) and this meant that the majority of the parafoveal word (the disambiguating word in the noun-noun compound) was unlikely to fall inside the word identification span (7–8 characters to the right of fixation).

Semantic information

Studies of alphabetic languages (like English, Finnish, and Spanish) have not shown evidence for parafoveal preview benefits of semantic information (Altarriba, Kambe, Pollatsek, & Rayner, 2001; Hyönä & Haikio, 2005; Rayner, Balota, & Pollatsek, 1985; White, Bertram, & Hyönä, 2008), but there is some evidence that readers of character-based languages (like Chinese) obtain semantic information parafoveally (Yan, Richter, Shu, & Kliegl, 2009; Yang Rayner, Li, & Wang, in press). Additionally, evidence of semantic preview benefit with German was recently reported (Hohenstein et al., 2010). However, all of the target words were nouns, which in German have a capital letter in the first position. Whether or not this has an influence needs to be investigated, as does the issue of how awareness of the display change influenced the results.

Rayner, Balota, and Pollatsek (1985) conducted an experiment using the boundary change paradigm in English in which the target word (*song*) changed from a semantically related word (*tune*), an orthographically similar nonword (*sorp*), an unrelated word (*door*) or did not change (*song*). Only the orthographically similar and identical previews showed a preview benefit. Similar results were found in a study with Spanish-English bilinguals. Bilinguals provide a good test for semantic preview benefit because one can systematically vary the effects of orthographic similarity and semantic similarity. Altarriba et al. (2001) had bilinguals read English sentences in a boundary change experiment. The previews were either identical to the target (e.g., *sweet-sweet*), cognates of the target (words which are similar orthographically and semantically between the two languages; e.g., *crema-cream*), pseudo-cognates of the target (words that are orthographically similar but semantically unrelated across languages; e.g., *grasa-grass*), non-cognate translations of the target (words which are semantically similar but orthographically different across languages; e.g., *dulce-sweet*), or a control word which was both orthographically and semantically unrelated (e.g., *torre-cream*). Altarriba et al. reported that the identical previews, cognates, and pseudo-cognates provided a preview benefit, but the non-cognate translation words did not. These data provide evidence that the preview benefit is due to orthographic-phonological processing; they do not show evidence for semantic parafoveal processing.

Hyönä and Haikio (2005) conducted a boundary change paradigm in Finnish in which emotional words (sex-related, threat words, etc.) were used as previews. The previews were either identical to the target, an orthographically similar emotional word, or an orthographically similar but semantically unrelated and emotionally neutral word. They found that emotional previews were no different from neutral previews, both in fixation measures on the target word when it was ultimately fixated and on fixations on the word prior to the target. They predicted that if semantic information was obtained parafoveally that the eyes would move to the emotional word sooner. But they did not find a difference in the gaze on the prior word, indicating that semantic information was not obtained from the emotional word prior to fixation.

White et al. (2008) investigated whether the second constituent of a compound word can be processed parafoveally. They conducted a boundary change experiment in which the second constituent of a compound word in Finnish (where the words tend to be long) was the target. Therefore, the word (*vaniljakastike* – 'vanilla sauce') had a semantically related preview (e.g., *vaniljakasinappi* – 'vanilla mustard'), a semantically unrelated preview (e.g., *vaniljarovasti* – 'vanilla priest'), or a nonword preview (e.g., *vaniljaseoklii* – 'vanilla nonword'). They found no difference between first pass reading measures on both the first and second constituents when the preview was semantically related compared to semantically unrelated, indicating that parafoveal preview is not obtained within a word when the word is a long compound.

All the above studies were conducted in alphabetic languages and did not find evidence for parafoveal processing of semantic information. Yan et al. (2009) found different results when they conducted a boundary change experiment in Chinese. The previews were identical, orthographically similar, phonologically similar, semantically similar, and unrelated controls. They found both parafoveal preview benefits and PoF effects of semantically related words, indicating that the subjects had obtained semantic information parafoveally. As also noted by Yan et al. (2009) the words in the study were highly constrained and the conclusions may not be generalizable. First, the previews were the first character in a two-character compound word and the identical condition was the only condition in which the preview character formed a real word with the following character. Second, Yan et al. selected only non-compound characters as the previews in order to avoid sublexical/radical activation. Both of these restrictions exclude characters that would otherwise be commonly encountered in normal Chinese reading. Yan et al. suggest that Chinese readers obtain semantic preview benefit when readers of alphabetic languages seem not to because there is a stronger relationship between orthography and semantics in Chinese than in alphabetic languages, where orthography is more closely linked to phonology than semantics. Indeed, the effects of phonology, which are quite strong in alphabetic languages, are comparatively small in Chinese (Feng, Miller, Shu, & Zhang, 2001).

Serial vs parallel lexical processing

In this section, we will address the issues of lexical processing that are central to the debate over serial vs parallel processing in reading; mainly, these issues are (1) lexical parafoveal-on-foveal (PoF) effects, (2) inflated fixations prior to skipping, and (3) preview benefit for word n+2. What constitutes a lexical property of a word is not completely agreed upon by researchers. Variables of a word, which are known to affect fixation times (as we noted in an earlier section), that are considered lexical are *frequency, familiarity, age of acquisition, neighborhood size* (how many words can be formed by changing one letter in the word), and *predictability*. Before addressing the three central issues mentioned above, we must first briefly mention controversies surrounding the effect of word frequency.

Word frequency

As we stated above, it is well established that frequency of the fixated word affects fixation times on it. However, frequency effects based on parafoveal processing are more elusive (see Rayner, 2009, for a summary of studies that have not obtained frequency effects on word n, when readers are fixated on it, and word n+1 is a low or high frequency word). Engbert, Nuthmann, Richter, and Kliegl (2005) argued that *spillover effects* of word frequency suggest that word processing is not a strictly serial process. Spillover effects refer to the finding that reading times on a word are slower when the preceding word was lower frequency that when it was high frequency (Rayner & Duffy, 1986). But it is not clear if spillover effects are due to diminished parallel processing because more resources are allocated to the foveal word or due to continuing post-lexical/integrative processing of the previous word during fixation on the now-fixated word. Similarly, *successor effects* or PoF effects are inconsistent in the literature, and cause of the effect is debated (see discussion below).

Inflated fixations prior to word skipping

During normal silent reading, as noted above, approximately a third of the words in the text are skipped (Rayner, 1998, 2009). In light of this pervasive finding, it is almost impossible to argue that the upcoming word was not identified (Rayner White, Kambe, Miller, Liversedge, 2003a). However, it is important to note that the majority of words that are skipped are either short and relatively meaningless (closed class words, such as *to, for, in, the*, etc.; Blanchard, Pollatsek, & Rayner, 1989; Brysbaert & Vitu, 1998; Rayner & McConkie, 1976; Rayner et al., 1996) or words which are highly predictable based on prior context (Drieghe et al., 2005; Ehrlich & Rayner, 1981; Hyönä, 1993; Rayner & Well, 1996; Rayner et al., 2011) in which case, skipping may not necessarily be due to parafoveal semantic processing, but rather due to prior context constraining lexical candidates and orthographic information confirming one of the options. Furthermore, even if a word was identified parafoveally, the processing was not obligatorily parallel with the foveal word, but could have occurred during an attention shift to the word prior to the saccade (see discussion below).

The finding that fixations on a word prior to skipping the following word are longer (Kliegl & Engbert, 2005; Pollatsek, Rayner, & Balota, 1986; Rayner et al., 2003) has been used to argue on both sides of the serial vs parallel debate in reading. Kliegl and Engbert (2005) found with a corpus analysis of eye movements that fixation durations were inflated prior to skipping long and infrequent words, but were reliably shorter prior to skipping short and high frequent words. The serial model and the parallel model account for word skipping data in very different ways. Rayner et al. (2003) claimed that, according to the serial model, inflated fixations prior to skipping the parafoveal word are due to cancelling the saccade that had been planned to word n+1 and reprogramming the saccade to target word n+2. Engbert et al. (2005) disagreed, supporting the parallel model's claim that inflated fixations are a *cause* of skipping, not a *consequence* because more parafoveal information is obtained during longer fixations. Therefore, words following a long fixation are more likely to be skipped because they have more opportunity to be identified parafoveally.

Parafoveal-on-foveal effects

As mentioned above parafoveal-on-foveal (PoF) effects are hotly contested evidence used to argue for parallel processing in reading. Many PoF effects occur when the parafoveal word is skipped (Pollatsek et al., 1986) and, as mentioned above, the two models account for these data differently. Orthographic PoF effects (e.g., a nonsense letter string in the parafovea slowing fixations on the foveal word) are pervasively found in the literature, but they are predicted by both serial and parallel models because they are effects at the lowest, sublexical level of representation.

Many of the studies that find PoF effects do not use reading tasks, but rather, tasks that *approximate* reading, but are not reading (Kennedy, 1998, 2000; Kennedy, Pynte, & Ducrot, 2002; Murray & Rowan, 1998). Furthermore, many studies that involve reading failed to find PoF effects. For example, Inhoff, Starr, and Shindler, (2000a) conducted a display change study in which the preview of a target word (*light*) was either identical, an upper case version (*LIGHT*), an orthographically illegal letter string (*qvtqp*) or an unrelated word, which did not make sense in the sentence context (*smoke*). Fixation measures on the preceding word (i.e., PoF effects) were inflated in the uppercase condition and the illegal letter string condition, but not in the identical or unrelated word condition, indicating the PoF effects are solely orthographic, and not lexical or semantic in nature (but see Inhoff, Radach, Starr, & Greenberg, 2000b). Furthermore, Underwood, Binns, and Walker (2000) found that properties of the initial trigram of the parafoveal word affected fixations on the foveal word, but again, these are orthographic effects, not lexical or superlexical. Although PoF effects are used to argue for parallel processing and are claimed to be inconsistent with a serial account, PoF effects of an orthographic nature are allowed in serial models (Rayner & Juhasz, 2004; Rayner et al., 2003a; Starr & Rayner, 2001). Importantly, lexical PoF effects (i.e., effects of the parafoveal word's frequency) have not been widely reported (Carpenter & Just, 1983; Henderson & Ferreira, 1993; Rayner et al. 1998b). Elsewhere in this volume (Chapter 5), Heister, Würzner, and Kliegl discuss issues related to PoF and spillover effects in the context of a parallel lexical processing point of view (and for an exchange regarding the issues see Kliegl, Nuthmann, & Engbert, 2006; Rayner et al., 2007d; Kliegl, 2007).

Yang, Wang, Xu, and Rayner (2009) had subjects read Chinese sentences in a boundary change experiment. When the foveal character was the first character in a two-character word they found evidence for parafoveal-on-foveal effects. However, when the foveal character constituted a word on its own, they did not find evidence for PoF effects. Yang et al. argued that it is not clear whether the PoF effects are lexical or orthographic and so it is unclear whether they pose a problem for serial models. Even though PoF effects have traditionally been used to argue for parallel processing, they can be accounted for in a serial model under a *mislocated fixation account* (see below).

Preview of word *n+2*

Although there have only been a few studies on the topic, evidence for preview effects on word n+2 is mixed in the literature. The majority of studies did not find evidence for any preview benefit of word n+2 (Angele & Rayner, 2011; Angele, Slattery, Yang, Kliegl, & Rayner, 2008; Kliegl, Risse, & Laubrock, 2007; Rayner, Juhasz, & Brown, 2007a). One study, although it did not find any evidence for n+2 preview effect found a *delayed parafoveal-on-foveal*, in which the n+2 preview effect was revealed when the eyes landed on word n+1 (Kliegl et al., 2007). It is important to note that preview of word n+2 effects have only shown up in very controlled circumstances, in which words n and n+1 are short words and generally relatively meaningless, close-class, high frequency words such as *the*. Considering this fact, the claim that these results are compatible with parallel models and not compatible with serial models is inaccurate. In fact, a serial model would predict that under these circumstances one would find an n+2 preview effect (see below).

Furthermore, McDonald (2006) found that preview of the parafoveal n+1 word is only obtained when that word is the target of the current saccade. McDonald conducted a boundary change study in which the boundary that triggered the display change was either at the end of the pretarget word or in the middle of it. The pretarget word was long enough (9–10 letters) that there was a high probability that it was refixated. This meant that McDonald could compare the preview benefit of word n+1 when the saccade landed on it to when it was a refixation on the preceding word (word n). He only found a preview benefit in the condition in which the saccade that triggered the display change landed on the target word, indicating that attention was only on the parafoveal word when a saccade was programmed to it. These data are more supportive of a model in which attention and eye movements are tightly coupled. As this will be discussed below, this is more compatible with a serial model in which attention shifts before the eyes than with a parallel model in which attention is distributed.

Models of eye movement control during reading

The two sides of the debate between serial and parallel hypotheses of lexical identification during reading are represented by the two major competing models of eye movement control during reading: the E-Z Reader model (Reichle, Pollatsek, Fischer, & Rayner, 1998; Reichle, Rayner, & Pollatsek, 2003), which is a serial lexical model and the SWIFT model (Engbert et al., 2005), which is a parallel model. Of course, there are several other models,[5] but for simplicity, only the two aforementioned models will be discussed.

The E-Z Reader model

E-Z Reader posits that eye movements during reading are determined by two phases of word recognition on the foveal word. The first stage, called L_1, is a cursory processing of the word (sometimes called a *familiarity check*). Once this stage completes, a more thorough stage of processing, called L_2 commences and a saccade is programmed to the following word (stages M_1 and M_2, see below). After L_2 completes, attention shifts to the next word. This attention shift is what accounts for word skipping and parafoveal preview benefits. L_1 and L_2 may not be two distinct stages, but rather two different thresholds of identification of the word (Rayner, Li, & Pollatsek, 2007b). Once M_2 completes, the saccade is triggered and the eyes move from the word. The lexical identification stages are preceded by a stage of visual analysis (V), which occurs in parallel over all the words within the perceptual span. This stage accounts for why small windows in the moving window paradigm, odd spacing manipulations, or inappropriate word length information in boundary change paradigms cause such disruption in processing. Another important aspect of the model is that processing depends on eccentricity from fixation. For this reason, foveal words are processed more quickly than parafoveal words, gaze duration is related to distance from the center of the word, and (controlling for other factors) short words will be processed faster than long words.

In concert with the lexical processing stages, the model posits two saccade-programming stages, M_1 and M_2. M_1, which marks a plan to fixate n+1, commences when L_1 ends and causes the program to refixate the word to be cancelled. This aspect of the model accounts for the fact that words that are hard to identify (i.e., have a long L_1 stage) are refixated more often. M_1 is a labile stage, which means that the saccade that is programmed during this stage can be cancelled. The second stage, M_2, follows M_1 and triggers the saccade when it finishes. M_2 is a non-labile stage, which means that it cannot be cancelled. If word n+1 is easy to process (i.e., L_1 and L_2 are short) and M_2 has not commenced, the program to n+1 can be cancelled and the eyes will make a saccade to word n+2, in which case word n+1 will be skipped.

The last set of assumptions of the model regard *where* to move the eyes. Eye movements (whether saccades between words or refixations within a word) are assumed to target the center of the word, with some error. Because the saccade has already begun to be programmed when attention shifts to the parafoveal word, processing of the parafoveal word should not influence processing on the foveal word. Therefore, it has been argued that E-Z Reader does not predict that there would be PoF effects. However, there are certain circumstances in which fixation durations on a foveal word can be lengthened by an unusual letter string in the parafovea, under the *mislocated fixation account* (Drieghe, Rayner, & Pollatsek, 2008). According to this account, occulomotor error causes the saccade to undershoot the target and land on the word prior to the one being attended. Therefore, PoF effects are actually the result of attributing processing to the foveal word, when the parafoveal word is the one being processed. Evidence for this account comes from the finding that PoF effects were only present in instances where the eyes were fixating close to the parafoveal word (Drieghe et al., 2008). There is systematic range error in saccade execution so that long saccades tend to undershoot the target and short saccades tend to overshoot the target (Brysbaert & Vitu, 1998; McConkie, Kerr, Reddix, & Zola, 1988). Furthermore, Drieghe et al. (2008) found a relationship between saccade length and single fixation duration when the first few letters of the parafoveal word was an illegal letter string, but not when it was a legal letter string.

As mentioned before, the E-Z Reader model accounts for inflated fixations before skipping with the assertion that the saccade to word n+1 needs to be cancelled and a saccade to word n+2 needs to be programmed. This adds time to fixations on the word prior to skipping. E-Z Reader predicts that word n+2 is processed only in a very special case. Attention shifts in E-Z Reader are based on the completion of L_2 and saccade executions are based on the completion of L_1 (and then M_1 and M_2). Therefore, in the case that L_1 completes on word n and both L_1 and L_2 complete on word n+1, then attention will have shifted to word n+2 and there will be an n+2 preview effect. In fact, as mentioned before, the only documented cases in which an n+2 preview effect has been reported are cases in which word n+1 is a short, relatively meaning-less, closed-class word (cf. Kliegl et al., 2007; Risse & Kliegl, in press) such as *the*, which has the potential to complete L_2 before M_2 completes on the prior word.

The SWIFT model

SWIFT attempts to explain eye movements in many different tasks, not only reading. SWIFT is based on dynamic field theory. Simplistically put, the model defines levels of activation for each word as a function of its distance from the center of fixation and as a function of time. There is continuous cross-talk between cognitive systems (linguistic processing modules and saccade generating modules) and this continuous interaction accounts for why fixation durations are so short compared to the length of time it takes to plan and execute saccades. Saccade targets are selected in a biased-random fashion, so that words with higher levels of activation are more likely to be targeted. Saccade targets are selected and updated based on partial information obtained from perceptual and cognitive linguistic input. Because the model is based on continually changing activation fields, there is the important implication that processing is spatially distributed and therefore occurs in parallel over several words.

SWIFT posits that there is a random timer that triggers the saccade to the next-fixated word, which is not necessarily the word to the right of the currently fixated word. The difficulty of processing the foveal word can inhibit the saccade and make the fixation longer. SWIFT assumes that there are separate pathways for saccade timing and targeting, which implies that the decision of *when* to move the eyes is decoupled from the decision of *where* to move the eyes. Whereas *when* to move the eyes is determined by a random timer with foveal inhibition, *where* to move the eyes is determined by levels of lexical activation, which have been accumulating over time.

Like E-Z Reader, there are two stages of saccade programming; a labile stage, and a non-labile stage. Error in the saccadic execution system leads to the exact goal location (the center of the targeted word) to not always be landed on. This error can be broken down into random (Gaussian) error and systematic error. The systematic error is a function of launch site distance, so that long saccades tend to undershoot and short saccades tend to overshoot the target location. Because there is error in saccade targeting, and there is worse processing of words at further eccentricities from the optimal viewing location (the center of the word), SWIFT posits that saccade errors can be quickly corrected with a short, corrective saccade. Moreover, these corrective saccades are more likely to occur at word boundaries (further from the optimal viewing position). Following this, SWIFT posits that saccade latency is modulated by intended saccade length. Therefore, with a longer intended saccade there is a longer saccade latency (i.e., preceding fixation).

As mentioned above, SWIFT accounts for inflated fixations before word skipping by positing that parafoveal words are skipped *after* long fixations *because* there was more opportunity for them to be processed, rather than inflated fixations being caused by saccade cancellation. Parallel models, like SWIFT, posit that PoF effects are real and occur because lexical processing is distributed and the parafoveal word was processed to some extent and that parafoveal processing slows processing and gaze durations on the foveal word. SWIFT also predicts preview effects of word n+2 based on the assumption that processing is distributed over multiple words.

Comparing serial and parallel models of silent reading

Criticisms of parallel models (see Reichle et al., 2009) point out that it is difficult to account for how the model keeps the different word entries separate and there are currently no models of word identification that allow for concurrent identification of more than one word. Reichle et al. (2009) further argued for serial allocation of attention, citing that the system needs attention to bind information in visual search tasks (for conjunction searches) and this attention needs to be shifted serially (see also Treisman & Gelade, 1980). Reichle, Vanyukov, Laurent, and Warren (2008) compared reaction times and eye movements while subjects performed visual search tasks that represent different levels of processing (asterisk detection, letter detection, rhyme detection, semantic judgment). These levels of processing progress from more shallow to more deep processing, each one using more cognitive resources and more closely approximating the cognitive demands of silent reading. On each trial, the screen contained one, two, three, or four words. There were four different types of tasks subjects were asked to perform: detect whether an asterisk ('*') was present, whether a particular letter ('q') was present, whether a word rhymed with a particular word ('blue'), or whether a word was a member of a particular semantic category ('animal').

Reichle et al. (2009) found an increase in response times, number of fixations, and first fixation durations for increasing number of words, indicating additional cost associated with processing additional words. These effects were more pronounced with deeper levels of processing. This increased processing cost with increasing number of words did not occur with the asterisk detection task, which is what should be observed in all tasks if parallel processing is occurring. These results are even stronger given that there was no requirement for the subjects to process the words serially (i.e., there was no word order or syntactic frame as there is in silent reading), but even so, the results are more consistent with a serial model. Furthermore, the blocked design encouraged the subjects to take advantage of the design and adopt a parallel strategy, but they did not. In fact, because word order does matter in reading, the effects in this study might even be under-estimations.

Evidence from disappearing text studies lend strong insight into the issue of serial vs parallel processing (Liversedge & Blythe, 2007; Liversedge, Rayner, White, Vergilino-Perez, Findlay, & Kentridge, 2004; Rayner, Liversedge, & White, 2007c; Rayner, Liversedge, White, & Vergilino-Perez, 2003c; Rayner et al., 2011). In these studies, either the foveal word or the foveal and parafoveal word disappear (or are masked) shortly after fixation. Even though the word disappears after 60 ms, fixation durations are still sensitive to word frequency, indicating that once enough visuo-orthographic information is obtained from a word processing can continue normally even if the visual information disappears

- Readers make eye movements when reading to move their fovea (region of the retina with highest acuity) to the word they wish to process.
- Time spent fixating a word reflects the cognitive and linguistic processing required to identify it and to integrate it into the sentence. Fixation time is modulated by factors such as lexical frequency and predictability from prior context.
- Fixation times in reading are shorter than response times in other (isolated) word identification tasks because information about upcoming words is available to be processed in the parafovea before it is directly fixated. Generally, the type of information that is processed in the parafovea is orthographic and phonological but, in some languages like Hebrew, morphological. There is little evidence demonstrating that lexical or semantic information is obtained from the parafovea.
- Models of eye movement control during reading (specifically E-Z Reader and SWIFT) account well for most effects found in reading studies and differ in how they address a few issues, specifically parafoveal lexical processing and whether readers can lexically identify words in parallel.

(or is masked). Furthermore, these studies show that reading is unaffected if the foveal word disappears at SOAs as short as 60 ms but is greatly disrupted if the parafoveal word disappears at that SOA. Reichle et al. (2009) argued this is not a problem for serial models following the assumption that 60 ms is the minimal amount of time needed to convert visual information into orthographic codes. Therefore, 60 ms is sufficient to orthographically encode the foveal word, but it is not enough time to also shift attention to and orthographically encode the parafoveal word. They argued that parallel models cannot account for this because there should be enough time to convert the visual information of both the foveal word and the parafoveal word if attention is distributed.

A serial model of reading would more closely approximate how the speech perception system must process words in auditory input. Since words can only be produced one at a time, they can only be heard one at a time. Writing systems are a second-order of representation – they are a documentation of naturally occurring spoken language – and it seems reasonable to assume that the way we process spoken language might be similar to in many ways (or may even support) how we process written language.

Reichle et al. (2009) argued that parallel models can be modified to account for data that favors serial models (for instance, making the gradient largely focused on the foveal word) but this, in essence makes the parallel model a serial model. One possible criticism of serial models is that they have difficulty explaining how fixation durations can be so fast if lexical identification is serial. Saccades take 150–200 ms to program and words take 150–300 ms to identify. Therefore, fixations should be on the order of 300–500 ms instead of the observed 200–250 ms. Attentional gradients explain the phenomenon of very quick fixations by allowing words to be identified over multiple fixations (importantly, including fixations on other words). Reichle et al. (2009) argued that if lexical processing and saccadic programming are supported by anatomically distinct systems then it is reasonable to assume that both can occur concurrently. Therefore, it is not compulsory that the time needed for saccade programming (150–200 ms) and the time needed for word identification (150–300 ms) be additive. This assumption is integral to a serial model.

In summary, over the past 30 years, eye movements have been employed to investigate the underlying processes that support word identification during reading. In other chapters in this book, factors that influence single word recognition are discussed. One of the most striking findings in reading research (compared to single word recognition) is that, although words are mostly identified one at a time during reading, important information from words other than the currently fixated word is obtained on each fixation and facilitates reading. This information allows for incredibly rapid information processing, allowing skilled readers to read at speeds of 200–400 words per minute (Rayner, 1998, 2009). As reviewed in this chapter, whether the use of parafoveal information is due to a serial or parallel process is an ongoing debate, though obviously our bias is for serial lexical processing.

Acknowledgments

Preparation of this chapter was supported by Grant HD26765 from NIH and the Atkinson Fund.

Notes

1 Character/letter spaces is the appropriate metric to use in reading since how far the eyes move is relatively invariant when the same text is read at different distances even though the character/letter spaces subtend different visual angles (Morrison & Rayner, 1981).

2 In a clever recent experiment, Miellet et al. (2009) used a novel variation of the moving window paradigm in which parafoveal letters on each fixation were magnified to offset acuity limitations. They still found that the span was approximately 14–15 letter spaces to the right of fixation.

3 Word length has little influence on first fixation duration and the effect on gaze duration of word length is due to increased refixations on a word.

4 It is interesting to note that frequency effects (Yan, Tian, Bai, & Rayner, 2006) and predictability effects (Rayner et al., 2005) are evident in Chinese readers and are of comparable size to those in English.

5 For a discussion of the models, see Reichle et al. (2003).

References

Altarriba, J., Kambe, G., Pollatsek, A., & Rayner, K. (2001). Semantic codes are not used in integrating information across eye fixations in reading: evidence from fluent Spanish-English bilinguals. *Perception & Psychophysics, 63,* 875–890.

Angele, B. & Rayner, K. (2011). Parafoveal processing of word n + 2 during reading: Do the preceding words matter? *Journal of Experimental Psychology: Human Perception and Performance, 37,* 1210–1220.

Angele, B., Slattery, T., Yang, J., Kliegl, R., & Rayner, K. (2008). Parafoveal processing in reading: Manipulating n+1 and n+2 previews simultaneously. *Visual Cognition, 16,* 697–707.

Ashby, J. & Rayner, K. (2004). Representing syllable information during silent reading: Evidence from eye movements. *Language and Cognitive Processes, 19,* 391–426.

Ashby, J., Treiman, R., Kessler B., & Rayner, K. (2006). Vowel processing during silent reading: Evidence from eye movements. *Journal of Experimental Psychology: Learning, Memory and Cognition, 32,* 416–424.

Balota, D. A., Pollatsek, A., & Rayner, K. (1985). The interaction of contextual constraints and parafoveal visual information in reading. *Cognitive Psychology, 17,* 364–90.

Bertram, R. & Hyönä, J. (2007). The interplay between parafoveal preview and morphological processing in reading. In R. Van Gompel, M. Fischer, W., Murray & R. Hill (Eds), *Eye movements: a window on mind and brain* (pp. 391–407). Oxford, UK: Elsevier Science.

Blanchard, H., Pollatsek, A., & Rayner, K. (1989). The acquisition of parafoveal word information in reading. *Perception & Psychophysics, 46,* 85–94.

Brysbaert, M. & Vitu, F. (1998). Word skipping: Implications for theories of eye movement control in reading. In G. Underwood (Ed.), *Eye guidance in reading and scene perception* (pp. 125–148). Oxford, UK: Elsevier.

Cattell, J. (1886). The time it takes to see and name objects. *Mind, 11*, 63–65.

Carpenter, P. & Just, M. (1983). What your eyes do when your mind is reading. In K. Rayner (Ed.), *Eye movements in reading: Perceptual and language processes* (pp. 275–307). New York: Academic Press.

Carroll, P.J. & Slowiaczek, M.L. (1986). Constraints of semantic priming in reading: A fixation time analysis. *Memory & Cognition, 14*, 509–522.

Chace, K., Rayner, K., & Well, A. (2005). Eye movements and phonological parafoveal preview: Effects of reading skill. *Canadian Journal of Experimental Psychology, 59*, 209–217.

Chaffin, R., Morris, R.K., & Seely, R.E. (2001). Learning new word meanings from context: A study of eye movements. *Journal of Experimental Psychology: Learning, Memory, and Cognition, 27*, 225–235.

Clifton, C., Jr, Staub, A., & Rayner, K. (2007). Eye movements in reading words and sentences. In: R. van Gompel (Ed.), *Eye movements: A window on mind and brain* (pp. 341–372). Amsterdam: Elsevier.

Daneman, M. & Reingold, E. (1993). What eye fixations tell us about phonological recoding during reading. *Canadian Journal of Experimental Psychology, 47*, 153–178.

Deutsch, A., Frost, R., Pollatsek, S., & Rayner, K. (2000). Early morphological effects in word recognition in Hebrew: Evidence from parafoveal preview benefit. *Language and Cognitive Processes, 15*, 487–506.

Deutsch, A., Frost, R., Peleg, S., Pollatsek, A., & Rayner, K. (2003). Early morphological effects in reading: Evidence from parafoveal preview benefit in Hebrew. *Psychonomic Bulletin & Review, 10*, 415–422.

Deutsch, A., Frost, R., Pollatsek, A., & Rayner, K. (2005). Morphological parafoveal preview benefit effects in reading: Evidence from Hebrew. *Language and Cognitive Processes, 20*, 341–371.

Drieghe, D., Rayner, K., & Pollatsek, A. (2005). Eye movements and word skipping during reading revisited. *Journal of Experimental Psychology: Human Perception and Performance, 31*, 954–969.

Drieghe, D., Rayner, K., & Pollatsek, A. (2008). Mislocated fixations can account for parafoveal-on-foveal effects in eye movements during reading. *Quarterly Journal of Experimental Psychology, 61*, 1239–1249.

Duffy, S.A., Morris, R.K., & Rayner, K. (1988). Lexical ambiguity and fixation times in reading. *Journal of Memory and Language, 27*, 429–446.

Ehrlich, S. & Rayner, K. (1981). Contextual effects on word perception of eye movements during reading. *Journal of Verbal learning and Verbal Behavior, 20*, 641–655.

Engbert, R., Nuthmann, A., Richter, E., & Kliegl, R. (2005). SWIFT: A dynamical model of saccade generation during reading. *Psychological Review, 112*, 777–813.

Feng, G., Miller, K., Shu, H., & Zhang, H. (2001). Rowed to recovery: The use of phonological and orthographic information in reading Chinese and English. *Journal of Experimental Psychology: Learning, Memory, and Cognition, 27*, 1079–1100.

Frazier, L. & Rayner, K. (1982). Making and correcting errors during sentence comprehension: Eye movements in the analysis of structurally ambiguous sentences. *Cognitive Psychology, 14*, 178–210.

Henderson, J. & Ferreira, F. (1993). Eye movement control during reading: Fixation measures reflect foveal but not parafoveal processing difficulty. *Canadian Journal of Experimental Psychology, 47*, 201–221.

Huey, E. B. (1908). *The Psychology and Pedagogy of Reading*. New York: Macmillan.

Hyönä, J. (1993). Effects of thematic and lexical priming on reader's eye movements. *Scandanavian Journal of Psychology, 34*, 293–304.

Hyönä, J. & Haikio, T. (2005). Is emotional content obtained from parafoveal words during reading? An eye movement analysis. *Scandinavian Journal of Psychology, 46*, 475–483.

Inhoff, A.W. & Rayner, K. (1986). Parafoveal word processing during eye fixations in reading: Effects of word frequency. *Perception & Psychophysics, 40*, 431–439.

Inhoff, A., Starr, M., & Shindler, K. (2000a). Is the processing of words during eye fixations in reading strictly serial? *Perception & Psychophysics, 62*, 1474–1484.

Inhoff, A., Radach, R., Starr, M., & Greenberg, S. (2000b). Allocation of visuao-spatial attention and saccade programming during reading. In A. Kennedy, R. Radach, D. Heller & J. Pynte (Eds), *Reading as a perceptual process* (pp. 221–46).Oxford, UK, Elsevier Science.

Inhoff, A., Radach, R., Eiter, B., & Juhasz, B. (2003). Distinct subsystems for the parafoveal processing of spatial and linguistic information during eye fixations in reading. *Quarterly Journal of Experimental Psychology, 56*, 803–827.

Jared, D., Levy, B., & Rayner, K. (1999). The role of phonology in the activation of word meaning during reading: Evidence from proofreading and eye movements. *Journal of Experimental Psychology: General, 128*, 219–264.

Juhasz, B. & Rayner, K. (2003). Investigating the effects of a set of intercorrelated variables on eye fixation durations in reading. *Journal of Experimental Psychology: Learning, Memory, and Cognition, 29*, 1312–1318.

Juhasz, B. & Rayner, K. (2006). The role of age of acquisition and word frequency in reading: Evidence from eye fixation durations. *Visual Cognition, 13*, 846–863.

Juhasz, B., White, S., Liversedge, S., & Rayner, K. (2008). Eye movements and the use of parafoveal word length information in reading. *Quarterly Journal of Experimental Psychology, 34*, 1560–1579.

Hohenstein, S., Laubrock, J., & Kliegl, R. (2010). Semantic preview benefit during eye movements in reading: A parafoveal fast-priming study. *Journal of Experimental Psychology: Learning, Memory, and Cognition*, 36, 1150–1170.

Kambe, G. (2004). Parafoveal processing of prefixed words during eye fixations in reading. Evidence against morphological influences on parafoveal processing. *Perception & Psychophysics, 66*, 279–292.

Kennedy, A. (1998). The influence of foveal words on parafoveal inspection time: Evidence for a processing trade-off. In G. Underwood (Ed.), *Eye guidance in reading and scene perception* (pp. 149–179). Oxford, UK: Elsevier Science.

Kennedy, A. (2000). Parafoveal processing in word recognition. *The Quarterly Journal of Experimental Psychology, 53*, 429–455.

Kennedy, A., Pynte, J. & Ducrot, S. (2002). Parafoveal-on-foveal interactions in word recognition. *The Quarterly Journal of Experimental Psychology, 55*, 1307–1337.

Kliegl, R. (2007). Toward a perceptual-span theory of distributed processing in reading: A reply to Rayner, Pollatsek, Drieghe, Slattery, and Reichle (2007). *Journal of Experimental Psychology: General, 236*, 530–537.

Kliegl, R. & Engbert, R. (2005). Fixation durations before word skipping in reading. *Psychonomic Bulletin & Review, 12*, 132–138.

Kliegl, R., Nuthmann, A., & Engbert, R. (2006). Tracking the mind during reading: The influence of past, present, and future words on fixation durations. *Journal of Experimental Psychology: General, 135*, 12–35.

Kliegl, R., Risse, S., & Laubrock, J. (2007). Preview benefit and parafoveal-on-foveal effects from word n+2. *Journal of Experimental Psychology: Human Perception and Performance, 33,* 1250–1255.

Levy, R., Bicknell, K., Slattery, T. J., & Rayner, K. (2009). Eye movement evidence that readers maintain and act on uncertainty about past linguistic input. *Proceedings of the National Academy of Sciences of the United States of America, 106,* 21086–90.

Lima, S. (1987). Morphological analysis in sentence reading. *Journal of Memory and Language, 26,* 84–99.

Liu, W., Inhoff, A., Ye, Y., & Wu, C. (2002). Use of parafoveally visible characters during the reading of Chinese sentences. *Journal of Experimental Psychology: Human Perception and Performance, 28,* 1213–1227.

Liversedge, S. & Blythe, H. (2007). Lexical and sublexical influences on movements during reading. *Language and Linguistic Compass, 1,* 17–31.

Liversedge, S., Rayner, K., White, S., Vergilino-Perez, D., Findlay, J., & Kentridge, R. (2004). Eye movements while reading disappearing text: Is there a gap effect in reading? *Vision Research, 44,* 1013–1124.

McConkie, G.W. & Rayner, K. (1975). The span of the effective stimulus during a fixation in reading. *Perception & Psychophysics, 17,* 578–586.

McConkie, G.W. & Zola, D. (1979). Is visual information integrated across successive fixations in reading? *Perception & Psychophysics, 25,* 221–224.

McConkie, G., Kerr, P., Reddix, M., & Zola, D. (1988). Eye movement control during reading: The location of initial eye fixations on words. *Vision Research, 28,* 1107–1118.

McDonald, S. (2006). Parafoveal preview benefit in reading is only obtained from the saccade goal. *Vision Research, 46,* 4416–4424.

Miellet, S. & Sparrow, L. (2004). Phonological codes are assembled before word fixation: Evidence from boundary paradigm in sentence reading. *Brain and Language, 90,* 299–310.

Miellet, S., O'Donnell, P., & Sereno, S. (2009). Parafoveal Magnification: Visual acuity does not modulate the perceptual span in reading. *Psychological Science, 20,* 721–728.

Morris, R. (1994). Lexical and message-level sentence context effects on fixation times in reading. *Journal of Experimental Psychology: Learning, Memory, and Cognition, 20,* 92–103.

Morrison, R.E. & Rayner, K. (1981). Saccade size in reading depends upon character spaces and not visual angle. *Perception & Psychophysics, 30,* 395–396.

Murray, W. & Rowan, M. (1998). Early, mandatory, pragmatic processing. *Journal of Psycholinguistic Research, 27,* 1–22.

Nuthmann, A., Engbert, R., & Kliegl, R. (2005). Mislocated fixations during reading and the inverted optimal viewing position effect. *Vision Research, 45,* 2201–2217.

Nuthmann, A., Engbert, R., & Kliegl, R. (2007). The IOVP effect in mindless reading: Experiment and modeling. *Vision Research, 47,* 990–1002.

O'Regan, J. & Levy-Schoen, A. (1987). Eye movement strategy and tactics in word recognition and reading. In M. Coltheart (Ed.), *Attention and performance XII: The psychology of reading* (pp. 363–383). Hillsdale, NJ: Lawrence Erlbaum Associates, Inc.

Pollatsek, A., Rayner, K., & Balota, D. (1986). Inferences about eye movement control from the perceptual span in reading. *Perception & Psychophysics, 40,* 121–130.

Pollatsek, A., Lesch, M., Morris, R., & Rayner, K. (1992). Phonological codes are used in integrating information across saccades in word identification and reading. *Journal of Experimental Psychology: Human Perception and Performance, 18,* 148–162.

Rayner, K. (1975). The perceptual span and peripheral cues in reading. *Cognitive Psychology, 7,* 65–81.

Rayner, K. (1979). Eye guidance in reading: Fixation locations within words. *Perception, 8,* 21–30.

Rayner, K. (1998). Eye movements in reading and information processing: 20 years of research. *Psychological Bulletin, 124,* 372–422.

Rayner, K. (2009). Eye movements and attention in reading, scene perception and visual search. *The Quarterly Journal of Experimental Psychology, 62,* 1457–1506.

Rayner, K. & Bertera, J. H. (1979). Reading without a fovea. *Science, 206,* 468–469.

Rayner, K. & Duffy, S.A. (1986). Lexical complexity and fixation times in reading: Effects of word frequency, verb complexity, and lexical ambiguity. *Memory & Cognition, 14,* 191–201.

Rayner, K. & McConkie, G. (1976) What guides reader's eye movements? *Vision Research, 16,* 829–837.

Rayner, K. & Pollatsek, A. (1989). *The psychology of reading.* Englewood Cliffs, NJ: Prentice Hall.

Rayner, K. & Well, A.D. (1996). Effects of contextual constraint on eye movements in reading: A further examination. *Psychonomic Bulletin & Review, 3,* 504–509.

Rayner, K. & Juhasz, B. J. (2004). Eye movements in reading: Old questions and new directions. *European Journal of Cognitive Psychology, 16,* 340–52.

Rayner, K., McConkie, G.W., & Zola, D. (1980). Integrating information across eye movements. *Cognitive Psychology, 12,* 206–226.

Rayner, K., Well, A., Pollatsek, A., & Bertera, J. (1982). The availability of useful information to the right of fixation in reading. *Perception & Psychophysics, 31,* 537–550.

Rayner, K., Balota, D., & Pollatsek, A. (1985). Against parafoveal semantic processing during eye fixations during reading. *Canadian Journal of Psychology, 40,* 473–483.

Rayner, K., Pollatsek, A., Ashby, J., and Clifton, C. (2012). *The Psychology of Reading.* New York: Psychology Press.

Rayner, K., Sereno, S., Lesch, M., & Pollatsek, A. (1995). Phonological codes are automatically activated during reading: Evidence from an eye movement priming paradigm. *Psychological Science, 6,* 26–32.

Rayner, K., Sereno, S., & Raney, G. (1996). Eye movement control in reading: A comparison of two types of models. *Journal of Experimental Psychology: Human Perception and Performance, 22,* 1188–1200.

Rayner, K., Fischer, M., & Pollatsek, A. (1998b). Unspaced text interferes with both word identification and eye movement control. *Vision Research, 38,* 1129–1144.

Rayner, K., Kambe, G., & Duffy, S. (2000). The effect of clause wrap-up on eye movements during reading. *The Quarterly Journal of Experimental Psychology, 53,* 1061–1080.

Rayner, K., White, S., Kambe, G., Miller, B., & Liversedge, S. (2003a). On the processing of meaning from parafoveal vision during eye fixations in reading. In J. Hyönä, R. Radach, and H. Deubel (Eds), *The mind's eye: Cognitive and applied aspects of eye movement research* (pp. 213–234). Amsterdam: North Holland.

Rayner, K., Juhasz, B., Ashby, J., & Clifton, C. (2003b). Inhibition of saccade return in reading. *Vision Research, 43*, 1027–1034.

Rayner, K., Liversedge, S., White, S., & Vergilino-Perez, D. (2003c). Reading disappearing text: Cognitive control of eye movements. *Psychological Science, 14*, 385–388.

Rayner, K., Ashby, J., Pollatsek, A., & Reichle, E.D. (2004a). The effects of frequency and predictability on eye fixations in reading: Implications for the E-Z Reader model. *Journal of Experimental Psychology: Human Perception and Performance, 30*, 720–732.

Rayner, K., Warren, T., Juhasz, B.J., & Liversedge, S.P. (2004b). The effect of plausibility on eye movements in reading. *Journal of Experimental Psychology: Learning, Memory, and Cognition, 30*, 1290–1301.

Rayner, K., Li, X., Juhasz, B., & Yan, G. (2005). The effect of word predictability on the eye movements of Chinese readers. *Psychonomic Bulletin & Review, 12*, 1089–1093.

Rayner, K., Cook, A., Juhasz, B., & Frazier, L. (2006a). Immediate disambiguation of lexically ambiguous words during reading: Evidence from eye movements. *British Journal of Psychology, 97*, 467–482.

Rayner, K., Juhasz, B., & Brown, S. (2007a). Do readers obtain preview benefit from word n+2? A test of serial attention shift versus distributed lexical processing models of eye movement control in reading. *Journal of Experimental Psychology: Human Perception and Performance, 33*, 230–245.

Rayner, K., Li, X., & Pollatsek, A. (2007b). Extending the E-Z Reader model of eye movement control to Chinese readers. *Cognitive Science, 31*, 1021–1033.

Rayner, K., Liversedge, S. & White, S. (2007c). Eye movements when reading disappearing text: The importance of the word to the right of fixation. *Vision Research, 46*, 310–323.

Rayner, K., Pollatsek, A., Drieghe, D., Slattery, T., & Reichle, E. (2007d). Tracking the mind during reading via eye movements: Comments on Kliegl, Nuthmann, and Engbert (2006). *Journal of Experimental Psychology: General, 136*, 520–529.

Rayner, K., Castelhano, M.S., & Yang, J. (2009). Eye movements and the perceptual span of older and younger readers. *Psychology and Aging, 24*, 755–760.

Rayner, K., Slattery, T. J., & Belanger, N. N. (2010). Eye movements, the perceptual span, and reading speed. *Psychonomic Bulletin and Review, 17*, 834–839.

Rayner, K., Castelhano, M.S., & Yang, J. (2010). Preview benefit during eye fixations for older and younger readers. *Psychology and Aging, 25*, 714–718.

Rayner, K., Slattery, T. J., Drieghe, D. & Liversedge, S. P. (2011). Eye movements and word skipping during reading: Effects of word length and predictability. *Journal of Experimental Psychology: Human Perception and Performance, 37*, 514–528.

Rayner, K., Yang, J., Castelhano, M.S., & Liversedge, S.P. (2011). Eye movements of older and younger readers when reading disappearing text. *Psychology and Aging, 26*, 214–223.

Reicher, G. (1969). Perceptual recognition as a function of meaningfulness of stimulus material. *Journal of Experimental Psychology, 81*, 275–280.

Reichle, E., Pollatsek, A., Fischer, D., & Rayner, K. (1998). Toward a model of eye movement control in reading. *Psychological Review, 105*, 125–157.

Reichle, E., Rayner, K., & Pollatsek, A. (2003). The E-Z Reader model of eye-movement control in reading: Comparisons to other models. *Behavioral and Brain Sciences, 26*, 445–526.

Reichle, E., Vanyukov, P., Laurent, P., & Warren, T. (2008). Serial or Parallel? Using depth-of-processing to examine attention allocation during reading. *Vision Research*, *48*, 1831–1836.

Reichle, E., Liversedge, S., Pollatsek, A., & Rayner, K. (2009). Encoding multiple words simultaneously in reading is implausible. *Trends in Cognitive Science*, *13*, 115–119.

Risse, S. & Kliegl, R. (in press). Evidence for delayed parafoveal-on-foveal effects from word n+2 in reading. *Journal of Experimental Psychology*.

Schotter, E. R., Angele, B., & Rayner, K. (2012). Parafoveal processing in reading. *Attention, Perception & Psychophysics*, *74*, 5–35.

Slattery, T. J, Angele, B., & Rayner, K., (2011). Eye movements and display change detection during reading. *Journal of Experimental Psychology: Human Perception and Performance*, *37*, 1924–38.

Staub, A. & Rayner, K. (2007). Eye movements and on-line comprehension processes. In: G. Gaskell (Ed.), *The Oxford handbook of psycholinguistics* (pp. 327–342). Oxford, UK: Oxford University Press.

Staub, A., Rayner, K., Pollatsek, A., Hyönä, J., & Majewski, H. (2007). The time course of plausibility effects on eye movements in reading: Evidence from noun-noun compounds. *Journal of Experimental Psychology: Language, Memory, and Cognition*, *33*, 1162–1169.

Starr, M. & Rayner, K. (2001). Eye movements during reading: Some current controversies. *Trends in Cognitive Science*, *5*, 156–163.

Triesman, A. & Gelade, G. (1980). A feature integration theory of attention. *Cognitive Psychology*, *12*, 97–136.

Tsai, J., Lee, C., Tzeng, O., Hung, D., & Yen, N. (2004). Use of phonological codes for Chinese characters: Evidence from processing of parafoveal preview when reading sentences. *Brain and Language*, *91*, 235–244.

Underwood, G., Binns, A., & Walker, S. (2000). Attentional demands on the processing of neighboring words. In A. Kennedy, R. Radach, D. Heller & J. Pynte (Eds), *Reading as a perceptual process*. Oxford, UK: Elsevier Science.

Vitu, F., O'Regan, J., & Mittau, M. (1990). Optimal landing position in reading isolated words and continuous text. *Perception & Psychophysics*, *47*, 583–600.

Vitu, F., McConkie, G., Kerr, P., & O'Regan, J. (2001). Fixation location effects on fixation durations during reading: An inverted optimal viewing position effect. *Vision Research*, *41*, 25–26.

Vitu, F., Lancelin, D., & Marrier d' Unienville, V. (2007). A perceptual-economy account for the inverted-optimal viewing position effect. *Journal of Experimental Psychology: Human Perception and Performance*, *33*, 1220–1249.

Wheeler, D. (1970). Processes in word recognition. *Cognitive Psychology*, *1*, 59–85.

White, S., Rayner, K., & Liversedge, S. (2005). Eye movements and the modulation of parafoveal processing by foveal difficulty: A reexamination. *Psychonomic Bulletin & Review*, *12*, 891–896.

White, S., Bertram, R., & Hyönä, J. (2008). Semantic processing of previews within compound words. *Journal of Experimental Psychology: Learning, Memory and Cognition*, *34*, 988–993.

Yan, M., Richter, E., Shu, H., & Kliegl, R. (2009). Readers of Chinese extract semantic information from parafoveal words. *Psychonomic Bulletin & Review*, *16*, 561–566.

Yan, G., Tian, H., Bai, X., & Rayner, K. (2010). The effect of word and character frequency on the eye movements of Chinese readers. *British Journal of Psychology*, *97*, 259–268.

Yang, J., Wang, S., Xu, Y., & Rayner, K. (2009). Do Chinese readers obtain preview benefit from word n+2? Evidence from eye movements. *Journal of Experimental Psychology*, *35*, 1192–1204.

Yang, J., Rayner, K., Li, N., & Wang, S. (in press). Semantic and plausibility effects on preview benefit during eye fixations in Chinese reading, *Reading and Writing*.

5 Analysing large datasets of eye movements during reading

Julian Heister, Kay-Michael Würzner, and Reinhold Kliegl

Most of the time, visual word recognition occurs in the context of reading. Eye movements and fixations provide necessary perceptual and language-related information; prior knowledge and sentence context guide our expectations about this input. Obviously, not only the *process* of word recognition during reading, but also *research* on this topic is a highly complex undertaking. One very successful approach to deal with this complexity has been to study the recognition of isolated words, often measured in recognition times. Typically, subjects and words are assigned to each other in some form of a (counter-)balanced design. The ensemble of chapters in this volume summarizes the state of the art.

In this chapter, we take an alternative starting point: fixation durations during continuous reading of sentences. We review research based on an analysis of a large corpus of fixation durations which allows the simultaneous consideration of a large number of influences. Such corpus-based reading research departs strongly from the principles of orthogonal experimental design, which is the aim of research that draws inferences from measurements of one to three target words (see, e.g., Schotter and Rayner, this volume, Chapter 4). In the following two sections, we describe conceptual and statistical frameworks for the analyses of eye movements that use fixations on (almost) all words. Within these frameworks, we build on earlier reports about the 'big three' word factors influencing fixation durations (type frequency, predictability from prior sentence context, and word length). We carry out these analyses from a perspective of distributed processing, taking into consideration not only the properties of the fixated word, but also those of its left and right neighbors (Kliegl, Nuthmann, & Engbert, 2006; Kliegl, 2007). We expand the previous research by including not only the properties of the word triplet but those of the word quintet centered at the fixated word.

A conceptual framework for the analyses of fixation durations in reading

Visual word recognition occurs in the context of reading, involving eye movements and fixations in the service of providing the necessary perceptual and language-related information. We distinguish roughly three types of effects: (1) Effects that arise from the oculomotor process and low-level processes of eye guidance leading to effects related to preferred viewing locations or launch sites. (2) Effects that arise from language-related processes. Many of the over 50 linguistic properties of words contributing to processing efficiency in isolated word recognition have also been established for fixation durations or probabilities in normal reading. In addition, during reading of sentences, fixation durations and probabilities are influenced by variables coding the context of words, such as the predictability of words from prior words of the sentence or corpus-based statistics such as transition probabilities or context diversity. (3) Finally, corpus analyses have provided reliable evidence that some indicators of language-related processes exert their effects during at least three successive fixations.

A three-dimensional taxonomy of fixations

The ocular dynamics of reading can be cast along three dimensions, comprising the *number of fixations* on a word, the *direction of saccades* bordering these fixations, and the *duration of fixations*. In Figure 5.1, we display fixation patterns for three successive fixations defined by the first two of these three dimensions (see Hogaboam, 1982, for an earlier taxonomy). The columns depict single, first, or second of two fixations. This covers almost all fixations, because very few words host more than two fixations during reading. The rows differentiate between eight different patterns of forward and backward movements. The figure panels inform about the absolute number and percentages of the corresponding fixations. The most frequent events are single fixations preceded and followed by a forward saccade (32%) and fixations preceding a forward skipping (12%). Regressions out of and into words (9% and 8% respectively) are much more common than regressions within words (2%).

Single fixations account for more than half (57%) of all fixation patterns, whereas the second and third column add up to just about 20%. Single fixations entering the analyses in the next section represent a subset from 125 515 single fixations in the highlighted panels of Figure 5.1.[1] Note that the panels in Figure 5.1 do not distinguish between first- and second-pass reading (see below). Analyses on gaze durations (the sum of all fixations on a word prior to movement to another word) actually include more single-fixation than double-fixation cases, even if we include cases with three or more fixations (Rayner, 1998).

The statistics in Figure 5.1 are based on 223 099 fixations, however 11 127 fixations (5%) fell into different fixation patterns (mostly three or more fixations on one word) leaving 211 972 fixations.[2] They were recorded from 273 subjects reading 144 sentences of the first Potsdam Sentence Corpus (PSC I, Kliegl, Grabner, Rolfs, & Engbert, 2004). Sentences with blinks or any loss of measurement were deleted, leaving 90% of the sentences for the analyses. Obviously, the presumably random loss of sentences varied across subjects, leaving 42–144 sentences across subjects. Conversely, sentences randomly differ in how many subjects contributed fixations, ranging from 229 to 257 subjects. Therefore, from the outset of analyses, the initial crossing of subject and sentence factors is lost; the design ends up being highly imbalanced.

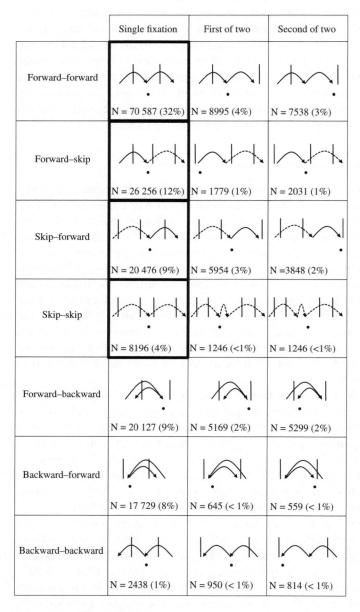

Figure 5.1 Different patterns of three successive fixations. N = 211 972 fixations (•) classified. Fixations are classified by forward/backward movements including
skippings (rows) and single, first, and second fixations (columns). Vertical
lines represent word boundaries, dashed lines indicate skippings. The LMM-
model (see Appendix 5.A) includes a subset (namely firstpass) of fixations in
the highlighted panels. N = 11 127 (5%) fixations unclassified.

Since we include (almost) all words (i.e., not only selected target words) into the analyses, we must also distinguish between variance that is due to differences between sentences and variance that is due to differences between words. Obviously, words are not crossed with sentences, but only partially crossed at best. Fortunately, statistical programs which estimate the variance components of such sparse designs in linear mixed models (LMMs) for continuous dependent variables (such as fixation durations) or generalized linear mixed models (GLMMs) for binary dependent variables (e.g., skipping vs fixating a word) have become available during recent years. We use Bates and Maechler's (2010) *lme4* package in the R environment for statistical computing and graphics (R Development Core Team, 2010) for our analyses.

A descriptive statistical model for single-fixation durations

At the level of the eyes, reading consists of an alternating sequence of fixations and saccades with information uptake during fixations. Most saccades are forward saccades to the next word (50%), but in about 25% of the cases the next word is skipped. For the remainder of this chapter, we focus on durations of fixations that were the only fixation during first-pass reading, that is fixations that were preceded by a saccade from a previous word and followed by a saccade to a subsequent word that had not been fixated or skipped before. Such a fixation is called a single fixation duration (SFD; see Figure 5.1, first column; Figure 5.2, top part). This definition covers roughly 50% of all fixations during leisurely reading for comprehension (see Figure 5.1, also e.g., Kliegl et al., 2006).

Immediate lexical effects

Past research has shown that fixation durations and skipping are influenced by word frequency, word length and predictability (Rayner & McConkie, 1976;

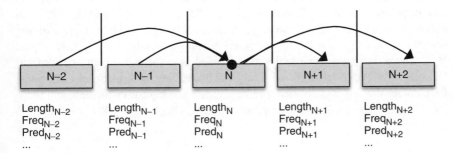

Figure 5.2 Distributed processing framework for possible influences on single-fixation duration (•) on word N; arrows represent possible incoming (left) or outgoing (right) saccades (i.e., word N–1 and word N+1 are fixated or skipped). Influences of length, frequency (Freq), and predictability (Pred) of word N–2, N–1, N, N+1, and N+2 (…) = additional predictors. Vertical lines represent word boundaries.

Kliegl et al., 2004; Brysbaert, Drieghe, & Vitu, 2005). Assuming *immediacy of processing*, properties of the fixated word are the primary determinants of fixation and gaze durations (Just & Carpenter, 1980). Together with the dominant role of frequency in psycholinguistic research, word length and a word's predictability from prior context occupy prominent roles in reading research (Rayner, 2009; see Rayner, 1998 for a review). Frequency, predictability, and the inverse of length[3] correlate negatively with fixation duration and refixation probability and positively with skipping probability (Kliegl et al., 2004). Besides frequency, length, and predictability, a wide range of linguistic variables influencing lexical word identification have been distinguished by means of enhanced computational methods and large, easily accessible digital resources. Graf, Nagler, and Jacobs (2005) identified effects of 57 linguistic word properties contributing to processing efficiency in isolated word recognition. Influences of lexical variables derived from surface frequency like lemma (Brysbaert & New, 2009; Beauvillain, 1996), rank (Murray & Forster, 2004), and document frequency (e.g., contextual diversity, see Adelman, Brown, & Quesada, 2006) have been shown to influence reaction times in naming and lexical decision tasks.

Fovea and parafovea

In reading we pick up information from more than just the currently fixated word. Word N−1, word N+1, and possibly also word N+2 fall into the so-called parafoveal region extending from the foveal region to about 5 degrees on either side of fixation. Starting with McConkie and Rayner (1975), numerous experiments have shown that parafoveal visual properties covering the area from 4 characters to the left to a maximum of 15 characters to the right of the current fixation location influence fixation durations. Consequently, during reading of sentences, fixation durations and probabilities depend also on variables coding the context of words, such as the predictability or plausibility of words from prior words of the sentence or corpus-based statistics such as transition probabilities and surprisal measures (cf. Boston, Hale, Kliegl, Patil, & Vasishth, 2008). In Figure 5.2, we list type frequency, predictability (given prior words of the sentence) and length for the fixated word N and for words N−2, N−1, N+1, and N+2. These independent variables are included as grand-mean centered continuous measures (covariates) in our analyses. In keeping with prior specifications, frequencies are log-transformed, predictabilities are logit-transformed, and word lengths are entered with their reciprocal values (Kliegl et al., 2004, 2006).

Lag effects

Analyses based on a large set of eye movements (e.g., Kliegl et al., 2006) have shown reliable influences of frequency, length, and predictability of word N−1 on fixations measured on word N. Word N−1 usually falls outside the foveal region comprising 2 degrees in the centre of vision (i.e., about 5 letters, presuming a distance to the monitor of 60 cm). There are (at least) two possible explanations for the influence of properties of word N–1. First, prolonged fixation durations on word N may reflect incomplete processing of word N–1. This spillover or lag effect is reflected in longer fixation durations after long, low-frequency, or unpredictable words. A second explanation follows from the foveal load hypothesis (Henderson & Ferreira, 1990) to word N–1: Longer fixations occur on word N after difficult (e.g., low-frequency) words N–1 because the difficulty of word N–1 causes a narrowing of the attention span which in turn reduces parafoveal preprocessing of word N. The interaction of frequency of word N–1 and N is in agreement with this view: The frequency effect on word N is more pronounced if word N–1 is a low-frequency word (Kliegl et al., 2006; Rayner & Duffy, 1986).

Influences from upcoming words

In reading we pick up information from more than just the currently fixated word. Words N+1 and, depending on the length of word N+1, possibly also word N+2 fall into the parafoveal region extending from the foveal region to about 5 degrees in the reading direction. Gaze-contingent masking of parafoveal text increases fixation durations (McConkie & Rayner, 1975; Rayner, 1975). Thus, efficient reading requires parafoveal preview of the upcoming words (e.g., Balota, Pollatsek, & Rayner, 1985; Binder, Pollatsek, & Rayner, 1999; McConkie & Rayner, 1975; Rayner, 1975; Rayner & Bertera, 1979; Underwood & McConkie, 1985). Which properties of upcoming words are extracted during preview is an active area of current research. Lexical effects of upcoming words on the currently fixated words are still controversial. In their corpus analyses, Kliegl et al. (2006) found an effect of word frequency and predictability of the word N+1 on fixations on word N. There was also an interaction of frequency of word N+1 and length of word N with a reliable N+1-frequency effect only after short words N, replicating Kennedy and Pynte (2005). Kennedy and Pynte also reported that for long words N, the parafoveal effect was limited to the initial trigram informativeness of word N+1, defined as the number of words sharing its initial three letters. Interestingly, whereas the N+1-frequency effect is always in the canonical direction with high-frequency words N+1 leading to short fixations, high-predictability words N+1 prolong fixations on word N (despite a positive correlation of frequency and predictability or words). Kliegl et al. (2006) explain this with memory retrieval of the upcoming word with prior sentence context as retrieval cue. In a corpus analyses by Pynte and Kennedy (2006) the parafoveal frequency effect also appeared, but White (2008) reported no effect of parafoveal frequency with control for orthographic familiarity. We emphasize again that the N+1-frequency effect has been questioned and only Kennedy and Pynte (2005; also Pynte & Kennedy, 2006, and Kliegl et al., 2006) found an effect (but see Inhoff, Radach, Starr, & Greenberg, 2000; Kennedy, Pynte, & Ducrot, 2002; Rayner, White, Kambe, Miller, & Liversedge, 2003; Rayner & Juhasz, 2004). In contrast, effects of sublexical effects of orthographic familiarity of word N+1 are well established (Pynte, Kennedy, & Ducrot, 2004; Starr & Inhoff, 2004;

Underwood, Binns, & Walker, 2000; but see Rayner, Juhasz, & Brown, 2007; White & Liversedge, 2004).

Polynomial trends

Some of the ambiguity of corpus-analytic results, such as those just described for N+1-frequency effects, may be due to nonlinearities underlying the relation between SFD and lexical predictors in multiple regression. In Figure 5.3, we illustrate the non-monotonicity of the function relating SFDs of word N to the log of the frequencies of word N (middle), word N−1 (left), and word N+1 (right). The top row is based on the fixations of 273 readers of the first PSC (144 sentences); the bottom row is based on 144 different sentences of the second PSC (159 readers). The similarities of the profiles across different readers and

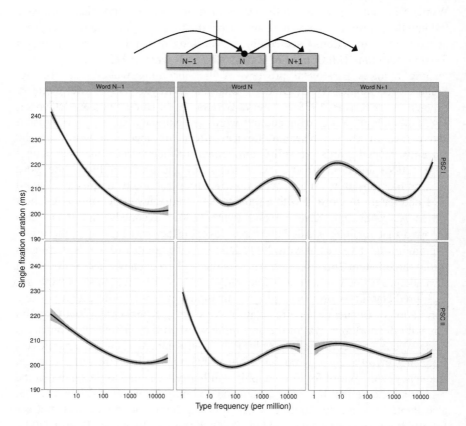

Figure 5.3 (top) Effects of frequency of word N−1, word N, and word N+1 on single-fixation duration on word N based on data from PSC I (first set of 144 sentences; 273 readers). (bottom) As (top), but based on data from PSC II (second set of 144 sentences; 149 readers). Lines are third-order polynomials.

different sentences suggest that the different non-linearities associated with the three different frequencies are reliable. Obviously, an explanation of such statistically reliable non-linear profiles represents the most formidable challenge for theoretical accounts of eye-movement control during reading, ideally validated with simulations in computational models.

Skipping

Starr and Rayner (2001) list word skipping as one of the major areas of research in reading besides regressions and the question of distributed processing and processing of upcoming words. In experimental designs word length accounts for most of the variance in skipping probabilities. As the length of a word increases, the probability that it will be skipped decreases (Brysbaert et al., 2005; Rayner & McConkie, 1976; Rayner, Sereno, & Raney, 1996). In their meta-analysis, Brysbaert and Vitu (1998), conclude that about one-fourth of the variance in skipping probabilities is determined by word length. Thus, 3-letter words are skipped about 67% of the time, whereas 7–8-letter words are skipped only about 20% of the time; Krügel and Engbert (2010) estimate that about 90% of 2-character words would be skipped if fixation locations are corrected for mislocated fixations. While there is agreement on the fact that word length influences skipping probability, it remains controversial to what extent lexical and sublexical properties of the skipped word influence the fixation duration prior to a skipped word. In Pynte and Kennedy (2006) skipping probability increases for high-frequency words and words with an informative beginning (see also White, 2008). In their first experiment, Pynte et al. (2004) revealed decreased skipping probabilities before words with misspelled first letters. In their second and third experiments, misspellings induced shorter first-fixation and gaze durations on word N–1 and there was no longer an effect on skipping probability. Similar to word frequency, words are also skipped more often if they are highly predictable (Ehrlich & Rayner, 1981; Brysbaert & Vitu, 1998; Kliegl, et al., 2004; McConkie et al., 1994; Rayner, Ashby, Pollatsek, & Reichle, 2004; Rayner & Well, 1996; Vitu et al., 1995). Kliegl and Engbert (2005) also examined the influence of skippings on prior fixation durations. They find that single-fixation durations before skippings vary with the length and frequency of the word to be skipped. Fixations before skipped words are shorter before short or high-frequency words and longer before long or low-frequency words in comparison with control fixations.

Oculomotor variables

Single-fixation durations also depend on oculomotor factors. We include (a) skipping of word N–1 or skipping of word N+1 (no-skip coded with '0', skipping coded with '1'); (b) launch site (i.e., the letter distance between the last fixation location and the beginning of the fixated word) and outgoing saccade amplitudes; and (c) the relative position of the fixation in the word (using a quadratic term) in our model. Of course, as reviewed for skipping in the last paragraph, these variables also reflect the effects of lexical processing (e.g., skipping of three-letter determiners is more frequent than skipping of three-letter verbs, O'Reagan, 1979). Here we examine them not as dependent, but as independent, variables of SFDs. In this context, oculomotor processes may not be of primary concern for word recognition *per se*. For example, there is no reliable effect of word frequency on landing positions (Rayner, Binder, Ashby, & Pollatsek, 2001). Including oculomotor variables in a regression model statistically removes the influence of low-level factors on SFDs from the residual error. This should increase our chances of detecting theoretically small effects related to lexical processing. For example, given the rapid decline of visual acuity relative to the fixation position, effects of lexical processing of parafoveal words are expected to be small. If they can be established reliably, these effects are of much relevance for constraining not only models of eye-movement control during reading, but also models of visual word recognition.

Oculomotor influences: launch site and landing site

Single-fixation durations are influenced by two oculomotor factors, namely saccadic amplitude and landing site. Several experiments have demonstrated the importance of parafoveal word properties by masking words outside the fovea (parafoveal masking), increasing subsequent fixation durations (e.g., Balota et al., 1985; Binder et al., 1999; McConkie & Rayner, 1975; Rayner, 1975; Rayner & Bertera, 1979; Underwood & McConkie, 1985). The further away, that is the longer an incoming saccade, the less preview is possible due to the drop-off in visual acuity and associated lateral inhibitions. Thus, the greater the amplitude of the incoming saccade, the longer the subsequent fixations on word N (Radach & Heller, 2000; Vitu, McConkie, Kerr, & O'Regan, 2001; see also Heller & Müller, 1983; Pollatsek, Rayner, & Balota, 1986). In the same way, long words N−1 lead to less preview and, consequently, longer fixation durations on word N (Kliegl et al., 2006). Consequently, fixations after skippings are longer. Fixation duration also depends on the landing position within a word. The effect that fixation durations in the middle of words are longer than those at the edges has been called the inverted optimal viewing position effect (IOVP) (Vitu et al., 2001, McConkie et al., 1989). Nuthmann, Engbert, & Kliegl (2005) argue that this effect is due to mislocated fixations and the immediate triggering of a new saccade program (see also Nuthmann, Engbert, & Kliegl, 2007).

Interactions

There are very strong interactions between lexical and oculomotor variables. Most importantly, the effect of lexical factors on SFDs depends strongly on whether word N−1 or word N+1 was skipped (e.g., Kliegl & Engbert, 2005; Kliegl, 2007). Below we will report analyses on such interactions and discuss their implications. Past research has also established a number of reliable interactions among the lexical variables (e.g., Kennedy & Pynte, 2005; Kliegl et al., 2006).

From this research we keep the following previously significant interactions in the model: (a) frequency of word N with frequency of word N–1, (b) frequency of word N with length of word N, (c) length of word N with frequency of word N+1, and (d) length of word N with predictability of word N+1.

Figure 5.2 represents the framework for possible influences on SFDs for the present analysis. As indicated by the ellipses, the framework may be expanded with other variables as their influence is established; this is not a closed set. Clearly, we are looking at a large number of variables simultaneously and this requires a defensible perspective for statistical inferences. We propose to analyze the relation of SFDs to the oculomotor and lexical variables with LMMs, covering at least the fixated word and its two left and right neighbors respectively and a selection of interactions between them. In the next section we review the key components of LMMs and how they relate to SFDs during reading.

A linear mixed model of single fixation durations during reading

We report LMM results for the statistical model of SFDs represented in Figure 5.2, focussing on the largest effects. The complete output of the *lmer* function (Bates & Maechler, 2010) is provided in Appendix 5A. Data and R scripts will be made available at a project website (http://www.dlexDB.de or http://read. psych.uni-potsdam.de/pmr2/) and enable not only the replication of the present model, but also the pursuit of alternatives.

Synopsis of methodological advantages of LMM

LMMs are rapidly gaining acceptance in psycholinguistic experimental research (e.g., Baayen, Davidson, & Bates, 2008; Kliegl, Masson, & Richter, 2010). Baayen (2008), Faraway (2007), and Gelman and Hill (2007) contain chapters which offer a general introduction to LMMs with an applied perspective. We suspect that LMMs are likely to replace traditional analyses of variance for inferential statistics. Three advantages of LMMs are of special relevance for the present purpose.

First, they suffer from much less loss in statistical power incurred by an imbalance in the number of observations than, for example, repeated-measures ANOVA (e.g., Quené & van den Bergh, 2008, for simulations). In eye-movement research, we have no control over whether a word is skipped or fixated once or several times; we also have to accept blinks and loss of measurement during the experiment. Thus, any experimental design, nicely counterbalanced at the outset, will end up highly unbalanced after about 2 seconds of measurement.

Second, traditionally experiments are specified as factorial designs; continuous lexical indicators such as printed frequency are often forced into discrete categories of, for example, low and high frequency. Alternatively, continuous predictors (such as log printed frequency) have been used in multiple regression analysis (MRA), but the clustering of fixations by subjects requires separate MRAs for each subject (i.e., repeated-measures MRA; Kliegl et al., 2006; Lorch & Myers, 1990), limiting the number of predictors in a model by the number of fixations measured per subject. LMMs overcome this distinction between ANOVA and MRA analyses. Effects of factors and covariates can be specified along with variances of these effects associated with random factors of subjects, sentences, and words.

Third, in psycholinguistic research we typically distinguish two random factors: subjects and items (sentences or words). The (presumably) random selection of subjects and items affords generalizability for these dimensions. As we want to generalize across subjects and items, we are usually not interested in how much a certain subject's, say, average fixation duration departs from the overall mean; nor are we interested in average fixation durations of individual items. What we do need to know for test-statistics, however, are the variances of subjects' and items' average fixation durations. Therefore, psycholinguistic experiments report two ANOVAs, one using subjects (F1 ANOVA) and one using items (F2 ANOVA) as random factors. LMMs, covering both random factors, are to be preferred for obvious reasons, such as the avoidance of ambiguities relating to significant F1 and F2 effects. More importantly, simultaneous estimates of fixed effects (i.e., effects analogous to unstandardized regression coefficients in multiple regression) and of between-subject, between-sentence, and between-word variance components (and correlation parameters) yield not only appropriate inferential test statistics for fixed effects, but offer additional insights in the dynamics of reading. In the next three sections we elaborate on this distinction between model parameters of the design matrix (fixed effect estimates), random factors, and parameters specifying variance components and correlation parameters associated with (some of) the fixed effects.

Fixed effects

In the last section, we introduced the lexical, visual, and oculomotor independent variables (including also polynomial trends and interactions among them) that are known to affect SFDs. These effects are represented in the unstandardized regression coefficients of a multiple regression model. Adding also the intercept (i.e., an estimate of the mean log SFD), we count a total of 44 fixed-effects parameters. While such a large number of parameters may appear to be daunting, especially after adding 12 parameters (plus 1 for the residual) for variance components (see below), their estimation is feasible, given that the analysis will be based on 80 625 SFDs (i.e., 1414 observations per parameter). Fixed effects will be presented in detail further below. We describe results for SFDs measured in the right eye.

Random factors

For a rather simple reason we cannot analyze SFDs with a standard MRA: SFDs are not independent observations, but they are clustered according to three factors: subjects, sentences, and words.

Subjects

In psychological research, subjects are considered to be drawn at random from an underlying population. In our study, SFDs were measured in 273 readers who varied widely in age, size of vocabulary, and cognitive ability. On average a reader contributed 295 fixations with a range from 78 to 444 fixations. If we proceed from the reasonable assumption that at least five observations should be available per parameter, the minimum number of observations given our fixed-effect regression model with 44 parameters is $1.8 = 78/44$. Forty subjects had less than 220 fixations, that is, less than five observations per parameter of the 44 fixed-effect model. Thus, we could hardly specify a repeated-measures MRA for a model with 44 predictors. LMMs take care of this problem by 'borrowing strength' from the estimates of population values. Individual differences in SFDs are reliable. Consequently, the fixations measured in a person are more similar to each other than those between these different persons. LMM take this intra-class correlation into account.

Sentences

The sentences constructed for the original Potsdam Sentence Corpus (PSC I; Kliegl et al., 2004) are also a presumably random sample from the population of sentences one may encounter in simple prose. The sentences did not provide particular difficulty for comprehension, but they varied widely in syntactic structure and semantic content. Consequently, the SFDs measured on a given sentence are more similar to each other than fixations measured on different sentences. LMMs also take into account the intra-class correlation associated with sentences. As each subject read the same 144 sentences of the PSC I, sentences are specified as crossed with subjects. Of course, given loss of measurement, this crossing is highly imbalanced.

Words

We also assume that the words selected to compose the sentences are a random sample from the population of words. When we restrict the analyses to SFDs as described in Figure 5.2, sentences are composed from 369 different words; many words occur in more than one sentence (i.e., determiners, conjunctions, and prepositions), whereas others appear only once. Of course, frequently occurring words are typically also short and, consequently, they are skipped very often. In contrast, words that occur once are typically longer and skipped less frequently. Therefore, the repetition across sentences partially compensates for the high skipping rate. Aggregating across subjects and sentences, we have sufficient information for the LMM to take into account the intra-class correlation of words.

Variance components

LMMs 'remove' the dependencies between observations that are due to the clustering of SFDs 'belonging' to a subject, a sentence, or a word. They do this on the assumption of independence between the three random factors and on the assumption that the deviations of the 'levels' of these factors from the fixed effect are normally distributed.

Varying intercepts

The main difference and advantage of LMM over traditional ANOVAs relates to estimates of parameters specifying the variance components associated with random factors. For the analysis of reading eye movements, we specify three random factors: subjects, sentences, and words. We assume that subjects yield a normal distribution of mean SFDs (actually, the log-transform of them). The mean of this distribution is returned as a fixed effect (see Appendix 5.A, block of fixed effects: (Intercept) = 5.25). The variance of the between-subject SFD distribution is estimated as a first variance component (see Appendix 5.A, block of random effects, subjects (Intercept)). Specifically, the square root of this variance, the standard deviation for between-subject differences of mean log SFD, is 0.152 for the present data. Similarly, we assume that sentences and words yield normal distributions of SFDs distributed around the same intercept. The variances of these two between-sentence SFD distributions are estimated as a second and third variance component. The square roots of these variances are listed with a value of 0.055 for sentences (see Appendix 5.A, top block, sentences (Intercept)) and with a value of 0.094 for words (see Appendix 5.A, top block, words (Intercept)). Thus, the SFD variance for subjects is larger than the SFD variance for words which is larger than the SDF variance for sentences. These three estimates represent independently varying intercepts for subjects, sentences, and words: An increase of the variance between subjects (e.g., by sampling from a broad range of reading ability) may leave the SFD variances of sentences and of words unchanged; an increase of the variance between sentences (e.g., by including sentences of particularly great syntactic difficulty – for example, multiple embedding of relative clauses) could be independent of the SFD variance between subjects and the SFD variance between words.

Varying slopes

We estimate a second group of variance components that relates to within-subject effects of three frequency effects linked to words N–1, N, and N+1. Overall, the linear trends are three slopes that are returned as three fixed effects (i.e., N freq. linear = 0.039, N–1 freq. linear = –0.041, N+1 freq. linear = –0.019; see Appendix 5.A, block of fixed effects). The LMM allows us to test the hypothesis that there are reliable differences between subjects in how strongly their SFDs respond to the difference between low- and high-frequency words on the assumption that these slopes are normally distributed around the overall fixed effect. The between-subject variances of these three frequency effects yield three additional variance components estimated as LMM parameters. They are given in the random-effects block of Appendix 5.A as N–1 freq. (linear), N freq. (linear), and N+1 freq. (linear); the standard deviations are 0.00044, 0.00085, and 0.00020, respectively.

Covariances between varying intercepts and varying effects
(correlation parameters)

So far, we have introduced the concept of varying intercepts and varying slopes. These are variance component parameters. In LMM, we can also estimate the associated covariances (or correlation parameters) if there are two or more components for a random factor. In the present model, this is the case for subjects. These correlation parameters tell us, for example, whether subjects with short average fixation durations tend to have strong or weak word-N frequency effects or whether there is a correlation between N+1-frequency, N-frequency, and N−1 frequency effects across subjects (Risse, Engbert, & Kliegl, 2008). These correlation parameters are listed in the random-effects block of Appendix 5.A. Kliegl et al. (2008) proposed that the two negative correlation parameters between N-frequency effects with N−1-frequency and N+1-frequency effects (i.e., −0.33 and −0.45, respectively) together with the positive correlation parameters between the latter two effects (i.e., 0.20) are consistent with an assumption of individual differences in perceptual span. Four variance components (1 intercept + 3 slopes) yield six model parameters to reconstruct the subject-related correlation parameters. Thus, there is a total of 12 model variance/correlation parameters (i.e., 4 variances + 6 correlation parameters for subjects + 1 variance for sentences + 1 variance for words). Finally, the model also returns a parameter for the estimate of the residual variance, 0.27 for the standard deviation in the present data (see random-effects block of Appendix 5.A).

Random effects

The deviations of subjects, sentences, and words from the intercept and subjects' deviations of frequency effects from the corresponding six effects are the random effects in the LMM, but, we iterate, they are *not* the model parameters. The distributions of the random effects can be described as unconditional distributions and as conditional distributions. The model parameters afford a description of the model in terms of the unconditional distribution. The actual random effects are from the conditional distribution, given the data and the values of the model parameters. In our LMM example, there are only 12 model parameters denoting variance components and associated correlation parameters, but 1605 random effects (i.e., 273 for subjects + 144 for sentences + 369 for words = 786 intercept deviations; 273 subjects × 3 different types of slopes = 819 slope deviations). The model parameters are the variances of the various regression coefficients associated with each of these factors (and possibly also their correlations). Consequently, adding data from new subjects to a data base does not change the number of model parameters to be estimated; we are still estimating the same number of fixed effects and parameters for variance components. Of course, the increase in number of observations due to SFDs of additional subjects increases the precision of the parameters for the variance components. In contrast, adding a subject in a repeated MRA requires that all regression coefficients are estimated for this person. Thus, in an LMM, adding data from additional subjects increases only the number of random effects that can be generated conditional on the data and the model parameters.

Fixed effects of type frequencies of the fixated word and its left and right neighbors

LMM framework

The model (as sketched in Figure 5.2) represents the baseline LMM model of the Potsdam Sentence Corpus (PSC I) in Kliegl (2007), extended with lexical and contextual as well as oculomotor variables for three successive words. We use reciprocal values of launch site to reduce the colinearity with skipping status of word N−1 ($r = 0.40$ instead of 0.61) and likewise for outgoing saccade amplitude to reduce the correlation with skipping status of word N+1 ($r = 0.42$ instead of 0.48). Motivated by the ongoing debate on lexical influences in the parafovea reviewed above and using a larger sample of readers (N = 273), we test additional effects of frequency of word N−2 and word N+2 as additional predictors, conditional on whether word N−1 or word N+1 were skipped or not. The complete model output is provided in the fixed-effects block of Appendix 5.A; it serves to document consistency of the present with earlier analyses and statistical control of effects not in the current focus of analysis (e.g., oculomotor variables). Differences between previous and current results will be discussed.

Illustration of effects

We use LMM statistics to guide our theoretical arguments and use figures to illustrate the core LMM results. The figures are not in a one-to-one correspondence with the statistics. For example, we present the effects in the original, not the log-transformed metric SFDs. We also fit polynomial functions to subsets of data, ignoring intra-class correlations due to random factors. We discuss divergences between test statistics and parts of the figure. Figure 5.4 summarizes the five frequency effects on a SFD measured on word N associated with words N−2 to word N+2 and their interactions with skipping status of word N−1 and word N+2; Figure 5.5 contains the analogous information for the five predictability effects.

Canonical fixation pattern: Fixations on word N−1, word N, and word N+1

The first row of Figure 5.4 reflects the pattern when the SFD on word N was preceded and followed by a fixation on word N−1 and word N+1, respectively. Roughly half of all SFDs (49%) are in this category. The first set of fixed effects

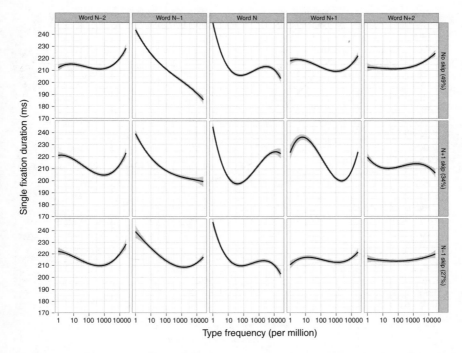

Figure 5.4 Dependent variable: Single-fixation durations on word N. Independent variables: Log type frequency of word N–2, word N–1, word N, word N+1, and
word N+2 (columns) conditional on whether word N–1 and word N+1 were
fixated (top row) or skipped (other rows). Lines are third-order polynomials.
All fits are for the subset of fixations in the respective panel. Fixations after
skipping word N–1 and before skipping word N+1 (9%) enter both skipping
conditions. This results in a total of 110% fixations entering the plot.

in Appendix 5.A lists the regression coefficients associated with this category of
fixations. Replicating previous results, there are significant cubic trends for
the N-frequency and significant linear N+1 and N–1-frequency effects (see
Figure 5.3). Here, to keep matters simple, we included a cubic trend only for
the N-frequency effect and linear trends for everything else. New results of
the present LMM are a lack of evidence for significant N+2-frequency and
N–2-frequency effects. Interestingly, inclusion of N+2-predictability in the LMM
renders the previously reported N+1-predictability effect as not significant
(Kliegl et al., 2006). In a way, however, this shift corroborates the interpretation
of the non-canonical direction of this effect (i.e., high predictability of word N+2
leads to long SDF on word N) as an effect of memory retrieval during the fixation
on word N. In summary and in general, given three fixations on successive words,
SFDs on word N relate to the frequencies of these three words in a complex and
clearly non-monotonic pattern; SFDs on word N are not significantly related to

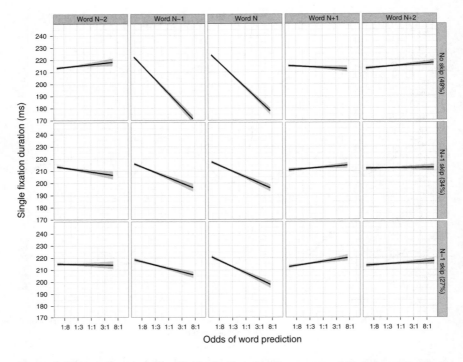

Figure 5.5 Dependent variable: Single-fixation durations on word N. Independent variables: Logit predictability of word N–2, word N–1, word N, word N+1, and word N+2 (columns) conditional on whether word N–1 and word N+1 were fixated (top row) or skipped (other rows). All lines are linear trends for the respective subset of fixations in the panel. Fixations after skipping word N–1 and before skipping word N+1 (9%) enter both skipping conditions. This results in a total of 110% fixations entering the plot.

the frequencies of the words outside this 3-word window (i.e., words N–2 and N+2). Does this pattern also hold for skipped words N–1 or N+1?

Interactions of frequency and predictability with skipping

The no-skip category of SFDs serves as the reference category for the following tests of interactions with skipping status of words N+1 and N–1. All coefficients 'S2 × *Coeff*' in Appendix 5.A (third block of fixed effects) test whether the effect indicated by *Coeff* is significantly different from the corresponding coefficient estimated for no-skip reference category when word N+1 was skipped. Analogously, all coefficients 'S1 × *Coeff*' in the fourth block of fixed effects test the difference between the effect reported for the no-skip reference category and the case when word N–1 was skipped. Importantly, the signs of these regression coefficients reflect whether an effect is weaker or stronger for no-skipping or skipping category.

N+1 skipping (2nd row in Figure 5.4 and 3rd block in Appendix 5.A)

Overall, there are significantly longer fixation durations prior to skipped words N+1 (S2; $t = 7.1$). This skipping cost is at odds with the non-significant skipping benefit reported in Kliegl and Engbert (2005), but the skipping effect returned by the current LMM is estimated under the assumption that all other covariates in the model assume a value of zero. Kliegl (2007) documented interactions between skipping and length and frequency of to-be-skipped word. Also, there are considerable individual differences in the skipping behavior between subjects that are caught in the random effect of subject in the LME. Most importantly, the cubic function relating SFD to the frequency of word N is of a significantly different shape if word N+1 is skipped (S2 × N-freq; $t = 3.4$) than the no-skip reference function. This difference is clearly visible in Figure 5.4. Indeed, much of the cubic shape is replaced by an almost symmetric quadratic function. In addition, there is a significantly stronger negative linear N+1-frequency effect for skipped than fixated words N+1 (S2 × N+1-freq; $t = -2.4$). Together these two interactions reflect that word N+1 is processed during the fixation on word N when word N is of high frequency and word N+1 is of low frequency, as in noun phrases.

N–1 skipping (3rd row in Figure 5.4 and 4th block in Appendix 5.A)

Fixations following a skipped word are longer (N–1-skip; $t = 23.0$). Moreover, the significant effect associated with the N-frequency effect (S1 × N-freq; $t = -4.9$) reflects the difference in the shape of the corresponding curves shown in Figure 5.4. Basically, after skipping word N–1, the cubic trend of the N-frequency effect is weaker (more montonic) compared to fixations following a fixation on word N–1. Thus, assuming that skipping word N–1 indicates little additional processing need for this word, the non-monotonic shape of the N-frequency effect in the canonical condition is at least partly due to spillover of processing from word N–1. Consistent with this interpretation is also the significantly weaker N–1-frequency effect (S1 × N–1-freq; $t = 3.1$).

Finally and surprisingly, after skipping of word N–1, there is a significant negative effect of word N–2 on fixation durations on word N (S1 × N–2 freq; $t = -5.8$). Although this lag-2 effect is much weaker than the lag-1 effect, the frequency of the word last fixated (at position N–1 or N–2) lingers on in the fixation on word N. The reverse pattern of significant effects was obtained for the predictability of word N–2: No significant N–2-predictability effect for the reference case, but a significant positive effect if word N–1 was skipped (S1 × N–2 pred; $t = 2.9$). Given the absence of a positive trend in the respective panel of Figure 5.5, it is likely related to the N–2-frequency effect through a suppressor constellation (which also explains the statistically large negative N–2 frequency effect in the presence of a weak negative trend in the respective panel of Figure 5.4).

Discussion

Most research on visual word recognition is carried out with narrowly defined experimental paradigms of word naming or lexical decision. Much has been learned with eye-movement measures during reading collected from a few target words in experimental designs based on the variation of some close set constraints. Only a minority of research in eye movements is based on the analyses of entire large sentence corpora (e.g., Pynte & Kennedy, 2006; Kliegl et al., 2006; Rayner & McConkie, 1976; Radach & Heller, 2000). Our results are in line with the proposal of a processing gradient that affords distributed processing across more than the fixated word, but they offer little on the precise mechanisms that generate the profiles. In the following sections, we highlight some of the methodological issues and challenges facing the corpus-analytic perspective and the theoretical issues that need to be addressed. In the end, the frequency and predictability signatures represented in Figures 5.4 and 5.5 need to emerge from general dynamical principles linking eye guidance and lexical processing.

Methodological issues and challenges

Lack of parsimony

We consider it conceptually simpler to formulate baseline models on the assumption that, as a rule, we will need a third-order polynomial function for lexical properties such as frequency. In an ensemble of, say, 12 covariates describing all of them as third-order polynome is simpler than describing, say, 1 of them with a linear, 2 with a quadratic, and 9 with a cubic function. A 'generous' model specification, keeping possibly non-significant terms, runs counter to current practice, according to which models should be specified as parsimoniously as possible. The aim for parsimony is often motivated not only by conceptual simplicity but also by statistical limitations (e.g., not enough observations), or numerical or computational limits of the software we use to estimate the parameters. The abundance of SFDs and the current generation of software render these problems as not relevant for our situation. Conceptually, we forego the attempt to interpret all model parameters, but use them for a statistically adequate description. We justify this decision with reference to the argument that the statistical description achieved with an LMM must be complemented with computational modeling for the control of eye movements during sentence reading such as SWIFT (Engbert, Nuthmann, Richter, & Kliegl, 2005; Richter, Engbert, & Kliegl, 2006) or E-Z Reader (Reichle, Pollatsek, Fisher, & Rayner, 1998; Reichle, Rayner, & Pollatsek, 2006). Indeed, we propose that the descriptive functions may constitute better simulation targets than the observed SFDs (see below).

LMM limits

In principle, variance components of frequency, predictability, and length effects cannot only be specified for subjects, but also for sentences. In practice, however, there are serious limitations on the number of variance components and correlation parameters that can be estimated in a single model. Moreover, in our admittedly limited experience, such between-sentence variance components are statistically not reliable; including them does not significantly improve the goodness of model fit in a LRT. Obviously, such variance components can only be estimated for within-subject, within-sentence, or within-word effects. Thus, as far as words are concerned, only predictability qualifies as a within-word effect whereas length and frequency are between-word effects and cannot be specified in such a model.

How do we cumulate knowledge across different analyses of the same corpus?

One of the lures of eye-movement corpora is their almost complete representation of the peripheral behavioral process of reading. The richness of the data affords analyses from countless different perspectives. Almost all observables (e.g., SFD, skipping status) serve as a dependent variable in one context and as a covariate in another. Advances in computational linguistics provide new indicators of lexical processing for eye movements collected many years back. For example, measures of syllable and lemma frequency as well as measures of orthographic neighborhood are already available as predictors for the present SFDs; many new ones will become available soon (Heister et al., 2011). In other words, with the addition of new predictors, the same measures can be recycled for new analyses. This is all welcome, but the maintainers of such corpora will have to set up a system that keeps track of the various analyses that are being carried out and, as accurately as possible, document the overlap of the analyses in a responsible way. If such a system is not put in place, it may become very difficult to recognize the degree to which supposedly new results are basically old results presented with new labels. Another difficulty relates to the evaluation and pursuit of alternatives of complex models like the one presented in this chapter. Such models generate a large number of test statistics. Communicating such models is probably a greater challenge than fitting them. We present the summary output of the model as Appendix 5.A and describe the results pertaining to the theoretical questions that motivated the analyses; other results serve as a statistical control. Different theoretical perspectives, equally plausible and interesting, would necessarily motivate a different foregrounding and backgrounding of information. In our opinion, it is necessary that such alternatives can be pursued without reliance on the present authors. Consequently, this type of analysis requires that data and scripts are available on a public website (in our case: http://www.dlexDB.de, which provides a wide variety of German word statistics for psychological and linguistic experiments).

Simultaneous estimation of fixation durations and probabilities

So far, we concentrated the analyses on SFDs, but eye movements during reading represent a dynamic interplay of fixation duration and fixation probability, that is, of both 'when' and 'where' decisions. Consequently, whether a word is skipped, fixated once, twice, or three or more times is just as valid a dependent variable as fixation duration. For purposes of statistical inference this requires the specification of generalized linear mixed models (GLMMs), using either the binomial or poisson family for the description of the error distribution along with a suitable link function (e.g., logit link for binomial family). In principle, any progress in specification of a comprehensive LMM model transfers to GLMM specification, even though some variables change their status from predictor to dependent variable and vice versa; most notably, for example, fixation duration is included as a co-variate in GLMMs. In perspective, we expect that fixation durations and fixation probabilities will be merged in so-called rate models. At present, however, the increase in complexity is unlikely to translate into a commensurate increase in theoretical progress. Again, complex models probably need to grow rather than being legislated top-down.

Compatibility between gaze-contingent display change experiments and corpus analysis

Most experiments in the field of reading rely on designs based on the variation of some close set constraints (for an overview, see Rayner, 1998). The focus is on processing a few open-class words like nouns, adjectives, or verbs; comparisons typically hold the syntactic structure constant (unless it is the target of the experimental manipulation). Research on syntactical parsing, as opposed to lexical or orthographic effects, in reading, necessitates analyses based on whole sentences, but only a few global measures are typically considered (e.g., total reading time, re-reading time). The *corpus-analytic approach* comprises analyses based on large sets of sentences with statistical – not experimental – control of different lexical, oculomotor, and possibly also syntactic, factors (see Kliegl, 2007). This approach allows one to generalize across word categories and syntactical structures, complementing analyses of specific target words. At this point in time, corpus analyses as presented in this chapter are based on single fixation durations (or likewise on gaze durations) only. In the future, analyses will aim at including multiple dependent measures or categorical outcomes.

Theoretical proposals about eye guidance in reading

The reported results have consequences for theoretical proposals about eye guidance in reading. We mention three controversial topics relating to whether lexical processing occurs with sequential shifts of attention or is better characterized by processing gradients covering not only one, but several words.

Evidence for distributed processing

Figures 5.4 and 5.5 corroborate our earlier claims (e.g., Kliegl et al., 2006; Kliegl, 2007) that SFDs during reading are reflective of the processing of not only the fixated word, but also of the processing of the neighboring words. Here we established that the zone of influence extends at least to two words to the right and two words to the left of the currently fixated one. The results also show that the size of effects strongly decline as we move away from the center triplet, but that the effect sizes of the neighboring words can be as large as the effect sizes of the fixated word. The cubic trend associated with the fixated word N appears to be largely a consequence of the spillover from or anticipatory processing of last and next word, respectively.

Non-monotonic effect profiles and LMM-parameters as targets for computational models

Much cognitive research may be characterized by ordinal data patterns. As the task gets more difficult or skill is reduced, reading or reaction time increases and accuracy drops. Ordinal data profiles of this kind are comparatively easy simulation targets for computational models. Consequently, such data profiles are often compatible with all competing models. We submit that the non-monotonic profiles reported in this chapter for N−1-, N-, and N+1-frequency effects during reading represent a formidable challenge for computational models. At the same time, computational models are the best hope we have to deliver explanations of non-monotonic data profiles on the basis of the theoretical principles that guided their construction. For example, we consider it plausible that cubic trends for N- and N+1-frequency effects on SFD on word N are the consequence of the nonlinear dynamical principles guiding saccade-target selection from a field of fluctuating activation levels associated with the words of a sentence, as implemented in a future version of SWIFT. Indeed, the parameters of the polynomial function may turn out to be a more suitable simulation target than individual fixation durations. Analysing large corpora of eye movements with linear mixed models will help us understand and model individual differences in readers and further unravel lexical, sub-lexical, and oculomotor processes.

- Visual word recognition occurs in the context of reading, involving eye movements and fixations in the service of providing the necessary perceptual and language-related information.
- This chapter reviews research based on analyses of a large corpus of fixation durations that allows the simultaneous consideration of a large number of influences. We distinguish roughly three sources:
  - There are contributions that arise from language-related processes. By now effects of many of the over 50 linguistic properties of words contributing to processing efficiency in isolated word recognition have been established for fixation durations or probabilities in normal reading. In addition, during reading of

sentences, fixation durations and probabilities are influenced by variables coding the context of words, such as the predictability of words from prior words of the sentence or corpus-based statistics such as transition probabilities or surprisal measures.

o   There are contributions from the oculomotor process and low-level processes of eye guidance leading to effects related to preferred viewing locations or launch sites.

o   Finally, corpus analyses have provided reliable evidence that some indicators of language-related processes exert their effects during successive fixation durations. For example, the effect of the frequency of the next word depends strongly on whether this word will be skipped or not. We also provide evidence for an N+2-effect for word predictability in cases when three subsequent words are fixated. Regarding fixations after skippings, we find an influence of the frequency of the last fixated word (which could be word N–2) on the current fixation duration.

- We illustrate how such distributed processing of visual word recognition can be analyzed with state-of-the-art multivariate statistical techniques such as linear mixed models. We discuss the consequences of these results for theoretical proposals about eye guidance in reading.

Acknowledgments

This research was supported by DFG Grant KL 955/12-1 to Reinhold Kliegl, Alexander Geyken and Thomas Hanneforth.

Notes

1 The main analysis reported in this chapter includes a total of 80 625 first-pass single-fixation durations, with durations ranging from 18 to 1372 ms. Only 139 fixations were shorter than 50 ms and only 66 were longer than 750 ms – two typical lower and upper bounds used in other research, but an analysis of model residuals strongly suggested keeping all fixations.

2 70 892 fixations on first and last words as well as 67 fixations below 15 or above 1500 ms were deleted beforehand. This leads to different percentages of first and second fixations in two fixation cases.

3 We typically use the reciprocal of word length to counteract the positive skew of the word-length distribution in German. Using the reciprocal of word length, renders the multiplicative interaction of frequency and length or predictability and length as a ratio or relative frequency and predictability measure (i.e., normalized on word length).

References

Adelman, J. S., Brown, G. D. & Quesada, J. F. (2006). Contextual diversity not word frequency determines word naming and lexical decision times. *Psychological Science,* *17*, 814–823.

Baayen, R. H. (2008). Analyzing Linguistic Data. *A Practical Introduction to Statistics Using R*. Cambridge: Cambridge University Press.

Baayen, R. H., Davidson, D. J., & Bates, D. M. (2008). Mixed-effects modeling with crossed random effects for subjects and items. *Journal of Memory and Language, 59*, 390–412.

Balota, D. A., Pollatsek, A., & Rayner, K. (1985). The interaction of contextual constraints and parafoveal visual information in reading. *Cognitive Psychology, 17*, 364–390.

Bates, D. M. & Maechler, M., (2010). *lme4: Linear mixed-effect models using S4 classes*. R package version 0.999375-33.

Binder, K. S., Pollatsek, A., & Rayner, K. (1999). Extraction of information to the left of the fixated word in reading. *Journal of Experimental Psychology: Human Perception and Performance, 25*, 1162–1172.

Beauvillain, C. (1996). The integration of morphological and whole-word form information during eye fixations on prefixed and suffixed words. *Journal of Memory and Language, 35*, 801–820.

Boston, M. F., Hale, J., Kliegl, R., Patil, U. & Vasishth, S. (2008). Parsing costs as predictors of reading difficulty: An evaluation using the Potsdam Sentence Corpus. *Journal of Eye Movement Research, 2*, 1–12.

Brysbaert, M. & Vitu, F. (1998). Word skipping: Implications for theories of eye movement control in reading. In G. D. M. Underwood (Ed.), *Cognitive processes in eye guidance* (pp. 125–147). Oxford: Oxford University Press.

Brysbaert, M., Drieghe, D., & Vitu, F. (2005). Word skipping: Implications for theories of eye movement control in reading. In G. D. M. Underwood (Ed.), *Cognitive processes in eye guidance* (pp. 53–78). Oxford: Oxford University Press.

Brysbaert, M. & New, B. (2009). Moving beyond Kučera and Francis: A critical evaluation of current word frequency norms and the introduction of a new and improved word frequency measure for American English. *Behavior Research Methods, 41*, 977–990.

Ehrlich, S. F. & Rayner, K. (1981). Contextual effects on word perception and eye movements during reading. *Journal of Verbal Learning and Verbal Behavior, 20*, 641–655.

Engbert, R., Nuthmann, A., Richter, E., & Kliegl, R. (2005) SWIFT: A dynamical model of saccade generation during reading. *Psychological Review, 112*, 777–813.

Faraway, J. J. (2007). *Changes to the mixed effects models chapter in ELM*. Available at: http://www.maths.bath.ac.uk/~jjf23/ELM

Gelman, A. & Hill, J. (2007). *Data Analysis Using Regression and Multilevel/Hierarchical Models*. Cambridge, UK: Cambridge University Press.

Graf, R., Nagler, M., & Jacobs, A. M. (2005). Factor analysis of 57 variables in visual word recognition. *Zeitschrift für Psychologie, 213*, 205–218.

Heister, J., Würzner, K.-M., Bubenzer, J., Pohl, E., Hanneforth, T., Geyken, A., & Kliegl, R. (2011). dlexDB – eine lexikalische Datenbank für die psychologische und linguistische Forschung [dlexDB – a lexical database for psychological and linguistic research]. *Psychologische Rundschau, 62*, 10–20.

Henderson, J. M. & Ferreira, F. (1990). Effects of foveal processing difficulty on the perceptual span in reading: Implications for attention and eye movement control. *Journal of Experimental Psychology: Learning, Memory and Cognition, 16*, 417–429.

Heller, D. & Müller, H. (1983). On the relationship of saccade size and fixation duration in reading. In R. Groner, C. Menz, D. F. Fisher, & R. A. Monty (Eds), *Eye movements and psychological functions: international views* (pp. 287–302). Hillsdale, NJ: Erlbaum.

Hogaboam, T. W. (1982). Reading patterns in eye movement data. In K. Rayner (Ed.), *Eye movements in reading: Perceptual and language processes* (pp. 309–332). New York: Academic Press.

Inhoff, A. W., Radach, R., Starr, M., & Greenberg, S. (2000). Allocation of visuo-spatial attention and saccade programming during reading. In A. Kennedy, R. Radach, D. Heller, & J. Pynte (Eds), *Reading as a perceptual process* (pp. 221–246). Amsterdam: Elsevier.

Just, M. A. & Carpenter, P. A. (1980). A theory of reading: From eye fixations to comprehension. *Psychological Review, 87*, 329–354.

Kennedy, A. & Pynte, J. (2005). Parafoveal-on-foveal effects in normal reading. *Vision Research, 45*, 153–168.

Kennedy, A., Pynte, J., & Ducrot, S. (2002). Parafoveal-on-foveal interactions in word recognition. *Quarterly Journal of Experimental Psychology: Human Experimental Psychology, Section A, 55A*, 1307–1337.

Kliegl, R. (2007). Towards a perceptual-span theory of distributed processing in reading: A reply to Rayner, Pollatsek, Drieghe, Slattery, & Reichle (2007). *Journal of Experimental Psychology: General, 138*, 530–537.

Kliegl, R. & Engbert, R. (2005). Fixation durations before word skipping in reading. *Psychonomic Bulletin & Review, 12*, 132–138.

Kliegl, R., Grabner, E., Rolfs, M., & Engbert, R. (2004). Length, frequency, and predictability effects of words on eye movements in reading. *European Journal of Cognitive Psychology, 16*, 262–284.

Kliegl, R., Nuthmann, A., & Engbert, R. (2006). Tracking the mind during reading: The influence of past, present, and future words on fixation durations. *Journal of Experimental Psychology: General, 135*, 12–35.

Kliegl, R., Risse, S., & Engbert, R. (2008). Reading strategies and their implementation in the SWIFT model of eye-movement control. *International Journal of Psychology, 43*, 190. [Abstract].

Kliegl, R., Masson, M. E. J., & Richter, E. M. (2010). A linear mixed model analysis of masked repetition priming. *Visual Cognition, 18*, 655–681.

Krügel, A. & Engbert, R. (2010). On the launch-site effect for skipped words during reading. *Vision Research, 50*, 1532–1539.

Lorch, R. & Myers, J. (1990). Regression analyses of repeated measures data in cognitive research: A comparison of three different methods. *Journal of Experimental Psychology: Learning, Memory, and Cognition, 16*, 149–157.

McConkie, G. W. & Rayner, K. (1975). The span of the effective stimulus in during a fixation in reading. *Perception & Psychophysics, 17*, 578–586.

McConkie, G. W., Kerr, P. W., Reddix, M. D., Zola, D., & Jacobs, A. M. (1989). Eye movement control during reading: II. Frequency of refixating a word. *Perception & Psychophysics, 46*, 245–53.

McConkie, G. G., Kerr, P. W., and Dyre, B. P. (1994). What are 'normal' eye movements during reading: Toward a mathematical description. In J. Ygge and G. Lennestrand (Eds.), *Eye movements in reading* (pp. 315–27). Oxford: Elsevier.

Murray, W. S. & Forster, K. I. (2004). Serial mechanisms in lexical access: The rank hypothesis. *Psychological Review, 111*, 721–756.

Nuthmann, A., Engbert, R., & Kliegl, R. (2005). Mislocated fixations during reading and the inverted optimal viewing position effect. *Vision Research, 45*, 2201–2217.

Nuthmann, A., Engbert, R., & Kliegl, R. (2007). The IOVP-effect in mindless reading: Experiment and modeling. *Vision Research, 47*, 990–1002.

O' Regan, J. K. (1979). Eye guidance in reading: Evidence for the linguistic control hypothesis. *Perception and Psychophysics, 25*, 501–509.

Pollatsek, A., Rayner, K., & Balota, D. A. (1986). Inferences about eye movement control from the perceptual span in reading. *Perception & Psychophysics, 40*, 123–130.

Pynte, J. & Kennedy, A. (2006). An influence over eye movements in reading exerted from beyond the level of the word: Evidence from reading English and French. *Vision Research, 46*, 3786–3801.

Pynte, J., Kennedy, A., & Ducrot, S. (2004). The influence of parafoveal typographical errors on eye movements in reading. *European Journal of Cognitive Psychology, 16*, 178–202.

Quené, H. & van den Bergh, H. (2008). Examples of mixed-effects modeling with crossed random effects and with binomial data. *Journal of Memory and Language, 59*, 413–425.

R Development Core Team (2010). *R: A language and environment for statistical computing.* (version 2.11.1). [Software].

Radach, R. & Heller, D. (2000). Relations between spatial and temporal aspects of eye movement control. In A. Kennedy, R. Radach, D. Heller, & J. Pynte (Eds), *Reading as a perceptual process* (pp. 165–191). Amsterdam: Elsevier.

Rayner, K. (1975). The perceptual span and peripheral cues in reading. *Cognitive Psychology, 7*, 65–81.

Rayner, K. (1998). Eye movements in reading and information processing: 20 years of research. *Psychological Bulletin, 124*, 372–422.

Rayner, K. (2009). The Thirty Fifth Sir Frederick Bartlett Lecture: Eye movements and attention during reading, scene perception, and visual search. *Quarterly Journal of Experimental Psychology, 62*, 1457–1506.

Rayner, K. & Bertera, J. H. (Oct 26, 1979). Reading without a fovea. *Science, 206*, 468–469.

Rayner, K. & Duffy, S. A. (1986). Lexical complexity and fixation times in reading: Effects of word frequency, verb complexity, and lexical ambiguity. *Memory & Cognition, 14*, 191–201.

Rayner, K. & Juhasz B. J. (2004). Eye movements in reading: Old questions and new directions. *European Journal of Cognitive Psychology, 16*, 340–352.

Rayner, K. & McConkie, G. W. (1976) What guides a reader's eye movements. *Vision Research, 16*, 829–837.

Rayner, K. & Well, A. D. (1996). Effects of contextual constraint on eye movements in reading: A further examination. *Psychonomic Bulletin & Review, 3*, 504–509.

Rayner, K., Sereno, S. C., & Raney, G. E. (1996). Eye movement control in reading: A comparison of two types of models. *Journal of Experimental Psychology: Human Perception and Performance, 22*, 1188–1200.

Rayner, K., Binder, K. S., Ashby, J., & Pollatsek, A. (2001). Eye movement control in reading: word predictability has little influence on initial landing positions in words. *Vision Research, 41*, 943–954.

Rayner, K., White, S., Kambe, G., Miller, B., & Liversedge, S. (2003). On the processing of meaning from parafoveal vision during eye fixations in reading. In J. Hyönä, R. Radach, & H. Deubel (Eds), *The mind's eye: Cognitive and applied aspects of eye movement research*, (pp. 213–234). Amsterdam: Elsevier.

Rayner, K., Ashby, J., Pollatsek, A., & Reichle, E. D. (2004). The effects of frequency and predictability on eye fixations in reading: Implications for the E-Z Reader model. *Journal of Experimental Psychology: Human Perception and Performance, 30*, 720–732.

128   *Julian Heister et al.*

Rayner, K., Juhasz, B. J., & Brown, S. J. (2007). Do readers obtain preview benefit from word n + 2? A test of serial attention shift versus distributed lexical processing models of eye movement control in reading. *Journal of Experimental Psychology: Human Perception and Performance, 33*, 230–245.

Reichle, E. D., Pollatsek, A., Fisher, D. L., & Rayner, K. (1998). Toward a model of eye movement control in reading. *Psychological Review, 105*, 125–157.

Reichle, E. D., Rayner, K., & Pollatsek, A. (2006). E-Z Reader: A cognitive-control, serial-attention model of eye-movement control during reading. *Cognitive Systems Research, 7*, 4–22.

Richter, E., Engbert, R., & Kliegl, R. (2006) Current advances in SWIFT. *Cognitive Systems Research, 7*, 23–33.

Risse, S., Engbert, R., & Kliegl, R. (2008). Eye-movement control in reading: Experimental and corpus-analytic challenges for a computational model. In K. Rayner, D. Shen, X. Bai, & G. Yan (Eds) *Cognitive and cultural influences on eye movements.* (pp. 65–92). Tianjin: Tianjin People's Publishing House/Psychology Press.

Starr, M. S. & Inhoff, A. W. (2004). Attention allocation to the right and left of a fixated word: Use of orthographic information from multiple words during reading. *European Journal of Cognitive Psychology, 16*, 203–225.

Starr, M. S. & Rayner, K. (2001). Eye movements during reading: Some current controversies. *Trends in Cognitive Science, 5*, 156–163.

Underwood, N. R. & McConkie, G. W. (1985). Perceptual span for letter distinctions during reading. *Reading Research Quarterly, 20*, 153–162.

Underwood, G., Binns, A., & Walker, S. (2000). Attentional demands on the processing of neighbouring words. In A. Kennedy, R. Radach, D. Heller, & J. Pynte (Eds), *Reading as a perceptual process* (pp. 247–268). Amsterdam: Elsevier.

Vitu, F., O'Regan, J. K. Inhoff, A., & Topolski, R. (1995). Mindless reading: Eye Movement characteristics are similar in scanning strings and reading texts. *Perception & Psychophysics, 57*, 352–64.

Vitu, F., McConkie, G. W., Kerr, P., & O'Regan, J. K. (2001). Fixation location effects on fixation durations during reading: An inverted optimal viewing position effect. *Vision Research, 41*, 3513–3533.

White, S. J. (2008). Eye movement control during reading: Effects of word frequency and orthographic familiarity. *Journal of Experimental Psychology: Human Perception and Performance, 34*, 205–223.

White, S. J. & Liversedge, S. P. (2004) Orthographic familiarity influences initial eye fixation positions in reading. *European Journal of Cognitive Psychology, 16*, 52–78.

Appendix 5.A

Table 5.A.1 Linear mixed model results, estimated with *lmer* (Bates & Maechler, 2010)

AIC	BIC	logLik	deviance	REMLdev
21 465	22 014	−10 674	20 965	21 347

Random effects:

Groups	Name	Variance	SD	Corr.
Words	(Intercept)	0.00881	0.09385	
Subjects	(Intercept)	0.02300	0.15166	

Table 5.A.1 Cont'd

N−1-freq (lin)	0.00044	0.02109		−0.338		
N-freq (lin)	0.00085	0.02908		0.113	−0.327	
N+1-freq (lin)	0.00020	0.01429		−0.254	0.179	-0.448
Sentences	(Intercept)	0.00304	0.05509			
Residual	0.07258	0.26941				

	Number of observations	80625
Groups	Words	369
	Subjects	273
	Sentences	144

Fixed effects:

Predictor	Coefficient	SE	t	
(Intercept)	5.25116	0.01301	402.21	*Mean log(SFD)*
N-freq (linear)	0.03878	0.01218	3.18	*Effects of word-N properties*
N-freq (quadr)	0.00595	0.00579	1.03	
N-freq (cubic)	−0.02010	0.00384	−5.23	
N-pred	−0.04033	0.00297	−13.56	
1/N-length	−0.08175	0.08238	−0.99	
N−1-freq	−0.04112	0.00364	−11.29	*Effects of word-N−1 properties*
N−1-pred	−0.01498	0.00298	−5.03	
1/N−1-length	−0.00981	0.03803	−0.26	
N+1-freq	−0.01921	0.00368	−5.22	*Effects of word-N+1 properties*
N+1-pred	0.00062	0.00312	0.20	
1/N+1-length	0.29004	0.03393	8.55	
N−2-freq	−0.00392	0.00329	−1.19	*Effects of word-N−2 properties*
N−2-pred	−0.00364	0.00345	−1.06	
1/N−2-length	−0.05489	0.03739	−1.47	
N+2-freq	−0.00142	0.00304	−0.47	*Effects of word-N+2 properties*
N+2-pred	0.00765	0.00204	3.76	
1/N+2-length	0.06684	0.03359	1.99	
1/launch site	0.24856	0.00562	44.23	*Oculomotor variables*
1/sacc. Ampl.	0.34264	0.02854	12.01	
IOVP (linear)	0.09485	0.00430	22.06	
IOVP (quadr)	−0.11264	0.01086	−10.37	
N-freq × N−1-freq	0.00881	0.00171	5.14	*Interactions*
N-freq × 1/N-length	0.31309	0.06163	5.08	*(see Kliegl et al., 2006)*
N+1-freq × 1/N-length	0.05023	0.02483	2.02	
N+1-pred × 1/N-length	−0.11911	0.02403	−4.96	

(*Continued*)

Table 5.A.1 Cont'd

Predictor	Coefficient	SE	t	
N+1-skip (S2)	0.02406	0.00340	7.07	*Effect of skipping word N+1*
S2 × N-freq	0.00916	0.00266	3.44	*... x word-N properties*
S2 × N-pred	0.00120	0.00247	0.48	
S2 × N−1/length	0.13062	0.03204	4.08	
S2 × N+1-freq	−0.00631	0.00266	−2.37	*... x word-N+1 properties*
S2 × N+1-pred	−0.00387	0.00232	−1.67	
S2 × 1/N+1-length	−0.19559	0.02961	−6.61	
S2 × N+2-freq	−0.00276	0.00259	−1.07	*... x word-N+2 properties*
S2 × N+2-pred	0.00098	0.00201	0.49	
S2 × N+2-1/length	0.01641	0.02962	0.55	
N−1-skip (S1)	0.07671	0.00333	23.03	*Effect of skipping word N−1*
S1 × N-freq	−0.01307	0.00266	−4.92	*... x word-N properties*
S1 × N-pred	0.02795	0.00254	11.02	
S1 × 1/N-length	−0.12015	0.03314	−3.63	
S1 × N−1-freq	0.00867	0.00283	3.06	*... x word-N−1 properties*
S1 × N−1-pred	−0.00308	0.00268	−1.15	
S1 × 1/N−1-length	0.33280	0.03187	10.44	
S1 × N−2-freq	−0.01733	0.00301	−5.75	*... x word-N−2 properties*
S1 × N−2-pred	0.00908	0.00314	2.89	
S1 × 1/N−2-length	−0.02433	0.03140	−0.77	

6 Bilingual visual word recognition in sentence context

Ana I. Schwartz and Janet G. Van Hell

Researchers in cognitive science have a long history of answering questions about the nature of mental processes through the examination of word recognition. For example, one of the best-known connectionist models of human cognition (the Interactive Activation framework) is a model of word identification (McClelland & Rumelhart, 1988). Research on word recognition has demonstrated that lexical retrieval is a highly interactive process, characterized by parallel activation of competing representations before resolution to a single lexical entry (see also, for example, Coltheart, accompanying volume, Chapter 1; Sibley and Kello, accompanying volume, Chapter 2; Forster, accompanying volume, Chapter 3; Balota et al., accompanying volume, Chapter 5; Grainger and Dufau, accompanying volume, Chapter 8; Halderman, Ashby, and Perfetti, accompanying volume, Chapter 10; Feldman and Weber, this volume, Chapter 1). However, models and theories of word identification focused exclusively on processing within a monolingual lexicon despite the fact that most of the world's population is bilingual. This began to change in the 1990s in which there was a sudden heightened interest in examining the nature of lexical co-activation across languages. The central question of interest was whether lexical activation proceeds selectively by language such that only competitors in the target language can be activated. The answer, based on much evidence accrued throughout the 1990s to today, is a resounding 'No'.

Many studies using different variations of single word recognition paradigms such as lexical decision and naming have demonstrated that when bilinguals recognize words, there is parallel co-activation of lexical entries from both languages. To test for cross-language lexical co-activation the common strategy has been to manipulate the orthographic, phonological or semantic similarity of words from the two languages of the bilinguals (and in some cases the three languages of trilinguals) being tested. The most frequently used comparison has been that between cognates, that is, words that share a high degree of meaning and form overlap (e.g., the Spanish–English translations 'piano-piano' or 'palace-palacio') and noncognate control words. If cognates are processed differently (i.e., showing different reaction times and/or accuracy rates) than noncognates (matched on lexical factors including frequency, length, and orthographic neighbors), it is assumed that representations of the cognate from both languages were simultaneously co-activated prior to the completion of lexical access, thereby altering the time-course and/or ease of access. The majority of studies have presented cognates and noncognates in the bilinguals' L2, and have found facilitated performance (faster reaction times and/or greater accuracy) than noncognate controls (e.g., Blumenfeld & Marian, 2007; Caramazza & Brones, 1979; Cristoffanini, Kirsner, & Milech, 1986; Costa, Caramazza, & Sebastian-Galles, 2000; De Groot & Nas, 1991; Dijkstra, Van Jaarsveld, & ten Brinke, 1998a; Dijkstra, Grainger, & Van Heuven, 1999; Lalor & Kirsner, 2001; Lemhöfer, Dijkstra, & Michel, 2004; Sánchez-Casas, Davis, & García-Albea, 1992; Schwartz, Kroll, & Diaz, 2007). Cognate facilitation effects have been found when the words were presented in the first, and dominant, language, L1 as well (Van Assche, Duyck, Hartsuiker, & Diependaele, 2009; Van Hell & Dijkstra, 2002). For example, Van Hell and Dijkstra (2002) presented Dutch–English–French trilinguals (with relatively high proficiency in both English-L2 and French-L3) with L1 Dutch words that were either cognates with English, cognates with French, or noncognate controls in a Dutch lexical decision task. The trilinguals' performance showed a cognate facilitation effect for both L1 Dutch-L2 English cognates and for L1 Dutch-L3 French cognates. This study demonstrates that cognate facilitation effects are not restricted to L2 processing (in which a weaker L2 is affected by the stronger L1), but can also occur in L1 processing (even a stronger L1 can be affected by a weaker L2). Cognate facilitation is one of the most robust effects of cross-language non-selectivity in lexical processing and has been observed across a wide variety of paradigms and languages, even languages that differ in script like Hebrew–English (Gollan, Forster, & Frost, 1997), Greek–English (Dimitropoulou et al., 2011; Voga & Grainger, 2007), Korean-English (Kim & Davis, 2003), or Japanese–English (Hoshino & Kroll, 2008).

Effects of non-selectivity in lexical processing have also been observed for words in two languages that do not share semantics but do share either orthography (interlingual homographs such as the Dutch word 'angel' meaning 'stinger' in Dutch) or phonology (interlingual homophones such as the Dutch word 'kou' pronounced as 'cow' but meaning 'cold'). Many studies found that lexical access of interlingual homographs and homophones differs from that of matched control words, and can be either facilitated or inhibited depending on factors like the composition of the stimulus list or specific task demands (Brenders, Van Hell, & Dijkstra, 2011; Brysbaert, Van Dyck, & Van de Poel, 1999; de Bruijn, Dijkstra, Chwilla, & Schriefers, 2001; De Groot , Delmaar, & Lupker, 2000; Dijkstra et al., 1999; Dijkstra, De Bruijn, Schriefers, & Brinke, 2000; Van Heuven, Dijkstra, & Grainger, 1998; Von Studnitz & Green, 2002).

It should be noted that the effects observed with interlingual homographs and homophones have been far less consistent than those observed for cognates, suggesting a critical role of shared semantics in augmenting and/or sustaining cross-language activation. For example, one study showed that interlingual homographs may be recognized slower than or as fast as monolingual control words depending on task requirements and language intermixing (Dijkstra et al., 1998). Dutch–English bilinguals were presented with cognates and interlingual homographs in an L2 lexical decision task. While recognition performance was facilitated for cognate items, no effects on performance were observed for inter-lingual homographs. In a second experiment, Dutch–English bilinguals again performed an English lexical decision task on homographs, but the stimulus set included, Dutch words which required a 'no' response, in addition to nonwords. In this case, recognition of the interlingual homographs showed strong homo-graph inhibition effects, which were dependent on the relative frequency differ-ence of the two readings of the homograph in the two languages.

For effects of language non-selectivity to be observed in word recognition performance the words in the bilinguals' two languages do not necessarily need to have identical orthography or phonology. For example, effects of the co-activation of languages have also been observed in the processing of cross-language ortho-graphic or phonological neighbors, and these effects vary with the degree of orthographic and phonological overlap across languages (e.g., Font, 2001; Schwartz et al., 2007). In a word-naming study, Schwartz and colleagues presented Spanish–English bilinguals with cognates that varied on orthographic and phonological similarity across languages and noncognate controls. L2 naming of orthographically-similar cognates (e.g., piano, base) was faster and more accurate than naming times of orthographically dissimilar cognates (train-tren, mark-marca). Furthermore, naming orthographically-similar cognates (e.g., piano, base) was slower and less accurate when the corresponding phonological codes in the two languages were more distinct (e.g., 'base' in Spanish is pronounced as /ba' se/) than when the phonological codes were more similar (as in piano). Such an effect of phonology was not obtained in the orthographically dissimilar cognates (e.g., train-tren, mark-marca). This indicates that cognate processing is influenced by the consistency of the orthographic to phonologi-cal mappings in the bilinguals' two languages, such that competition from inconsistent phonology is most likely to be observed when the phonological representations map on to the same orthographic representations across languages. Likewise, Font (2001) showed that cognate effects were larger in identical than in non-identical cognates (cf. Duyck, Assche, Drieghe, & Hartsuiker, 2007). Interestingly, recent studies using sign-speech bilinguals showed that the co-activation of languages in bilingual lexical processing is not restricted to languages in the oral modality, but extends to languages from the spoken and visual modalities, speech and sign (Morford, Wilkinson, Villwock, Piñar, & Kroll, 2011; Shook & Marian, 2010; Van Hell, Ormel, Van der Loop, & Hermans, 2009) or speech and gesture (Brown & Gullberg, 2008).

Observing consistent and robust effects of non-selectivity that persist irrespec-tive of the language mode of the experimental situation, participant expectations, task demands, language-script or language-modality leaves unanswered the ques-tion of how bilinguals eventually do select language. Not finding a mechanism or source of selectivity in single word paradigms, some researchers turned their attention to possible influences from context. There are several possible sources of selectivity from context. First, the language of the written context itself might allow for earlier language selection based on activation within the target lexicon. Second, conceptual or semantic constraints in a sentence context may facilitate language selection via top-down activation of appropriate lexical entries, above and beyond the language cue the sentence context provides. Third, syntactic constraints in the sentence may help rule out cross-language competitors that cannot be accommodated within a particular syntactic structure. We next review evidence for each of these different potential sources to constrain lexical activation to a single language.

Language cues from context

Available evidence suggests that the first potential source, language of the surrounding words, is not an effective mechanism for language selection. For example, highly-proficient Dutch–English bilinguals performed a language-general lexical decision on word triplets (responding 'no' only if one or more stimuli in the triplet was not a word in either language) (De Bruijn et al., 2001). The first word could be in either language and, on critical trials, the second was an interlingual homograph and the third word was semantically related to the English-specific meaning (e.g., *HOUSE-ANGEL-HEAVEN*). Lexical decision times and N400 priming of the English-specific meaning instantiated by the third word were unaffected by the language membership of the first word in the triplet. Thus, the simple presence of words in a specified language is not sufficient to allow for selective activation of one language.

Later studies using full sentences as context produced convergent findings demonstrating a limited role of the language membership of context. [1] In fact, two separate studies using different language pairs (Dutch–English and Spanish–English) and bilingual populations showed persistent effects of cross-language lexical activation when critical cross-language competitors were embedded in a semantically-neutral sentence context. In one study, highly-proficient and intermediate proficient Spanish–English bilinguals were presented with all-L2 sentences word by word on a computer screen using a Rapid Serial Visual Presentation (RSVP) paradigm (Schwartz & Kroll, 2006). Their task was to name a target word (marked with a red font) out loud into a microphone. On critical trials the target words were either cognates in Spanish and English (e.g., piano) or interlingual homographs (e.g., pan in Spanish means 'bread'). Analyses on the naming latencies revealed significantly shorter naming latencies for cognates relative to noncognate controls when these were embedded in a semantically–neutral context which did not bias the meaning of the upcoming target word (e.g., 'When we entered the dining hall we saw the *piano* in the corner of the room.'). This result demonstrated continued language non-selectivity within a semantically–neutral sentence context. Van Hell and De Groot (2008; see also Van Hell, 1998) also presented bilinguals (native Dutch speakers who were highly proficient in English) with target cognate words within an all-L2 sentence context, this time with the lexical decision and word translation tasks. They observed significant cognate facilitation for both lexical decision and translation when cognates were in semantically-neutral contexts. Both studies also converged in finding an elimination of cognate facilitation when the cognates were embedded in sentence contexts that highly biased the meaning of the cognate (described in more detail below).

Recent eye-tracking studies have failed to observe any constraining influence on non-selectivity from the language context of a sentence. In a lexical decision and eye-tracking study by Duyck et al. (2007), Dutch–English bilinguals were presented with cognates and noncognates in their L2 English, preceded by a low constraint sentence context (e.g., 'I would like you to repeat that 'dance' (cognate) / 'smile'.' (noncognate). They found that the cognate facilitation effect observed when the words were presented in isolation remained significant when the cognates and noncognates were presented after a low constraint sentence context which did not contain semantic cues that could bias the meaning of upcoming target words. This finding has recently been extended to reading in the L1, which should be particularly resilient to influences from the weaker L2 (Van Assche et al., 2009). Also in L1, the relative constraint of the sentence contexts did not modulate the processing advantage of cognates over noncognates.

Even hearing the language-specific phonology and phonotactics of the target language seems not to be sufficient to allow for language selective access. In an eye-movement investigation of the effects of context for auditorily presented sentences containing interlingual homophones (e.g., the French word, *poule* in French, meaning 'chicken' and *pool* in English), highly proficient French–English bilinguals made more saccades to objects depicting the non-target meaning of the homophones within a visual array, but only when the preceding sentence context was semantically plausible for both the target and non-target (e.g., 'Marie va décrire la poule' (Marie will describe the chicken)) (Chambers & Cooke, 2009). Taken together these studies provide a strong case against the language of the context in and of itself as a source for selective activation of a single language.

However, in one study on bilingual sentence processing the ambient language of the experimental context did have an observable influence on language non-selectivity (Elston-Güttler, Gunter, & Kotz, 2005). In that study proficient German–English bilinguals performed a lexical decision on target words that were preceded by purely English sentences. On critical trials the sentences (e.g., 'The woman gave her friend a pretty') ended in an interlingual homograph (e.g., 'gift' in German means 'poison') and the follow-up target was related to the German meaning of the homograph (e.g., *POISON*). Critically, participants watched a short film in either English or German right before performing the lexical decision task. Both behavioral reaction time and Event Related Potentials (ERP) data showed priming of the German meaning of the homograph but only for participants who viewed the film in German and only during the first block of trials. Thus, unlike previous isolated-word paradigms, this sentence priming study revealed that the surrounding language mode can influence non-selectivity.

Semantic cues from context

Does semantic information from context modulate the co-activation of words in the non-target language? Stated differently, can information activated top-down from the semantic representation of the sentence influence the bottom-up processes of lexical access? Research on the influence of semantic constraints for monolingual readers has shown that sentence context can influence lexical access and modulate word frequency effects (e.g., Van Petten & Kutas, 1990), lexical ambiguity effects (e.g., Simpson & Krueger, 1991), concreteness effects (see Schwanenflugel, 1991, for a review), and eye movements during reading (Rayner & Well, 1996). For bilingual reading, a sentence context contains semantic cues that bias a particular meaning, and thus can potentially constrain the activation of upcoming words. Relatively few studies have directly examined the role that semantic information from a sentence context may play in modulating cross-language activation in bilingual lexical processing (Elston-Güttler et al., 2005; Libben & Titone, 2009; Schwartz & Kroll, 2006; Van Hell & De Groot, 2008). As we shall see, the available evidence suggests that the degree of language non-selective activation is affected by semantic characteristics of the sentence. So, as with monolingual processing, top-down processes of sentence comprehension and bottom-up processes of lexical activation interact in bilingual reading.

As discussed above, Elston-Güttler et al. (2005), Duyck et al. (2007), and Van Assche et al. (2009) had used one type of sentential context, weakly predictive sentences that did not strongly bias the activation of upcoming words (i.e., many words can complete the low constraining sentence 'I would like you to repeat that …' as used by Duyck et al., 2007). To gain more insight into the role of contextual constraint on bilingual lexical access both Schwartz and Kroll (2006) and Van Hell and De Groot (2008) manipulated the semantic bias of the sentential context preceding the target word. Schwartz and Kroll observed an elimination of the cognate facilitation effect in word naming when the to-be-named cognates were embedded in a sentence context that biased its meaning (e.g., 'Before playing the composer first wiped the keys of the *piano* at the beginning of the concert.' versus 'When they entered the large room they saw the *piano* that had been shipped from Italy'.)

To examine whether the top-down influences of semantic constraint is sensitive to subtle variations in semantic overlap of the target words, Van Hell and De Groot (2008) manipulated the concreteness of cognate and noncognate target words in addition to the semantic bias of the sentence context (an earlier study indicated that concrete translations, in particular concrete cognates, share more semantic features across languages than abstract words; Van Hell and De Groot, 1998). They found that in both lexical decision and translation, the cognate facilitation effect was modulated when these words were embedded in a high constraint sentence context, but not when embedded in a low constraint sentence context. The magnitude of the facilitation effect was not qualified by the concreteness of the cognates and noncognates, suggesting that the top-down influence of semantic constraint is not modulated by subtle differences in the degree of semantic overlap of target words' lexical representations across languages.

Libben and Titone (2009) provided more insight into the time course of lexical activation of words embedded in semantically biased and non-biased sentence context. They recorded eye-movements of French–English bilinguals while reading a high constraint or low constraint sentence context, followed by a cognate, an interlingual homograph, or a matched control word. When reading a low constraint sentence, both early-stage reading measures (first fixation, first pass gaze duration, and skipping rate; from initial fixation to approximately 350 ms later) and late-stage reading measures (go-past time, total reading time; approximately 350–600 ms after first fixation on target word) showed a cognate facilitation and a homograph inhibition effect. This finding indicates that low constraint sentence contexts do not modulate nonselective lexical access and cross-language activation, and corroborates the findings of Schwartz and Kroll (2006), Duyck et al. (2007), and Van Hell and De Groot (2008). Interestingly, in the high constraint sentences, Libben and Titone also observed effects of cross-language activation, but only in the early-stage reading measures (first fixation and gaze duration) and not in the late-stage reading measures. This study thus indicates that while a constraining semantic context does not fully eliminate cross-language activation, it does restrain parallel activation to the early stages of target processing.

Syntactic cues from context

A third source of contextual constraint that may guide lexical access in bilingual word recognition are syntactic cues. For every possible combination of two languages there will be syntactic features that are unique to one language alone, some that are not present, and others that are expressed differently in the other language. Such syntactic features potentially restrict lexical activation to one language only, thereby constraining activation of lexical alternatives in the nontarget language. Remarkably, there is little empirical work that examines whether, and if so how, syntactic constraints affect bilingual lexical access, and how syntactic constraints may facilitate selection of lexical entries in a particular language.

Language specificity of syntactic structures has been found to affect bilingual language processing in other domains, including the acquisition of syntactic structures in the L2 (e.g., Tokowicz & MacWhinney, 2005; for a review, see Van Hell & Tokowicz, 2010) and code-switching (e.g., Deuchar, 2005; Kootstra, Van Hell, & Dijkstra, 2010; Poplack, 1980). More specifically, the ease of learning syntactic structures in a second language depends on the similarity of structures in the learners' first language, L1. For example, in an ERP study, Tokowicz and MacWhinney (2005) asked native English speakers who had just started to learn Spanish as an L2 to read Spanish sentences with and without syntactic violations. Sentences had syntactic structures that were either similar in Spanish and English (auxiliary omission), different in Spanish and English (determiner number agreement), or unique to Spanish (determiner gender agreement). The learners demonstrated P600s in response to violations for the similar and unique constructions, but not for the different constructions. This indicates that whether or not syntactic structures are similar, different, or unique across languages affects their acquisition in a second language. The language specificity of syntactic structures has also been found to influence code-switching, the switching between languages which is a hallmark of fluent bilingual processing (e.g., Deuchar, 2005; Kootstra et al., 2010; Poplack, 1980). Linguistic corpora of code-switched utterances suggest that syntax constrains code-switching in the sense that switching is more likely to occur at positions where the syntax of the two languages is the same (e.g., Deuchar, 2005; Poplack, 1980). In a series of experiments, Kootstra et al. (2010) asked Dutch–English bilinguals to describe a picture after being cued with word orders that were similar across the two languages, or unique to one language. Although this was not the main question of this study, the data indicated that bilinguals were more likely to switch between languages after the shared syntactic cue than after the language-specific cue. In contrast, they more often used only one language when cued by language-specific syntax as compared to shared syntax. Language-specific syntactic cues thus evoked bilinguals to more often use only one language.

On the basis of research in these other domains of bilingual language processing, we can infer that syntactic constraints also potentially modulates lexical access in word recognition. Conceivably, sentences with high syntactic constraint (with language-specific, or unique syntactic features) constrain lexical access as opposed to sentences with low syntactic constraint (sentences with language non-specific features, syntactic features that are shared between two languages). Do syntactic constraints function like semantic constraints in reducing cross-language competition? A first study suggests that this may indeed be the case. Gullifer, Dussias, and Kroll (2010) presented Spanish–English bilinguals with cognates and noncognates embedded in sentences with language specific syntax (high syntactic constraint) or language non-specific syntax (low syntactic constraint). Bilinguals were asked to name the cognates and noncognate targets. The bilinguals' naming data showed that cognate effects were only present in the low syntactic constraint sentences, where the sentence syntax was not specific to only one language. This first study thus suggests that syntactic constraints can function like semantic constraints in reducing but not eliminating cross-language competition in lexical processing.

Implications for models of bilingual lexical access

One of the first and most-often-cited connectionist models of bilingual lexical access is the Bilingual Interactive Activation Model (BIA; Grainger & Dijkstra, 1992; Dijkstra, Van Heuven, & Grainger, 1998b) and its successor the BIA+ (Dijkstra & Van Heuven, 2002). A fundamental assumption of the BIA is that there is an integrated bilingual lexicon. Thus, when the system is provided with an input string word candidates from both languages are simultaneously activated. The assumption of parallel activation in two languages allows the model to account for the non-selectivity observed in bilingual word recognition. Most central to the present review on sentence context effects is the structure and operation of 'language nodes' in the two models, one node for each of the bilingual's languages. The language nodes are connected to all the words of its language in the lexicon and they are the mechanism in the model that allows for the *potential* of language selection. In its first formulation, the language nodes of the BIA collect activation from both linguistic (activation of lexical entries) and non-linguistic (e.g., language context of the experiment) sources of information. As a language node collects activation, it sends top-down inhibition to words from the other, competing language. This top-down inhibitory mechanism is what allows the system to operate in a language selective manner after an initial period of non-selectivity.

A fundamental change from the BIA to the BIA+ involved the operation of the language nodes. More specifically, in the later BIA+ the language nodes were no longer designated to collect activation from non-linguistic sources of information (such as the particular demands or instructions involved in the experimental task). Instead, extralinguistic sources of information operated outside of the lexicon within a task-decision system. This modification was motivated by accruing evidence that factors such as participant knowledge of the language of the task or language exclusivity of a task did not reduce observed effects of cross-language activation.

Findings from the studies reviewed here provide us with additional insight regarding the specific ways in which activated language nodes may allow for language selection. According to the BIA+ model, semantic information from a surrounding context can influence language selection in fundamentally two mutually interacting ways: First, it can allow for the language nodes to collect sufficient activation for lexical access to operate selectively. Second, the boosted activation of a language node for one language can allow it to more efficiently inhibit words from the competing language. Although it would be difficult to completely disentangle these two actions (activation of the language node is what allows for top-down inhibition), the available evidence suggests that context acts more directly on the second mode of action, top-down inhibition. Evidence from eye-movement studies is revealing that even in semantically highly constraining sentences there is an initial period of non-selectivity. This suggests that there is little opportunity for the language nodes to become sufficiently pre-activated to allow for selective access based on semantics from the onset. Instead, what the biasing semantic context can do is allow the language nodes to exert top-down inhibition more quickly, consequently narrowing the time-course over which non-selective activation is observed. Thus, in eye-tracking studies such as Libben and Titone (2009) cognate facilitation and homographic inhibition were only observed in early measures of the eye-movement record such as first fixation and gaze duration. Emerging findings from sentence context studies also highlight ways in which current models can be further developed. For example, it is not clear if there are types of linguistic context other than the semantic context that the language nodes in the BIA+ are sensitive to. For example, are they sensitive to fine-grained distinctions in semantic constraint? Or are they exclusively responsive to more coarse-grained sources of information such as language membership of preceding words? And to what extent is the activation of language nodes affected by syntactic constraints in the sentence?

Modeling sentence context and lexical access

Research on sentence context effects on lexical access has been specifically concerned with whether context can allow for selective access of a word's meaning within a language. This focus has been fueled by on-going debates regarding the degree to which language processing is modular or interactive across different levels of processing. If language operates in a modular fashion, top-down semantic integration processes of sentence comprehension should not directly influence the bottom-up process of lexical access. If, on the other hand, processing across levels is interactive, then semantic information activated through prior context should have the potential to directly modify lexical access. There are a variety of models of lexical access in sentence context and they differ most fundamentally in whether they assume exhaustive access of homonym meanings or allow for potential selective access. To discriminate between these two hypotheses researchers have used the general strategy of embedding semantically ambiguous homonyms in sentence contexts.

In a classic study, Swinney, Onifer, Prather, and Hirshkowitz, (1979) had participants listen to auditorily presented sentences containing lexical ambiguities (e.g., bugs) such as 'Rumor had it that for years the government building had been plagued with problems. The man was not surprised when he found several spiders, roaches and other *bugs* in the corner of the room.' At the offset of the ambiguous words participants performed a visual lexical decision on target words that were either related to the context-appropriate interpretation of the ambiguous word (e.g., *ant*), or related to the inappropriate meaning (e.g., *spy*) or were completely unrelated (e.g., *sew*). Participants' responses to the words relating to the contextually appropriate and inappropriate meaning were both facilitated, suggesting that the multiple meanings of 'bugs' were activated irrespective of contextual constraint. Findings such as those from Swinney et al. (1979) have been interpreted as strong evidence for modular theories of language. If the multiple meanings of ambiguous words are activated, irrespective of context, this would mean that the bottom-up lexical processes that lead to their activation are autonomous from top-down processing. The implication is that any observed semantic priming from sentence context that would seemingly support interactivity is in fact due to either intra-lexical priming and/or post lexical processing.

However, the assumption that effects of sentence context are due to intra-lexical priming has been challenged (Simpson, Peterson, Casteel, & Burgess, 1989). In one study participants read visually presented sentences and named target words out loud. On critical trials the to-be-named target words (e.g., table) were preceded by an associatively related prime (e.g., chairs). The authors manipulated whether these words were presented in a normal sentence context (e.g., 'John bought new *chairs* to go with his new *table*') or a scrambled context (e.g., 'Four with to *chairs* his go John new bought *table*'). They reasoned that, if speeded lexical access of the target words (e.g., table) were due solely to intra-lexical priming, than naming latencies should have been equally fast for targets, irrespective of whether they were embedded in normal or scrambled sentences.

In contrast, if contextual priming was indeed due to the higher level, semantic information of the sentences, than priming should have only been observed in the normal sentence conditions. The results showed significant priming for targets, only when they were embedded in normal sentences. In a second experiment the scrambled sentences were replaced with sentences that followed English syntax, but did not make sense (e.g., 'The *author* tried many whispers on his back *book*'). Once again there was significant priming for targets only when they were embedded in normal sentences. These findings, overall, provided a strong argument against the claim that effects of priming in sentence context were due solely to intra-lexical, associative priming.

Several hybrid models have since been formulated which assume a combined influence of rapid activation of alternative meanings and the surrounding semantic context of a sentence (e.g., Duffy, Morris, & Rayner, 1988; Simpson & Burgess, 1985) (see Morris, 2002 for a review). In this chapter we highlight one such model in particular, the Re-ordered Access Model (RAM) (Duffy et al., 1988). Because this model provides an account for a reliable effect (the subordinate bias effect, described below) which lends itself easily to cross-language extensions, Schwartz and colleagues have recently extended its assumptions to bilinguals processing (Arêas & Schwartz, 2011; Arêas, Yeh, Schwartz, 2010; Schwartz & Arêas, 2010; Schwartz, Yeh, & Shaw, 2008). Thus, this model in particular is described in further detail below.

One assumption of the RAM is that access of homonym meanings in context is exhaustive. Thus, all meanings receive activation, irrespective of semantic constraint. Second, the RAM assumes that the relative frequency of individual meanings influences the degree of activation. Thus, a dominant meaning will be more strongly activated than a subordinate meaning. Third, activation levels of the contextually–instantiated homonym meaning are influenced by the extent to which the sentence context semantically biases that meaning. In this way, a subordinate meaning of a homonym can be more strongly activated if it is strongly biased by the sentence. A fourth assumption of the model is that activation of the non-instantiated meaning is unaffected by context. This implies that even if a dominant meaning is not biased by a sentence context, its relatively high frequency allows it to still be sufficiently activated to compete with other meanings.

Initial evidence for the RAM came from Duffy and others (1988). The authors compared eye fixations for two types of ambiguous words: words for which the frequency of the multiple meanings was similar (balanced words) (e.g., *bark*) and words for which one of the meanings was of a much higher frequency (biased words) (e.g., *port*). These words were presented in either neutral sentences, sentences that biased the dominant meaning, or sentences that biased the subordinate meaning. When biased words were presented in neutral context fixations were similar to non-ambiguous control words, suggesting that the highly dominant meaning was automatically activated and since the frequency of the subordinate meaning was comparably lower, it did not compete for activation. When these same biased words were presented in sentences biasing the *subordinate* meaning, strong inhibitory effects emerged. Duffy et al. reasoned that the additional semantic support of the subordinate meaning provided by the sentence allowed the subordinate meaning to become activated within the same window of time as the dominant meaning. The resulting competition delayed eye fixations. Duffy and colleagues referred to the delayed eye fixations observed in contexts biasing the subordinate meaning of ambiguous words as the 'subordinate bias effect' and it has been replicated across several studies (Binder, 2003; Binder & Rayner, 1998; Kambe, Rayner, & Duffy, 2001).

Modeling sentence context and lexical access: implications for bilingual word recognition

The emerging finding that sentence context does not eliminate cross-language non-selectivity but rather alters its time-course is convergent with the major premise of the RAM. In a recent set of studies Schwartz and colleagues have examined how cross-language non-selectivity might further influence the time-course with which homonym meanings are activated, thus proposing a way to extend the RAM to account for bilingual processing (Arêas & Schwartz, 2011; Schwartz & Arêas, 2010; Schwartz et al., 2008). The general strategy across these studies has been to present bilinguals with sentences containing a cognate that is semantically-ambiguous ('homonym cognates') within the target language of the sentence (e.g., the cognate pair *arms-armas*: in Spanish *armas* shares the subordinate meaning of 'weapon'; the cognate pair *novel-novela*: in Spanish *novela* shares the dominant meaning of 'story') and to systematically manipulate the semantic bias of the preceding sentence context. In one study (Schwartz et al., 2008), highly–proficient Spanish–English bilinguals read all-English sentence contexts (the entire sentence with the last word absent) on a computer screen and made a button press to see the last word (the prime), which after 250 ms was followed by a target word. The participants' task was to decide as quickly and accurately as possible whether the target word was related in meaning to the sentence they had just read. On critical trials the prime word was a semantically–ambiguous English homonym that was either a cognate with Spanish (e.g., *novel-novela*) or a noncognate (e.g., *fast*) and the preceding context biased its subordinate meaning (e.g., 'She is an original thinker and her ideas are' [prime word 'novel']; 'In observance of the religious holiday the family observed the' [prime word: 'fast']). The follow-up target word was related to the contextually-irrelevant but dominant meaning (e.g., novel: *BOOK*; fast: *SPEED*) (thus requiring a 'no' response). Bilinguals were slower and made more errors in rejecting the follow-up target word when the homonym prime word was also a cognate with Spanish (e.g., 'novel'). The increased competition observed from cognate homonyms relative to noncognate homonyms suggests that cross-language co-activation of the dominant meaning increased the strength of its activation. In a variation of this study a new group of highly proficient Spanish–English bilingual performed the same task, however, this time the participants' task was to decide whether the follow-up target words were related to any meaning of the preceding homonym prime (e.g., *arms* in English can mean either a 'body part' or a 'weapon') (Arêas et al., in press). On critical trials the sentence contexts biased the dominant meaning of the homonyms (e.g., 'Tim fell out of the tree and broke his' [prime word: '*arms*]') and the target was related to the non-instantiated subordinate meaning (e.g., *WEAPON*) (thus requiring a 'yes' response). Bilinguals were faster and more accurate in accepting the follow-up targets as being related to a meaning of the prime word when the prime was a cognate homonym and the subordinate meaning was shared across languages (e.g., '*armas*' in Spanish shares the subordinate English meaning 'weapon').

Together these two reaction-time based studies provide converging evidence that cross-language activation affects the strength of activation of homonym meanings during sentence comprehension. This interpretation has recently received additional support from a study using eye-movement monitoring (Schwartz & Arêas, 2010). Highly proficient Spanish–English bilinguals read all-English sentences on a computer screen while their eye-movements were monitored. These sentences contained English homonyms that were either noncognates (e.g., *bullets*) or cognates (e.g., *arms*) with Spanish, and shared the subordinate meaning ('weapon'). When the sentence context up until the critical word was neutral (e.g., 'There were too many *bullets* under the heading and the slide was not clear', there was no difference in processing time for noncognate homonyms and nonhomonym controls. When these same noncognate homonyms were embedded in a context biasing the subordinate meaning (e.g., 'His slides had too many *bullets* and were difficult to understand.'), the mean first fixation duration was significantly longer than controls, thus replicating the subordinate bias effect. More critically, processing time for cognate homonyms was significantly *longer* than controls in both neutral and biasing contexts (e.g., 'The man placed his *arm* on the table to pass through security check', 'The man fired his *arm* when the robber entered his house'). This demonstrates that co-activation of the subordinate meaning was sufficient to allow this meaning to compete with the dominant meaning even in the absence of support from a biasing context.

Based on these studies Schwartz and colleagues have proposed an extension of the RAM – the Bilingual Re-ordered Access Model (B-RAM). This extended model adds a third factor, cross-language activation, which is assumed to influence the activation of homonym meanings for bilinguals. The B-RAM shares the four assumptions of the RAM listed above. However, critically it adds cross-language lexical activation as a third factor that influences activation levels of instantiated homonym meanings (in addition to relative frequency and sentential context). Thus, when a subordinate meaning of a homonym is a cognate meaning across a bilingual's two languages, the coactivation will allow it to become sufficiently activated to compete with the dominant meaning, even in the absence of a biasing context, as observed by Schwartz and Arêas (2010). This phenomenon has not been previously observed with any of the monolingual investigations of the subordinate bias effect cited above. The key implication is that due to language non-selectivity bilinguals can activate subordinate meanings early on, in the absence of a biasing context.

Future directions

Published systematic and focused investigations on the effects of sentence context on bilingual lexical access have only recently begun to appear, with most studies appearing after the year 2000. This is despite the fact that psycholinguistic studies on the effects of sentence context on lexical access have more than a 30-year history. From the relatively few studies published to date it is clear that our understanding of the cognitive dynamics guiding sentence comprehension will be incomplete without the inclusion of bilingual manipulations. For example, for years there has been a debate regarding whether information from sentence context directly influences lexical access. Yet only very recently have we learned that language membership does not provide a powerful cue to allow for selective access within a language but rich, semantic information can constrain the time-course of language non-selectivity. Emerging evidence provides some suggestion that syntactic information can have a similarly constraining effect on language non-selectivity, but more research is clearly needed. Yet another example of the need for bilingual research is the fact that studies dating back 20 years demonstrated that a critical component of fluent reading is the ability to efficiently sustain activation of weaker meanings of ambiguous words (e.g., Gernsbacher & Faust, 1991). Yet only recently have we learned that bilinguals might be at an advantage for activation weaker meanings when these are co-activated across languages.

The lack of studies that specify the features of contextual information that constrain lexical activation is another gap in the available bilingual literature. Such studies are needed in order to fine-tune theoretical models on lexical activation in bilingual word recognition. In the last decade, many studies on isolated word processing studies appeared in the literature on bilingualism, the next step is to extend this to perceiving words in more naturalistic contexts. Furthermore, bilingual sentence context studies have focused on two oral languages from the same script. In order to develop theories and models of bilingual sentence processing that fully specify the relative contributions of different potential sources of constraint, more evidence is needed on coactivation in different-script languages, and sign-speech or gesture-speech. Another dimension of sentence processing that requires further specification is the time-course with which lexical competitors are activated during sentence processing. Recent eye-tracking studies have produced effects of cross-language activation even in semantically-rich sentences but only in aspects of the eye-movement record that tap into earlier stages of processing. There is a need for more studies using methodologies that can further elucidate the time-course of activation such as eye-tracking and ERPs. Finally, a hallmark of bilingual language processing is the flexible switching between languages, both in the production and the perception of language. However, as of yet, the majority of studies on lexical access in context focused on studies in which the language of the context was the same as the language of the target. To what extent does our current knowledge on lexical activation in bilinguals apply to lexical access in code-switched sentences?

- How do bilinguals recognize words within their two languages? Does bilingual word recognition necessarily involve activation of both languages or is there some sort of a language switch that allows for selective activation of just the relevant language? These questions gained considerable empirical attention in the 1990s, which continues today.

- Initial studies examined whether bilingual access of individual words presented in isolation involves parallel activation of word representations across both languages (termed 'language non-selectivity'). The general methodological strategy was to compare bilinguals' performance (reaction time and accuracy) when recognizing words with a high degree of lexical form overlap across languages (e.g., the English–Spanish cognate translation pair piano/piano; the English–Spanish interlingual homograph pan, meaning 'bread' in Spanish) with non-lexically overlapping controls in tasks such as single word naming and visual lexical decision. The vast majority of these studies consistently revealed effects of non-selective activation. For example, across various experimental tasks, language populations and proficiency levels cognate translations were found to be recognized more quickly and accurately than frequency-matched control words. The magnitude and nature of these effects is influenced by the type of overlap (e.g., phonological, orthographic) and degree (full, partial).

- Consistent observation of effects like cognate facilitation demonstrated that bilingual lexical access is by nature language-non-selective and bilinguals cannot avoid activating competing lexical entries across their languages. The remaining question is how bilinguals are able to communicate in just one language despite this non-selectivity. Recent studies have focused on the role that a surrounding linguistic context might play in allowing for language selection. The emerging finding is that a semantically-rich context that biases towards one reading of a word can significantly constrain non-selective cross-language activation. Most recent eye-movement studies do not show a complete elimination of non-selectivity but they do demonstrate a decrease in the amount of time word representations from the other language are active, allowing for earlier selection of the target language representation. Therefore, bilingual word recognition is fundamentally language non-selective. However, the nature and magnitude of co-activation is influenced by the type of lexical form overlap and surrounding linguistic context.

Note

1 We will restrict the discussion to studies in which the target words and sentence context were presented in the same language. For studies that examined code-switched reading by presenting bilinguals with words embedded in sentences in the other language, see Altarriba, Kroll, Sholl, and Rayner (1996), Moreno, Federmeier, and Kutas (2002), Proverbio Leoni, and Zani (2004). For a review, see Van Hell and Witteman (2009).

References

Altarriba, J., Kroll, J. F., Sholl, A., & Rayner, K. (1996). The influence of lexical and conceptual constraints on reading mixed-language sentences: Evidence from eye. *Memory and Cognition, 24*, 477–492.

Arêas A. B. & Schwartz, A.I. (2011). Working memory influences on cross-language activation during bilingual lexical disambiguation. *Bilingualism: Language and Cognition, 14*, 360–370.

Arêas, A. B., Yeh, L., & Schwartz, A. I. (2010). Bilingual lexical disambiguation: The nature of cross-language activation effects. *Lectrônica, 3*, 107–127.

Binder, K. (2003). Sentential and discourse topic effects on lexical ambiguity processing: An eye movement examination. Memory & Cognition, *31*, 690–702.

Binder, K. & Rayner, K. (1998). Contextual strength does not modulate the subordinate bias effect: Evidence from eye fixations and self-paced reading. *Psychonomic Bulletin & Review, 5*, 271–276.

Blumenfeld, H. & Marian, V. (2007). Constraints on parallel language activation in bilingual spoken language processing: Examining proficiency and lexical status using eye-tracking. *Language and Cognitive Processes, 22*, 633–660.

Brenders, P., Van Hell, J. G., & Dijkstra, T. (2011). Word recognition in child second language learners: Evidence from cognates and false friends. *Journal of Experimental Child Psychology, 109*, 383–396.

Brown, A. & Gullberg, M. (2008). Bidirectional crosslinguistic influence in L1-L2 encoding of manner in speech and gesture. *Studies in Second Language Acquisition, 30*, 225–251.

Brysbaert, M., Van Dyck, G., & Van de Poel, M. (1999). Visual wordrecognition in bilinguals: evidence from masked phonological priming. *Journal of Experimental Psychology: Human Perception and Performance, 25*, 137–148.

Caramazza, A. & Brones, I. (1979). Lexical access in bilinguals. *Bulletin of the Psychonomic Society, 13*, 212–214.

Chambers, C. G. & Cooke, H. (2009). Lexical competition during second-language listening: Sentence context, but not proficiency, constrains interference from the native lexicon. *Journal of Experimental Psychology: Learning, Memory, and Cognition, 34*, 1029–1040.

Costa, A., Caramazza, A., & Sebastian-Galles, N. (2000). The cognate facilitation effect: Implications for models of lexical access. *Journal of Experimental Psychology: Learning, Memory, and Cognition, 26*, 1283–1296.

Cristoffanini, P., Kirsner, K., & Milech, D. (1986). Bilingual lexical representation: The status of Spanish-English cognates. *Quarterly Journal of Experimental Psychology, 38A*, 367–393.

De Bruijn, E. R. A., Dijkstra, T., Chwilla, D. J., & Schriefers, H. J. (2001). Language context effects on interlingual homograph recognition: Evidence from event-related potentials and response times in semantic priming. *Bilingualism: Language and Cognition, 4*, 155–168.

De Groot, A. M. B., Delmaar, P., & Lupker, S. J. (2000). The processing of interlexical homographs in translation recognition and lexical decision: Support for non-selective access to bilingual memory. *Quarterly Journal of Experimental Psychology: Human Experimental Psychology, 53A*, 397–428.

De Groot, A. M. B. & Nas, G. L. J. (1991). Lexical representation of cognates and noncognates in compound bilinguals. *Journal of Memory and Language, 30*, 90–123.

Deuchar, M. (2005). Congruence and Welsh-English code-switching. *Bilingualism: Language and Cognition, 8*, 255–269.

Dijkstra, T. & Van Heuven, W. (2002). The architecture of the bilingual word recognition system: From identification to decision. *Bilingualism: Language and Cognition, 5*, 175–197.

Dijkstra, T., Van Jaarsveld, H., & ten Brinke, S. (1998a). Interlingual homograph recognition: Effects of task demands and language intermixing. *Bilingualism: Language and Cognition, 1*, 51–66.

Dijkstra, T., Van Heuven, W., & Grainger, J. (1998b). Simulating cross-language competition with the bilingual interactive activation model. *Psychologica Belgica, 38*, 177–196.

Dijkstra, T., Grainger, J., & Van Heuven, W. J. B. (1999). Recognition of cognates and interlingual homographs: The neglected role of phonology. *Journal of Memory and Language, 41*, 496–518.

Dijkstra, T., De Bruijn, E., Schriefers, H., & Brinke, S. T. (2000). More on interlingual homograph recognition: Language intermixing versus explicitness of instruction. *Bilingualism: Language and Cognition, 3*, 69–78.

Dimitropoulou, M., Duñabeitia, J. A., & Carreiras, M. (2011). Phonology by itself: Masked phonological priming effects with and without phonological overlap. *Journal of Cognitive Psychology, 23*, 185–203.

Duffy, S., Morris, R., & Rayner, K. (1988). Lexical ambiguity and fixation times in reading. *Journal of Memory and Language, 27*, 429–446.

Duyck, W., Assche, E., Drieghe, D., & Hartsuiker, R. (2007). Visual word recognition by bilinguals in a sentence context: Evidence for nonselective lexical access. *Journal of Experimental Psychology: Learning, Memory, and Cognition, 33*, 663–679.

Elston-Güttler, K. E., Gunter, T. C., & Kotz, S. A. (2005). Zooming into L2: Global language context and adjustment affect processing of interlingual homographs in sentences. *Cognitive Brain Research, 25*, 57–70.

Font, N. (2001). Rôle de la langue dans l'accès au lexique chez les bilingues: Influence de la proximité orthographique et sémantique interlangue sur la reconnaissance visuelle de mots. *Unpublished Doctoral Thesis of the Université Paul Valery*, Montpellier, France.

Gernsbacher, M. A. & Faust, M. (1991). The mechanism of suppression: A component of general comprehension skill. *Journal of Experimental Psychology: Learning, Memory, and Cognition, 17*, 245–262.

Gollan, T. H., Forster, K. I., & Frost, R. (1997). Translation priming with different scripts: Masked priming with cognates and noncognates in Hebrew–English bilinguals. *Journal of Experimental Psychology: Learning, Memory, and Cognition, 23*, 1122–1139.

Grainger, J. & Dijkstra, T. (1992). On the representation and use of language information in bilinguals. *Cognitive processing in bilinguals* (pp. 207–220). Oxford, England: North-Holland.

Gullifer, J., Dussias, P., & Kroll, J. (2010). Bilingual sentence processing: The role of syntactic constraints in modulating cross-language lexical activity. Poster presented at the 23rd Annnual CUNY conference on Human sentence processing, March 18–20. New York University, NY.

Hoshino, N. & Kroll, J. F. (2008). Cognate effects in picture naming: Does cross-language activation survive a change of script? *Cognition, 106*, 501–511.

Kambe, G., Rayner, K., & Duffy, S. (2001). Global context effects on processing lexically ambiguous words: Evidence from eye fixations. *Memory & Cognition, 29*, 363–372.

Kim, J. & Davis, C. (2003). Task effects in masked cross-script translation and phonological priming. *Journal of Memory and Language, 49*, 484–499.

Kootstra, G. J., Van Hell, J. G., & Dijkstra, T. (2010). Alignment in the production of code-switched sentences: The role of word order and dialogue partner. *Journal of Memory and Language, 63*, 210–236.

Lalor, E. & Kirsner, K. (2001). The representation of 'false cognates' in the bilingual lexicon. *Psychonomic Bulletin & Review, 8*, 552–559.

Lemhöfer, K., Dijkstra, T., & Michel, M. C. (2004). Three languages, one ECHO: Cognate effects in trilingual word recognition. *Language and Cognitive Processes, 19*, 585–611.

Libben, M. & Titone, D. (2009). Bilingual lexical access in context: Evidence from eye movements during reading. *Journal of Experimental Psychology: Learning, Memory, and Cognition, 35*, 381–390.

McClelland, J. L. & Rumelhart, D. E. (1988). An interactive activation model of context effects in letter perception: Part 1: an account of basic findings. In A. M. Collins (Ed.), *Readings in cognitive science: A perspective from psychology and artificial intelligence* (pp. 580–596). San Mateo, CA: Morgan Kaufmann, Inc.

Moreno, E. M., Federmeier, K. D. & Kutas, M. 2002. Switching languages, switching palabras: An electrophysiological study of code switching. *Brain and Language, 80*, 188–207.

Morford, J. P., Wilkinson, E., Villwock, A., Piñar, P. & Kroll, J. F. (2011). When deaf signers read English: Do written words activate their sign translations? *Cognition, 118*, 286–292.

Morris, R. K. (2002). Lexical processing and sentence context effects. In M. J. Traxler & M. A. Gernsbacher (Eds) *Handbook of psycholinguistics* (2nd Edn) (pp. 377–402). London: Elsevier.

Poplack, S. (1980). Sometimes I'll start a sentence in Spanish Y TERMINO EN ESPAÑOL: Toward a typology of code-switching. *Linguistics, 18*, 581–618.

Proverbio, A. M., Leoni, G., & Zani, A. (2004). Language switching mechanisms in simultaneous interpreters: An ERP study. *Neuropsychologia, 42*, 1636–1656.

Rayner, K. & Well, A. (1996). Effects of contextual constraint on eye movements in reading: A further examination. *Psychonomic Bulletin & Review, 3*, 504–509.

Sánchez-Casas, R., Davis, C. W., & García-Albea, J. E. (1992). Bilingual lexical processing: Exploring the cognate/non-cognate distinction. *European Journal of Cognitive Psychology, 4*, 311–322.

Schwanenflugel, P. J. (1991). Contextual constraint and lexical processing. In: G. B. Simpson (Ed.) *Understanding word and sentence. Advances in Psychology*, No 77 (pp. 23–45). Oxford: North Holland.

Schwartz, A. I. & Arêas A. B. (2010). The Bilingual Re-Ordered Access Model (B-RAM): A model of bilingual semantic disambiguation. Paper presented at the 7th International Conference on the Mental Lexicon, Windsor, Canada.

Schwartz, A. & Kroll, J. (2006). Bilingual lexical activation in sentence context. *Journal of Memory and Language, 55,* 197–212.

Schwartz, A. I., Kroll, J. F., & Diaz, M. (2007). Reading words in English and Spanish: Mapping orthography to phonology in two languages. *Language and Cognitive Processes, 22,* 106–129.

Schwartz, A. I., Yeh, L., & Shaw, M. P. (2008). Lexical representation of second language words: Implications for second language vocabulary acquisition and use. *The Mental Lexicon, 3,* 309–324.

Shook, A. & Marian, V. (2010). Interactivity during spoken word recognition: Evidence from bimodal bilinguals. Poster presented that the Cognitive Science Meeting, Portland.

Simpson, G. & Burgess, C. (1985). Activation and selection processes in the recognition of ambiguous words. J*ournal of Experimental Psychology: Human Perception and Performance, 11,* 28–39.

Simpson, G. & Krueger, M.A. (1991). Selective access of homograph meanings in sentence context. *Journal of Memory and Language, 30,* 627–643.

Simpson, G., Peterson, R., Casteel, M., & Burgess, C. (1989). Lexical and sentence context effects in word recognition. *Journal of Experimental Psychology: Learning, Memory, and Cognition, 15,* 88–97.

Swinney, D., Onifer, W., Prather, P., & Hirshkowitz, M. (1979). Semantic facilitation across sensory modalities in the processing of individual words and sentences. *Memory & Cognition, 7,* 159–165.

Tokowicz, N. & MacWhinney, B. (2005) Implicit and explicit measures of sensitivity to violations in second language grammar: An event-related potential investigation. *Studies in Second Language Acquisition, 27,* 173–204.

Van Assche, E., Duyck, W., Hartsuiker, R. J., & Diependaele, K. (2009). Does bilingualism change native language reading? Cognate effects in a sentence context. *Psychological Science, 20,* 923–927.

Van Hell, J. G. (1998). Cross-language processing and bilingual memory organization. Unpublished dissertation, University of Amsterdam, Amsterdam, The Netherlands.

Van Hell, J. G. & De Groot, A. M. B. (1998). Conceptual representation in bilingual memory: Effects of concreteness and cognate status in word association. *Bilingualism: Language and Cognition, 1,* 193–211.

Van Hell, J. G. & De Groot, A. M. B. (2008). Sentence context modulates visual word recognition in bilinguals. *Acta Psychologica, 128,* 431–451.

Van Hell, J. G. & Dijkstra, T. (2002). Foreign language knowledge can influence native language performance in exclusively native contexts. *Psychonomic Bulletin and Review, 9,* 780–789.

Van Hell, J. G. & Witteman, M. J. (2009). The neurocognition of switching between languages: A review of electrophysiological studies. In L. Isurin, D. Winford, and K. de Bot (Eds), *Multidisciplinary approaches to code switching* (pp. 53–84). Amsterdam / Philadelphia: John Benjamins.

Van Hell, J. G., Ormel, E., Van der Loop, J., & Hermans, D. (2009). Co-activation of phonology in bimodal and unimodal bilinguals. Poster presented at the 50th Annual Meeting of the Psychonomic Society, Boston.

Van Hell, J. G. & Tokowicz, N. (2010). Event-related brain potentials and second language learning: Syntactic processing in late L2 learners at different L2 proficiency levels. *Second Language Research, 26,* 43–74.

Van Heuven, W. J. B., Dijkstra, T., & Grainger, J. (1998). Orthographic neighbor-hood effects in bilingual word recognition. *Journal of Memory and Language, 39*, 458–483.

Van Petten, C. & Kutas, M. (1990). Interactions between sentence context and word frequency in event-related brain potentials. *Memory & Cognition, 18*, 380–393.

Voga, M. & Grainger, J. (2007). Cognate status and cross-script translation priming. *Memory & Cognition, 35*, 935–952.

Von Studnitz, R. E. & Green, D. (2002). Interlingual homograph interference in German-English bilinguals: Its modulation and locus of control. *Bilingualism: Language and Cognition, 5*, 1–23.

7 Individual differences in skilled visual word recognition and reading

The role of lexical quality

Sally Andrews

In the century since Huey (1908) identifyed skilled reading as 'one of the most remarkable feats of the human mind', we have learned a lot about how skilled readers identify words. The chapters in this book testify to the large, rich body of evidence that has been accumulated about visual word recognition in skilled readers. The 'chronometric' approaches of early experimental psycholinguistics continue to be widely employed, using faster computers with more refined software to increase precision of measurement along with more sophisticated and valid measures of stimulus attributes (e.g., Davis, accompanying volume, Chapter 9; Feldman and Weber, this volume, Chapter 1). Increasingly, these methods are complemented by psychophysiological and neuropsychological techniques, including event-related potentials (Halderman et al., accompanying volume, Chapter 10), eye movement methods (Schotter & Rayner, this volume, Chapter 4) and measures of lateralized processing (Brysbaert et al., accompanying volume, Chapter 7). This accumulated body of research has established a number of robust phenomena that have been used to develop and refine theories of the representations and processes underlying skilled word recognition.

With advances in computing power, many of these theories have been implemented as large-scale computational simulations (e.g., Coltheart, accompanying volume, Chapter 1; Sibley and Kello, accompanying volume, Chapter 2), or as mathematical models that provide a principled account of the parameters predicting performance in specific tasks (e.g., Gomez, accompanying volume, Chapter 4; Schotter and Rayner, this volume, Chapter 4). The adoption of computational approaches has forced tighter specification of the underlying theories and generated new predictions that have stimulated further empirical research. Direct comparisons of human data with model predictions have also provided a new source of evidence for theory-testing and refinement.

However, the vast majority of research on skilled word recognition is built on an implicit *uniformity assumption*: that the cognitive architecture of the skilled reading system is relatively constant across individuals, at least among the population of above-average readers from which undergraduate students are drawn. This assumption is reflected in the use of measures of average reaction time (RT) and accuracy for samples of around 25 student participants to provide 'benchmarks' against which to evaluate computational models of reading aloud (e.g., Coltheart, Rastle, Perry, Langdon, & Ziegler, 2001; Perry, Ziegler, & Zorzi, 2007). Similarly, the average performance of 25–35 university students is assumed to provide a reliable and valid index of skilled readers' responses to the large samples of items tested in the megastudies of word recognition performance reviewed by Balota et al., (accompanying volume, Chapter 5).

The virtually universal reliance on measures of average performance for relatively small samples of university student readers to test theories of skilled word recognition and reading implies that all skilled readers read in essentially the same way. However, there is considerable variability in measures of written language proficiency in samples of university students, even when bilinguals are excluded. For example, Table 7.1 presents means, standard deviations and ranges for two tests of reading (a 10-minute passage comprehension test and a cloze measure of reading speed), two tests of spelling (dictation and recognition) and a vocabulary test for a sample of 97 students tested by Andrews and Hersch (2010). The fastest reader read nearly 15 times as many words in the 3-minute cloze test as the slowest reader, and spelling dictation ranged from 25% to 100% correct. Substantial variability was also evident in mean RT and error rate for a lexical decision task. This sample is not unusual. We have found similar variability in many other samples from this undergraduate population (e.g., Andrews & Bond, 2009; Hersch & Andrews, in press). This evidence indicates that there *are* substantial differences in both psychometric measures of written language proficiency and in experimental measures of word recognition within samples of university students who, in general, fall above the mean on standardized tests of reading comprehension. This variability raises questions about the validity of conclusions based on average RT for unselected samples of skilled readers.

The uniformity assumption has served the field of visual word recognition well to this point. The chapters in these two volumes demonstrate that the accumulated evidence about how stimulus and task attributes influence average performance has made significant contributions to the development and refinement of theories of word recognition and reading. It was necessary to establish phenomena that can be robustly observed in average data before attempting to address nuances in its functioning. Many of the subtle effects of stimulus and task factors that have been established may have been difficult to tease out against the welter of individual differences in general cognitive capability and reading-specific skills that might potentially have been measured.

Table 7.1 Mean, standard deviation and range on measures of written language proficiency and lexical decision performance from Andrews and Hersch (in press)

	Reading compre-hension	*Reading speed (3 mins)*	*Spelling dictation (Max.=20)*	*Spelling recognition (Max.=88)*	*Vocabulary (Max.=30)*	*Lexical decision RT (ms)*	*Lexical decision (% errors)*
Mean	14.70	554.84	12.49	75.24	17.94	611	10.5
St Dev	7.60	155.39	3.80	6.31	4.19	100	11.2
Range	3–28	66–944	4–20	62–86	8–30	424–1026	0–30

However, the field has reached the point at which individual differences need to be systematically investigated. This is, in part, because both the empirical database and the major models have reached a level of maturity and robustness that allows consideration of parameter variations that are related to individual differences. With well-specified theories of how visual word recognition works on average, we are in a better position to conduct theoretically-grounded investigations of individual differences among skilled readers. Acknowledging the potential contribution of individual differences is also important to ensure that reliance on average data does not lead us to false conclusions and inappropriate adjustments to models. Many established computational models are at the stage where their developers are 'tweaking' them to fit ever-increasing sets of empirical data (e.g., Davis, 2010; Perry et al., 2007). If at least some of the generalizations derived from average data are undermined by systematic sources of individual differences, as suggested by the evidence discussed below (Andrews & Hersch, 2010), model refinements based on average data may be misguided.

The development of individual differences in reading

Insight into the sources of individual variability that are likely to persist amongst competent readers can be gleaned from the literature on reading development (see McClung et al., this volume, Chapter 8). It is widely accepted that phonological awareness is a critical cognitive prerequisite for effective reading acquisition because it is essential for extraction of the alphabetic principle (Byrne, 1998) which, in turn, provides a self-teaching mechanism (Share, 1995) that allows children to link new written words with their existing spoken vocabulary. However, a number of questions remain about the causality of the role played by phonological awareness (e.g., Castles & Coltheart, 2004) and about exactly how and why phonological information contributes to the development and use of lexical knowledge.

Dual-route frameworks assume that phonological knowledge is independent of the orthographic forms stored in the lexical route, although the two neurally independent systems play an inter-dependent role during reading development (Jackson & Coltheart, 2001). However, attempts to identify individual differences among skilled readers in relative reliance on these two systems have had little success (see Brown, Lupker, & Colombo, 1994, for review).

Stage models of reading development emphasize the intimate relationship between phonological and orthographic information in the development of lexical knowledge (see Ehri, 2005, for review). Phonological awareness is a critical prerequisite for the early stages of successful reading acquisition, but it is not sufficient for optimal reading development. Very few children with low levels of phonological awareness acquire reading efficiently, but not every child with high phonological awareness becomes a good reader (e.g., Juel, Griffith, & Gough, 1986). Children need to progress beyond the relatively laborious decoding process of the alphabetic stage to develop the fluent, automated lexical retrieval that characterizes skilled reading. Frith (1986) referred to the final state as the 'orthographic' stage of reading development to distinguish it from the earlier alphabetic stage. However, as Ehri (1992) emphasized, the dominant assumption of stage models is that, rather than being purely orthographic, the lexical representations supporting skilled reading are 'paved with phonology'. Ehri (2005) proposed a sequence of phases characterized by gradual refinement of 'the predominant type of connection that bonds written words to their other identities in memory' (p. 14). Readers progress from a 'partial alphabetic' stage, which only codes salient letters and sounds, to a 'full alphabetic' representation 'involving complete connections between all the graphemes and ... phonemes' and finally to a 'consolidated alphabetic' representation that adds syllabic and morphemic connections.

Within such frameworks, phonological awareness is a necessary but not sufficient condition for transition to a fluent orthographic approach to reading. Moreover, the factors determining the later stages of lexical development may be different from those responsible for variations in the early stages of reading acquisition leading to another 'cognitive 'sticking point' where reading acquisition can run aground' (Stanovich, 1992, p. 318) and impede the transition to a fully efficient orthographic approach to reading.

Developmental research suggests that some form of orthographic representation is acquired quite quickly. Share (2004) showed that as few as four opportunities to read a novel Hebrew word aloud in a short text led to development of a sufficiently detailed orthographic representation to allow children to reliably discriminate it not just from a new unfamiliar word but also from a homophone. Bowey and Muller (2005) extended this evidence to silent reading of new English words in text providing strong support for Share's (1995) arguments for the 'self-teaching' role of phonological recoding. But it remains unclear whether the orthographic representations developed in these studies correspond to the 'consolidated alphabetic representations' described by Ehri (2005). Indeed, there is good reason to believe that many competent readers have not developed such fully specified representations, or at least not for all the words they are able to read. However, rather than requiring a metacognitive insight like phonological awareness, the mechanisms underlying the development of these representations are likely to be gradual and therefore susceptible to the impact of both individual differences and environmental influences.

One obvious source of environmental influence is reading experience. As reviewed by McClung et al. (this volume, Chapter 8), exposure to print is a robust predictor of reading development across the primary years. Individual differences in reading experience continue to exert an influence across adolescence and adulthood. Even in a university student sample, who presumably read more than the average adult, measures of print exposure predicted unique variance in a composite measure of verbal ability and reading (Acheson, Wells, & MacDonald, 2008). Martin-Chang and Gould (2008) found even stronger relationships with 'primary print knowledge', defined by the number of authors for whom university students reported they had read at least one book. This measure of 'personal reading experience' predicted additional unique variance in vocabulary, reading comprehension and reading speed over and above the standard author recognition measure suggesting that 'it is the act of reading over and above memory for reading-related information that furthers the development of linguistic skill' (Martin-Chang & Gould, 2008, p. 273).

Confirming the contribution of print exposure to predicting the efficiency of skilled readers' word identification, Sears, Siakuluk, Chow and Buchanan (2008) found that higher print exposure was associated with faster lexical classification and reduced sensitivity to both word frequency and orthographic similarity to other words. To separate the unique contribution of print exposure to predicting skilled readers' word identification performance, Chateau and Jared (2000) compared groups of university students who were matched on reading comprehension ability but differed significantly on measures of print exposure. The high-print-exposure group was faster and more accurate at pseudoword reading, lexical decision and homophone choice tasks, indicating greater efficiency at both phonological decoding and activating orthographic codes. In the masked form priming paradigm, which is discussed in more detail below, the high-print-exposure group showed fast, facilitatory priming from orthography followed by slower phonological activation, while the low-print-exposure group showed no significant priming. The differences in word recognition performance between the two print exposure groups are quite striking given the equivalent reading comprehension of the two groups and provide strong evidence that 'even among successful students, differences in exposure to print lead to large differences in the efficiency of both orthographic and phonological word recognition processes' (Chateau & Jared, 2000, p. 143).

If experience reading words directly contributes to the refinement and consolidation of lexical representations, the lexical representations *within* an individual reader's lexicon will differ in the extent to which they have been consolidated (Perfetti, 2007). These differences will not solely be a function of experience with individual words but also of ongoing changes in the demands of the word recognition system as reading vocabulary increases. As readers learn more words that are similar to each other, they must 'tighten the input criteria' of their lexical representations to avoid confusing orthographically similar words (Castles, Davis, Cavalot, & Forster, 2007). That is, rather than necessarily reflecting different developmental stages, individual variability in word recognition amongst skilled readers may also arise from item-based differences in the 'tuning' of lexical representations (Castles et al., 2007).

Thus, the notion of a discrete 'orthographic stage' of reading development may be inappropriate. Rather, developing a lexicon of consolidated alphabetic representations is a gradual process in at least two senses: it depends on frequent exposure to print and it requires ongoing refinement of lexical representations to adapt to the increase in written vocabulary. A coding strategy that allows effective discrimination between the words of a small vocabulary may prove inadequate for discriminating between increasing numbers of orthographically similar words. In the same way that early growth in written vocabulary forces abandonment of a logographic strategy and triggers a shift to an alphabetic strategy in children who have developed phonological awareness (Freebody & Byrne,

1988), exposure to similar orthographic forms may drive the tuning of lexical representations to allow discrimination between similar words (Castles et al., 2007). The remainder of this chapter reviews theory and evidence suggesting that the extent of this tuning is a systematic source of individual differences amongst above-average readers that influences both the lexical retrieval processes that support word identification and the role played by word identification in reading comprehension.

Individual differences among skilled readers: the lexical quality hypothesis

As outlined above, the average data for unselected samples of university students that have provided the empirical grounding for theories and models of skilled reading may not arise from a uniform cognitive architecture. Rather, competent adult readers may be at different points along the continuum of Ehri's (2005) developmental sequence from 'partial' through to 'consolidated' alphabetic representations. This focus on the refinement of lexical representations is central to Perfetti's (1992, 2007; Perfetti & Hart, 2001) *lexical quality hypothesis.* Perfetti's (1985) earlier 'verbal efficiency theory' focused on how the speed and efficiency of lexical retrieval *processes* facilitate reading by reducing demands on working memory. The lexical quality hypothesis shifts the emphasis to lexical representations:

> ... the thing to understand is not speed but rather the ability to retrieve word identities that provide the meanings the reader needs in a given context. The source of this ability is the knowledge a reader has about words, specific lexical representations
>
> (Perfetti, 2007, p. 359).

High-quality representations are defined by the principles of 'precision' and 'redundancy' (Perfetti, 2007). Precise representations are fully rather than partially specified so that the input features directly activate a single correct representation with minimal activation of orthographically similar words. There is therefore little need to make use of context to facilitate lexical retrieval. With increasing precision, representations become more redundant as orthographic and phonological features of words become 'amalgamated' (Ehri, 1992). Precision and redundancy yield lexical retrieval that is reliable and 'coherent' in the sense that the multiple constituents (e.g., orthographic, phonological, semantic) that define a word 'are available synchronously at retrieval ... [in a] unitary word perception event'. Word identity is therefore 'both unitary and compositional' (Perfetti & Hart, 2001, p. 69) yielding the potential for flexibility in the pattern of activation across constituents according to the demands of the task.

The development of high-quality representations is a gradual process that operates at the item level. Highly skilled reading depends on tuning a high proportion of lexical representations, presumably through reading experience, to foster development of 'a context-free autonomous lexicon' (Perfetti, 1992, p. 162) populated by precise representations that can be activated by visually presented words deterministically, without any requirement for contextually based prediction. Context and higher order knowledge only exert their influence on the integrative processes that operate on the *outputs* of the autonomous lexical retrieval process. The notion of lexical autonomy clearly overlaps with the well accepted assumption that word identification is 'automatic', but the terms are not synonymous. Autonomy does not entail resource-independence (Logan, 2002) – processing is ballistic and resistant to interference, but not necessarily resource-free. Consistent with this assumption, reading skill is not associated with the greater Stroop interference predicted by the simple view of automaticity. Instead, more skilled readers show *less* Stroop interference, suggesting that their more autonomous word recognition allows them to exert more effective cognitive control when the task requires it (Protopapas, Archonti, & Skaloumbakas, 2007).

The assumption that a set of mental representations of orthographic word forms is critical to skilled reading is supported by recent brain-imaging data which has identified an isolable system in posterior left fusiform gyrus that is selectively activated by words and well-structured nonwords, but not by non-linguistic or poorly structured linguistic stimuli (Cohen, Dehaene, Vinckier, Jobert, & Montavont, 2008). This visual word form system (VWFS) is argued to serve as the 'primary gateway between the visual system and core components of the pre-existing language apparatus' (Carr, 1999). Critically, in the present context, the VWFS appears to play a greater role in the processing of competent readers than disabled readers (see Pugh, Mencl, Jenner, Lee, Katz, Frost, et al., 2001, for review). Pugh et al. (2001) argue that successful reading relies on two consolidated left hemisphere (LH) posterior systems: a temporo-parietal area that 'performs the function of learning to decode print for normally developing young readers', and the extrastriatal VWFS region which 'develops with reading experience into a system that recognizes printed words in a fast, automatic manner'. Disabled readers, by contrast, appear to use compensatory strategies that rely on bilateral activity in the inferior frontal gyrus and in right hemisphere posterior sites homologous to the VWFS. The increased involvement of VWFS in more proficient readers is consistent with the hypothesis that the development of reading skill depends on gradual refinements in the representation of lexical knowledge.

Investigating lexical quality

Investigating the contributions of variability in lexical quality to the behavioural performance of skilled readers requires a different approach to assessing individual differences than those used in most of the existing literature on these issues – both in terms of the measures used to assess reading skill and the tasks used to assess word identification and its contribution to reading. Developmental studies have consistently shown that the variance in reading comprehension that is predicted by word recognition decreases with development, in parallel with an increase in the variance predicted by listening comprehension (Catts, Adlof, &

Weismer, 2006) leading researchers to claim that 'in later grades, language skills other than word recognition replace decoding as the primary factors to successful reading comprehension' (Eason & Cutting, 2009, p. 265). However, this conclusion may be too strong. Although the variance accounted for word identification decreases from 3rd to 8th grade relative to that predicted by listening comprehension, both measures predict significant variance at all grade levels (Catts et al., 2006). To use Gough and Wren's (1998) analogy: 'Breathing may not account for much of the variance in quality of life, but life without it would not be possible. The same can be said for decoding: We could not read without it.' (p. 19). Moreover, if competent readers vary in the extent to which they have established high-quality representations of many of the words in their reading vocabulary, the balance between reliance on automatic lexical retrieval and comprehension processes, such as inference and integration, will remain a source of individual differences in on-line reading even among samples of above-average readers.

However, standard measures of decoding efficiency, such as the accuracy of word or nonword reading, may not effectively capture the more subtle differences implicated by lexical quality. Although faster word identification is a predicted consequence of lexical quality, comparisons of fast and slow participants in word identification tasks do not necessarily shed light on the basis of their superior performance. For example, Brown et al.'s (1994) comparison of groups defined by the relationship between indices of lexical and nonlexical processing provided no evidence for the independent routes assumed by the dual route model. Instead their data demonstrated effects of general proficiency leading to the rather uninteresting conclusion that 'faster subjects are just more skilled at reading' (Brown et al., 1994, p. 546).

There are also a number of problems with relying on measures of reading comprehension. Keenan, Olson, and Betjemann's (2008) recent largescale comparison of six commonly used measures of reading comprehension in 8–18-year-old twins showed that 'different reading comprehension tests measure different skills' (p. 242). Reading ability in adults is usually assessed with passage comprehension tests in which participants answer multiple-choice questions about short texts (e.g., Nelson–Denny Reading Test; Brown, Fishco, & Hanna, 1993). Such tests were developed as global measures of general reading-related skills and some passage comprehension tests can be answered with above-chance accuracy without reading the passages (e.g., Keenan et al., 2008). The general verbal ability and world knowledge demonstrated by effective performance on such tests presumably contribute to reading comprehension in more naturalistic contexts, but tests that are susceptible to such influences are unlikely to be sensitive to lexical quality, particularly given that they have not usually been developed to discriminate among a highly skilled population. Thus, effective reading comprehension is a necessary but not sufficient indicator of high-quality lexical representations.

Nevertheless, Perfetti and Hart (2001) used a short version of the Nelson–Denny test to evaluate the lexical quality hypothesis by comparing 'more-skilled' and 'less-skilled' readers (the top and bottom third of a large sample) in a task requiring judgements of the relatedness in meaning of word pairs presented at

150-ms, 450-ms and 2-s delays. The critical stimuli were homophones paired with a word related to their homophonic mate (e.g., *night royalty*; *knight dark*). Only poorer readers showed homophone interference on 'no' judgements for the higher frequency homophone (e.g., *night royalty*), while for the lower frequency member (e.g., *knight-dark*) better readers showed a more rapid build-up and a more rapid release from homophone interference than poorer readers. Perfetti and Hart (2001) interpreted these data as demonstrating that better readers show 'more rapid confusion and more rapid release from confusion' (p. 80) from the homophonic mate and argued that the presence of effects of reading ability as early as 150 ms was consistent with the prediction that higher quality lexical representations support more rapid lexical retrieval. Attempts to predict homophone interference from other individual difference measures showed that accuracy of pseudoword reading was the best predictor at the short delay, but Perfetti and Hart (2001) acknowledged that their battery of measures provided only a crude assessment of lexical quality. Their use of extreme-reading-ability groups, rather than a sample covering the full range of reading ability, also limits the validity of the correlations with other measures. Questions can also be raised about how effectively Perfetti and Hart's (2001) task assessed the early stages of lexical retrieval. Eye-movement data show that the average fixation time on a word during sentence reading for skilled readers is 200–250 ms, but perceptual information is extracted much more quickly than that because text reading proceeds normally when words disappear, or are replaced with masks, 50–60 ms after the reader fixates on them (Rayner, Yang, Castelhano, & Liversedge, 2011). Thus, even the shortest (150 ms) delay used by Perfetti and Hart (2001) may tap relatively late stages of lexical retrieval.

A novel approach to assessing individual differences in the timecourse of lexical retrieval has recently been applied by Yap, Tse, and Balota (2009) using measures of vocabulary to index 'lexical integrity', which they identified with the attributes of coherence and stability that form part of the definition lexical quality. Yap et al. (2009) compared the joint effects of semantic priming and word frequency in the average data for samples of participants from different universities which differed in average vocabulary. They used a relatively long prime-target delay (800 ms) but assessed the timecourse of the observed effects by using RT distributional analysis (e.g., Andrews & Heathcote, 2001) to determine which aspects of the RT distribution were responsible for observed differences between the high and low vocabulary samples. Their results showed that the higher vocabulary sample showed additive effects of frequency and semantic priming, reflecting a consistently larger semantic priming effect for low- than high-frequency items across the whole RT distribution. However, the low-vocabulary sample showed an interaction between frequency and semantic priming due principally to a larger semantic priming effect for low- than high-frequency words in the slow tail of the RT distribution. These findings challenge many theories of semantic priming by showing that the interaction between semantic priming and frequency is not as robust as suggested in the average data for samples of skilled readers (e.g., Borowsky & Besner, 2000). Yap et al. (2009) argue that the additive effects shown by high-vocabulary participants support the lexical quality account by implicating a relatively modular system in which all target words receive an automatic boost in activation from the 'headstart' provided by an associatively related prime. Lexical processing is more difficult for lower vocabulary participants with lower quality lexical representations so they rely more heavily on the prime, particularly for low-frequency words, leading to stronger priming effects especially for the slowest, most difficult words.

Yap, Balota, Sibley, and Ratcliff (2012) have recently extended this approach using the measures of vocabulary obtained for all participants tested in the English Lexicon megastudy (Balota et al., accompanying volume, Chapter 5). Individual vocabulary scores for 1289 participants were used to predict performance in single word naming and lexical decision tasks for very large sets of items. In addition to analyzing how vocabulary modulates the impact of a range of stimulus attributes on different parameters of the RT distributions, Ratcliff et al.'s (2004) diffusion model was used to estimate parameters for each participant's lexical decision data to investigate their relationship to vocabulary scores. Consistent with Yap et al.'s (2009) semantic priming data, vocabulary was most strongly related to variability in the slow tail of the RT distribution for both tasks, showing that vocabulary effects are more marked for more difficult items. Vocabulary was also strongly related to the drift rate parameter of the diffusion model which was interpreted as showing that higher vocabulary is associated with more efficient stimulus processing in the lexical decision task. Consistent with this interpretation, higher vocabulary was associated with a reduced influence of both structural stimulus attributes and word frequency in the speeded naming task, but these relationships were weaker, and even reversed, for the lexical decision task. Yap et al. (in press) argued that the reduced sensitivity to such stimulus attributes is consistent with the view that lexical retrieval is more automatic in more proficient readers, but acknowledge that the differences between naming and lexical decision require further investigation and that the data do not provide any insight into the mechanisms underlying the shift to a more automatic process. They also acknowledge that their choice of vocabulary to index aspects of lexical quality was a pragmatic rather than a conceptual decision and that a broader range of measures is necessary to fully evaluate the contribution of lexical quality to word identification performance.

None of the individual difference measures discussed so far captures the full specification of orthographic word forms that define Ehri's (2005) consolidated alphabetic representations. Perfetti (1992) argued that spelling performance provides the best index of this aspect of lexical quality because effective spelling implies precision of lexical representations. Accurate spelling requires a level of detailed knowledge about lexical form while many reading tasks can be achieved on the basis of partial lexical information supplemented by context. Reading and spelling skills correlate quite strongly in unselected samples ($r = 0.5$–0.8; Kahmi & Hinton, 2000), but many competent adult readers are poor spellers (Frith, 1986). Although evidence from brain-injured populations has been argued to show that reading and spelling rely on separate representations (e.g., Patterson,

1986), investigations of healthy adult readers provide strong evidence that they rely on common lexical representations (e.g., Burt, 2006). Within the lexical quality framework, differences in spelling ability amongst good readers reflect variations in the quality of lexical representations.

Consistent with this conclusion, Frith (1986) found that individuals who show a discrepancy between reading and spelling – Good Readers/Poor Spellers (GR/PS) – differ from Poor Readers/Poor Spellers (PR/PS) because their spelling errors are phonologically plausible, indicating that they have acquired alphabetic insight but failed to successfully progress to the orthographic stage. She suggested that unexpectedly poor spelling in good readers reflects the adoption of a reading strategy that relies on 'partial cues', in combination with contextual prediction, to recognize words. This is fast and efficient for reading, but does not involve the detailed attention to the internal structure of words necessary to acquire fully specified orthographic representations of words. Subsequent comparisons of GR/GS and GR/PS groups have, however, yielded contradictory data. Although poor spellers' tendency to make phonologically plausible errors has been confirmed, they nevertheless show subtle deficits in phonological processing (e.g., Masterson, Laxon, Lovejoy, & Morris, 2007) which may impede their development of consolidated alphabetic representations. However, a number of attempts to identify differences between the groups in visual, orthographic or sequential processing have failed to clearly identify the mechanisms responsible for GR/PS groups failure to acquire the word-specific knowledge required for effective spelling (e.g., Holmes, Malone, & Redenbach, 2008).

According to the lexical-quality hypothesis, GR/PS subgroups consist of individuals who have achieved their reading competence without developing an optimally expert lexical representational system. Their above-average reading comprehension relies on strong contextual reliance, which is effective in many naturalistic reading situations. There are a number of reasons that readers may develop a contextually-based reading strategy including exposure to top-down instruction methods, low-level deficits in phonological processing that impede development of orthographic representations and reduced reading experience. Conversely, effective reading comprehension in association with accurate spelling performance is a marker of high quality lexical representations that support autonomous, context-independent retrieval of the multiple constituents of a word.

Thus, the lexical quality hypothesis provides a framework to guide investigations of individual differences among skilled readers that goes beyond the general prediction that their word identification should be fast and accurate to claim that high-quality representations are more precise and fully specified, and yield more coherent activation of the various 'constituents' of lexical representations. To investigate these predictions, researchers need to include specific indicators of the various criteria for lexical quality. This requires measures of both reading comprehension and spelling in order to identify 'lexical experts' who show evidence of both effective reading comprehension and precise word-specific representations (Andrews, 2008). Measures of vocabulary are also critical to capture the semantic coherence emphasized by Yap et al.'s (2009) concept of lexical integrity. To tap differences amongst skilled readers, who are all relatively fast and accurate in identifying words, it is also necessary to use experimental tasks that are sensitive to early lexical retrieval processes and to differences in the timecourse of activation of different constituents.

Using masked priming to investigate lexical precision

An ideal paradigm for investigating how the quality of lexical representations, and particularly lexical precision, affects early lexical retrieval has been developed within the experimental psycholinguistic literature on skilled readers. This 'masked priming' paradigm, presents a very brief (~50 ms) lowercase prime between a neutral forward mask (e.g., ####) and an uppercase target (Forster & Davis, 1984). It has become a popular vehicle for investigating the early stages of lexical processing (see Kinoshita & Lupker, 2003) both because it reduces the contaminating effects of consciously mediated strategies and because it allows performance for the same target item to be compared across different priming conditions. Consistent with the claim that the paradigm provides insight into the early stages of lexical retrieval, masked priming is usually found only for word targets, and not for nonwords (e.g., Forster & Davis, 1984). Thus, the paradigm provides the perfect vehicle for investigating individual differences in the precision of lexical representation.

Castles, Davis, & Letcher, (1999) used the 'form priming' variant of the masked priming task, in which priming from a 1-letter different 'neighbour' prime is compared to an unrelated prime (e.g., *dask DARK* vs *meit DARK*), to investigate the tuning of lexical representations across reading development. Consistent with their hypothesis that lexical representations gradually become less vulnerable to being activated by a similar, but not identical, prime, they found that 2nd, 4th and 6th grade readers showed a form-priming benefit for 'high neighbourhood (N)' target words with many 1-letter neighbours[1] which do not yield form priming in adults. More direct evidence for a developmental tuning process was provided by a longitudinal comparison reported by Castles et al. (2007) which showed that the same children who showed strong priming from a neighbour prime in 3rd grade showed no priming when tested on the same stimuli in 5th grade, by which point their null priming effects were equivalent to those of adults. However, both 3rd grade and 5th grade readers showed priming from transposed-letter primes (e.g., *paly PLAY*) that was not shown by adults, suggesting that lexical tuning continues between 5th grade and adulthood and that sensitivity to letter order takes longer to be developed than sensitivity to letter identity. Castles et al. (2007) interpreted their data as 'evidence for a transition from more broadly tuned to more finely tuned word recognition mechanisms' (p. 165).

Masked-neighbor priming has also provided evidence of differential tuning within the average data for skilled readers. Forster, Davis, Schoknecht, and Carter (1987) found neighbor priming effects for 8-letter words, which have an average of less than 1 neighbour, but not for 4-letter words, which have an average of 7.2

neighboring words in English (Andrews, 1997). They showed that the critical stimulus attribute is neighbourhood size rather than length *per se* because significant facilitatory neighbour priming occurred for 'Low-N' 4-letter words (e.g., *eble ABLE*) whereas 'High-N' 4-letter words (e.g., *tand SAND*) yielded a non-significant inhibitory effect. This evidence was interpreted as showing that the detectors for words in high-density neighbourhoods are more narrowly tuned and therefore less vulnerable to being activated by a prime containing a mismatching letter. Forster and Taft (1994) conducted a more refined investigation of patterns of priming for High-N and Low-N words which revealed a very complex pattern of priming that varied with target N and the nature of the overlap between the prime and target. However, if skilled readers vary in the precision of their lexical representations, these average priming data may be misleading.

Consistent with this possibility, recent research from my laboratory has revealed that masked form priming amongst skilled readers is systematically modulated by spelling ability. Andrews and Hersch (2010) compared neighbour priming of High- and Low-N word targets by both word and nonword primes. The average data for our student sample replicated Forster et al. (1987) by showing facilitatory form priming only for Low-N targets. They also confirmed recent evidence that masked neighbour priming is influenced by prime lexicality (Davis & Lupker, 2006) because the facilitatory priming for Low-N words in the average data only occurred for nonword prime; word neighbours yielded no priming.

Supporting the predictions derived from the lexical quality hypothesis, our data showed that the average pattern of priming obscured a strong effect of spelling ability. As summarized in Figure 7.1, better spellers showed *inhibitory* priming from higher frequency, orthographically similar word neighbours (e.g., *node-NOTE*), while poor spellers showed facilitation. The inhibitory priming for good spellers was restricted to High-N target words. This is consistent with Castles et al.'s (2007) claim that lexical representations become more finely tuned for words that are confusable with many other words, but shows that this is not true for all skilled readers. Measures of reading, spelling and vocabulary jointly accounted for 26% of variance in priming of High-N words, but spelling was the only variable that accounted for unique variance (9%). The differential inhibitory neighbour priming for better and poorer spellers was replicated in a second experiment (Figure 7.2) which also included 'partial primes' constructed to be consistent only with the target word (unambiguous primes: e.g., *cr#wn CROWN*) or with at least one other word (ambiguous primes: e.g., *crow# CROWN*). Better spellers, but not poorer spellers, showed less facilitation for ambiguous than for unambiguous primes. These results are consistent with the lexical quality hypothesis's prediction that more skilled readers have more precise lexical representations which are less vulnerable to being activated by similar stimuli and able to exert fast inhibition of similar words, and that the precision of lexical representations is best indexed by spelling.

These findings also converge with recent claims (Perry, Lupker, & Davis, 2008) that masked priming reflects independent facilitatory effects due to sublexical overlap and inhibitory effects reflecting lexical competition because spelling

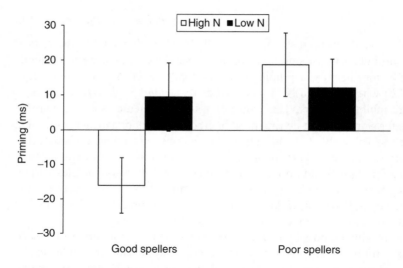

Figure 7.1 Average priming effects for above average (Good) and below average (Poor) spellers for High-N and Low-N target words preceded by 1-letter different neighbour primes. Positive values indicate that neighbour primes yielded facilitation relative to unrelated primes. Adapted from Andrews, S. and Hersch, J. (2010). Lexical precision in skilled readers: Individual differences in masked neighbor priming. Adapted with permission from *Journal of Experimental Psychology: General, 139*, 299–318, published by American Psychological Association.

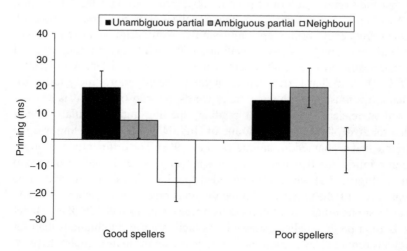

Figure 7.2 Average priming effects for above average (Good) and below average (Poor) spellers for target words preceded by Unambiguous or Ambiguous partial primes (see text for explanation) or 1-letter different word Neighbour primes. Positive values indicate that related primes yielded facilitatory priming relative to unrelated primes. Adapted from Andrews, S. and Hersch, J. (2010). Lexical precision in skilled readers: Individual differences in masked neighbor priming. Adapted with permission from *Journal of Experimental Psychology: General, 139*, 299–318, published by American Psychological Association.

was selectively related to lexical competition. Andrews and Hersch's data strongly suggest that the lexical precision indexed by spelling is selectively related to lexical competition. In our first experiment, inhibitory priming was restricted to high-N words which, for the 4-letter stimuli we used, have many neighbours that have the potential to compete with the target word. The partial priming data for Experiment 2 showed that good and poor spellers showed equivalent facilitatory priming from unambiguous primes, which are not compatible with any competing neighbours. However, only good spellers showed significantly reduced facilitatory priming from ambiguous partial primes that potentially activate word competitors. Thus good and poor spellers appear to benefit equally from the sublexical facilitatory priming, but for good spellers this is counteracted by lexical competition (Andrews & Hersch, 2010). These findings suggest that high-quality representations support very fast activation of the prime representation which inhibits activation of its neighbours, including the target.

We have recently replicated the finding of greater inhibitory neighbour priming in better than poorer spellers using a mixed sample of 4- and 5-letter words and showed that it is specific to a more difficult lexical decision environment. When hermit nonwords with no neighbours were used, both good and poor spellers showed facilitatory priming (Andrews & Hersch, 2009). Thus, better spellers were only sensitive to lexical competition when the task required fine-grained lexical discrimination and could not be performed on the basis of orthographic knowledge alone.

My claim that high quality lexical representations are associated with sensitivity to lexical competition may seem incompatible with the assumption that lexical quality supports more efficient lexical retrieval since, in the masked priming task, competition often leads to poorer performance relative to the unrelated control prime condition. The resolution to this apparent paradox lies in the fact that masked priming taps the very early stages of the lexical retrieval process during which multiple word candidates are activated in parallel. The inhibitory priming shown by better spellers indicates very efficient access to the prime, leading to fast inhibition of other similar words. This would usually be desirable to allow identification of the prime stimulus, but, when the prime is replaced by another word that is a lower-frequency neighbour, it causes interference. The masked priming paradigm also 'tricks' the lexical system by presenting two stimuli under conditions that provide no clues to the fact that the prime and target are separate events, leading to responses based on the combined perceptual input from the two stimuli (e.g., Norris & Kinoshita, 2008). From this perspective, the results for better spellers might provide evidence that inhibitory priming occurs when the representation of the prime word is activated quickly enough to be differentiated from the target.

In addition to their relevance to understanding individual differences among skilled readers, investigations of how masked priming varies with spelling and reading ability also contribute to an ongoing debate in the psycholinguistic literature about orthographic coding in skilled readers. As demonstrated by a recent special issue on this topic (Grainger, 2008), there are a number of different theories that vary in a range of assumptions about how perceptual information is extracted from words and matched with representations in lexical memory. A large body of evidence has been accumulated conducting increasingly refined tests of these different theoretical accounts using average data from student samples. However, if skilled readers vary in the precision of their lexical representations, the question of what is the 'correct' theory of orthographic coding may be misguided. Contradictory evidence may, in part, reflect averaging across individuals who vary in the precision of representation of letter identity and order. We have recently confirmed that the inhibitory form priming shown by good spellers is magnified for transposed-letter (TL) word pairs (e.g., *calm-CLAM*) while poor spellers show facilitation from both neighbour (e.g., *clap-CLAM*) and TL primes (Andrews and Lo, under review). The complicated patterns of sensitivity to manipulations of the order of prime letters that have been reported for unselected samples of skilled readers (e.g., Guerrera & Forster, 2008) may, therefore, arise from averaging over readers who vary in their sensitivity to letter order.

Lexical quality and sentence comprehension

Masked priming effects provide an ideal method for probing how high–quality lexical representations influence early lexical retrieval. However, such evidence does not address the broader prediction of the lexical quality hypothesis that high-quality representations contribute to effective reading comprehension. To investigate how the fast efficient retrieval supported by high-quality lexical representations contributes to reading comprehension, I have been using Rapid Serial Visual Processing (RSVP) sentence-processing tasks to assess how individual differences modulate the interplay between bottom-up and top-down processes. Andrews and Bond (2009) assessed implicit sensitivity to sentence meaning using a probe memory task in which sentences ending with an ambiguous word (e.g., *They danced at the ball*) were presented in RSVP, one word at a time at rates of 150 ms and 300 ms/word, followed by a probe word. On critical trials, probes were related to the sentence's congruous (e.g., *WALTZ*) or incongruous meaning (e.g., *THROW*) of the final ambiguous word, or matched unrelated words. Participants simply decided whether the probe occurred in the sentence. Participants were assessed on the same measures of reading and spelling used by Andrews and Hersch (2010; see Table 7.1). Analyses of subgroups classified as above and below the median according to composite measures of reading (reading comprehension and reading speed) and spelling (dictation and spelling recognition) showed that the 'lexical expert' group, who were above average on both reading and spelling (GR/GS), performed the task more quickly and accurately than groups who were above average on reading but not spelling (GR/PS), spelling not reading (PR/GS), or below average on both (PR/PS). More importantly the GR/GS group showed substantially less interference for related probe words (i.e., rejecting WALTZ as having occurred in the sentence *They danced at the ball*), particularly at fast (150 ms/word) RSVP rates. Interference for related relative to unrelated probes implicates a top-down influence of context that leads to 'false memories' of words that are related to the meaning of the sentence. At fast presentation rates, the GR/GS group showed a non-significant interference effect of 19 ms compared to significant effects of 74 and 73 ms for GR/PS and PR/PS, respectively. Good spellers who were below average at reading (PR/GS), showed a significant, intermediate interference effect of 42 ms, suggesting that better spelling is generally associated with reduced contextual reliance. However, lexical expertise, defined as the combination of good reading and good spelling, was associated with a complete absence of contextual influence when it was disadvantageous to task performance (Andrews & Bond, 2009).

We have recently reported converging evidence for this conclusion using a double word selection task (Potter, Stiefbold, & Moryadas, 1998) in which readers were presented with an RSVP sentence containing a pair of words, only one of which fit the sentence (Hersch & Andrews, in press). The critical context disambiguating between the words came either before or after the 'double word' pair (e.g., 'The ink on the *bush/note* was smeared and hard to read' vs 'On the *bush/note* the ink was smeared and hard to read'). In one condition, participants were required to read the sentence including only the contextually appropriate member of the double word pair; in another they only had to report the contextually appropriate word. The results for both conditions showed that lexical experts were more accurate at reading the words of the double word display in the absence of supporting context, confirming their more efficient lexical retrieval. They also made less use of context to select which word best fit the sentence (Hersch & Andrews, in press). Regression analyses including reading, spelling, vocabulary and reading span accounted for 40% of variance in the accuracy of reporting the correct word, but only reading and spelling accounted for unique variance, and spelling was the only unique predictor of reduced reliance on context. Confirming the importance of including multiple measures of written language proficiency, analyses including only vocabulary and reading span as predictors showed that higher vocabulary significantly predicted higher accuracy and reduced contextual reliance but when measures of reading and spelling were added, vocabulary was no longer a significant predictor of any aspect of performance and spelling was the only variable that predicted contextual reliance. This suggests that significant effects of a single individual difference measure, like Yap et al.'s (2009, in press) findings for vocabulary, need to be interpreted cautiously.

Thus, the results of the RSVP sentence reading tasks used by Andrews and Bond (2009) and Hersch and Andrews (in press) confirm that lexical expertise, defined by the combination of above-average reading and spelling, is associated with more efficient, context-independent processing of the individual lexical constituents of a sentence, as well as with more effective integration of their meanings. We are currently extending our individual differences approach to eye-movement data collected under more naturalistic sentence-reading conditions.

Conclusions

The theories of skilled word recognition and reading elaborated in other chapters of this book have been built almost entirely on average data obtained from samples of university students. This strategy has been heuristically useful because it has allowed us to establish general principles of skilled reading behaviour without the distraction and complication of individual differences. However, there *is* considerable variability within the population of skilled readers on both psychometric measures of written language proficiency and performance in experimental psycholinguistic tasks. Such variability suggests that the development of the consolidated, orthographic representations that define fluent, skilled reading is a protracted process that depends on reading experience, rather than a discrete stage. Lexical representations are gradually tuned by reading experience to facilitate discrimination between orthographically similar words (Castles et al., 2007). The differential success and extent of this tuning is still evident in the behavioural data for samples of above-average readers, when early lexical retrieval is tapped using the masked priming task, and is most uniquely predicted by measures of spelling (Andrews & Hersch, 2010; Andrews and Lo, 2012). Readers' success in developing high-quality lexical representations also determines the extent to which they need to use context to identify words and therefore the balance between bottom-up and top-down processes in on-line reading (Andrews & Bond, 2009; Hersch & Andrews, in press).

These findings address an important gap in the literature on visual word recognition. Systematic psycholinguistic research has yielded a deep understanding of the 'average skilled reader'. But we know little about individual differences amongst competent readers. Addressing this gap in our knowledge is, however, important. At a theoretical level, we need to ensure that the ongoing refinements of detailed, computational accounts of word identification are not based on a misleading 'average reader' that obscures important theoretical distinctions that should influence model refinement. At a practical level, evidence from highly skilled readers can provide insight into the causal role played by high-quality lexical representations that are difficult to detect at earlier stages of reading development but have potentially important implications for how reading should be taught.

- Most theories of skilled visual word recognition have been based on average data for relatively small samples of university students, despite the wide variability in reading, spelling and vocabulary known to exist in such samples.
- Results for 'the average reader' might obscure systematic individual differences in the cognitive processing that could challenge current theories of visual word recognition.
- Developing the precise orthographic representations of words that most theories assume to be essential for skilled reading is likely to be a slow, gradual process that remains a source of individual differences among skilled readers.

- The masked form priming task provides a window on the early stages of lexical retrieval. Evidence that spelling ability predicts the direction of form priming confirms that the task taps individual differences in lexical precision.
- Readers who fail to develop precise lexical representations must rely more heavily on context to identify words. This prediction is confirmed by evidence that above average reading and spelling is associated with less reliance on context in tasks requiring rapid processing of sentences.

Note

1 Orthographic neighbours have been most frequently defined using Coltheart, Davelaar, Jonasson, and Besner's (1977) N metric which counts the number of words that can be created by changing one letter of the target word. Words with many vs few such neighbours will be referred to as 'High N' and 'Low N', respectively.

References

Acheson, D.J., Wells, J.B., & MacDonald, M. (2008) New and updated tests of print exposure and reading abilities in college students. *Behavior Research Methods*, *40*, 278–279.

Andrews, S. (1997) The role of orthographic similarity in lexical retrieval: Resolving neighborhood conflicts. *Psychonomic Bulletin and Review*, *4*, 439–461.

Andrews, S. (2008) Lexical expertise and reading skill. In B.H. Ross (Ed.), *The psychology of learning and motivation: Advances in research and theory (Vol. 49)* (pp. 247–281). San Diego: Elsevier Academic Press.

Andrews, S. & Bond, R. (2009) Lexical expertise and reading skill: Bottom-up and top-down processing of lexical ambiguity. *Reading and Writing*, *22*, 687–711.

Andrews, S. & Heathcote, A. (2001) Distinguishing common and task-specific processes in lexical retrieval: A matter of some moment? *Journal of Experimental Psychology: Learning Memory and Cognition*, *27*, 514–544.

Andrews, S. & Hersch, J. (2009) Individual differences in masked neighbour priming: Lexical precision or different decision strategies? Paper presented at the Australian Language and Speech Conference, University of New South Wales, December 2009.

Andrews S. & Hersch, J. (2010) Lexical precision in skilled readers: Individual differences in masked neighbor priming. *Journal of Experimental Psychology: General*, *139*, 299–318.

Andrews, S., & Lo, S. (2012) Not all skilled readers have cracked the code: Individual differences in masked form priming. *Journal of Experimental Psychology: Learning Memory and Cognition*, *38*, 152–163.

Borowsky, R. & Besner, D. (2000). Lexical access codes in visual word recognition: Are the joint effects of context and stimulus quality diagnostic? *Canadian Journal of Experimental Psychology*, *54*, 196–207.

Bowey, J., & Muller, D. (2005) Phonological recoding and rapid orthographic learning in third-graders' silent reading: A critical test of the self-teaching hypothesis. *Journal of Experimental Child Psychology*, *92*, 203–219.

Brown, J.L., Fishco, V.V., & Hanna, G. (1993) *Nelson-Denny Reading Test (Forms G&H)*. Austin, TX: Pro-Ed.

Brown, P., Lupker, S.J., & Colombo, L. (1994) Interacting sources of information in word naming: A study of individual differences. *Journal of Experimental Psychology: Human Perception and Performance, 20*, 537–554.

Burt, J. S. (2006). Spelling in adults: The combined influences of language skills and reading experience. *Journal of Psycholinguistic Research, 35*, 447–470.

Byrne, B. (1998) *The foundation of literacy: The child's acquisition of the alphabetic principle*. Hove, England: Psychology Press.

Carr, T.H. (1999) Trying to understand dyslexia: Mental chronometry, individual differences, cognitive neuroscience and the impact of instruction as converging sources of evidence. In R.M. Klein and P.A. McMullen (Eds), *Converging methods for understanding reading and dyslexia*. Cambridge, MA: MIT Press.

Castles, A. & Coltheart, M. (2004). Is there a causal link from phonological awareness to success in learning to read? *Cognition, 91*, 77–111.

Castles, A., Davis, C., & Letcher, T. (1999) Neighborhood effects on masked form priming in developing readers. *Language and Cognitive Processes, 14*, 201–224.

Castles, A., Davis, C., Cavalot, P., & Forster, K. (2007) Tracking the acquisition of orthographic skills in developing readers: Masked priming effects. *Journal of Experimental Child Psychology, 97*, 165–182.

Catts, H.W., Adlof, S.M., & Weismer, S.E. (2006). Language deficits in poor comprehenders: A case for the simple view of reading. *Journal of Speech Language and Hearing Research, 49*, 278–293.

Chateau, D. & Jared, D. (2000) Exposure to print and word recognition process. *Memory & Cognition, 28*, 143–153.

Cohen, L., Dehaene, S., Vinckier, F., Jobert, A., & Montavont, A. (2008). Reading normal and degraded words: Contribution of the dorsal and ventral visual pathways. *Neuroimage, 40*, 353–366.

Coltheart, M., Davelaar, E., Jonasson, J.T., & Besner, D. (1977). Access to the internal lexicon. In S. Dornic (Ed.), *Attention and performance VI* (pp. 535–555). Hillsdale, NJ: Erlbaum.

Coltheart, M., Rastle, K., Perry, C., Langdon, R., & Ziegler, J. (2001) DRC: A dual route cascaded model of visual word recognition and reading aloud. *Psychological Review, 108*, 204–256.

Davis, C.J. (2010) The spatial coding model of visual word identification. *Psychological Review, 117*, 713–758.

Davis, C.J & Lupker, S.J. (2006) Masked inhibitory priming in English: Evidence for lexical inhibition. *Journal of Experimental Psychology: Human Perception and Performance, 32*, 668–687.

Eason, S.H. & Cutting, L.E. (2009) Examining sources of poor comprehension in older poor readers. In R.K. Wagner, C. Schatschneider, & C. Phythian-Sence (Eds), *Beyond decoding: The behavioral and biological foundations of reading comprehension* (pp. 263–286). NY: Guilford.

Ehri, L.C. (1992) Reconceptualizing the development of sight word reading and its relationship to decoding. In P. Gough, L.C. Ehri, and R. Treiman (Eds), *Reading acquisition*. Hillsdale, NJ: Erlbaum.

Ehri, L. (2005) Development of sight word reading: Phases and findings. In M.J. Snowling and C. Hulme (Eds), *The science of reading*. Cornwall, UK: Blackwell.

Forster, K.I. & Davis, C. (1984) Repetition priming and frequency attenuation in lexical access. *Journal of Experimental Psychology: Learning, Memory and Cognition, 10,* 680–686.

Forster, K.I. & Taft, M. (1994) Bodies, antibodies and neighborhood-density effects in masked form priming. *Journal of Experimental Psychology: Learning, Memory, and Cognition, 20,* 844–863.

Forster, K.I., Davis, C., Schoknecht, C., & Carter, R. (1987) Masked priming with graphemically related forms: Repetition or partial activation? *Quarterly Journal of Experimental Psychology, 39,* 211–251.

Freebody, P. & Byrne, B. (1988) Word reading strategies in elementary school children: Relations to comprehension, reading time, and phonemic awareness. *Reading Research Quarterly, 23,* 441–453.

Frith, U. (1986) A developmental framework for developmental dyslexia. *Annals of Dyslexia, 36,* 69–81.

Gough, P. B. & Wren, S. (1998). The decomposition of decoding. In C. Hulme and Joshi, R. M. (Eds), *Reading and spelling: Development and disorders* (pp. 19–32). Mahwah, NJ: Lawrence Erlbaum Associates.

Grainger, J. (2008) Cracking the orthographic code: An introduction. *Language and Cognitive Processes, 23,* 1–35.

Guerrera, C. & Forster, K. I. (2008). Masked form priming with extreme transpositions. *Language and Cognitive Processes, 23,* 117–142.

Hersch, J. & Andrews, S. (in press) Lexical expertise and reading skill: Bottom-up and top-down contributions to sentence processing. *Scientific Studies of Reading.* DOI:10.1080/10888438.2011.564244

Holmes, V.M., Malone, A.M., & Redenbach, H. (2008) Orthographic processing and visual sequential memory in unexpectedly poor spellers. *Journal of Research in Reading, 31,* 136–156.

Huey, E.B. (1908/1968) *The psychology and pedagogy of reading.* Cambridge, MA: MIT Press (reprinted 1968).

Jackson, N. E. & Coltheart, M. (2001). *Routes to reading success and failure: Toward an integrated cognitive psychology of atypical reading.* New York: Psychology Press

Juel, C., Griffith, P.L., & Gough, P.B. (1986) Acquisition of literacy: A longitudinal study of children in first and second grade. *Journal of Educational Psychology, 78,* 243–255.

Kamhi, A.H. & Hinton, L.N. (2000) Explaining individual differences in spelling ability. *Topics in Language Disorders, 20,* 37–49.

Keenan, J.M., Olson, R.K. & Betjemann R.S. (2008) Assessment and etiology of individual differences in reading comprehension. In R.K. Wagner, C. Schatschneider, & C. Phythian-Sence (Eds), *Beyond decoding: The behavioral and biological foundations of reading comprehension* (pp. 227–245). New York: Guilford.

Kinoshita, S. & Lupker, S. (Eds) (2003) *Masked priming: The state of the art.* New York: Psychology Press.

Logan, G.D. (2002) An instance theory of attention and memory. *Psychological Review, 109,* 376–400.

Martin-Chang, S.L. & Gould, O.N. (2008) Revisiting print exposure: Exploring differential links to vocabulary, comprehension and reading rate. *Journal of Research in Reading, 31,* 273–284.

Masterson, J., Laxon, J., Lovejoy, S., & Morris (2007) Phonological skill, lexical decision and letter report in good and poor adult spellers. *Journal of Research in Reading, 30,* 429–442.

Norris, D. & Kinoshita, S. (2008). Perception as evidence accumulation and Bayesian inference: Insights from masked priming. *Journal of Experimental Psychology: General*, *137*, 434–455.

Patterson, K. (1986) Lexical but nonsemantic spelling. *Cognitive Neuropsychology*, *3*, 341–367.

Perfetti, C.A. (1985) *Reading ability*. New York: Oxford University Press.

Perfetti, C.A. (1992) The representation problem in reading acquisition. In P.B. Gough, L.C. Ehri, & R. Treiman (Eds), *Reading acquisition* (pp. 145–174). Hillsdale, NJ, England: Lawrence Erlbaum Associates.

Perfetti, C.A. (2007) Reading ability: Lexical quality to comprehension. *Scientific Studies of Reading*, *11*, 357–383.

Perfetti, C. & Hart, L. (2001) The lexical basis of comprehension skill. In D. Gorfein (Ed.), *On the consequences of meaning selection: Perspectives on resolving lexical ambiguity* (pp. 67–86). Washington DC: American Psychological Association.

Perry, C., Ziegler, J.C., & Zorzi, M. (2007). Nested incremental modeling in the development of computational theories: The CDP+ model of reading aloud. *Psychological Review*, *114*, 273–315.

Perry, J.R., Lupker, S.J., & Davis, C.J. (2008) An evaluation of the interactive-activation model using masked partial-word priming. *Language and Cognitive Processes*, *23*, 36–68.

Potter, M.C., Stiefbold, D., & Moryadas, A. (1998) Word selection in reading sentences: Preceding versus following contexts. *Journal of Experimental Psychology: Learning, Memory, and Cognition*, *24*, 68–100.

Protopapas, A., Archonti, A., & Skaloumbakas, C. (2007) Reading ability is negatively related to Stroop interference. *Cognitive Psychology*, *54*, 251–282.

Pugh, K.R, Mencl, W.E., Jenner, A.R., Lee, J.R., Katz, L., Frost, S.J, Shaywitz, S.E., & Shaywitz, B.A. (2001) Neuroimaging studies of reading development and reading disability. *Learning Disabilities Research & Practice*, *16*, 240–249.

Ratcliff, R., Gomez, P., and McKoon, G. (2004). A diffusion model account of the lexical decision task. *Psychological Review*, *111*, 159–182

Rayner, K., Yang, J., Castelhano, M.S., & Liversedge, S.P. (2011) Eye movements of older and younger readers when reading disappearing text. *Psychology and Aging*, *26*, 214–223.

Sears, C. R., Siakaluk, P. D., Chow, V., and Buchanan, L. (2008). Is there an effect of print exposure on the word frequency effect and the neighborhood size effect? *Journal of Psycholinguistic Research*, *37*, 269–291.

Share, D.L. (1995) Phonological recoding and self-teaching: *sine qua non* of reading acquisition. *Cognition*, *55*, 151–218.

Share D.L. (2004) Orthographic learning at a glance: On the time course and developmental onset of self-teaching. *Journal of Experimental Child Psychology*, *87*, 267–298.

Stanovich, K.E. (1992) Speculations on the causes and consequences of individual differences in early reading acquisition. In P.B. Gough, L.C. Ehri, & R. Treiman (Eds), *Reading acquisition* (pp. 307–342). Hillsdale, NJ: Lawrence Erlbaum Associates.

Yap, M.J., Tse, C., & Balota, D.A. (2009) Individual differences in the joint effects of semantic priming and word frequency revealed by RT distributional analyses: The role of lexical integrity. *Journal of Memory and Language*, *61*, 303–325.

Yap, M.J., Balota, D.A., Sibley, D.E., & Ratcliff, R. (2012) Individual differences in visual word recognition: Insights from the English Lexicon Project. *Journal of Experimental Psychology: Human Perception and Performance*, *38*, 53–79.

8 Orthographic learning and the development of visual word recognition

Nicola A. McClung, Colleen R. O'Donnell, and Anne E. Cunningham

The ability to effortlessly recognize words is arguably the most critical skill one develops while learning to read. Automatic word recognition allows the reader to allocate cognitive resources to higher-level reading processes such as adopting a high standard of story coherence, attending to the syntactic and semantic structure of language, and evaluating and integrating text (Perfetti, 1985, 2007; Perfetti, Landi, & Oakhill, 2005; Stanovich, 1980). Simply, the development of well-specified representations of the written and spoken forms of words and their meanings supports efficient word recognition and thereby allows the reader to attend to the primary purpose of reading: gaining meaning from text. Conversely, when knowledge about a word is not fully specified, word recognition is laborious and resource demanding, meaning may be obstructed and reading unrewarding. Because word recognition is central to the ability to successfully comprehend text, it is thought to be the primary determinant of individual differences in reading performance throughout schooling (Cunningham & Stanovich, 1997; Perfetti & Bolger, 2004; Vellutino & Scanlon, 1987).

Given the importance of word recognition in overall reading proficiency, it is essential that we develop our understanding of the various processes that underlie and influence the development of this important skill. Although phonological processing has widely been held as the primary determinant of word identification (NICHD, 2000; Share, 1995; Stanovich, 1986, 2000), it is becoming increasingly clear that phonological skills cannot single-handedly explain the development of skilled word recognition. Instead, a comprehensive model of reading must also reflect the role of other components such as orthographic processing – the way that individuals process and encode the specific sequences of letters in written language (Cunningham, Perry, & Stanovich, 2001). All current major cognitive theories of word recognition – the connectionist models (Harm & Seidenberg, 1999; Plaut, 2005; Seidenberg & McClelland, 1989; Sibley and Kello, accompanying volume, Chapter 2), the dual-route model (Coltheart, accompanying volume, Chapter 1), the self-teaching model (Share, 1995, 2008), the lexical quality hypothesis (Perfetti, 1985, 2007) and developmental models (e.g., Ehri, 1992, 2005a) – although different in their accounts of skilled reading, emphasize the fact that efficient word recognition requires the acquisition of a large supply of well-specified orthographic representations that are securely linked to semantic and phonological information. In addition, they all suggest that weaknesses in the ability to acquire detailed, print-specific, knowledge of words leads to reading difficulty. Thus, developing and refining our collective understanding of how orthographic representations are acquired and how they subsequently support word recognition is of great interest in reading research.

The purpose of this chapter is to review what is currently understood about the development of orthographic skills and orthographic knowledge. To begin, we discuss the unique role of orthographic processing in word recognition and our current theoretical understanding of the way that orthographic learning occurs. We then move on to a description of the most current empirical data that both supports and enhances our understanding of the specific manner in which children acquire orthographic knowledge and orthographic learning occurs. We conclude with a brief examination of the language-specific factors that influence orthographic skills and a discussion of the challenges our field faces as we prepare to move forward in our quest to further elucidate the complicated process of becoming literate.

For the purpose of this review, we define *orthographic processing* as the ability to form, store, and access orthographic representations, which (1) specify the allowable order of letters within the orthography of a specific language; and (2) are themselves securely linked to phonological, semantic, morphological, and syntactic information within the language in which they operate (Cassar & Treiman, 1997; Cunningham, Nathan, &, Raher, 2010; Ehri, 1980; Perfetti, 1992; Reitsma, 1983a; Share, 1995; Stanovich & West, 1989). That is, we employ a definition that includes both procedural and declarative aspects of orthographic knowledge.

Establishing orthographic processing as a critical construct

Over the last three decades, we have made considerable progress in our understanding of reading development, and it is now widely accepted that phonological processing is the most influential cognitive skill involved in children's word recognition abilities (e.g., Rutter, 1978; Stanovich, 1982, 1992; Vellutino, 1979). Substantial empirical evidence has shown that the bulk of the variability in reading skill is the result of individual differences in phonological skills (Bradley & Bryant, 1983; Byrne & Fielding-Barnsley, 1993; Cunningham, 1990; Ehri, Nunes, Willows, Schuster, Yaghoub-Zadeh, & Shanahan, 2001; Hatcher, Hulme, & Ellis, 1994; Kjeldsen, Niemi, & Olofsson, 2003; Lundberg, Frost, & Peterson, 1988; NICHD, 2000; Stanovich, 1986), with dyslexics evidencing extreme difficulties in the ability to attend to the phonological structure of language (Stanovich, 2000; Vellutino & Scanlon, 1987).

Although phonological skills are generally believed to be the primary determinant of the development of skilled word identification, a growing body of research has also suggested that they cannot single-handedly explain variability in the ability to recognize words. This research has suggested that, in addition to phonological processes, visual processes represent a secondary, but significant, source of variation in word recognition, operating in a subtle, localized, and inter-active fashion (Reitsma, 1983a; Stanovich & West, 1989). Specifically, it appears that the capacity to form, store, and access orthographic representations, and the ability to connect them to phonological and semantic information, plays a unique and significant role in both reading and spelling ability (Badian, 2001; Baron & Treiman, 1980; Barker, Torgesen, & Wagner, 1992; Booth et al., 1999; Bourke & Adams, 2010; Bryant & Impey, 1986; Cunningham et al., 2001; Cunningham & Stanovich, 1990, 1993; Freebody & Byrne, 1988; Share & Shalev, 2004; Treiman, 1984; Wagner & Barker, 1994).

For example, in an early study, Cunningham and Stanovich (1990) found that although phonological processing accounted for a substantial amount of the variance in third- and fourth-grade word recognition abilities (20%), orthographic processing abilities uniquely accounted for an additional 10% of the variance. Similarly, Barker and colleagues (1992) found that when controlling for phonological processing and general cognitive ability, orthographic processing significantly predicted the speed and accuracy of word-reading in third-grade children. In another study, Cunningham and colleagues (2001) found that after the influence of phonological processing had been accounted for, a composite measure of orthographic processing coherently loaded onto a single factor that explained a considerable portion of the variance in word recognition. These findings help to substantiate theories emphasizing the importance of orthographic processing in word recognition.

Orthographic learning

Given that orthographic processing skills appear to be uniquely related to word reading, a complete understanding of reading development requires knowledge of how orthographic representations are acquired. Ultimately, our current theoreti-cal understanding suggests that the development of high-quality orthographic representations comes from experience with the very orthography one is seeking to master. Although letter names and sound-symbol correspondences can be (and should be) directly taught, for many readers, knowledge about the orthographic structure of words is acquired incidentally while reading. Specifically, each successful attempt at translating a written word into its spoken form attunes the reader to the regularities of written language and their relation to phonological, morphological, and semantic information. It is argued that the process of translat-ing written words into their spoken forms through decoding, and more specifi-cally phonological recoding, acts as a *self-teaching* device and is thought to be the central means by which detailed knowledge about the orthographic structure of words is acquired (Share, 1995, 2008). Thus, orthographic learning is thought to reflect a connection-forming process between the orthographic, phonological, and semantic aspects of words (Ehri, 1980, 1992, 2005b), or in other words, the acquisition of well-specified orthographic representations and their bindings to a word's other constituent identities that are strengthened by reading experience (Perfetti, 1985, 1992, 2007).

Theoretically, it is posited that while reading, self-teaching works as unfamiliar words are computed via spelling-to-sound translation (Share, 1995). This process generates candidate pronunciations that can be matched to words that already exist in the reader's spoken lexicon. After a word has been successfully decoded and identified, relatively few encounters are necessary to commit its printed form to memory and secure it in the orthographic lexicon (Share, 1999, 2004). Over time, a gradual tuning process helps the reader develop precise, high-quality lexical representations (Andrews, this volume, Chapter 7). Eventually, when a word's 'fully specified orthographic representation is bonded to the phonemic representation' it can be accessed efficiently (Perfetti, 1992, p. 160); that is, it can be read quickly without competing with other similar and partly activated word candidates. Once orthographic word recognition is automatic, the process becomes subconscious, and the reader cannot help but to automatically recognize words (Ehri, 2005b). As the number of words in the reader's print-based lexicon grows, the overall reading process becomes increasingly efficient (Share, 2004). Thus, it is the amalgamation of orthographic, phonological, and semantic knowledge, that comes about through reading experience, that is the foundation of automatic word identification (Ehri, 2005a; Nation, 2009).

Furthermore, theory suggests that experiences with print facilitate a growing body of orthographic knowledge. The initially useful one-to-one letter correspondences become increasingly lexicalized, through an evolving self-refining process (Andrews, this volume, Chapter 7; Perfetti, 1992; Share, 2008). For example, initially the reader must process each of the individual letter-sound correspondences in the words *bat, cat,* and *hat*. However, over time, he or she recognizes that, with very few exceptions, the *-at* letter combination has the same pronunciation when found at the end of a word. Henceforward, it is no longer necessary to process these words letter by letter. Along with additional words such as *fat, mat,* and *sat*, they can now be processed in onset-rime fashion, hastening the word identification process. Additionally, this new piece of orthographic knowledge gives the reader a leg up when reading more sophisticated words like *attitude* and *Saturday*. Eventually, after sufficient experience decoding and attending to orthographic patterns, even complicated, multisyllabic words can be automatically recognized by sight (Ehri, 2005b).

Although most of the theory and research on the acquisition of orthographic knowledge emphasizes the importance of phonological recoding, some work has drawn attention to its relationship with the spelling process (Ouellette, 2010; Treiman, 1984; Shahar-Yames & Share, 2008). Shahar-Yames and Share (2008) suggest that it is the repetitive act of connecting the spoken and written forms of language, via decoding *or* spelling, that helps to bring about the large collection of well-specified orthographic representations that are vital to skilled reading. Additionally, spelling, which requires the production, rather than merely recognition, of meaningful letters and letter patterns, may be an even more powerful mechanism for orthographic learning.

Evidence for the self-teaching hypothesis

Much of what has been described to this point are theoretical accounts of ortho-graphic learning as a means of developing efficient word recognition skills. Yet over the last two decades, an abundance of research has helped to substantiate the theoretical explanations detailed above, and, as a result of these scientific inves-tigations, the relationships between phonological recoding, spelling, and ortho-graphic learning (i.e., self-teaching) are now well documented (Bowey & Muller, 2005; Cunningham, 2006; Cunningham et al., 2002; de Jong & Share, 2007; Ehri & Saltmarsh, 1995; Kyte & Johnson, 2006; Nation, Angell, & Castles, 2007; Reitsma, 1983a; Share, 1999, 2004; Sprenger-Charolles, Siegel, Béchennec, & Serniclaes, 2003).

Much of the research investigating orthographic learning and its relation to overall word learning has relied on a methodology first designed and imple-mented by David Share (1999). In this paradigm, children read short passages embedded with unknown target words simulating the experience of a novice reader encountering an unfamiliar word in text. Target words are guaranteed to be unknown to children through the use of pseudowords designed to be both orthographically and phonologically plausible (e.g., *sloak*, introduced and defined in the text as 'the hottest town in the world'; Share, 2008). Typically, children are asked to read aloud the passages containing the target word, and then various post-test measures are implemented to determine whether they have acquired detailed word-specific orthographic knowledge of each novel stimulus. For example, the *homophone choice task* is a post-test measure that assesses the child's ability to correctly identify the spelling of the target words when he or she is presented with a homophonic alternative (e.g., *sloak* and *sloke*). Given that both words sound the same when they are decoded, and that both spelling patterns are common in print, the assumption is that correct identification of the target words over the foils at above-chance levels indicates that the child must be responding on the basis of functional orthographic representations rather than knowledge of the phonological structure of the word or general knowledge of orthographically plausible spellings (Share, 1999).

Employing the above-mentioned design, a number of studies have provided evidence for the self-teaching hypothesis. Share's seminal study demonstrated that children could distinguish a target word from a homophonic foil and two nonhomophonic, but visually similar spellings (i.e., one with two adjacent letters transposed, and the other with a visually-similar single-letter substitution) 74% of time. In addition, he found that naming times for the target words were signifi-cantly faster than for foils, and in spelling production tasks, target words were correctly spelled a significantly greater portion of the time (41%), compared to foils (10%). In a second experiment, Share exposed children to target words while they engaged in irrelevant concurrent vocalization or articulation (i.e., the child was asked to repeat the pseudoword *dubba* when viewing the target word), which was presumed to minimize phonological recoding. Post-tests showed that the children had acquired significantly less orthographic knowledge of the targets during the concurrent articulation condition than in the read-aloud condition, suggesting that mere visual exposure was not enough to stimulate orthographic learning. Share's initial study provided supportive evidence for the self-teaching hypothesis: the act of phonologically recoding novel stimuli leads to acquisition of knowledge about the detailed orthographic structure of words.

Subsequent investigations have extended and provided converging evidence for Share's initial study. In 2002, Cunningham and colleagues examined orthographic learning and the self-teaching hypothesis in second-grade children. They found evidence of self-teaching in a substantial correlation ($r = 0.52$) between orthographic learning and the number of target homophones correctly decoded during story reading. When children went through the decoding process necessary to accurately identify the unfamiliar words, they were also more likely to correctly identify their correct spelling in post-tests.

Kyte and Johnson (2006) provided further evidence for the role of the self-teaching mechanism in word learning. Replicating Share's initial investigation, they compared orthographic learning after children were presented with target words in a read-aloud condition promoting phonological recoding, and a concurrent articulation condition presumed to diminish phonological recoding. Results indicated that reading aloud facilitated greater orthographic learning than the concurrent articulation condition. Together, these studies' results converge, thus supporting Share's (1995, 2008) hypothesis that phonological recoding is the primary mechanism or 'self-teacher' by which children acquire information about the orthographic structure of words.

Refining our understanding of self-teaching, Shahar-Yames and Share (2008) suggested that spelling might be an even more powerful self-teaching mechanism than reading because it requires closer attention to the order and identity of letters and their relation to their phonological counterparts. In order to test this hypothesis, third graders were assigned to one of three conditions: (1) a spelling condition in which the children were asked to read a passage containing novel pseudoword targets and immediately following were asked to spell them; (2) a reading condition in which the children read a passage and immediately following were asked to respond to simple questions about the passage; or (3) a control condition in which the children did not participate in a learning trial (i.e., participated in the post-test session only). Controls were in place to ensure that the length of training sessions was consistent across the first two conditions and that children were exposed to the target words (orally and in writing) the same number of times. As predicted, significantly more orthographic learning was evidenced in the spelling condition compared to the reading and control conditions. Similarly, in a subsequent study, Ouellette (2010) found that significantly more orthographic learning occurred when second-grade children practiced spelling words compared to when they were asked to read them. Although additional research is necessary to confirm our understanding of spelling as a significant mechanism for orthographic learning, these recent studies provide preliminary evidence of the powerful role of spelling in self-teaching, beyond that of phonological recoding.

Exploring the precise nature of orthographic learning

Overall, once children have developed a degree of phonological sensitivity and knowledge of symbol-sound correspondences, phonological recoding and spelling enable them to master word-specific orthographic patterns and become more efficient at word identification. However, the process of learning to effortlessly identify words is immensely complicated, and self-teaching does not occur one word at a time in simulated, controlled learning trials. Instead, orthographic learning and self-teaching occur during everyday reading and learning experiences and are thus impacted by the wide variety of factors present in these contexts. A comprehensive understanding of the orthographic learning process must be dynamic and reflect the complexities of the conditions in which the learning occurs. Over the last decade, researchers have made substantial progress towards identifying the features of authentic reading experiences that impact orthographic learning and refining our understanding of the orthographic learning process.

Print exposure

Given knowledge that orthographic learning occurs during the process of reading itself (and not simply as a prerequisite to the ability to read), it is reasonable to assume that general experiences with reading might have an impact on the orthographic learning process. It is likely that variation in the quality of developing orthographic representations 'arise[s] through literacy and language experiences ... [including] ... learning to decode printed words, practice in reading and writing, and engagement with concepts and their language forms' (Perfetti, 2007, p. 380). For this reason, the relationship between general exposure to print and orthographic learning has been thoroughly examined.

Several studies demonstrate that experience with print makes a significant contribution to the development of orthographic processing skills (Barker et al., 1992; Braten, Lie, Andreassen, & Olaussen, 1999; Booth et al., 1999; Cunningham & Stanovich, 1990; Chateau & Jared, 2000; Ehri & Saltmarsh, 1995; Mesman & Kibby, 2011; Olson, Forsberg, Wise, & Rack, 1994). For example, Cunningham and Stanovich (1990) initially proposed that exposure to print plays a key role in the growth of children's orthographic processing skills. They administered a battery of assessments including measures of general intellectual functioning, word recognition, phonological processing, orthographic processing, and exposure to print to third- and fourth-grade children to test their hypothesis. As discussed above, hierarchical multiple regression analyses indicated that, indeed, individual differences in orthographic processing accounted for unique variance in word recognition abilities. Results of subsequent analyses, aimed at establishing the determinants of orthographic processing, revealed a unique role for print exposure, independent of other cognitive and reading-related skills. Cunningham and Stanovich's findings suggest that the more volume a child reads, the more orthographic representations are strengthened and refined, and ultimately, the more they support the comprehension of text.

Research has also indicated that repeated exposures to individual words are necessary to allow the self-teaching process to occur. However, even after the self-teaching process has transpired, and the reader begins to recognize a word by sight, further experience reading the word as a single unit continues to enhance and strengthen detailed knowledge about its written form. That is, multiple exposures to a word in authentic text secure orthographic information in memory, making it *autonomous* (identifiable without reliance on phonological recoding or context), *precise* (well-specified), and *redundant* (secured to phonological and semantic information; Ehri, 1980, 1992; Perfetti & Hart, 2001; Share, 1995). As a result, increased levels of exposure to print (i.e., more reading experience) hone orthographic knowledge and make reading more efficient.

Silent versus oral reading

Most of the experimental research on self-teaching has involved children reading short passages *aloud* and has thus shown that phonological recoding aids the reader in forming reliable knowledge about the orthographic structure of words. However, most authentic reading, at least after about the third grade, is done silently. Given this contrast, Bowey and Muller (2005) raised the question of whether the read-aloud procedure utilized in previous investigations of self-teaching, that explicitly activates the phonological system, is representative of the majority of natural (i.e., silent) reading. In other words, perhaps self-teaching as described by Share and others occurs when children are reading aloud, but not when they are reading silently – the very condition under which learning must occur in order for children to master the volume of orthographic knowledge that is necessary to read skillfully. To explore this issue, Bowey and colleagues conducted an experiment involving silent reading of short texts containing target psuedowords. Post-tests, both immediately following the text reading and after a 6-day delay, demonstrated that children were able to name target pseudowords significantly faster than homophonic alternatives, indicating the formation of functional orthographic representations seemingly through the recoding process. Additionally, in an orthographic-choice task, children showed a significant preference for target pseudowords over homophonic alternatives. This result suggests that children had phonologically recoded targets during silent reading, which was enough to stimulate sensitivity to the orthographic features of words. Subsequent work by Bowey and Miller (2007), de Jong and Share (2007), and de Jong et al. (2009) provide converging evidence that silent reading also engages the powerful self-teaching mechanism, thereby bringing about detailed knowledge of the printed word.

Context

One criticism of the research investigating self-teaching has been its use of artificial stimuli. When pseudowords are utilized to assess orthographic learning, participants are unable to use contextual and meaning-based information to aid in the word identification process as they might in authentic reading situations. Because we suspect that the vast majority of orthographic learning occurs during independent reading, it is equally important to examine the facilitative or limiting role that context may play.

To investigate this issue, Cunningham (2006) analyzed the effects of context in a study designed to simulate everyday reading. In this study, first graders were designated to one of two conditions: (1) a story condition in which participants were exposed to real-word targets embedded within the context of a real story; or (2) a scrambled condition in which participants were exposed to real-word targets, but the words in the story had been scrambled such that the text was nonsensical (i.e., provided no contextual support). Targets were words likely to be familiar in spoken language but not yet automatized in print. The children were then evaluated in their ability to distinguish targets from their pseudohomophonic mates (e.g., bored/bord, chews/chooze, course/corse). When the impact of context was examined, a reliable difference was observed between conditions in children's accuracy of word identification. Children in the story condition outperformed their peers in the scrambled condition 84–67% in their ability to accurately decode words in the passage. Furthermore, in comparison to their peers who were asked to read words out of context, children who had the support of context were more likely to subsequently demonstrate evidence of orthographic learning, likely due to the higher accuracy of word identification during passage reading. However, even in the scrambled condition, children displayed evidence of self-teaching in that, on post-test measures, they were also significantly more likely to successfully identify target words that had been correctly decoded during passage reading. Cunningham maintained that while context may be facilitative, its absence does not preclude the reader from phonologically recoding novel words and engaging in the self-teaching process. Thus, self-teaching and orthographic learning persist regardless of whether a child has the benefit of contextual reading.

In a subsequent study, Nation et al. (2007) examined the role of context among similarly aged children, ranging from 7 to 8 years of age. The design of this experiment was slightly different than that employed by Cunningham (2006) in that children were exposed to real-word targets in either a meaningful story (i.e., context) condition or in an isolated word reading (i.e., no context) condition. Consistent with Cunningham (2006), Nation et al. (2007) found evidence of durable orthographic learning in both the context and no-context conditions. In contrast to Cunningham, however, Nation and her colleagues found no evidence that context was any more facilitative of self-teaching than no-context was. When Ricketts, Bishop, Pimperton, and Nation (2011) examined orthographic learning in a similar group of children in two different context conditions – words embedded in text such that their meanings could be directly inferred or in a story context that gave clues about the general category of the word – they found that context did not have an effect on word learning.

It is also useful to consider whether readers engage different sets of cognitive skills depending on the demands of the reading task. For example, readers may rely more on contextual information when reading irregular words than they do when regular words (Zeigler & Goswami, 2005). Exploring this possibility, Wang, Castles, Nickels, and Nation (2011) presented second-grade children with regular and irregular words in context (i.e., stories) and no-context (i.e., word lists) conditions. They found a significant facilitative effect of context during irregular word reading but not for regular word reading. These findings suggest that readers deploy decoding skills when a word's spelling is regular, while they may rely more on context when phonological information is not readily available in the word's orthography (i.e., in the case of irregular words).

The results of the studies presented thus far would suggest that while context may or may not provide added value, it certainly does not limit or hinder orthographic learning in any way. In contrast, a study conducted by Landi, Perfetti, Bolger, Dunlap, and Foorman (2006) suggested otherwise. These researchers found that although context facilitated decoding and word identification, children's retention of word forms (i.e., orthographic knowledge) was better when the word was read in isolation. They hypothesized that because context facilitated the identification of unfamiliar words, children were less likely to attend to the word's unique phonological and orthographic structure and, thus, context had a limiting effect on the orthographic learning process. However, Landi et al. found that the benefit of isolated word reading was greater for less skilled readers than for more skilled readers. Readers with weaker decoding skills might be more likely to rely on context for accurate word identification (Perfetti, 1985; Stanovich, 1980, 1986), and as a result, during contextual reading, they fail to engage in the letter-by-letter analysis that is necessary for durable orthographic learning. Yet, when these same children read words in isolation they are forced to employ their decoding skills and attend to the orthographic and phonological features of the word, hence improving their word retention. It is evident that the discrepant results obtained in the projects described above highlight the need for additional research in this area.

Semantics

Given that semantic factors may play a role in cognitive learning processes (Plaut, McClelland, Seidenberg, & Patterson, 1996; Seidenberg & McClelland, 1989), it is useful to consider the influence of semantics on orthographic learning. As mentioned previously, one of the critiques of research on orthographic learning has been the use of artificial stimuli or pseudowords. Critics have suggested that the use of pseudowords does not allow for the potential use of context and word meanings (including morphological information) in the word identification process. A related question is the extent to which the absence of semantic information, inherent in the use of pseudowords, might also jeopardize the generalizability of the current empirical data. Even when pseudowords are embedded within connected text, which might allow context to provide support to the reader in ascertaining word meanings, texts vary in the extent to which the context supports the development of word knowledge (Ouelette & Fraser, 2009). As a result, it is difficult to know whether context is sufficient to allow a child to infer a word's meaning and, accordingly, whether that information aids the child in his or her ability to form and maintain orthographic representations.

While the studies presented thus far represent the most current information available about the general role of context, research on the specific impact of semantics is relatively recent. There is some evidence, however, to suggest that orthographic learning is, in fact, enhanced when information about a word's meaning is available. Investigating the role of semantics during the acquisition of word-specific orthographic representations, Ouellette and Fraser (2009) devised a study whereby children were presented with 10 target pseudowords, five of which were accompanied by semantic information – a short definition and a drawing that depicted the target as described by the definition. Orthographic learning was significantly greater for words that were presented with the semantic information than words that were presented in isolation. Furthermore, children's phonological and semantic skills were found to be significantly predictive of orthographic learning. These findings, along with additional work by Ouellette (2010) and Taylor, Plunkett, and Nation (2011), suggest that word learning involves the amalgamation of phonological, orthographic, and semantic processes.

In contrast, Ricketts et al. (2011) found that semantic knowledge did not relate to orthographic learning after controlling for target decoding and nonverbal reasoning and that decoding (i.e., self-teaching) was the strongest predictor of word learning. However, they also noted that there were differences in control variables (e.g., independent measures of decoding versus target word decoding) and inconsistencies in the items across the different studies; in sum, findings on the role of semantics in orthographic learning are mixed and further research in this area is warranted.

Orthographic processing across languages

At this point, we have discussed many of the factors involved in the general orthographic learning process. Although the development of well-specified orthographic representations is a universal aspect of skilled reading, learning occurs within the context of a particular linguistic system, and thus can be impacted by the characteristics of the orthography (Ehri, 2005a, 2005b; Zeigler & Goswami, 2005). Accordingly, our understanding of word recognition is greatly enhanced by theoretical and empirical work that accounts for differences in learning across orthographies. Alphabetic languages differ significantly in the extent to which individual phonological units are identifiable in the spoken language (i.e., *syllabic complexity*), in the consistency of spelling-to-sound correspondences (i.e., *orthographic depth*[1]), and in the size of the most regular units of the orthography (i.e., whether the language is regular at the individual letter level or if larger units of the language lead to greater regularity; *granularity* of the language); as a result, there is considerable variation in how learning occurs across languages (Frost, 2005; Seymour, Aro, Erskine, and in Collaboration with COST Action A8 network, 2003; Zeigler & Goswami, 2005).

Although there is mounting evidence that the ability to form, store, and access orthographic information is a universal aspect of reading, readers of regular orthographies (e.g., pointed Hebrew) may have less of a need to attend to word-specific orthographic detail early in the learning process. Facilitated by the regularity of small units in their orthography, they operate on a primarily bottom-up level. That is, they are able to focus almost exclusively on the relatively straightforward (typically one-to-one) relationship between letters and sounds in their script (Share, 2004, 2008). Conversely, in an irregular orthography like English, where knowledge of a small set of one-to-one grapheme-phoneme correspondences may bootstrap the learning process, the reader must become quickly attuned to the fact that the orthography is more consistent at the level of the spellings-bodies/pronunciations-rimes than at the level of the individual letter (Zeigler & Goswami, 2005). For example, while most individual letters represent multiple sounds (e.g., the letter 'c' maps to both the /k/ sound and the /s/ sound), there is more spelling-to-pronunciation consistency in larger units of the orthography. As a result, in many cases, it is more reliable to use rhyme analogy (e.g., using *fight* to read *tight* and *light*) than to employ a serial letter-by-letter decoding strategy (Goswami, 1986, 1988).

Deep orthographies, such as that of English, which have multiple scales of correspondence between their written and spoken forms (i.e., symbols correspond to sounds at the letter/sound, spelling-body/pronunciation-rime, and whole-word levels) require the emerging reader to learn a vast number of both small and large orthographic units (Van Orden & Kloos, 2005). For example, 'to decode the most frequent 3,000 monosyllabic English words…a child needs to learn mappings between approximately 600 different orthographic patterns and 400 phonological rimes' (Zeigler & Goswami, 2005, p. 19). Needless to say, this is dramatically more than the mere 26 mappings they would need to learn if the language had one scale of correspondence and each letter mapped to only one sound. As a result, deep orthographies such as English appear to force the phonological recoding mechanism to operate flexibly at multiple scales of correspondence between spelling and sound. That is, skilled readers of a deep orthography must employ a decoding strategy that makes use of both the small and large units in the orthography (Goswami, Ziegler, Dalton, & Schneider, 2001). For comparison, in the Finnish orthography, phoneme-grapheme correspondences are highly regular with only 16 consonant phonemes and eight vowel phonemes; with only one exception, these phonemes correspond to single-letter graphemes and, thus, once a Finnish child has learned the 23 symmetrical phoneme/grapheme correspondence rules, he or she has a tool for reading or spelling any word encountered in text (Lyytinen, Aro, Holopainen, Leiwo, Lyytinen, & Tolvanen, 2006).

Differences in the letter-sound consistency across words within the same language may also affect the acquisition of orthographic knowledge. For example, the English language contains both regular and irregular words, and it is thought that the establishment of precise and autonomous representations of irregular words may require more exposures than regular words and may be more challenging to acquire (Burt & Blackwell, 2008; McKague, Davis, Pratt, & Johnston, 2008; Ricketts, Bishop, & Nation, 2008). Overall, the development of well-specified orthographic knowledge in a deep orthography may, out of necessity, require greater cognitive flexibility, continual adjustment to the higher-order regularities of the script, and more learning trials (Share, 2004).

The developmental onset of self-teaching

The onset of the orthographic learning process is an area that is perhaps best explored within the context of cross-linguistic data. The acquisition of orthographic knowledge has consistently been evidenced in young children; however, there is some indication that the need to develop early sensitivity to print-specific information may be unique to the demands of irregular orthographies. For example, Cassar and Treiman (1997) found that English-speaking children are sensitive to orthographic patterns very early in the process of learning to read. In this study, kindergarten children were shown pairs of pseudowords, one created with a legal double-letter spelling and one with an illegal doublet (e.g. *pess/ppes and baff/ bbaf*). They were then asked to identify which of the two words looked more like a real word. Results indicated that the children were significantly more likely to choose the orthographically legal spelling, suggesting that even at the very early stages of formal reading instruction, English-speaking children have already begun to attend to the dominant orthographic patterns in their orthography. Similarly, in a study examining printed word learning in beginning readers of the moderately irregular Dutch language, Reitsma (1983a) asked young (i.e., 7- and 8-year-old) children to read aloud meaningful sentences containing target words that were considered familiar in spoken language but not in print. They named targets significantly more quickly than homophonic foils (both targets and homophonic foils were equally plausible phonologically), providing evidence that the children had acquired word-specific orthographic knowledge of the target words.

In contrast, when Share (2004) examined orthographic learning in the highly regular pointed Hebrew writing system, he found that although beginning Hebrew readers (i.e., first graders) had greater decoding skill than the children in the previously mentioned English and Dutch studies, they were relatively insensitive to the orthographic features of words. Share concluded that young Israeli children might not have a need to attend to orthographic surface information because of the Hebrew language's straightforward relationship between spelling and sound. That is, a competent beginning reader of Hebrew can make use of the orthography's reliable letter-sound algorithm to read almost any unknown word. Furthermore, he hypothesized that letter-by-letter decoding may initially exhaust cognitive resources and thus prevent readers of shallow orthographies from attending to orthographic information.

Nevertheless, although readers of highly consistent orthographies may have less of a need or capability to attend to spelling patterns early on, as they advance through schooling, experience with text enables, and skilled reading requires, their attunement to the orthographic structure of the printed word. While Share's (2004) study suggested that novice readers were insensitive to orthographic structures, the study also provided evidence of a print-specific processing advantage in older Hebrew readers. Results of an experiment with third-grade children suggest that most typical readers of Hebrew (and possibly other highly consistent scripts) exhibit orthographic learning after considerable reading experience. Share hypothesized that extensive reading experience in a regular script brings about an important shift in orthographic sensitivity, whereby the more experienced and efficient reader absorbs item-specific sublexical orthographic information that is beyond the level of the novice.

Speed of acquisition and durability of orthographic learning

Share's (2004) findings not only enhance our understanding of when orthographic learning begins, but also our understanding of how quickly the learning occurs and how durable it is. His work also demonstrated that Hebrew-speaking third graders had gained orthographic knowledge after a single exposure to a novel word and that the learning was maintained for up to 30 days. Share argued that this finding was consistent with logistic learning algorithms postulated by the connectionist models, where the first learning trial is thought to be the most powerful (e.g., Harm & Seidenberg, 1999, 2004). In an attempt to explore this exposure issue further, Nation and colleagues (2007) provided English-speaking children with one, two, and four exposures to words and evaluated their ability to retain print-specific information after 1 and 7 days. Children exhibited slight orthographic learning after a single exposure to a target word when assessed after 1 day; however unlike Share's results, it was not maintained after 7 days. Two trials produced moderate learning outcomes after 7 days, and four appeared to be sufficient to retain knowledge of spelling patterns. Although these findings raise doubts about the efficiency of single-trial learning (or at least the efficiency of single-trial learning in an irregular orthography), durable learning in typically developing readers has consistently been detected after four exposures (Ehri & Saltmarsh 1995; Reitsma, 1983a, 1989; Share, 1999), and there is some evidence of learning following just three (Hogaboam & Perfetti, 1978) or even two exposures (Reitsma, 1983a,b, 1989).[2] Regardless of whether the specific number of exposures necessary varies slightly across languages, these results indicate that only a few learning trials appear to be sufficient to secure the printed forms of words in memory.

Phonology primary and orthography secondary

It is clear from the studies described above that if we are to understand the role of orthographic learning in word recognition, we must take into account how various aspects of reading may be dependent on the demands of the particular orthography. It has also been suggested that readers respond to the characteristics of their script and, therefore, in part, the language itself may shape the learning process. For example, in shallow orthographies, phonological recoding may be sufficient for successful word identification, whereas in deep orthographies, the reader may need to rely more heavily on the ability to draw on contextual and orthographic information (Zeigler & Goswami, 2005). As a result, researchers have began to explore the universality of the widely accepted notion that phonology is the primary constituent of word recognition and that orthography is an important, yet secondary source of variance in word recognition.

For example, examining the relative roles of phonology and orthography across dimensions of orthographic depth, Share (2007) utilized a within-subjects self-teaching design in two scripts. He presented a group of third-grade children with pointed and unpointed Hebrew passages containing unknown target words and assessed them on array of cognitive measures. (Pointed Hebrew is thought to be relatively shallow compared to deeper unpointed Hebrew.) Although decoding and orthographic learning were roughly the same in both orthographies, results indicated that there were fundamental differences in how the children processed the scripts. Specifically, the primary role of phonology and a secondary role for orthography were confirmed in the pointed Hebrew, yet did not hold in the deeper unpointed Hebrew. Instead, orthographic processing (as measured by an orthographic choice and a word boundaries task), accounted for a substantial portion of variance in word learning, above and beyond phonological processing, which itself was not a strong or statistically reliable predictor. Share concluded that word reading in the shallow script was primarily dependent on sublexical processes – phonology and rapid automatized naming – while in the deeper script it was linked to 'sublexical, lexical (word-level) and supra-lexical factors' (Share, 2007, p. 34). Share's findings highlight the reader's ability to flexibly draw on the appropriate cognitive resources to maximize efficiency in his or her reading environment.

In a similar study, Arab-Moghaddam and Sénéchal (2001) studied the orthographic and phonological predictors of reading performance in English-Persian bilingual second- and third-grade children living in Canada. Persian was employed as a contrast to English because it is considered to have a relatively shallow orthography. Arab-Moghaddam and Sénéchal found that, although phonological and orthographic skills were consistently highly correlated (highlighting their interdependence and mutual support of word recognition), they both independently predicted word reading and spelling ability in both languages. However, orthographic processing explained a greater portion of the variance in these literacy skills in both English and Persian than phonological processing. In another cross-linguistic study, Georgiou, Parrila, and Papadopoulos (2008) compared English and Greek reading (accuracy and fluency) through the use of structural equation modeling and found that both orthographic and phonological skills were important in reading in both languages. Interestingly, although orthographic skill predicted both accuracy and fluency in English, it was only associated with fluency in Greek. The authors concluded that Greek readers made use of their orthographic skills only when the reading task required a fast automatic whole-word unit response. These studies, once again provide evidence that across languages, orthographic processing is an important ingredient in word recognition. They also highlight the fact that the deployment of orthographic skills during word recognition may depend on the demands of the reading task.

Orthographic processing deficits and competencies

Given that phonological and orthographic processes appear to be separable and unique components of variance in word recognition (Cunningham et al., 2001), researchers have hypothesized that both phonological and orthographic processes contribute differentially to reading difficulties (Cunningham & Stanovich, 1990; Cunningham et al., 2001). Exploring the possibility of orthographic processing deficits and competencies in word recognition across languages, Miller-Guron and Lundberg (2000), van der Leij and Morfidi (2006), and Bekebrede, van der Leij, and Share (2009) studied the cognitive skills of bilingual dyslexic readers. It was hypothesized that dyslexic readers share a core phonological deficit yet may vary in their orthographic skills such that there are qualitatively different subgroups of dyslexic readers: readers with poor phonological skills and poor orthographic skills (Poor/Poor) and readers with poor phonological skills and adequate orthographic processing skills (Poor/Good; van der Leij & Morfidi, 2006).

Examining the reading and cognitive skills of Swedish college students (who also read English), Miller-Guron and Lundberg (2000) indentified a statistically distinct subgroup of Poor/Good dyslexic readers, who had significantly better orthographic skills than Poor/Poor readers. This group read better in English than Swedish even though Swedish is a highly regular orthography and it was their native language. The authors maintained that the students favored English reading because their strong orthographic skills created a tendency to prefer the large orthographic unit approach to decoding that was especially effective during English reading. Similarly, van der Leij and Morfidi (2006) observed a unique subgroup of Poor/Good dyslexic readers that performed unexpectedly well in English relative to their poor Dutch reading skill as a result of their strong orthographic processing skills. Investigating the reading-related skills of bilingual Dutch and English readers, Bekebrede et al. (2009) found further evidence that dyslexic readers share a core phonological deficit yet vary in their orthographic ability. Similar to the previous studies, Poor/Good readers outperformed Poor/Poor readers on speeded reading tasks – which presumably draw on the ability to recognize words as larger units. However, in contrast to the previous studies, Bekebrede et al. (2009) did not observe any evidence of superior reading in English among their participants. The authors concluded that variability in orthographic competence may differentiate groups of dyslexic readers, yet these differences affect reading regardless of the language being read.

The results of the studies discussed in this chapter not only demonstrate that orthography universally, uniquely, and importantly supports word recognition, but they also provide support for Cunningham and Stanovich's (1990) and Cunningham et al.'s (2001) hypothesis that constitutional differences in the ability to form, store, and access orthographic information may be a unique cause of reading difficulties. In contrast, findings are mixed as to whether orthographic processing abilities interact with orthographic depth in a predictable way such that orthographic competencies are particularly advantageous in deep languages and orthographic deficits less of an obstacle in shallow languages. Certainly, future research will have to explore the relationship between orthographic processing and orthographic depth one language at a time.

Conclusion

The goal of this chapter was to analyze and review what is currently understood about orthographic learning. We sought to discuss the evidence underlying how children move from a slow, laborious word identification process to effortless and instantaneous word recognition ability. Ironically, to date, our best understanding of this process suggests that, in many ways, it is the participation in the initial stages of word identification that enables a child to become a skilled reader. It is the effortful decoding that characterizes early reading, which brings about the reader's attunement to the regularities of written language and provides the opportunity to secure detailed word-specific orthographic information in memory and ultimately to read words by sight. This 'self-teaching' mechanism is powerful and appears to become activated quickly and persist long term regardless of whether words are read silently or aloud, and with the support of context or in its absence. In fact, it is the multitude of different types of reading experiences that allows the reader to continue to develop and refine the print lexicon throughout adulthood.

We have also attempted to contextualize the discussion of orthographic learning by highlighting the underlying role that language-specific factors play in determining orthographic learning. Although orthography is a universal constituent of word recognition, readers of deep orthographies may be more dependent on orthographic information and the ability to develop well-specified orthographic representations than readers of shallow orthographies. Nevertheless, the study of the differences in orthographic learning between languages is in its infancy and in this review we have discussed only *some* of the differences in orthographic learning across the *alphabetic* languages. We have not addressed instructional methods that vary across languages and cultures, the differing morphological structures of languages, and the unique characteristics of non-alphabetic writing systems. Clearly these factors play an important role in orthographic learning, and a deeper understanding of these processes would enhance our understanding of the universal and language-specific aspects of word recognition as well. Although it is evident from what we have reviewed that efficient readers of all languages deploy orthographic processes as they develop the ability to recognize words by sight, there is nonetheless much ground to still cover. The recent inclusion of cross-linguistic research in our study of orthographic learning is heartening, but as we make progress in our ability to draw conclusions and state the absolutes that we seek, our broadened research lens often simultaneously uncovers considerably more gaps in our understanding. Nonetheless, one of the few universals we can assume is that learning to read involves a two-way interplay between the reader and the orthography that is mediated by the reader's ability to adapt to the demands of the environment.

In sum, an emerging body of empirical evidence has bolstered our understanding of the unique role of orthographic processing in word recognition and our theoretical understanding of the way that orthographic learning occurs. While phonological processes remain primary, orthographic processes represent an understudied frontier in the study of word recognition processes.

- Learning to read words is the process of understanding how writing represents speech.
- One of the first steps in becoming literate is learning to map spelling to sound. This skill, which has been called phonological recoding, has been assigned a critical role in the reading acquisition process.
- Phonological recoding acts as a self-teaching device: Each successful attempt facilitates children's attunement to the regularities of written language and provides the opportunity to secure word-specific orthographic information in memory. Once children learn to convert spelling into sound, they can read many words that already exist in their spoken lexicons.
- Skilled reading depends on the formation of precise orthographic representations and their amalgamation to phonological, semantic, syntactic, and morphological information, which allow children to achieve the final goal of reading: comprehension.

Notes

1 Languages have been classified along an orthographic depth continuum (i.e., shallow-to-deep/transparent-to-opaque/regular-to-irregular; see Frost, 2005; Seymour et al., 2003).
2 The acquisition of well-specified orthographic knowledge may require more learning trials in disabled readers (Share & Shalev, 2004).

References

Arab-Moghaddam, N. & Sénéchal, M. (2001). Orthographic and phonological processing skills in reading and spelling in Persian/English bilinguals. *International Journal of Behavioral Development, 25*, 140–147.

Badian, N. A. (2001). Phonological and orthographic processing: Their roles in reading prediction. *Annals of Dyslexia, 51*, 179–202.

Barker, T. A., Torgesen, J. K., & Wagner, R. K. (1992). The role of orthographic processing skills on five different reading tasks. *Reading Research Quarterly, 27*, 334–345.

Baron, J. & Treiman, R. (1980). Some problems in the study of differences in cognitive processes. *Memory & Cognition, 8*, 313–321.

Bekebrede, J., van der Leij, A., & Share, D. L. (2009). Dutch dyslexic adolescents: Phonological-core variable-orthographic differences. *Reading and Writing, 22*, 133–165.

Booth, J. R., Perfetti, C. A., & MacWhinney, B. (1999). Quick, automatic, and general activation of orthographic and phonological representations in young readers. *Developmental Psychology, 35*, 3–19.

Bourke, L. & Adams, A. M. (2010). Cognitive constraints and the early learning goals in writing. *Journal of Research in Reading, 3*, 94–110.

Bowey, J. A. & Miller, R. (2007). Correlates of orthographic learning in third-grade children's silent reading. *Journal of Research in Reading, 30*, 115–128.

Bowey, J. A. & Muller, D. (2005). Phonological recoding and rapid orthographic learning in third-graders' silent reading: A critical test of the self-teaching hypothesis. *Journal of Experimental Child Psychology, 92*, 203–219.

Bradley, L. & Bryant, P. E. (1983). Categorizing sounds and learning to read: A causal connection. *Nature, 301*, 419–421.

Braten, I., Lie, A., Andreassen, R., & Olaussen, B. S. (1999). Leisure time reading and orthographic processes in word recognition among Norwegian third- and fourth-grade students. *Reading and Writing: An Interdisciplinary Journal, 11*, 88.

Bryant, P. E. & Impey, L. (1986). The similarities between normal readers and developmental and acquired dyslexics. *Cognition, 24*, 121–137.

Burt, J. S. & Blackwell, P. (2008). Sound–spelling consistency in adults' orthographic learning. *Journal of Research in Reading, 31*, 77–96.

Byrne, B. & Fielding-Barnsley, R. (1993). Evaluation of a program to teach phonemic awareness to young children: A 2- and 3-year follow-up and a new preschool trial *Journal of Educational Psychology, 87*, 488–503.

Cassar, M. & Treiman, R. (1997). The beginnings of orthographic knowledge: Children's knowledge of double letters in words. *Journal of Educational Psychology, 89*, 631–644.

Chateau, D. & Jared, D. (2000). Exposure to print and word recognition process. *Memory & Cognition, 28*, 143–153.

Cunningham, A. E. (1990). Explicit versus implicit instruction in phonemic awareness. *Journal of Experimental Child Psychology, 50*, 429–444.

Cunningham, A. E. (2006). Accounting for children's orthographic learning while reading text: Do children self-teach? *Journal of Experimental Child Psychology, 95*, 56–77.

Cunningham, A. E. & Stanovich, K. E. (1990). Assessing print exposure and orthographic processing skill in children: A quick measure of reading experience. *Journal of Educational Psychology, 82*, 733–740.

Cunningham, A. E. & Stanovich, K. E. (1993). Children's literacy environments and early word recognition subskills. *Reading and Writing, 5*, 193–204.

Cunningham, A. E. & Stanovich, K. E. (1997). Early reading acquisition and its relation to reading experience and ability 10 years later. *Developmental Psychology, 33*, 934–945.

Cunningham, A. E., Perry, K. E., & Stanovich, K. E. (2001). Converging evidence for the concept of orthographic processing. *Reading and Writing, 14*, 549–568.

Cunningham, A. E., Perry, K. E., Stanovich, K. E., & Share, D. L. (2002). Orthographic learning during reading: Examining the role of self-teaching. *Journal of Experimental Child Psychology, 82*, 185–199.

Cunningham, A. E., Nathan, R. G., & Raher, K. S. (2010). Orthographic processing in models of word recognition. In M. L. Kamil, P. D. Pearson, E. Birr Moje, & P. P. Afflerbach (Eds), *Handbook of reading research, volume IV* (pp. 259–285). New York: Taylor & Francis.

de Jong, P. F. & Share, D. L. (2007). Orthographic learning during oral and silent reading. *Scientific Studies of Reading, 11*, 55–71.

de Jong, P. F., Bitter, D. J. L., van Setten, M., & Marinus, E. (2009). Does phonological recoding occur during silent reading, and is it necessary for orthographic learning? *Journal of Experimental Child Psychology*, *104*, 267–282.

Ehri, L. C. (1980). The development of orthographic images. In U. Frith (Ed.), *Cognitive processes in spelling* (pp. 311–338). London, England: Academic Press.

Ehri, L. C. (1992). Reconceptualizing the development of sight word reading and its relationship to recoding. In C. Gough, L. Ehri, & R. Treiman (Eds), *Reading acquisition* (pp. 107–143). Hillsdale, NJ: Lawrence Erlbaum Associates, Inc.

Ehri, L. (2005a). Development of sight word reading: Phases and findings. In M. J. Snowling, & C. Hulme (Eds), *The science of reading: A handbook* (pp. 135–154). Malden, MA: Blackwell.

Ehri, L. (2005b). Learning to read words: Theory, findings, and issues. *Scientific Studies of Reading*, *9*, 167–188.

Ehri, L. C. & Saltmarsh, J. (1995). Beginning readers outperform older disabled readers in learning to read words by sight. *Reading and Writing*, *7*, 295–326.

Ehri, L. C., Nunes, S., Willows, D., Schuster, B., Yaghoub-Zadeh, Z., & Shanahan, T. (2001). Phonemic awareness instruction helps children learn to read: Evidence from the national reading Panel's meta-analysis. *Reading Research Quarterly*, *36*, 250–287.

Freebody, P. & Byrne, B. (1988). Word-reading strategies in elementary school children: Relations to comprehension, reading time, and phonemic awareness. *Reading Research Quarterly*, *23*, 441–453.

Frost, R. (2005). Orthographic systems and skilled word recognition processes in reading. In M. J. Snowling & C. Hulme (Eds), *The science of reading: A handbook* (pp. 272–95). Malden, MA: Blackwell Publishing.

Georgiou, G., Parrila, R., & Papadopoulos, T. (2008). Predictors of word decoding and reading fluency in English and Greek: A cross-linguistic comparison. *Journal of Educational Psychology*, *100*, 566–580.

Goswami, U. (1986). Children's use of analogy in learning to read: A developmental study. *Journal of Experimental Child Psychology*, *42*, 73–83.

Goswami, U. (1988). Orthographic analogies and reading development. *Quarterly Journal of Experimental Psychology*, *40*, 239–268.

Goswami, U., Ziegler, J., Dalton, L., & Schneider, W. (2001). Pseudohomophone effects and phonological recoding procedures in reading development in English and German. *Journal of Memory and Language*, *45*, 648–664.

Harm, M. W. & Seidenberg, M. S. (1999). Phonology, reading acquisition, and dyslexia: Insights from connectionist models. *Psychological Review*, *106*, 491–528.

Harm, M. W. & Seidenberg, M. S. (2004). Computing the meanings of words in reading: Cooperative division of labor between visual and phonological processes. *Psychological Review*, *111*, 662–720.

Hatcher, P. J., Hulme, C., & Ellis, A. W. (1994). Ameliorating early reading failure by integrating the teaching of reading and phonological skills: The phonological linkage hypothesis. *Child Development*, *65*, 41–57.

Hogaboam, T. W. & Perfetti, C. A. (1978). Reading skill and the role of verbal experience in decoding. *Journal of Educational Psychology*, *70*, 717–729.

Kjeldsen, A., Niemi, P., & Olofsson, Å. (2003). Training phonological awareness in kindergarten level children: Consistency is more important than quantity. *Learning and Instruction*, *13*, 349–365.

Kyte, C. S. & Johnson, C. J. (2006). The role of phonological recoding in orthographic learning. *Journal of Experimental Child Psychology*, *93*, 166–185.

Landi, N., Perfetti, C. A., Bolger, D. J., Dunlap, S., & Foorman, B. R. (2006). The role of discourse context in developing word form representations: A paradoxical relation between reading and learning. *Journal of Experimental Child Psychology*, *94*, 133.

Lundberg, I., Frost, J., & Peterson, O. (1988). Effects of an extensive program for stimulating phonological awareness in preschool children. *Reading Research Quarterly*, *23*, 263–284.

Lyytinen, H., Aro, M., Holopainen, L., Leiwo, M., Lyytinen, P., & Tolvanen, A. (2006). Children's language development and reading acquisition in a highly transparent orthography. In R.M. Joshi & P.G. Aaron (Eds), *Handbook of orthography and literacy* (pp. 47–62). Mahwah, NJ: Lawrence Erlbaum.

McKague, M., Davis, C., Pratt, C., & Johnston, M. (2008). The role of feedback from phonology to orthography in orthographic learning: An extension of item-based accounts. *Journal of Research in Reading*, *31*, 55–76.

Mesman, G. R. & Kibby, M. Y. (2011) An examination of multiple predictors of orthographic functioning. *Journal of Learning Disabilities*, *44*, 50–62.

Miller-Guron, L. & Lundberg, I. (2000). Dyslexia and second language reading: A second bite at the apple? *Reading and Writing*, *12*, 41–61.

Nation, K. (2009). Form-meaning links in the development of visual word recognition. *Philosophical Transactions of the Royal Society, B.*, *364*, 3665–3674.

Nation, K., Angell, P., & Castles, A. (2007). Orthographic learning via self-teaching in children learning to read English: Effects of exposure, durability, and context. *Journal of Experimental Child Psychology*, *96*, 71–84.

NICHD: National Institute of Child Health and Human Development, NIH, DHHS. (2000). *Report of the National Reading Panel: Teaching Children to Read.* Washington, DC: U.S. Government Printing Office.

Olson, R., Forsberg, H., Wise, B., & Rack, J. (1994). Measurement of word recognition, orthographic, and phonological skills. In G. Reid Lyon (Ed.), *Frames of reference for the assessment of learning disabilities: New views on measurement issues* (pp. 243–268). Baltimore: Paul H. Brooks.

Ouellette, G. (2010). Orthographic learning in learning to spell: The roles of semantics and type of practice. *Journal of Experimental Child Psychology*, *107*, 50–58.

Ouellette, G. & Fraser, J. R. (2009). What exactly is a yait anyway: The role of semantics in orthographic learning. *Journal of Experimental Child Psychology*, *104*, 239–251.

Perfetti, C. A. (1985). *Reading ability.* New York: Oxford University Press.

Perfetti, C. A. (1992). The representation problem in reading acquisition. In C. Gough, L. Ehri & R. Treiman (Eds), *Reading acquisition* (pp. 145–174). Hillsdale, NJ: Erlbaum.

Perfetti, C. A. (2007). Reading ability: Lexical quality to comprehension. *Scientific Studies of Reading*, *11*, 357–383.

Perfetti, C. A. & Bolger, D. J. (2004). The brain might read that way. *Scientific Studies of Reading*, *8*, 293–304.

Perfetti, C. A. & Hart, L. (2001). The lexical quality hypothesis. In L. Vehoeven, C. C. Elbro & P. Reitsma (Eds), *Precursors of functional literacy* (pp. 189–214). Amsterdam/Philadelphia: John Benjamins.

Perfetti, C. A., Landi, N., & Oakhill, J. (2005). The acquisition of reading comprehension skill. In M. J. Snowling & C. Hulme (Eds), *The science of reading: A handbook* (pp. 227–247). Malden, MA: Blackwell.

Plaut, D. C. (2005). Connectionist approaches to reading. In M. J. Snowling & C. Hulme (Eds), *The science of reading: A handbook* (pp. 24–38). Malden, MA: Blackwell.

Plaut, D. C., McClelland, J. L., Seidenberg, M. S., & Patterson, K. (1996). Understanding normal and impaired reading: Computational principles in quasi-regular domains. *Psychological Review, 103*, 56–115.

Reitsma, P. (1983a). Printed word learning in beginning readers. *Journal of Experimental Child Psychology, 36*, 321–339.

Reitsma, P. (1983b). Word-specific knowledge in beginning reading. *Journal of Research in Reading, 6*, 41–56.

Reitsma, P. (1989). Orthographic memory and learning to read. In P. G. Aaron & R. M. Joshi (Eds), *Reading and writing disorders in different orthographic systems* (pp. 51–73). Dordrecht/Norwell, MA: Kluwer Academic.

Ricketts, J., Bishop, D. V. M., & Nation, K. (2008). Investigating orthographic and semantic aspects of word learning in poor comprehenders. *Journal of Research in Reading, 31*, 117–135.

Ricketts, J., Bishop, D. V. M., Pimperton, H., & Nation, K. (2011). The role of self-teaching in learning orthographic and semantic aspects of new words. *Scientific Studies of Reading, 15*, 47–70.

Rutter, M. (1978). Prevalence and types of dyslexia. In A. Benton & D. Pearl (Eds), *Dyslexia: An appraisal of current knowledge* (pp. 5–28). New York: Oxford University Press.

Seidenberg, M. & McClelland, J. (1989). More words but still no lexicon: Reply to Besner et al. *Psychological Review, 97*, 447–52.

Seymour, P., Aro, M., Erskine, J., and in Collaboration with COST Action A8 network. (2003). Foundation literacy acquisition in European orthographies. *British Journal of Psychology, 94*, 143–174.

Shahar-Yames, D. & Share, D. L. (2008). Spelling as a self-teaching mechanism in orthographic learning. *Journal of Research in Reading, 31*, 22–39.

Share, D. L. (2007). Sources of individual differences in orthographic learning: A comparison of deep and shallow scripts. Manuscript submitted for publication.

Share, D. L. (1995). Phonological recoding and self-teaching: Sine qua non of reading acquisition. *Cognition, 55*, 151–218.

Share, D. L. (1999). Phonological and orthographic learning: A direct test of the self-teaching hypothesis. *Journal of Experimental Child Psychology, 72*, 95–129.

Share, D. L. (2004). Orthographic learning at a glance: On the time course and developmental onset of self-teaching. *Journal of Experimental Child Psychology, 87*, 267–298.

Share, D. L. (2008). Orthographic learning, phonological recoding, and self-teaching. *Advances in Child Development and Behavior, 36*, 31–82.

Share, D. L. & Shalev, C. (2004). Self-teaching in normal and disabled readers. *Reading and Writing, 17*, 769–800.

Sprenger-Charolles, L., Siegel, L. S., Béchennec, D., & Serniclaes, W. (2003). Development of phonological and orthographic processing in reading aloud, in silent reading, and in spelling: A four-year longitudinal study. *Journal of Experimental Child Psychology, 84*, 194–217.

Stanovich, K. E. (1980). Toward an interactive-compensatory model of individual differences in the development of reading fluency. *Reading Research Quarterly, 16*, 32–71.

Stanovich, K. E. (1982). Individual differences in the cognitive processes of reading: 1. word decoding . *Journal of Learning Disabilities, 15*, 485–493.

Stanovich, K. E. (1986). Matthew effects in reading: Some consequences of individual differences in the acquisition of literacy. *Reading Research Quarterly, 21*, 360–407.

Stanovich, K. E. (1992). Speculation on the causes and consequences in individual differences in early reading acquisition. In P. P. Gough, L. Ehri & R. Trieman (Eds), *Reading acquisition* (pp. 307–342). Hillsdale, NJ: Lawrence Erlbaum Associates, Inc.

Stanovich, K. E. (2000). *Progress in understanding reading: Scientific foundations and new frontiers*. New York: Guilford Publications.

Stanovich, K. E. & West, R. F. (1989). Exposure to print and orthographic processing. *Reading Research Quarterly, 24*, 402–433.

Taylor, J. S. H., Plunkett, K., & Nation, K. (2011). The influence of consistency, frequency, and semantics on learning to read: An artificial orthography paradigm. *Journal of Experimental Psychology: Learning, Memory, and Cognition, 37*, 60–76.

Treiman, R. (1984). Individual differences among children in spelling and reading styles. *Journal of Experimental Child Psychology, 37*, 463–477.

van der Leij A. & Morfidi E. (2006). Core deficits and variable differences in Dutch poor readers learning English. *Journal of Learning Disabilities, 39*, 74–90.

Van Orden, G. & Kloos, K. (2005). The question of phonology and reading. In M. J. Snowling & C. Hulme (Eds), *The science of reading: A handbook* (pp. 61–78). Malden MA: Blackwell.

Vellutino, F. R. (1979). *Dyslexia: Theory and research*. Cambridge, MA: MIT press.

Vellutino, F. R. & Scanlon, D. M. (1987). Phonological coding, phonological awareness, and reading ability: Evidence from a longitudinal and experimental study. *Merrill-Palmer Quarterly, 33*, 321–363.

Wang, H., Castles, A., Nickels, L., & Nation, K. (2011). Context effects on orthographic learning of regular and irregular words. *Journal of Experimental ChildPsychology, 109*, 39–57.

Wagner, R. K. & Barker, T. A. (1994). The development of orthographic processing ability. In V. W. Berninger (Ed.), *The variety of orthographic knowledge I: Theoretical and developmental Issues* (pp. 243–276). Dordrecht, Netherlands: Kluwer Academic Publishers.

Ziegler, J. C. & Goswami, U. (2005). Reading acquisition, developmental dyslexia, and skilled reading across languages: A psycholinguistic grain size theory. *Psychological Bulletin, 131*, 3–29.

9 How visual word recognition is affected by developmental dyslexia

Yusra Ahmed, Richard K. Wagner, and Patricia Thatcher Kantor

Developmental dyslexia refers to unexpected difficulty in learning to read that is not due to sensory or motor impairments, emotional disturbance, mental deficiency, economic or cultural disadvantage, or inadequate reading instruction (Adams & Bruck, 1993; Lyon, Shaywitz, & Shaywitz, 2003; Siegel, 2003). A number of important historical figures were believed to have dyslexia (West, 1992), illustrating that an unexpected inability to read is characteristic of dyslexia. Word-level reading typically is impaired in individuals with dyslexia (Piasta & Wagner, 2007), and the impairment is characterized by (a) an inability to sound out new words and (b) an impoverished set of sight words that are decoded automatically (Ehri, 1998; Fox, 1994; Snow, Burns, & Griffin, 1998; Rack, Snowling, & Olson, 1992). Lyon et al. (2003) provide the following definition of dyslexia:

> Dyslexia is a specific learning disability that is neurobiological in origin. It is characterized by difficulties with accurate and/or fluent word recognition and by poor spelling and decoding abilities. These difficulties typically result from a deficit in the phonological component of language that is often unexpected in relation to other cognitive abilities and the provision of effective classroom instruction. Secondary consequences may include problems in reading comprehension and reduced reading experience that can impede growth of vocabulary and background knowledge.
>
> (p. 2)

Reading disability or dyslexia appears to represent the low end of normal variation in reading ability as opposed to a qualitatively distinct disorder (Fletcher, Lyon, Fuchs, & Barnes, 2007; Plomin & Kovas, 2005). Given this continuum of variability, a difficult issue that has occupied researchers and practitioners alike is at what point in the distribution a reading problem is severe enough to be considered a reading disability.

Developmental dyslexia is distinguished from acquired dyslexia in that developmental dyslexia refers to the failure to acquire sufficient reading skills, whereas acquired dyslexia refers to impaired reading due to brain injury or illness that typically occurs subsequent to a normal history of learning to read. As the definition implies, many individuals with developmental dyslexia (hereafter referred to as dyslexia) have impaired reading comprehension and word decoding. Problems in reading comprehension often are a direct effect of the decoding difficulty (Aaron, 1989; Stanovich & Siegel, 1994). In addition to this direct effect, a long-term indirect effect is likely as the inability to decode words affects vocabulary development and other aspects of oral language comprehension, which in turn affects reading comprehension. Additional support for the primacy of deficits in word-level reading as the core reading problem for most individuals with dyslexia comes from the fact that adults who have compensated for their reading difficulty and are not impaired at reading comprehension nevertheless continue to struggle with word recognition (Bruck, 1990, 1993; Scarborough, 1984).

Approximately half of older readers who struggle with reading comprehension do so despite adequate word-level decoding skills. For these poor readers, reading problems appear to represent deficiencies in vocabulary and oral language comprehension more generally as opposed to deficiencies that are specific to reading. Their problem lies in the domain of language comprehension rather than dyslexia (Nation, 2005).

In the remaining sections of this chapter, we review theories of dyslexia focusing on visual and linguistic impairments that have been argued to be the origin of the disorder. Given that there is considerable variability in the characteristics of oral languages throughout the world, and even more variability in the writing systems that have been developed, we consider implications of cross-cultural research on dyslexia. Then we review research on subtypes of dyslexia. Finally, we draw some conclusions.

Theories of developmental dyslexia

Quite a few theories of the origin of dyslexia have been proposed over the years (Fletcher et al., 2007; Ziegler, 2011). Given the fact that reading involves both vision and language, it is not surprising that deficits in either vision or language have been proposed as origins of dyslexia. Other explanations have focused on more fundamental causes. Examples include a deficit in rapid temporal processing that purportedly affects both speech and nonspeech perception (Tallal & Piercy, 1973), and a deficit in cerebellar functioning (Nicolson, Fawcett, & Dean, 2001). However, accounts based on more fundamental purported causes of dyslexia have received less support in the literature (see Fletcher et al., 2007) and therefore we focus upon some influential visual- and language-based accounts of dyslexia in the next two sections.

Visual deficit accounts of developmental dyslexia

The most influential visual deficit-based account of dyslexia was proposed by Orton during the 1920s. Orton argued that individuals with dyslexia make reversal errors in letter perception and read words backwards due to a lack of left-hemispheric dominance for processing linguistic symbols (Fletcher et al.,

2007). In the United States, this remains the common belief among laypeople, with dyslexia associated with seeing things backwards.

Poor readers at the end of first grade or in second grade indeed make reversal errors such as confusing 'b' and 'd' and reading 'was' as 'saw.' However, beginning normally-developing readers commonly make reversal errors as well. The letters 'b' and 'd' are visually confusable. They also are confusable in how they sound, as both are categorized as voiced stop consonants because they are produced by stopping, then releasing the flow of air in the vocal tract. Additionally, children must learn to read in a direction appropriate to the conventions of their written language. For English, it is left to right, but this is not universal. Arabic, for example, is read from right to left. Although poor readers in second grade stand out by virtue of making reversal errors, the critical fact is that second-grade readers with dyslexia make no more reversal errors than do younger normal readers who are matched for reading level (Crowder & Wagner, 1992; Werker, Bryson, & Wassenberg, 1989). What explains the popularity of the mistaken view that reversals are a sign of dyslexia is that teachers and parents of second-grade readers only see children with reading problems making these errors. In reality, reversal errors are a by-product of still being at the beginning stage of reading acquisition where such errors are common (Wagner, Piasta, & Torgesen, 2006). Furthermore, reversal errors can be explained from an evolutionary perspective. Although humans evolved to speak, we recruit brain regions that are used for vision and speech for reading. Specifically, a portion of the left fusiform gyrus is particularly responsive to visual words, and has been termed the 'Visual Word Form Area' (McCandliss, Cohen, & Dehaene, 2003). Thus, as with other visual activities, vertical reversals are less discernible than horizontal reversals as they are less essential for survival (e.g., a lion on its back is less threatening than a lion on its feet) (see also Brysbaert, Cai, and Van der Haegen, accompanying volume, Chapter 7).

Another popular visual account of dyslexia is that it results from faulty eye-movements. Reading requires sophisticated and finely orchestrated eye-movements (Rayner & Pollatsek, 1989; Schotter & Rayner, 2011). As you read these words, it feels as though your eyes are gliding smoothly across the page. In fact, your eyes are propelled across the page a little bit at a time in a series of tiny ballistic movements called saccades. When the eyes are moving, little can be seen clearly. Almost all visual input comes during brief fixations that separate the saccades. The fact that our eyes do not glide smoothly across the page when reading but rather in a series of saccades and fixations can be observed in a casual experiment. Ask someone to sit across from you and read. Look carefully at the individual's eyes and you will observe the saccades and fixations. Perform the same experiment on an individual with dyslexia and it will be apparent that the individual's eyes move much more erratically, even moving in the wrong direction at times. Observations like these were viewed as confirmation of the deficient-eye-movement account of dyslexia, and led to interventions that trained smooth-pursuit eye-movements such as holding your head steady and following a moving target with your eyes.

Faulty eye-movements turn out not to be a cause of dyslexia but rather a byproduct of it. The eye-movements of individuals with dyslexia do not move across the page as smoothly as do those of normal readers simply because they are having trouble reading the words. The fact that faulty eye-movements are a byproduct rather than a cause of dyslexia was confirmed by experiments in which normal readers were given passages that were difficult for them to read, and individuals with dyslexia were given easy passages that they could read at a normal rate with minimal errors. The eye-movements of the normal readers resembled the previously reported faulty eye-movements of individuals with dyslexia. Conversely, the eye-movements of individuals with developmental dyslexia who were given easy passages now appeared normal. Additional confirmation of the fact that faulty eye-movements do not cause dyslexia came from the results of eye-movement training studies. Eye-movement training improved performance on eye-movement tasks that did not involve reading such as accuracy in tracking a moving object with the eyes, but reading performance did not improve (Crowder & Wagner, 1992).

Other visual-processing-based accounts of dyslexia have involved low-level visual perceptual deficits (Eden, Stern, Wood, & Wood, 1995; Lovegrove, Stern, Wood, & Wood, 1986; Stein, 2001; Vidyasagar & Pammer, 2010; see Stein, this volume, Chapter 10, for a review of low-level processing based accounts of dyslexia, including magnocellular system deficits, and visual motion sensitivity).

Language deficit accounts of dyslexia

Although earlier theories of dyslexia focused on deficient visual perceptual processing, the present consensus is that the primary origin of dyslexia lies in language rather than vision (Ramus, Rosen, Dakin, Day, Castellote, White, & Frith, 2003; Vellutino, 1979). The language system that appears to be implicated is the phonological processing system. Phonological processing refers to using speech-based codes in processing written and oral language (Wagner & Torgesen, 1987). The term phonological derives from the Greek root *phone* which means as 'voice' or 'sound.' Phonological processing can be thought of as using speech-sound-based codes for processing both oral and written language. Phonological processing can be categorized on the basis of levels of phonological representation and the specific kind of processing that a task requires. From the smallest to largest, these levels are the acoustic (or sound waves), phonetic (universal set of speech tones found in all languages), phonological (speech sounds correspond roughly to the letters in the alphabet), and morphophonological (sounds that represent meaning as well as pronunciation). Phonological representations in speech are refined during development, such that children start out by mapping relatively large acoustic segments and gradually refine them to the level of phonemes to match regularities in language (Snowling & Hulme, 1994). The phonological-core variable-difference model of reading disability (Stanovich, 1994; Stanovich & Siegel, 1994) was key in establishing that a discrepancy between IQ and achievement was not a necessary criterion for identifying children with dyslexia. Rather, Stanovich established that both garden-variety poor readers and individuals with dyslexia presented phonological problems. The differences between them were that garden-variety poor readers were also characterized by deficits in other domains, including vocabulary and language comprehension. Hence, their poor performance on reading was expected.

Longitudinal studies that utilized a latent variable approach to compare alternative models of phonological processing abilities showed that three kinds of phonological processing appear to be related yet distinct factors (Wagner & Torgesen, 1987; Wagner et al., 1994, 1997). The three kinds of phonological processing are phonological awareness, phonological memory, and rapid naming. Impaired performance in phonological awareness and rapid naming are implicated in dyslexia.

Phonological awareness

Phonological awareness refers to an awareness of and access to phonological elements that make up the sound structure of oral language (Fletcher et al., 2007; Wagner & Torgesen, 1987). At the phonological level, speech is represented by abstract phonemes, which refer to sound distinctions that signal changes in meaning for a given language. The sounds represented by the 'f' in 'fan' and the 'p' in 'pan' are different phonemes, which leads to different meanings associated with the words 'fan' and 'pan' (Wagner et al., 2006). Approximately 40 phonemes can be strung together in various combinations to make up every word in the English language, with some variability associated with different dialects. For example, the phonemes of Midwestern American English (i.e., the dialect used by most national news anchors on television) are presented in Table 9.1. There is a rough correspondence between phonemes and the letters in an alphabetic system of writing. For example, the spoken words 'cat,' 'rat,' and 'hat' each have three phonemes. They have different initial phonemes and identical medial and final phonemes. The similarity and differences among these three spoken words are reflected in their spellings: They have different initial letters, and identical middle and final letters. The awareness that all words can be decomposed into basic elements of language (phonemes) makes learning to read an alphabetic system a more manageable task for normally developing readers, and the lack of this awareness is the core imbalance in poor readers (Lyon et al., 2003). See the chapter by Halderman, Ashby and Perfetti in the accompanying volume (Chapter 10) for a discussion of the role of phonology in word recognition.

Individuals with dyslexia typically perform poorly on measures of phonological awareness compared to younger reading-age matched controls (Wagner et al., 2006). An example of a task that measures phonological awareness is elision (Wagner et al., 1999). A word or nonword is presented to an individual who is asked to repeat it. Then, the individual is asked to cut out a particular phonological segment and pronounce what remains (e.g., 'Say click.' 'Now say click without saying /l/.' Correct answer is 'kick.'). Poor readers consistently perform below normally developing readers on measures of phonological awareness and letter-sound decoding task (Wagner & Torgesen, 1987; Wagner, Torgesen, Rashotte, Hecht, Barker, Burgess, & Garon, 1997).

Table 9.1 Phonemes of Midwestern American English

Vowels									
Front		zebra	kit	hen	cat				
Middle	*dart*	tern	pup	about					
Back		cod	pork	poodle	hood				
Dipthongs		cow	python	goat	koi	deer	poor	ferret	*snake*
Consonants									
Stops	Voiced	bat	dog	goat					
	Voiceless	pig	turtle	cat					
Fricatives	Voiced	dove	*these*	zebra	measure				
	Voiceless	*farm*	thistle	snake	*sheep*	hippopotamus			
Affricatives	Voiced	jump							
	Voiceless	*chirp*							
Nasals		mouse	night	wing					
Liquids		lamb	rooster						
Glides		yak	wombat						

Two converging lines of evidence support the fact that phonological awareness is causally related to reading. The first line of evidence comes from causal modeling studies of longitudinal data with normally developing readers (de Jong & van der Leij, 2003; Parrila, Kirby, & McQuarrie, 2004; Parrila, Aunola, Leskinen, Nurmi, & Kirby, 2005; Perfetti, Beck, Bell, & Hughes, 1991; Wagner et al., 1997). The second line of evidence comes from studies that train poor readers on phonological awareness and then look for the effects of training on decoding (e.g., Byrne, Fielding-Barnsley, & Ashley, 2000; Ehri, Nunes, Stahl, & Willows, 2001a; Ehri, Nunes, Willows, Schuster, Yaghoub-Zadeh, & Shanahan, 2001b; Foorman, Chen, Carlson, Moats, Francis, & Fletcher, 2003; Lovett, Steinbach, & Frijters, 2000; Rashotte, MacPhee, & Torgesen, 2001; Schneider, Roth, & Ennemoser, 2000; Torgesen, Alexander, Wagner, Rashotte, Voeller, & Conway, 2001). These studies have found that direct instruction on phonological awareness and letter sound correspondence has facilitated word recognition and reading ability in general for poor readers.

Some of the evidence that is cited in support of a causal relation between phonological awareness and learning to read words has been challenged (Castles & Coltheart, 2004). For example, if both phonological awareness and letter knowledge are trained in an intervention, as is commonly done, can we be sure it is the phonological awareness training that is responsible for a boost in word reading? Although individual studies can be challenged on various grounds, the overall pattern of results, and in particular the longitudinal correlational studies that have included an autoregressor effect and training studies that include a well-chosen control group, support the existence of a causal influence of phonological awareness on word reading (Hulme, Snowling, Caravolas, & Carroll, 2005).

Rapid naming

The efficiency with which phonological codes associated with visual objects are retrieved is commonly measured by speeded naming tasks. Although it is likely that rapid naming tasks measure additional processes, such as processing speed or orthographic awareness (Wolf, Pfeil, Lotz, & Biddle, 1994), rapid naming tasks have a phonological component because they require retrieving and voicing the phonological codes associated with the objects or symbols that are named (Wagner et al., 1997). Rapid automatized naming (RAN) tasks require individuals to name pictures of objects, colors, digits, or letters, either individually or in a series. Some individuals with dyslexia show deficits in rapid naming in addition to deficits in phonological awareness, and both appear to make relatively independent contributions to predicting reading ability and dyslexia (Fletcher et al., 2007; Schatschneider, Fletcher, Francis, Carlson, & Foorman, 2004; Wolf & Bowers, 1999). Individuals with dyslexia who have deficits in both phonological awareness and rapid naming (i.e., a 'double' deficit) appear to decode more poorly than do individuals with a single deficit in either area, although interpretation of this finding is complicated by the fact that individuals who are impaired in both phonological awareness and rapid naming tend to have more severe impairments in phonological awareness than do individuals who only have deficits in phonological awareness (Schatschneider, Carlson, Francis, Foorman, & Fletcher, 2002; Schatschneider et al., 2004).

Rapid naming may be more closely related to reading performance for orthographies that are more transparent than English. Rapid naming is strongly related to fluent reading of single words (Fletcher et al., 2007). In transparent writing systems such as German and Finnish, poor readers tend to be more accurate than English poor readers but tend to be primarily impaired in fluency. Because of the one-to-one correspondence between letters and sounds, accurate decoding is more easily achieved. Once there is a ceiling effect on accuracy, variability in reading skill can only be expressed by differences in fluency. Rapid naming performance predicts reading in German better than it does in English (Wimmer & Mayringer, 2002), although phonological awareness still makes an independent contribution to prediction of reading performance even in transparent languages.

Dyslexia in other languages

Cross-cultural comparisons of reading problems can inform our understanding of the fundamental nature of word recognition deficits. The linguistic properties of specific languages influence the difficulty with which children learn to read and write, as was just noted for the case of rapid naming being more predictive of performance for transparent orthographies such as German. Therefore, it is important to consider dyslexia from the vantage point of different systems of print. We have discussed phonology, or the speech sounds of oral languages that are represented in print (see also Halderman, Ashby, & Perfetti, 2011). Two other constructs are key in understanding letter-sound correspondences in other scripts: (a) morphology, which is relevant to meaning, and (b) orthography, which is relevant to print.

Morphology

Morphology refers to the 'minimal meaningful elements' that make up words (Bloomfield, 1933). Morphemes include word roots, suffixes, prefixes, and inflections which are parts of words that indicate number, person, tense, or case (Arnbak & Elbro, 2000). For example, the suffix 'er' is a morpheme that denotes 'one who does something,' as in the words 'baker,' 'sailor,' and 'tailor' (Wagner et al., 2006).

As beginning readers transition into skilled readers, morphological knowledge becomes more important to reading acquisition. With increasing frequency, newly encountered written words happen to be morphologically related to already known words. Being able to use morphology to figure out the likely meaning of new words from knowledge of known words that are morphologically related to the new words is essential. For example, a student who encounters the unknown word 'enthusiastically' in print can use knowledge of the known root word 'enthusiasm' and perhaps also knowledge about the likely role of the suffix 'ically' to infer the meaning of 'enthusiastically.' English is referred to as a morpho-phonemic system of writing because printed English words convey information about the pronunciations of words but also information about meaning.

Thus, the morphological relation between the printed words 'heal' and 'healthy' is represented by their shared spelling of 'heal,' despite the fact that this segment is pronounced differently in the two words.

Orthography

Orthography refers to the system of symbols used to represent pronunciation and meaning in print. There are essentially three major kinds of orthography or writing systems used in the world today: alphabetic writing systems, syllabaries, and morpho-syllabic writing systems (Crowder & Wagner, 1992; DeFrancis, 1989, Gelb, 1952; Rayner, Foorman, Perfetti, Pesetsky, & Seidenberg, 2001; Rayner & Pollatsek, 1989).

Alphabetic writing systems rely on a relatively small number of orthographic units or letters that map roughly onto the phonemes of speech. The single letter 'p' is used to represent what actually are different speech sounds or phones associated with the 'p' in 'pot,' 'top,' and 'spot.' You can prove to yourself that these are different though related speech sounds by holding your hand in front of your mouth and saying the words 'pot,' 'top,' and 'spot.' You will feel the largest burst of air associated with the sound of the 'p' in 'top,' somewhat less of a burst associated with the sound of the 'p' in 'pot,' and the smallest burst of air associated with the sound of the 'p' in 'spot.' English orthography consists of the 26 upper and lower case letters, the numerals 0 through 9, punctuation marks, and a small number of other symbols (e.g., & to represent 'and,' and more recently, @ to represent 'at' in email addresses). Examples of other alphabetic writing systems include Chinese *pin yin*, French, German, Italian, Korean, Finnish and Spanish. One important difference among alphabets is the consistency of relations between letters and sounds. Consistency refers to the number of sounds associated with a given letter and the number of letters associated with a given sound. Alphabets with consistent mappings, called *shallow orthographies*, include Finnish, Italian, Spanish, German and Dutch. Alphabets with inconsistent mappings, called *deep orthographies*, include English and French. Russian is an example of an alphabet that falls in between shallow and deep (Frost, Katz, & Bentin, 1987).

Syllabaries, the second kind of writing system, have orthographic units that correspond to syllables rather than phonemes. An example of a syllabary is the Japanese Kana. Finally, morpho-syllabic systems have orthographic units that represent syllables that also are morphemes. Examples of morpho-syllabic writing systems include Chinese and the Japanese Kanji system.

Regardless of the oral language and writing system involved, the task for the beginning reader is to connect the orthographic representations or script on the printed page to their corresponding morphological and phonological representations (Wagner et al., 2006). Cross-linguistic studies of both normal reading development and dyslexia reveal two remarkable similarities (Snowling, 2000; Goulandris, 2003; Ziegler & Goswami, 2005). First, in every language and writing system that has been studied to date, a roughly comparable percentage – between 3 and 5 percent – of individuals have serious reading problems despite having normal intelligence, adequate instruction, and no sensory or other known impairments. Second, regardless of the oral language or writing system involved, impaired phonological processing is observed in individuals with dyslexia, although skills such as orthographic and morphological awareness may also be implicated, depending on the nature of the script that must be learned.

Perhaps the major difference observed across oral languages and writing systems is that it is much easier to learn to read words accurately in shallow writing systems compared to deep writing systems (Caravolas, 2005; Seymour et al., 2003). Although individuals with dyslexia who read shallow orthographies do so with higher levels of accuracy than do comparable individuals with dyslexia who read deep orthographies, their decoding problem is evident in the slow rate at which they read.

The search for subtypes of dyslexia

Although it is generally agreed that individuals with dyslexia are heterogeneous, whether there are two primary subtypes, more than two subtypes, or variability that is mostly individual in nature remains unclear. In this section we review research that addresses possible subtypes of dyslexia.

Phonological and surface dyslexia subtypes

Good readers have a large number of words they recognize relatively automatically and also are skilled at sounding out unknown words. Might there be a subtype of dyslexia that is characterized by a deficit in sounding out unknown words, and another subtype that is characterized by a deficit in recognizing known words relatively automatically? Regardless of whether one assumes a model of decoding that explicitly includes a lexical route that would handle decoding words relatively automatically and a nonlexical route that would handle sounding out new words such as Coltheart, Rastle, Perry, Langdon, and Ziegler's (2001) dual-route cascaded (DRC) model of decoding, or a model that handles both tasks using only a lexical route such as Seidenberg and McClelland's (1989), Harm and Seidenberg's (2004), and Plaut, McClelland, Seidenberg, and Patterson's (1996) triangle models, the empirical question remains as to whether there are two primary subtypes of dyslexia.

The plausibility of two subtypes of dyslexia has been suggested by results from the acquired dyslexia literature. Although individuals who once could read but later have difficulty due to brain injury or illness often show complex patterns of strengths and weaknesses, individuals are found on occasion whose problems are limited to one of the two kinds of decoding (Baddeley, Ellis, Miles, & Lewis, 1982; Coltheart, 1987). Individuals characterized as surface dyslexics have selective impairment in decoding known words relatively automatically but are able to sound out new words. Conversely, individuals characterized as phonological (or deep) dyslexics have a selective impairment in sounding out new words but are able to decode known words relatively automatically (Newcombe & Marshall,

1981; Shallice, Warrington, & McCarthy, 1983). It should be noted that the examples of individuals with purely phonological or surface acquired dyslexia who have featured prominently in the literature on acquired dyslexia are the exception rather than the rule; most individuals with acquired dyslexia are properly classified as 'mixed' as they exhibit some deficits in both phonological and orthographic processing.

The existence of phonological and surface acquired dyslexia motivated investigation of comparable subtypes in developmental dyslexia (Baddeley et al., 1982; Bryant & Impey, 1986; Castles & Coltheart, 1993; Coltheart, 1987; Snowling, 1983). However, even if there are phonological and surface types of acquired dyslexia, the story might be different for developmental dyslexia for several reasons. The problem of being selectively impaired in a type of reading due to illness or injury after previously having developed the skill normally may be different from that of being impaired in developing the skill in the first place (Castles & Coltheart, 1993). It also is the case that a strong correlation exists between pseudoword and exception word reading for normal readers as well as individuals with dyslexia (e.g., Booth, Perfetti, & MacWhinney, 1999; Ehri, 1997, 1998; Manis, Custodio, & Szeszulski, 1993; Share, 1995, 1999).

Subtyping studies of individuals with dyslexia have used what have become known as hard and soft criteria for subtype identification (Stanovich, Siegel, & Gottardo, 1997a). The hard criterion is met if there is subnormal performance in either pseudoword or exception word performance and normal performance in the other type of decoding. The soft criterion is met if there is a relative discrepancy in pseudoword and exception word performance without the requirement that either type of decoding reaches a normal level of performance.

Castles and Coltheart (1993) gave lists of pseudowords and irregular words to students with dyslexia and a chronological-age-matched sample of normal readers. They used a regression procedure to predict pseudoword decoding performance from irregular word decoding performance and, conversely, used pseudoword decoding performance to predict irregular word decoding performance. Confidence intervals were drawn around the regression line based on control group performance. The results were that 15 percent of dyslexic individuals met the hard classification criteria for the phonological subtype and 19 percent met the hard criteria for the surface subtype. Using the soft classification criteria, 55 percent and 30 percent of the sample met the requirements for phonological and surface subtypes, respectively, and 6 percent of the sample showed a dual deficit, with impairments in both phonological and orthographic processing.

However, a concern about the Castles and Coltheart (1993) study is the use of a chronological-age-matched control group rather than reading-age-matched control group (Manis, Seidenberg, Doi, McBride-Chang, & Peterson, 1996; Stanovich et al., 1997a; Stanovich, Siegel, Gottardo, Chiappe, & Sidhu, 1997b). Using a chronological-age-matched control group will result in comparing good and poor readers who differ in overall amount of reading development, confounding general development and skill acquisition with differences that are specific to dyslexia. This problem can be solved by using a reading-age-matched control group (Stanovich, 1988; Stanovich, Nathan, & Zolman, 1988). Given the wide range in both chronological age and reading abilities within Castles and Coltheart's (1993) sample, Stanovich et al. (1997a) reanalyzed the original Castles and Coltheart data using a reading-age-matched control group of normal readers. The results changed dramatically. Now, 38 percent of the sample of poor readers met the soft phonological subtype criteria, but only 5 percent (two individuals) met the soft surface subtype criteria. Stanovich et al. (1997a) concluded that phonological subtype represents a deviant pattern of processing consistent with conceptualizations of dyslexia, but that the surface subtype could not be distinguished from younger normal readers. In other words, the surface 'subtype' resembled a developmental lag as opposed to a developmental difference in performance.

Manis et al. (1996) looked at hard and soft subtypes within a dyslexic group and both a chronological-age-matched and a reading-age-matched control group. Comparison of these disabled readers with their chronologically age-matched peers resulted in 10 percent of the sample meeting the hard classification criteria for each subtype. Using the soft classification scheme, 33 percent of the dyslexic group was categorized as the phonological subtype, 30 percent as the surface subtype, and 10 percent met the criteria for inclusion in both subtypes. However, when compared to the younger, reading-age-matched group, no surface subtype individuals remained.

Stanovich et al. (1997a) performed subtype analyses using the soft criteria with a sample of readers with dyslexia, normal readers matched on chronological age, and younger normal readers matched on reading age. Using the chronological age matched controls, they found that 25 percent, 22 percent, and 28 percent of the dyslexic sample could be classified as members of the phonological subtype, surface subtype, or both subtypes, respectively. After switching to a reading-age-matched control group, 25 percent of the dyslexic group was identified as representing the phonological subtype and only one disabled reader (less than 2 percent of the dyslexic sample) met the surface subtype criteria. The results were similar when Stanovich and Siegel (1994) performed subtype analysis on older children. Finally, Manis, Seidenberg, Stallings, Joanisse, Bailey, Freedman, et al. (1999) carried out a 2-year longitudinal study of subtypes of dyslexia. The results again supported a phonological subtype but not a surface subtype of dyslexia.

In summary, the results of studies of phonological and surface subtypes of dyslexia support the phonological subtype as a case of deviant development in which the ability to sound out new words is impaired. In contrast, the surface subtype of dyslexia appears to be a case of developmental lag in which impaired readers perform comparably to younger normally-developing readers.

Beyond phonological and surface subtypes of dyslexia

More recently, Ziegler and colleagues (2008; Ziegler, 2011) extended the study of possible subtypes of dyslexia downward to a more fine-grained level. Their novel approach combined assessing performance on sub-skills representing components of the DRC model of decoding (Coltheart et al., 2001) and then using computer simulation to model patterns of sub-skill and reading performance at the level of the individual subject. The DRC model begins decoding words using visual feature units that are connected to letter units. From there, the model branches: a nonlexical route relies on grapheme-phoneme correspondence rules to get to the phoneme and speech output system; a lexical route relies on an orthographic lexicon (i.e., a dictionary of word spellings) and a phonological lexicon (i.e., a dictionary of word pronunciations) to get to the phoneme and speech output system.

Three tasks were used to measure components of the DRC model. A letter-search task required participants to identify whether a target letter was present in either an unpronounceable consonant string (e.g., KWTLD) or a real word. Performance at searching for the target letter when it was embedded in the unpronounceable consonant strings was used to assess the functioning of position-specific letter processing and the orthographic lexicon. Also, from this same task, a measure of the word superiority effect was calculated as the difference in letter search performance when the target letter was embedded in a word as opposed to an unpronounceable consonant string. The word superiority effect was a second measure of the efficiency of the orthographic lexicon. A picture naming task was used as a measure of the efficiency of the phonological lexicon. Common pictures were shown individually on a computer screen and the time to name the picture was recorded. Although described as a measure of the efficiency of the phonological lexicon, presumably this measure also reflected the efficiency of the phoneme and speech output system because the pictures were named orally. Finally, an odd one out version of a phoneme matching task was used to measure the efficiency of an important aspect of the nonlexical route. For each trial, three spoken CVC words were presented, two of which shared either the initial or the final phoneme. The participants' task was to indicate which one did not share either the initial or the final phoneme that the other two shared. This, of course, does not fully capture the full grapheme-phoneme correspondence rule component of the nonlexical route, but arguably a deficit in phonemic awareness as evidenced by poor performance on the phoneme-matching task would be more consequential to the nonlexical route compared to the lexical route. The tasks, along with measures of regular word, irregular word, and nonword decoding were given to 24 individuals with dyslexia and 24 age-matched controls.

Beginning with group differences in average performance, the dyslexic group performed more poorly than the age-matched controls on letter search, picture naming, and phoneme matching. The effect sizes for picture naming and phoneme matching were considerably larger than that for letter search. No group difference was found for the word superiority effect. Turning to the decoding measures, the dyslexic group was less accurate in decoding the nonwords and irregular words but not the regular words. However, group differences in latency were found for regular words as well as irregular words and nonwords.

Surface and phonological subtypes were identified using Castles and Coltheart's regression procedure. Out of the 24 individuals in the dyslexic sample, seven (29 percent) were identified as surface dyslexics and four (19 percent) were identified as phonological dyslexics. However, the differences between surface and phono-logical dyslexics were not as expected, in that surface dyslexics showed clear phonological deficits. What makes this approach novel is that the profiles of individual participants with dyslexia were analyzed with respect to their perform-ance on the tasks representing components of the DRC model. A deficit in letter search was found for 40 percent of the dyslexic sample. A deficit in rapid object naming was found for 70 percent of the dyslexic sample, and a deficit in phoneme matching was found for 80 percent of the dyslexic sample. Eight individuals in the dyslexic sample had a single deficit, whereas seven had two deficits and nine had three deficits. The pattern of performance of each of the individuals in the dyslexic sample was then modeled computationally, and the results of the simulation accounted for a highly significant 48 percent of the variance in the behavioral data.

A potentially important limitation of this study is the use of a chronological-age-matched control group as opposed to a reading-age-matched control group. Given the pattern of results noted for the earlier series of studies that investigated the possibility of phonological and surface subtypes of dyslexia, it is possible that support for the surface subtype would diminish or vanish entirely if the study were to be replicated with a reading-age-matched control group.

Conclusions

The history of developmental dyslexia is characterized by reports of many purported causes that have turned out to be little more than myths. Part of the problem is the fact that many things are correlated with impaired reading. Ehri (1979) described four possible relations between a target skill and reading. First, a target skill might be a prerequisite in that normal reading is impossible unless the target skill has been acquired. Second, a target skill may facilitate the devel-opment of reading but may not actually be a prerequisite. Third, a target skill may be a consequence of either impaired or normal reading. Fourth and finally, a target skill might be an incidental correlate by virtue of relations between some third variable and both the target skill and reading.

Merely comparing the performance of individuals with dyslexia to normally developing, chronological-age-matched peers is not sufficient to distinguish which of the four possible relations exist between a target skill and reading. At least three kinds of studies support causal inferences to varying degrees. The reading-age-matched design (Bryant & Goswami, 1986) compares reading performance of children with dyslexia to a control group of younger normally developing readers who are at the same performance level. Longitudinal correla-tional studies can support causal inferences, particularly when the autoregressive effect of a variable at an earlier time point being a potential cause of individual differences in the same variable at a subsequent time point is included, and when the design of the study also makes possible the testing of reciprocal relations. Finally, intervention studies that involve manipulation of levels of performance on a target variable and then look for corresponding effects on reading can support causal inferences, especially when random assignment to intervention and control conditions is carried out.

Based on many studies that have used various designs and featured a wide variety of languages and written scripts, some conclusions about dyslexia are well established. First, dyslexia occurs in every language and type of writing system that has been studied to date. Second, word-level reading is the key weakness, as opposed to comprehension. Third, although some individuals with dyslexia have weaknesses in a variety of areas, impaired phonological processing appears to be a universal cause of dyslexia. Fourth, there is little support for subtypes of dyslexia. However, newer approaches that leverage existing models of decoding to identify potential causes of dyslexia have the potential to discover valid subtypes.

- Dyslexia represents low end of normal variation in reading ability where word-level reading is the key weakness, as opposed to comprehension. Given the fact that reading involves both vision and language, deficits in either vision or language have been proposed as origins of dyslexia.
- The language system that appears to be a universal cause of dyslexia is the phonological processing system. Phonological processing refers to using speech-based codes in processing written and oral language. Phonological awareness and rapid naming are two aspects of phonological processing that have been implicated in dyslexia. Phonological awareness refers to an awareness of phonological elements that make up the sound structure of oral language. Rapid naming refers to the efficiency with which phonological codes associated with visual objects, such as letters, are retrieved from long term memory.
- Regardless of the oral language or writing system involved, impaired phonological processing is observed in individuals with dyslexia although skills such as orthographic and morphological awareness may also be implicated, depending on the nature of the script that must be learned.
- Finally, there is little support for phonological and surface subtypes of dyslexia. The phonological subtype is a case of deviant development in which the ability to sound out new words is impaired. In contrast, the surface subtype of dyslexia appears to be a case of developmental lag in which impaired readers perform comparably to younger normally-developing readers.

Acknowledgments

Support for writing this chapter was provided by Grant P50 HD052120 from the *Eunice Kennedy Shriver* National Institute of Child Health and Human Development (NICHD).

References

Aaron, P. G. (1989). Qualitative and quantitative differences among dyslexic, normal, and nondyslexic poor readers. *Reading & Writing, 1*, 291–308.

Adams, M. J. & Bruck, M. (1993). Word recognition: The interface of educational policies and scientific research. *Reading & Writing, 5*, 113–139.

Arnbak, E. & Elbro, C. (2000). The effects of morphological awareness training on the reading and spelling skills of young dyslexics. *Scandinavian Journal of Educational Research, 44*, 229–251.

Baddeley, A. D., Ellis, N. C., Miles, T. R., & Lewis, V. J. (1982). Developmental and acquired dyslexia: A comparison. *Cognition, 11*, 185–199.

Bloomfield, L. (1933). *Language*. Oxford, England: Holt.

Booth, J. R., Perfetti, C. A., & MacWhinney, B. (1999). Quick, automatic, and general activation of orthographic and phonological representations in young readers. *Developmental Psychology, 35*, 3–19.

Bruck, M. (1990). Word recognition skills of adults with childhood diagnoses of dyslexia. *Developmental Psychology, 26*, 439–454.

Bruck, M. (1993). Word recognition and component phonological processing skills of adults with childhood diagnosis of dyslexia. *Developmental Review, 13*, 258–268.

Bryant, P. & Goswami, U. (1986). Strengths and weaknesses of the reading level design: A comment on Blackman, Mamen and Ferguson. *Psychological Bulletin, 100*, 101–103.

Bryant, P. E. & Impey, L. (1986). The similarities between normal readers and developmental and acquired dyslexics. *Cognition. 24*, 121–137.

Byrne, B., Fielding-Barnsley, R., & Ashley, L. (2000). Effects of preschool phoneme identity training after six years: Outcome level distinguished from rate of response. *Journal of Educational Psychology, 92*, 659–667.

Caravolas, M. (2005). The nature and causes of dyslexia in different languages. In M. Snowling & C. Hulme (Eds), *The science of reading: A handbook* (pp. 336–355) Malden, MA: Blackwell Publishing.

Castles, A. & Coltheart, M. (1993). Varieties of developmental dyslexia. *Cognition, 47*, 149–180.

Castles, A. & Coltheart, M. (2004). Is there a causal link from phonological awareness to success in learning to read? *Cognition, 91*, 77–111.

Coltheart, M. (1987). Varieties of developmental dyslexia: A comment on Bryant and Impey. *Cognition, 27*, 97–101.

Coltheart, M., Rastle, K., Perry, C., Langdon, R., & Ziegler, J. (2001). DRC: A dual route cascaded model of visual word recognition and reading aloud. *Psychological Review, 108*, 204–256.

Crowder, R. G. & Wagner, R. K. (1992). *The psychology of reading: An introduction* (2nd edn). London: Oxford University Press.

DeFrancis, J. (1989). *Visible speech: The diverse oneness of writing systems*. Honolulu, HI: University of Hawaii Press.

De Jong, P. F. & van der Leij, A. (2003). Developmental changes in the manifestation of a phonological deficit in dyslexic children learning to read a regular orthography. *Journal of Educational Psychology, 95*, 22–40.

Eden, G. F., Stern, J. F., Wood, M. H., & Wood, F. B. (1995). Verbal and visual problems in dyslexia. *Journal of Learning Disabilities, 28*, 282–290.

Ehri, L. C. (1979). Linguistic insight: Threshold of reading acquisition. In T. Waller & G. MacKinnon (Eds), *Reading research: Advances in theory and practice* (pp. 66–114). New York: Academic Press.

Ehri, L. C. (1997). Sight word learning in normal readers and dyslexics. In B. A. Blachman (Ed.), *Foundations of reading acquisition and dyslexia: Implications for early intervention* (pp. 163–189). Mahwah, NJ: Lawrence Erlbaum Associates.

Ehri, L. C. (1998). Grapheme-phoneme knowledge is essential to learning to read words in English. In J. L. Metsala & L. C. Ehri (Eds.), *Word recognition in beginning literacy* (pp. 3–40). Mahwah, NJ: Lawrence Erlbaum Associates.

Ehri, L. C., Nunes, S. R., Stahl, S. A., & Willows, D. M. (2001a). Systematic phonics instruction helps students learn to read: Evidence from the National Reading Panel's meta-analysis. *Review of Educational Research, 71*, 393–447.

Ehri, L. C., Nunes, S. R., Willows, D. M., Schuster, B. V., Yaghoub-Zadeh, Z., & Shanahan, T. (2001b). Phonemic awareness instruction helps children learn to read: Evidence from the National Reading Panel's meta-analysis. *Reading Research Quarterly, 36*, 250–287.

Fletcher, J. M., Lyon, G. R., Fuchs, L. S., & Barnes, M. A. (2007). *Learning disabilities: From identification to intervention.* New York: The Guilford Press.

Foorman, B. R., Chen, D.-T., Carlson, C., Moats, L., Francis, D. J., & Fletcher, J. M. (2003). The necessity of the alphabetic principle to phonemic awareness instruction. *Reading and Writing: An Interdisciplinary Journal, 16*, 289–324.

Fox, E. (1994). Grapheme-phoneme correspondence in dyslexic and matched control readers. *British Journal of Psychology, 85*, 41–53.

Frost, R., Katz, L., & Bentin, S. (1987). Strategies for visual word recognition and orthographical depth: A multilingual comparison. *Journal of Experimental Psychology: Human Perception and Performance, 13*, 104–115.

Gelb, I. J. (1952). *A study of writing.* Chicago: University of Chicago Press.

Goulandris, N. (2003) Introduction: developmental dyslexia, language and orthographies. In N. Goulandris (Ed.), *Dyslexia in different languages: Cross-linguistic comparisons.* Philadelphia, PA: Whurr Publishers.

Halderman, L. K., Ashby, J., & Perfetti, C. A. (2011). Phonology: an early and integral role in identifying words. In J. S. Adelman (Ed.), *Visual word recognition Vol. 1: Meaning and context, individuals and development.* Hove, UK: Psychology Press.

Harm, M. W. & Seidenberg, M. S. (2004). Computing the meanings of words in reading: Cooperative division of labor between visual and phonological processes. *Psychological Review, 111*, 662–720.

Hulme, C., Snowling, M., Caravolas, M., & Carroll, J. (2005). Phonological skills are (probably) one cause of success in learning to read: A comment on Castles and Coltheart. *Scientific Studies of Reading, 9*, 351–365.

Lovegrove, W., Martin, F., & Slaghuis, W. (1986). A theoretical and experimental case for a visual deficit in specific reading disability. *Cognitive Neuropsychology, 3*, 225–267.

Lovett, M. W., Steinbach, K. A., & Frijters, J. C. (2000). Remediating the core deficits of developmental reading disability: A double-deficit perspective. *Journal of Learning Disabilities, 33*, 334–358.

Lyon, G. R., Shaywitz, S. E., & Shaywitz, B. A. (2003). A definition of dyslexia. *Annals of Dyslexia, 53*, 1–14.

McCandliss, B. D., Cohen, L., & Dehaene, S. (2003). The visual word form area: expertise for reading in the fusiform gyrus. *Trends in Cognitive Science, 7*, 293–299.

Manis, F. R., Custodio, R., & Szeszulski, P. A. (1993). Development of phonological and orthographic skill: A 2-year longitudinal study of dyslexic children. *Journal of Experimental Child Psychology, 56*, 64–86.

Manis, F. R., Seidenberg, M. S., Doi, L. M., McBride-Chang, C., & Peterson, A. (1996). On the bases of two subtypes of development dyslexia. *Cognition, 58,* 157–195.

Manis, F. R., Seidenberg, M. S., Stallings, L., Joanisse, M., Bailey, C., Freedman, L., Curtin, S., & Keating, P. (1999). Development of dyslexic subgroups: A one-year follow up. *Annals of Dyslexia, 49,* 105–134.

Newcombe, F. & Marshall, J. C. (1981). On psycholinguistic classification of the acquired dyslexias. *Annals of Dyslexia, 31,* 29–46.

Nation, K. (2005). Children's reading comprehension difficulties. In M. J. Snowling & C. Hulme (Eds), *The science of reading.* Oxford, UK: Blackwell.

Nicolson, R. I., Fawcett, A. J., & Dean, P. (2001). Developmental dyslexia: The cerebellar deficit hypothesis. *Trends in Neurosciences, 24,* 508–511.

Parrila, R., Kirby, J. R., & McQuarrie, L. (2004). Articulation rate, naming speed, verbal short-term memory, and phonological awareness: Longitudinal predictors of early reading development? *Scientific Studies of Reading, 8,* 3–26.

Parrila, R., Aunola, K., Leskinen, E., Nurmi, J. E., & Kirby, J. R. (2005). Development of individual differences in reading: Results from longitudinal studies in English and Finnish. *Journal of Educational Psychology, 97,* 299–319.

Perfetti, C. A., Beck, I., Bell, L. C., & Hughes, C. (1991). Phonemic knowledge and learning to read are reciprocal: A longitudinal study of first grade children. In K. E. Stanovich (Ed.), *Children's reading and the development of phonological awareness.* Detroit, MI: Wayne State University Press.

Piasta, S. B. & Wagner, R. K. (2007). Dyslexia: Identification and classification. In E. Grigorenko & A. Napes (Eds,) *Single word reading: Behavioral and biological perspectives* (pp. 309–326). Mahwah, NJ: Erlbaum.

Plaut, D. C., McClelland, J. L., Seidenberg, M. S., & Patterson, K. (1996). Understanding normal and impaired word reading: Computational principles in quasi-regular domains. *Psychological Review, 103,* 56–115.

Plomin, R. & Kovas, Y. (2005). Generalist genes and learning disabilities. *Psychological Bulletin, 131,* 592–617.

Rack, J. P., Snowling, M. J., & Olson, R. K. (1992). The nonword reading deficit in developmental dyslexia: A review. *Reading Research Quarterly, 27,* 28–53.

Ramus, F., Rosen, S., Dakin, S., Day, B., Castellote, J., White, S., & Frith, U. (2003). Theories of developmental dyslexia: Insights from a multiple case study of dyslexic adults. *Brain, 126,* 841–865.

Rashotte, C. A., MacPhee, K., & Torgesen, J. K. (2001). The effectiveness of a group reading instruction program with poor readers in multiple grades. *Learning Disability Quarterly, 24,* 119–134.

Rayner, K. & Pollatsek, A. (1989). *The psychology of reading.* Upper Saddle River, NJ: Prentice Hall.

Rayner, K., Foorman, B. R., Perfetti, C. A., Pesetsky, D., & Seidenberg, M. S. (2001). How psychological science informs the teaching of reading. *Psychological Science in the Public Interest, 2,* 31–74.

Scarborough, H. S. (1984). Continuity between childhood dyslexia and adult reading. *British Journal of Psychology, 75,* 329–348.

Schatschneider, C., Carlson, C. D., Francis, D. J., Foorman, B. R., & Fletcher, J. M. (2002). Relationship of rapid automatized naming and phonological awareness in early reading development: Implications for the double-deficit hypothesis. *Journal of Learning Disabilities, 35,* 245–256.

Schatschneider, C., Fletcher, J. M., Francis, D. J., Carlson, C. D., & Foorman, B. R. (2004). Kindergarten prediction of reading skills: A longitudinal comparative analysis. *Journal of Educational Psychology, 96*, 265–282.

Schneider, W., Roth, E., & Ennemoser, M. (2000). Training phonological skills and letter knowledge in children at risk for dyslexia: A comparison of three kindergarten intervention programs. *Journal of Educational Psychology, 92*, 284–295.

Schotter, E. R. & Rayner, K. (2011). Eye movements and word recognition during reading. In J. S. Adelman (Ed.), *Visual word recognition Vol. 2: Meaning and context, individuals and development.* Hove, UK: Psychology Press.

Seidenberg, M. S. & McClelland, J. L. (1989). A distributed, developmental model of word recognition and naming. *Psychological Review, 96*, 523–568.

Seymour, P. H. K., Aro, M., & Erskine, J. M. (2003). Foundation literacy acquisition in European orthographies. *British Journal of Psychology, 94*, 143–174.

Shallice, T., Warrington, E. K., & McCarthy, R. (1983). Reading without semantics. *Quarterly Journal of Experimental Psychology, 35A*, 111–138.

Share, D. L. (1995). Phonological recoding and self-teaching: Sine qua non of reading acquisition. *Cognition, 55*, 151–218.

Share, D. L. (1999). Phonological recoding and orthographic learning: A direct test of the self-teaching hypothesis. *Journal of Experimental Child Psychology, 72*, 95–129.

Siegel, L. S. (2003). Basic cognitive processes and reading disabilities. In H. L. Swanson & K. R. Harris (Eds), *Handbook of learning disabilities* (pp. 158–181). New York: Guilford Press.

Snow, C. E., Burns, M. S., & Griffin, P. (Eds) (1998). *Preventing reading difficulties in young children.* Washington, D.C.: National Academy Press.

Snowling, M. J. (1983). The comparison of acquired and developmental disorders of reading: A discussion. *Cognition, 14*, 105–118.

Snowling, M. J. (2000). *Dyslexia.* Oxford: Blackwell.

Snowling, M. J. & Hulme, C. (1994). The development of phonological skills. *Philosophical transactions: Biological Sciences, 346* (1315), 21–27.

Stanovich, K. E. (1988). Explaining the differences between the dyslexic and the garden-variety poor reader: The phonological-core variable-difference model. *Journal of Learning Disabilities, 21*, 590–604, 612.

Stanovich, K. E. (1994). Does dyslexia exist? *Journal of Child Psychology & Psychiatry & Allied Disciplines, 35*, 579–595.

Stanovich, K. E. & Siegel, L. S. (1994). Phenotypic performance profile of children with reading disabilities: A regression based test of the phonological-core variable-difference model. *Journal of Educational Psychology 86*, 24–53.

Stanovich, K. E., Nathan, R. G., & Zolman, J. E. (1988). The developmental lag hypothesis in reading: Longitudinal and matched reading-level comparisons. *Child Development, 59*, 71–86.

Stanovich, K. E., Siegel, L. S., & Gottardo, A. (1997a). Converging evidence for phonological and surface subtypes of reading disability. *Journal of Educational Psychology, 89*, 114–127.

Stanovich, K. E., Siegel, L. S., Gottardo, A., Chiappe, P., & Sidhu, R. (1997b). Subtypes of developmental dyslexia: Differences in phonological and orthographic coding. In B. A. Blachman (Ed.), *Foundations of reading acquisition and dyslexia: Implications for early intervention* (pp. 115–141). Mahwah, NJ: Lawrence Erlbaum Associates.

Stein, J. (2001). The sensory basis of reading problems. *Developmental Neuropsychology, 20*, 509–534.

Tallal, P. & Piercy, M. (1973). Defects of non-verbal auditory perception in children with developmental aphasia. *Nature*, *241*, 468–469.

Torgesen, J. K., Alexander, A. W., Wagner, R. K., Rashotte, C. A., Voeller, K. K. S., & Conway, T. (2001). Intensive remedial instruction for children with severe reading disabilities: Immediate and long-term outcomes from two instructional approaches. *Journal of Learning Disabilities*, *34*, 33–58.

Vellutino, F. R. (1979). *Dyslexia: Theory and research*. Cambridge, MA: MIT Press.

Vidyasagar, T. R. & Pammer, K. (2010). Dyslexia: A deficit in visuo-spatial attention, not in phonological processing. *Trends in Cognitive Science*, *14*, 57–63.

Wagner, R. K. & Torgesen, J. K. (1987). The nature of phonological processing and its causal role in the acquisition of reading skills. *Psychological Bulletin*, *101*, 192–212.

Wagner, R. K., Torgesen, J.K., & Rashotte, C. A. (1994). Development of reading-related phonological processing abilities: New evidence of bidirectional causality from a latent variable longitudinal study. *Developmental Psychology*, *30*(1), 73–87.

Wagner, R. K., Torgesen, J. K., Rashotte, C. A., Hecht, S., Barker, T., Burgess, S., & Garon, T. (1997). Causal relations between the development of phonological processing and reading: A five-year longitudinal study. *Developmental Psychology*, *33*, 468–479.

Wagner, R. K., Torgesen, J.K., & Rashotte, C.A. (1999). *Comprehensive test of phonological processing*. Austin, TX: PRO-ED Publishing, Inc.

Wagner, R. K., Piasta, S. B., & Torgesen, J. K. (2006). Learning to read. In M. A. Gernsbacher & M. J. Traxler (Eds), *Handbook of psycholinguistics* (pp. 1111–1142). San Diego, CA: Academic Press.

Werker, J. F., Bryson, S. E., & Wassenberg, K. (1989). Toward understanding the problem in severely disabled readers: II. Consonant errors. *Applied Psycholinguistics*, *10*, 13–30.

West, T. (1992). A future of reversals: Dyslexic talents in a world of computer visualizations. *Annals of Dyslexia*, *42*, 124–139.

Wimmer, H. & Mayringer, H. (2002). Dysfluent reading in the absence of spelling difficulties: A specific disability in regular orthographies. *Journal of Educational Psychology*, *94*, 272–277.

Wolf, M. & Bowers, P. G. (1999). The double deficit hypothesis for the developmental dyslexias. *Journal of Educational Psychology*, *91*, 415–438.

Wolf, M., Pfeil, C. Lotz, R., & Biddle, K. (1994). Towards a more universal understanding of the developmental dyslexias: The contribution of orthographic factors. In V. W. Berninger (Ed.), *The varieties of orthographic knowledge 1: Theoretical and developmental issues*. Dordrecht, The Netherlands: Kluwer.

Ziegler, J. C. (2011). Understanding developmental dyslexia through computational modeling: An individual deficit-based simulation approach. In P. McCardle, B. Miller, J. R. Lee and O. J. L. Tzeng (Eds), *Dyslexia across languages*. Baltimore: Paul H. Brookes Publishing.

Ziegler, J. C. & Goswami, U. (2005). Reading acquisition, developmental dyslexia, and skilled reading across languages: A psycholinguistic grain size theory. *Psychological Bulletin*, *131*, 3–29.

Ziegler, J. C., Castel, C., Pech-Georgel, C., George, F., Alario, F.-X., & Perry, C. (2008). Developmental dyslexia and the dual route model of reading: Simulating individual differences and subtypes. *Cognition*, *107*, 151–178.

10   Biological-level account of developmental dyslexia

John F. Stein

Those who originally developed the concept of dyslexia were all doctors, such as the ophthalmologists, Berliner and Hinshelwood, and the neurologists Orton and Critchley. Therefore they viewed both acquired and developmental dyslexia as having a biological basis. More recently however, the study of developmental dyslexia has been strongly influenced by Chomsky's psycholinguistic movement. So now the dominant theory in the field is a linguistic one, namely that it is caused by a defect in representing the sounds of words in the brain to match with their written forms, a phonological deficit. Most people agree that these phonological representations are defective in dyslexics. But many now believe that this explanation does not go far enough and that we need a biological description of what brain differences cause the phonological failure. This would start with the genes that control development of the brain.

Genetics

The strong evidence that developmental dyslexia is hereditary means that nobody any longer believes that it is 'all in the mind'. Everybody agrees that genes play an important part in controlling the development of the brain; hence there must be some differences between the brains of dyslexics and good readers. But many still cling to the Chomskian idea that human language is the product of a separate genetically endowed brain module, Chomsky's 'encapsulated' linguistic processor, hence that human speech is somehow special (Chomsky, 1975). They argue that phonological difficulties are the result of inheriting a defective language module and can arise independently of any lower level auditory or visual processing difficulties. However I join de Haen in arguing that, like language itself, reading piggy-backed on pre-existing lower level visual and auditory processing capacities (Dehaene, 2010). Thus my basic argument is that reading difficulties ought to be traced back beyond phonology to fundamental differences in aspects of visual and auditory processing.

Twin studies put the heritability of dyslexia at ca. 60 per cent (Wadsworth, Olson, & DeFries, 2010). The most frequently replicated genes that have been linked with reading problems seem to be involved in the early development of the brain in utero. The very fundamental nature of these processes makes it unlikely, though not impossible, that these genes would have a selective effect on the development of language alone. Instead there is increasing evidence that many, if not all, dyslexics have mild deficits in basic sensory processing. It is possible that failure to show such deficits reliably in all dyslexics is because current techniques are not yet sensitive enough to show them.

Understanding how genes influence reading ability is beginning to illuminate how reading difficulties arise from such underlying sensorimotor deficiencies. But perhaps the most important gain that has already accrued is that acceptance of its genetic basis shows clearly that dyslexia is a real neurological condition, and not a euphemism to hide middle-class children's laziness or stupidity; the latter view is all too frequently maintained by some people. Demonstrating that dyslexia has a genetic basis makes it impossible to maintain that it is 'purely psychological'; rather it has a clear biological basis. Knowing that his dyslexia is a respectable neurological diagnosis, and not another word for laziness or stupidity can transform a child's self confidence.

One unexpected outcome of applying genetic techniques to the study of the development of reading skills was the small number of genes that appear to be involved. Unlike the 600 or so genes of small effect that have been implicated in, for example, schizophrenia (Porteous, 2008) less than a dozen with much larger effects have been associated with dyslexia, and their role in reading is steadily being unravelled (Williams & O'Donovan, 2006). This is probably because the reading phenotype is so much easier to define quantitatively than many other higher functions, such as emotion, motivation or delusional thinking.

Tony Monaco and I have taken advantage of the large number of children and families with reading problems that we have seen around Oxford to carry out quantitative trait linkage (QTL) whole genome association (WGA) studies. We collected nearly 400 Oxford families and replicated many of our findings in 200 Colorado families provided by Dick Olsen. Here I shall just discuss one new gene that these analyses have revealed.

This is a gene on the short arm of chromosome 6 in the middle of the major histocompatibility (MHC) set of genes. We found that this gene, already named KIAA 0319, is often under-expressed in dyslexia (Paracchini, Thomas, Castro, Lai, Paramasivam,Wang, et al., 2006). The protein it encodes is now known to be a partly extracellular, cell-to-cell signalling molecule involved in the control of neuronal migration. In the normal course of the early development of the cerebral cortex neuronal stem cells divide in the ventricular zone, into one radial glial cell and one neurone; this then divides and subdivides further. Under the control of a variety of signalling molecules, such as KIAA 0319 and other gene products that have been associated with dyslexia, neurones migrate up the radial processes of the glial cells to take up their correct positions on the surface, and thereby form the mature six layers of the cerebral cortex. The last cells to divide form the most superficial layer, passing through the earlier layers to get there.

If KIAA 0319 is completely switched off by local electroporation of a specific inhibitory RNAi into the ventricular zone in the rat embryo brain, the neurones fail to migrate at all and remain clustered around the ventricle (Paracchini et al., 2006).

The gene is not completely knocked out in dyslexia, but the allele found in dyslexia causes underexpression by about 30 per cent. Consistent with this, in dyslexic brains that had been donated to the Orton brain bank at Harvard, Galaburda, Sherman, Rosen, Aboitiz, and Geschwind (1985) found clear developmental migration abnormalities. These took the form of cortical ectopias, aberrant outgrowths of particularly large neurones out beyond layer 1 on the surface of the cortex. It seems likely that this over-migration results from these cells failing to synthesise enough KIAA 0319 cell–cell signal protein to respond correctly to migration control signals.

At least two of the other genes that have been associated with dyslexia (DCDC2 and ROBO) have also been found to be involved in the control of neuronal migration early in the development of the brain (Galaburda, LoTurco, Ramus, Fitch, & Rosen, 2006). Further unravelling of the precise function of these genes promises to revolutionise our understanding not only of dyslexia, but also development of the brain in general. Not only dyslexia, but also the whole gamut of neurodevelopmental conditions that overlap with it both genetically and phenotypically should benefit, such as developmental dysphasia (specific language impairment), dyscalculia, developmental dyspraxia (developmental coordination disorder – DCD), Attention deficit hyperactivity disorder (ADHD) and the autistic spectrum.

Autoimmunity

KIAA 0319 is situated within the MHC immune control gene complex. It has recently become clear that this system is involved in both the development of the brain and also its plasticity later in life (Needleman, Liu, El-Sabeawy, Jones, & McAllister, 2010). The MHC system seems to play a particularly important role in the development of 'magnocellular' neurones (Shatz, 2009). These are large cells found throughout the whole nervous system, in the visual, auditory, cutaneous, proprioceptive, memory (hippocampus) and motor systems (motor cortex and cerebellum). They all express specific surface 'magnocellular signature' antigens, such as the one known in cats as CAT 301, implying that they all arise from the same lineage. They are specialised for rapid conduction, fast responses and tracking transients in real time (i.e., for temporal processing). As we shall see they play a particularly significant role in reading. But they seem to be especially vulnerable to genetic, immune and environmental damage.

Antineuronal antibodies are found in the blood in many general autoimmune conditions such as systemic lupus erythromatosus (SLE; Lahita, 1988) The BSXB mouse has been bred to exhibit strong autoimmunity, as an animal model of such conditions as lupus. Ectopias similar to those seen in dyslexia develop in the brains of these mice and these are associated with antineuronal antibodies that appear to have occluded the normal migration control sites.

So it is not surprising to find that children of mothers with lupus have a very high incidence of dyslexia and other neurodevelopmental conditions. Interestingly also, dyslexic children and their families consistently report a higher prevalence of immunological problems, not only lupus which is rare, but also much commoner conditions such as eczema, asthma and allergies (Hugdahl et al., Synnevag, & Satz, 1990).

It seems therefore that dyslexia is often associated with abnormalities of the immune system. We therefore decided to see whether mothers with dyslexic children showed any signs of circulating anti-neuronal antibodies in their blood. We took serum from mothers who had had two or more dyslexic or autistic children and injected it into pregnant mice. We then tested the offspring for behavioural abnormalities and looked for anomalies in cerebellar metabolism by magnetic resonance spectroscopy (MRS) and in cerebellar antibody binding. We found that indeed these young mice showed deficits in motor coordination tests. These abnormalities were associated with antibodies binding to the pup's cerebellar Purkinje cells (many of which are magnocellular neurones that stain for CAT 301) and their severity correlated with MRS indices of impaired cerebellar metabolism (Vincent, Deacon, Dalton, Salmond, Blamire, Pendlebury, et al., 2002).

Reading pathways

How do these genetically and immunologically based abnormalities in the development of the brain lead to reading difficulties? First let us consider the main neural systems used for reading. Reading is in fact mainly a visual process. Most lay people think this is obvious; the first stage of reading, namely identifying letters, groups of letters or words is clearly visual. Blind people cannot read print.

Most people agree that there are two main routes to understanding written material: sublexical and lexical, though there is controversy about how separate they are, and there are clearly interactions between them (Manis, McBride-Chang, Seidenberg, Doi, & Petersen, 1997). Beginning readers need to use the longer sublexical or phonological route. First individual letters are identified and ordered visually and then they are translated into the sounds they stand for. Then these are melded into the word sound and its meaning becomes clear.

However practised readers already have many words in their visual lexicon. So they can use the whole word, lexical or visual semantic route. They can identify the whole word visually and thus rapidly gain its meaning, so they do not need to employ the probably more time consuming phonological route.

Visual requirements of reading

The important point here is that both these routes rely first and foremost on visual analysis, though this is relatively more important for the lexical route. Thus a very large proportion of the information processing required for reading is visual. It is pertinent therefore to focus more precisely on what the visual requirements of reading are.

Obviously letters have to be identified correctly, so it is often assumed that the crucial visual process for reading is the pathway that specialises in object identification, the so-called ventral or 'what' stream that projects from the primary visual cortex through areas V2, V4 to culminate in the anterior part of the left fusiform gyrus under the inferior temporal gyrus, in the so called 'visual word form area' (VWFA; Cohen & Dehaene, 2004). This area appears to be specialised for identifying written words, independently of their font, case, size, spacing, phonology or meaning.

It is equally important to be able to sequence the letters within a word in their right order. Dyslexics are more inaccurate and slow at sequencing series of letters than they are at identifying each individually. Correct sequencing depends on the properties of the other forward route from the primary visual cortex – the dorsal 'where' route that culminates in the parietal cortex. The ventral stream is specialised for identifying objects (what they are), whereas the dorsal stream is primarily devoted to determining where they are in relation to the observer, for the visual guidance of attention and of eye and limb movements (Goodale & Milner, 1992).

Visual magnocellular neurones

The visual input to this 'where' route is mainly, but not exclusively, provided by the visual magnocellular neurones. Retinal ganglion cells gather signals from the photoreceptors, bipolar, horizontal and amacrine cells and relay them to the lateral geniculate nucleus (LGN), thence to the primary visual cortex in the back of the occipital lobe. Ten percent of these retinal ganglion cells are much larger than the other 90 per cent of small parvocells – hence they are named magnocellular (m-) neurones. These project to the magnocellular layers of the LGN and to the superior colliculus to control eye movements (Maunsell, 1992).

The axons of these magnocells are heavily myelinated so that they conduct fast and their signals arrive at the visual cortex ca. 10 ms before the slower parvocell signals. Also their dendritic fields are 20–50 times the size of the parvocells'. At the reading distance this means that m- cells respond best to relatively large targets – around 5 mm in size; this is about half the average size of a word. Therefore they cannot identify the shapes of letters, which in small print subtend less than 1 mm. Still less can they detect letter features of 0.1 mm in size. But without identifying them they can rapidly indicate the positions of each letter. Thus they have high contrast and temporal frequency sensitivity, but low spatial frequency sensitivity; that is, they are specialised for indicating letter position, change, flicker and motion, even at very low light levels and contrasts, rather than detailed form or colour.

This combination of features makes their function not only to detect position, but also, in conjunction with motor signals they track self movements, in particular of the eyes. Knowing where the eyes are pointing in relation to your head and body enables you to locate objects in relation to your egocentre independently of their retinal position (Stein, 1992). Hence the m-system is extremely important, not only for identifying letters, but for correctly determining their order in a word.

Visual stabilisation

Because m- cells detect any unwanted image motion, they also provide crucial input to the systems that stabilise visual perception. Our eyes move around constantly, hence images move around the retina much of the time. Yet the world does not usually appear to move, because the predicted visual consequences of each eye movement are subtracted from the image motion it causes, to yield a stable percept.

Such compensation depends on the integrity of the visual magnocellular system, because this picks up the motion of images across the retina that is caused by eye movements. Between saccades from one object to the next the eyes are kept fixated to inspect each one by a negative feedback servo-control system. The eyes make small movements all the time; this is essential to prevent too much bleaching of the retinal pigments (Yarbus, 1965). But these miniature eye movements cause unwanted image motion. This is detected by retinal magnocells, and fed back to the ocularmotor servo system. This then brings the eyes back on target. So the integrity of the m- system is crucial not only for tracking eye movements to help indicate where they are pointing, but also for keeping them fixated on a single letter when required.

Even this servomechanism does not keep the eyes absolutely stationary. So images are always 'jittering' on the retina. This jitter would cause retinal images to blur if there were no mechanism to compensate for it. But most of us perceive a clear image. Murakami and Cavanagh (1998) proposed that normally the visual system removes jitter by estimating the minimal 'baseline' amount of retinal movement that is caused by the miniature eye movements. This is signalled by the m- ganglion cells. The retinal area showing the least motion then corresponds to features in the visual scene which are actually stationary. Hence we can subtract this 'motion minimum' from the motion signals coming from all over the retina; then any motion surviving this subtraction will denote real object motion in the outside world. This will correct for the small eye movements and allow a stable percept of truly stationary objects during fixation.

The dorsal visual pathway projects motion signals to the posterior parietal cortex (PPC), whose main function is to determine where things are in relation to the body's egocentre (Stein, 1992). At the same time a copy of the motor signals triggering the muscles to move the eyes is also sent to the posterior parietal cortex, to forewarn how the eyes will move. After the movement, eye muscle proprioceptors then signal to the PPC their new lengths. All these signals are used by the PPC to calculate how far the eyes will move, then how far they did in fact move. In this way they help to keep track of where each visual object is in relation to the body (Stein, 1992). Although crucial for attention and eye control, the motion of these images across the retina never reaches consciousness, so the world appears satisfactorily stationary.

Thus the magnocellular system plays crucial roles not only in sequencing small objects such as letters, but also in achieving stable visual perception. If it is deficient in any way these operations will be less precise and the subject will neither know precisely where his eyes are pointing, nor achieve a stable percept. He will not have accurate knowledge of where letters are positioned and his eyes will move around more than they should during fixation. Being unintended and uncontrolled these movements will not be accompanied by motor efference signals to indicate how large they were, so the image movements they cause may be treated as real movements of the external target. Hence letters may appear to move around and will be mislocated after each eye movement.

These problems will be exacerbated in the reading situation when the eyes need to converge at 25 cm away. If at one moment the right eye is looking at the d in the word dog and then a moment later it shifts to point at the g, the g will appear to have moved into the position previously occupied by the d. At the same time the other eye might be doing something different and so letters can appear to blur, go double, move in and out of the page or cross over each other.

Visual symptoms

These are exactly the kinds of 'visual stress' symptom of which many dyslexic children complain (Singleton & Henderson, 2007; Stein & Fowler, 1981). 'The letters blur'; 'they move over each other, so I can't tell what order they're meant to be in'. Half the children we see at our dyslexia clinics report such symptoms. In adult dyslexics such overt problems with clearly seeing text seem to be less common, and the dominant symptom in compensated adults is very poor spelling. Their inaccurate spellings probably reveal deficiencies in how their visual representations of words were laid down in their 'mind's eyes'. These are probably visual and attentional in origin and not 'phonological'.

Nevertheless at the moment the phonological theory of developmental dyslexia is still the most popular. Even though everyone agrees that at least some dyslexic children have visual problems, some put its prevalence very low – at less than 10 per cent of all dyslexics (Snowling, 2000). In contrast we find that 50 per cent of the children we see in our clinics have significant visual problems that often contribute to their phonological ones (Stein & Fowler, 2005).

These estimates also depend on what is counted as visual. If someone says that letters and words appear to move around, it is difficult to call this a phonological problem. But many children are so used to seeing the letters move around that they don't realise that it is abnormal, unless they are specifically asked. In adults apparent letter motion is much less common. But their visual word representations for spelling are often very poor, as noted earlier. Even without having symptoms of letters appearing to move around, not having a clear idea of the order of letters is also likely to have a visual origin.

Normally before you move your eyes something about it has attracted your attention. It grabs your attention; then you move your eyes. Accordingly the visual magnocellular system is engaged before any eye movements, to control the focus of your attention. Shifting attention accurately from one letter to another is therefore equally, if not more, important for determining letter order. The visual dorsal stream dominated by m- cell input shifts attention to each letter or word in order to determine what letter the ventral visual word form area should identify and in what order the letters appear (Cheng, Eysel, & Vidyasagar, 2004).

Magno impairments in dyslexia

Strictly speaking visual magnocells can only be defined in the subcortical visual system because they are only anatomically separated from the parvo system in the retina, LGN and layer 4c of the primary visual cortex. Thereafter magno and parvo systems converge and interact strongly. Hence the best way to test for deficits in dyslexics is to use stimuli that are selectively processed by the subcortical magnocellular areas.

Nevertheless visual magnocellular input dominates the dorsal 'where' corticofugal stream, so that tests focussing on these higher cortical areas can also provide evidence about impairments. Furthermore many of the neurones in the cortical dorsal stream may be termed magnocellular because they are large and express the magnocellular antigen, CAT 301, on their surfaces. However one always has to bear in mind that tasks involving higher area are functions of the whole dorsal stream; and this receives 10 per cent of its visual input from parvo and konio sources, not just the subcortical visual magnocellular input (Skottun, 1997). Therefore higher area visual tasks provide only circumstantial evidence for deficits of the subcortical visual magnocellular system. Nevertheless there is enough direct evidence from studying the subcortical visual m- stream specifically, together with the more circumstantial evidence from higher areas that receive large m- cell input, to conclude that many dyslexics do indeed have impaired visual m- cell function.

In fact there is evidence of m- abnormality in dyslexics at all subcortical magnocellular levels: retinal, LGN, primary visual cortex, and for the cortical dorsal 'where' stream from the primary visual cortex to MT/V5, posterior parietal cortex and the ultimate goal of both magno and parvo routes, the prefrontal cortex.

Retina

One of the most important features of m- cells is their non-linear character. They fire transiently not only when a light is switched on in their receptive field centre but also when it is switched off (rectification), so that if a grating is moved across the field they will fire at twice the temporal and spatial frequency of the grating. Since they are much more sensitive to low contrasts than parvo cells are, when contrast is increased from zero magno cells begin to respond much earlier than parvo cells. Since they signal at twice the frequency of the stimulus, this is interpreted visually as the grating not only moving at twice its true rate but as having twice the number of bars. This is called the spatial frequency doubling effect and it therefore constitutes a selective test of retinal magnocellular sensitivity (Maddess, Goldberg, Dobinson, Wine, Welsh, & James, 1999). Dyslexics consistently show a higher contrast threshold for perceiving such low spatial, high temporal frequency gratings (Pammer & Wheatley, 2001).

The same non-linearity can be seen in the visual evoked potential recorded from the primary visual cortex. If an oscillating grating or chequer board is used as a stimulus the m- cells fire twice each time a bar crosses their receptive field, that is, they fire at the 2nd harmonic of the stimulus frequency. Since parvo cells fire to the entry of the bar only and are inhibited by its exit they mainly respond just to the fundamental rather than the 2nd harmonic. So by measuring the ratio of the 2nd harmonic to the fundamental frequency in the evoked potential recorded over the occipital pole we can measure the sensitivity of an individual's m- system relative to his p- system. We have found that this ratio is very much lower in dyslexics; and this has turned out to be a very sensitive technique for detecting magnocellular impairment.

As discussed earlier another effect mediated by retinal m- cells is the 'jitter illusion'. When patterns imaged onto one part of the retina are jittered by a small amount equivalent to the size of miniature eye movements for several seconds, the m- cells there adapt and so give a falsely low estimate of the amplitude of the motion. Hence after the jitter is stopped images on unadapted adjacent parts of the retina will now appear to jitter. The duration of this illusion therefore gives a measure of the sensitivity of retinal m- cells. The more sensitive they are, the more adapted they will become, so the longer they will take to return to normal after the jitter stimulus, and the longer the subsequent jitter illusion will be (Murakami & Cavanagh, 1998). We have recently shown that in adult dyslexics this illusory percept is much shorter, and its duration correlates not only with another measure of m- cell function, visual motion sensitivity, but also with the dyslexics' reading accuracy and speed. These findings again support the view that dyslexics have deficits in visual magnocellular processing.

Lateral geniculate nucleus (LGN)

This is the main thalamic relay of visual information between the eye and the visual cortex. Here the m- retinal ganglion cells terminate in their own m- cell layers, separately from the parvo cell layers, one for each eye. Although the properties of the peripheral m- system have been mainly worked out by recording from the m- layers in the LGN in monkeys, we have as yet no non-invasive way of recording responses in the LGN directly in intact humans. But perhaps the best evidence for a magnocellular deficit came from Galaburda's post-mortem studies of five dyslexic human brains from the Orton brain bank. He found that the m- layers in the LGN in these brains were selectively impaired. Not only were the cells ca. 25 per cent smaller in the dyslexic compared with the control brains, but also they were not confined to their proper m- layers but many had mismigrated into the adjacent konio and parvo layers of the LGN (Livingstone, Rosen, Drislane, & Galaburda, 1991). Thus the LGN shows migration abnormalities similar to the ectopias found in the cerebral cortex in dyslexia (Galaburda et al., 1985). Probably all these result from inheriting the dyslexic alleles of the KIAA 0319, DCDC2 and ROBO genes.

Grating contrast sensitivity (CS) – primary visual cortex

Sensitivity to the contrast of black and white gratings is thought to be mediated mainly by the primary visual cortex (VI). Since Lovegrove's first report

(Lovegrove, Bowling, Badcock, & Blackwood, 1980; Turkeltaub, Flowers, Verbalis, Miranda, Gareau, & Eden, 2004) there have been several studies that have confirmed that the contrast sensitivity (CS) of many dyslexics is lower than that of controls, particularly at the low spatial and high temporal frequencies mediated by the m- system (Bednarek & Grabowska, 2002; Cornelissen, Richardson, Mason, Fowler, & Stein, 1995). Other tests of m- function involving the primary visual cortex in dyslexics that have been reported are: abnormal temporal gap detection for low contrast and low spatial frequency stimuli (Badcock & Lovegrove, 1981), reduced critical flicker frequency (Chase & Jenner, 1993; Talcott, 2003) and decreased low spatial frequency contrast sensitivity for flickering and moving stimuli (Edwards et al., 2004; Felmingham & Jakobson, 1995; Martin & Lovegrove, 1987; Mason et al., 1993);

However some studies have failed to confirm these differences. On the basis of his study with Gross-Glen of 18 adult dyslexics (Gross-Glen, Skottun, Glenn, Kushch, Lingua, Dunbar, et al., 1995) together with more than 25 reviews of others' work, Skottun has repeatedly criticised the hypothesis that dyslexics have specifically impaired m- stream processing, even though he accepts that many dyslexics have visual problems. The reading of Gross-Glen and colleagues' sample of dyslexics was actually better than normal for their age, but behind that expected from their IQ. Although they found that the dyslexics did have CS deficits when compared with good readers, these were not so marked at the low spatial frequencies that are expected to stimulate the magno- system best. Instead they were more impaired at higher ones. However Gross Glen et al. used very brief stimuli lasting only 17 or 34 ms (equivalent to temporal frequencies of 59 and 29 Hz respectively), frequencies that would preferentially stimulate the m- system. Thus Gross-Glen's results actually confirmed others' findings that if gratings are flickered at high temporal frequencies, dyslexics show lower CS than controls even at high spatial frequencies, hence that dyslexics often show m-weakness.

Williams, Stuart, Castles, and McAnally (2003) also failed to find any significant differences between dyslexics and controls at either low or high spatial frequencies. However they studied only a small number of subjects, and they chose to stimulate the m- system using a high-contrast grating at a temporal frequency of only 8 Hz. The p- system is not completely silenced at this high contrast and rate and can still respond, so large differences would not be expected, especially with such a small number of subjects.

Sperling and colleagues have suggested that dyslexics' visual problems are not the result of a magnocellular impairment, but of a failure to filter out 'visual noise' (Sperling, Lu, Manis, & Seidenberg, 2005). Clearly the source of such noise is crucial. Probably the impaired m- system in dyslexics spatially under-samples the visual world (Talcott, Assoku, & Stein, 2000a). This would leave response gaps between retinal m- cells that would clearly add noise to any visual processing, just as Sperling et al. found.

Like Gross-Glen et al. (1995) they failed to find lower contrast sensitivity in dyslexics at the low spatial frequencies which they expected of an m- impairment.

But they used stationary gratings; whereas for stationary gratings contrast sensitivity is not mediated by the m- system alone, even at low spatial frequencies (Merigan & Maunsell, 1990). Hence their dyslexics' surviving sensitivity to low spatial frequencies was probably mediated by the parvo system because this can signal even low spatial frequency gratings if they are stationary. In summary the great majority of studies that have specifically looked for subcortical visual m-cell deficits in dyslexics have shown that many do suffer from mild impairments, particularly at high-temporal and low-spatial frequencies.

Visual motion sensitivity

Although motion-sensitive neurons in the middle temporal visual motion area (V5/MT) do not receive their visual input exclusively from the m- system, probably 90 per cent is provided by the m- system and only 10 per cent comes from other sources. The best way of assessing the sensitivity of these MT neurons in individuals is to measure their responses to visual motion in 'random dot kinematograms' (RDKs). Clouds of dots moving in the same direction, 'coherently', are progressively diluted with noise dots moving in random directions until the subject can no longer detect any coherent motion in the display. This threshold therefore defines that individual's motion (visual dorsal stream) sensitivity. Several researchers have shown that this is reduced in many dyslexics (Cornelissen et al., 1995; Downie et al., 2003; Hill & Raymond, 2002; Samar et al., 2002; Talcott, Witton, McLean, Hansen, Rees, Green, et al., 2000b). Over the whole range of reading abilities from good readers to dyslexics, the lower a person's motion sensitivity the lower their reading ability (Talcott et al., 2000b). Other work has shown reduced velocity discrimination (Demb et al., 1998; Eden et al., 1996) and elevated speed thresholds for motion-defined form (Felmingham & Jakobson, 1995).

However some people with low motion sensitivity are still better readers than dyslexics (Skoyles & Skottun, 2004). Nevertheless even their reading is worse than those with high motion sensitivity. Individual differences in motion sensitivity explain over 25 per cent of the variance over the whole range of reading ability from good to bad (Talcott et al., 2000b). In other words, individuals' dorsal stream performance dominated by m- cell input plays an important part in determining how well their visual reading skills develop, and this is true of everybody, not just dyslexics.

Higher-level dorsal stream tasks

The posterior parietal cortex (PPC) receives its main visual input from the dorsal stream V5/MT; this input plays a crucial role in its functions of guiding visual attention, eye and limb movements (Vidyasagar, 2004). Dyslexics have been found to be worse than good readers at cueing visual attention (Facoetti, Turatto, Lorusso, & Mascetti, 2001; Kinsey, Rose, Hansen, Richardson, & Stein, 2004), visual search (Iles, Walsh, & Richardson, 2000; Facoetti, Paganoni, & Lorusso, 2000), visual short term 'retain and compare' memory (Ben-Yehudah, Sackett, Malchi-Ginzberg, & Ahissar, 2001) and attentional grouping in the Ternus test

(Cestnick & Coltheart, 1999). These findings again suggest that their dorsal stream function is impaired.

Since none of these tests stimulates the peripheral magnocellular system entirely selectively, taken by themselves these results do not prove that impaired magnocellular function is responsible (Skottun, 2001). Nevertheless, as the dorsal stream receives mainly m- input and it is composed of CAT 301 neurones, it is dominated by the magnocelluar system. Moreover many of the studies mentioned above incorporated control tests for parvo function, such as visual acuity and colour discrimination, and dyslexics usually proved to be as good or better at these. This suggests that their poor performance can be mainly attributed to m-system weakness even in the presence of robust parvocellular function (Fukushima, Tanaka, Williams, & Fukushima, 2005; Skoyles & Skottun, 2004).

Eye movement control by the dorsal stream

Normally the dorsal stream not only directs visual attention to a target but also redirects the eyes towards it. Hence numerous studies have found not only that the direction of visual attention is disturbed in dyslexics (Vidyasagar, 2004), but also that their eye control during reading is abnormal. This is generally accepted. But these abnormalities are often ascribed to the subject not understanding the text, rather than themselves helping to cause the reading problems. Yet poor eye control has also been demonstrated in several non-reading situations, by tests in children of fixation stability (Fischer, Hartnegg, & Mokler, 2000), smooth pursuit and saccadic control (Crawford & Higham, 2001). In one study however, although the dyslexics did display abnormal eye movements, these were not significantly associated with worse dorsal stream function as measured by coherent motion detection; but the number of dyslexics studied was very small (Hawelka & Wimmer, 2005).

Event-related potentials

Recording averaged EEG potentials in response to a moving, low-contrast visual target provides a more objective measure of cortical dorsal stream processing than psychophysical techniques. Of recent visual event-related potential (ERP) studies in dyslexics the great majority have either confirmed Livingstone et al.'s (1991) original observation that dyslexics have weaker responses to moving, low-contrast, targets than good readers (Kuba, Szanyi, Gayer, Kremlacek, & Kubova, 2001), or they have found that dyslexics show slower, smaller and spatially abnormal focused visual attentional ERP responses in line with the psychophysical results. Only one study with small numbers found no sensory or attentional abnormalities (Robichon, Besson, & Habib, 2002).

Visual treatments

The main purpose of trying to understand the mechanisms causing dyslexics to have reading problems is to develop rational means of helping them.

Although evidence that a particular technique works cannot usually be taken as evidence that the theory underlying it is necessarily correct, it does provide circumstantial evidence in its favour. Although there is a plethora of claims about visual treatments that help dyslexics to learn to read better, very few have been rigorously designed or properly controlled for placebo effects. The very fact that somebody is taking notice of their reading problems is often sufficient for children to try harder, to focus their attention more effectively and to feel better about themselves. So their reading may improve even if the treatment has no specific effect at all. Such placebo effects should not be denigrated; whatever their cause, any improvements should be welcomed. However they do not justify charging large sums for the treatment, as is often the case, and to be plausible they need to have a defensible rationale.

Here, therefore, I will only consider some techniques that have a rationale that is relevant to the magnocellular theory and that have been subjected to appropriate controls. In 1985 we published the results of a double-blind randomised controlled trial of monocular occlusion when reading (Stein & Fowler, 1985). We studied children with significant reading difficulties who also had unstable binocular control measured using a standard orthoptic test. Randomly selected children were given either spectacles with the left lens occluded with opaque tape or placebo clear plano spectacles. Those receiving the occlusion were more likely to achieve stable binocular control. If they did so they improved their reading highly significantly more than those receiving placebo who did not achieve stable control. Although this was not a double-blind trial because the children worked out pretty quickly that the placebo lenses were plano, nevertheless those who received the occluded lenses and did not achieve binocular stability served as additional controls for a placebo effect. Their reading improved no better than those who received the plano spectacles. In 2000, we repeated this study using pale yellow spectacles as the placebo and obtained similar results (Stein, Richardson, & Fowler, 2000). We argued that dyslexics' binocular instability was due to a significant visual magnocellular deficit, and that occluding the left eye when reading helped the ocular motor control system to overcome this deficit to achieve more stable fixation.

Yellow filters are often used by skiers to improve contrast under white-out conditions. We had noticed that the response to pale yellow filters in 2000 was considerably greater than the placebo response to plano clear lenses in 1985. We also found that we could improve amblyopia in some children using deep yellow filters (Fowler, Mason, Richardson, & Stein, 1991). We argued that all these effects were because yellow filters specifically stimulate the magnocellular system. This is because although the m- ganglion cells do not contribute to conscious colour vision, nevertheless they receive mainly from the long (red) and medium wavelength (green) cones, so that they are activated maximally by yellow light. Therefore we tested whether deep yellow filters designed to maximally activate m- cells, might be even more effective in improving m- cell function and reading in children with visual reading difficulties. In a double-blind randomised controlled trial we showed that this was indeed the case (Ray,

Fowler, & Stein, 2005). Those who received the yellow filters improved their m- responses, as indexed by their sensitivity to visual motion in random dot kinematograms, and this improvement was accompanied by improved single word reading. We have since confirmed that the yellow filters actually do increase the amount of long wavelength light falling on the retina because the pupil dilates significantly, hence m-cells are stimulated more,.

Serendipitously we also observed that some children benefited from wearing deep blue filters. We were mystified by this until we heard about a new class of intrinsically photosensitive retinal ganglion cells (IPRGCs) containing the blue sensitive pigment melanopsin (Hankins, Peirson, & Foster, 2008). These cells project, not to the conscious retinogeniculate visual system, but to the hypothalamus. Their function there is to synchronise the body's internal clock in the hypothalamic suprachiasmatic nucleus (SCN) to seasonally varying day length. We wake up earlier in the summer because the IPRGCs signal the amount of blue light entering the eye, which is maximal in the morning. The SCN activates the dorsal 'where' visual pathway and its magnocells specifically during arousal. Hence when we give children blue filters we facilitate the dorsal visual route and help the children to focus their attention and eye movements more reliably. Accordingly we have recently confirmed in another double-blind randomised control trial that some children with visual reading problems benefit significantly more from wearing blue filters than yellow.

Improving the synchronisation of diurnal rhythms appears to have other benefits as well. Many of the children with visual reading difficulties who benefited from using blue filters have disturbed sleep patterns, as might be expected because their diurnal rhythm control is impaired. Accordingly we found that not only did their reading improve with the blue filters, but also their sleeping. Likewise many of these children complain of headaches when they try to read. Migraine headaches are known to be accompanied by disturbed sleep rhythms. Hence we now have many anecdotal reports that successful treatment of reading difficulties with blue filters is also accompanied by fewer headaches, and we are now following this up more systematically.

There are now many commercial companies selling ranges of coloured filters for reading problems with the claim that each person needs an individually prescribed colour for best effect; hence using only yellow and blue is said to fail to meet individual requirements. In a study by Wilkins 68 children viewed text illuminated by coloured light in an apparatus that allowed the separate manipulation of hue (colour) and saturation (depth of colour), at constant luminance, and were asked which colour improved their reading of the text most. A pair of plastic spectacle lenses was then dyed so as to provide the chosen chromaticity under conventional white (F3) fluorescent light for each child. A placebo pair was also made that looked a similar colour but had a chromaticity outside the range which they had reported to improve their reading. Each pair was worn for 1 month. The children kept diaries recording any visual symptoms; but only 36 (53 per cent) were completed. As many as 31 (46 per cent) of the children dropped out of the study altogether, presumably because they found that the glasses did not help them at all. Of those who did complete the study however, slightly more reported reduction of symptoms of eye-strain and headache when the light had the chromaticity they had chosen, which was different for each individual. Thus symptoms were indeed slightly less frequent on days when the correct lenses had been worn but the difference was small and there is no evidence that simple yellow and blue would not have been equally or more efficacious. It was notable that most of the chromaticities chosen clustered around yellow or blue (Wilkins, Evans, Brown, Busby, Wingfield, Jeanes, et al., 1994).

Thus the evidence for requiring a large range of filter colours is slight; the individual colours chosen usually cluster around yellow and blue and if the m- theory outlined here is correct, only yellow and blue should suffice. In an as-yet unpublished head-to-head study comparing our Oxford blue and yellow filters with one company's much wider range, our Oxford filters actually achieved superior results.

In summary there are now a fair number of clinical trials showing that visual treatments derived from the visual magnocellular theory of reading problems have produced worthwhile improvements in children's reading. These will remain controversial until many more and larger, properly controlled, trials have been carried out. But they are at least consistent with the m- theory.

Auditory transient processing

Although we do it without thinking, identifying and ordering the sequences of sounds that make up speech is as difficult as sequencing letters visually. All doctors in training know this when they try to distinguish systolic from diastolic heart murmurs. For the novice whether a murmur comes before or after the second heart sound is very difficult to decide, and these events are far slower than in average speech. Analysis of sound sequences depends on being able to accurately detect changes in sound frequency and amplitude; these are what convey information in speech. Like the visual m- system this tracking of auditory transients in real time is mediated by a set of large auditory neurones specialised for rapid temporal processing that may be likened to m- cells; they also express the surface signature molecule CAT 301. These contrast with the smaller auditory neurones that are important for identifying different mixtures of frequencies, such as chords, by their spectral composition. These neurones work less rapidly, like visual parvo cells. Thus there are auditory equivalents to the visual m- and p- systems. Likewise there are analogous dorsal 'where' and ventral 'what' cortical streams projecting from the primary auditory cortex. However at no stage are they entirely separate; so they are not named magnocellular and parvocellular, as in the visual system (Rauschecker & Tian, 2000).

Paula Tallal was the first to suggest that developmental dysphasics may be poor at the auditory temporal processing that is mediated by this auditory equivalent of the visual m- pathways (Tallal & Piercy, 1973). We began testing dyslexic children's ability to detect simple amplitude or frequency changes to see whether they might have impaired sensitivity to sound amplitude and frequency transients (McAnally & Stein, 1996; Menell, McAnally, & Stein, 1999; Stein & McAnally, 1996, 1995). The dyslexics did display lower sensitivity to amplitude or frequency modulations of a 500-Hz carrier, up to modulation frequencies of 40 Hz. Above this rate there were no significant differences between dyslexics and controls, probably because the auditory system can no longer follow these high rates in real time. Instead the percept becomes qualitatively different; instead of hearing individual modulations we hear a single chord. Perception of these sounds is mediated by the smaller parvo-like neurones which identify the whole spectrum generated by the high-frequency modulations.

We also found that the sensitivity of individual children, whether dyslexic or not, predicted their ability to read non-words, which is regarded as a task that particularly tests their phonological skills (Snowling, Goulandris, Bowlby, & Howell, 1986). Auditory sensitivity to frequency and amplitude modulations accounted for nearly 50 per cent of individual differences in phonological skill (Witton, Stein, Stoodley, Rosner, & Talcott, 2002). In the last 5 years there have been over 100 studies testing basic auditory processing capabilities in dyslexics. Most have confirmed our finding that at least some dyslexics have auditory processing deficits (Banai, Nicol, Zecker, & Kraus, 2005; Boets, Wouters, van Wieringen, & Ghesquiere, 2006). These particularly involve the processing of transients in real time and their slowness and inaccuracy could help to explain dyslexics' phonological weaknesses.

Again however, there are wide discrepancies in the prevalences claimed, ranging from 10 to 70 per cent. Current psychophysical tests may not be sensitive enough to reveal the mild auditory deficits that may nevertheless cause reading problems. So it is still argued that there can be higher level phonological problems without any evidence of lower level auditory temporal processing impairments. However using a mismatch negativity paradigm, we were able to show that even when we could not demonstrate a deficit psychophysiologically, we could show a degree of low-level auditory processing impairment that correlates with subjects' phonological problems (Stoodley, Hill, Stein, & Bishop, 2006).

In general, ERP studies of auditory processing in dyslexics have proved more sensitive than psychophysical ones, and most people would now accept that dyslexics with phonological problems have some degree of underlying impaired low-level auditory processing of transient stimuli that helps to explain their phonological deficit.

Auditory magnocellular system?

This low-level auditory processing deficit may be the result of impaired development of large m- like neurones in the auditory brainstem; these mediate the processing of frequency and amplitude modulations in real time. In dyslexics poor visual magnocellular function is often accompanied by poor auditory temporal processing(Talcott et al., 2000b). As we have seen, these large neurones in the auditory system specialised for tracking frequency and amplitude transients can be termed magnocells because, like visual magnocells, they are recognised by m-specific antibodies, such as CAT 301 (Lurie, Pasic, Hockfield, & Rubel, 1997).

The development of these auditory m- like cells may be impaired in many dyslexics. In the dyslexic brains studied by Galaburda and colleagues, magnocellular neurones in the left thalamic auditory medial geniculate nucleus (MGN), like those in the dyslexic LGN, were found to be smaller (Galaburda, Menard, & Rosen, 1994). Impaired development of large m- like cells in the auditory system might therefore underlie dyslexics' problems with acquiring good phonological skills.

Since not all dyslexics who show phonological problems can be shown to have either auditory or visual weaknesses, these cannot be considered either necessary or sufficient to cause dyslexia. Some have argued from this that they cannot be considered causal at all (Ramus, Rosen, Dakin, Day, Castellote, White, & Frith, 2003). But this is like saying that because smoking is neither necessary nor sufficient to cause lung cancer, it can never cause it – patently false. The probability is that impaired auditory and visual temporal processing are important, but not the only, causes of impaired phonological processing.

Cutaneous sensation

The dorsal column division of the cutaneous sensory system is in many ways analogous to the dorsal visuomotor stream, and contains magnocellular neurones specialised for processing transients and staining for CAT 301. We therefore tested the vibration sensitivity of adult dyslexics compared with good readers. The dyslexics turned out to be significantly less sensitive to vibration at 3 Hz but showed no difference at 100 Hz (Stoodley, Talcott, Carter, Witton, & Stein, 2000). Cutaneous sensory fibres can follow frequencies of 3 Hz in real time, but not at 100 Hz. Thus our result suggests that magnocellular cutaneous sensory fibres are also impaired in dyslexia. This supports the hypothesis that a generalised, multisensory deficit of m- like cells underlies the temporal processing deficits in dyslexia.

The cerebellum

The cerebellum is the brain's autopilot responsible for automatising motor skills by building up internal models to represent their execution. Since accurate timing of sensory feedback and motor outflow is an essential requirement for this function, the cerebellum receives a rich input from visual, auditory, proprioceptive and motor magnocellular systems (Eckert et al., 2005; Stein, 1986). Furthermore many precerebellar nuclear cells and cerebellar Purkinje cells stain for the magnocellular specific antigen CAT301. Accordingly there is now a great deal of evidence that cerebellar function is mildly impaired in dyslexics and related neurodevelopmental conditions such as developmental coordination disorder (dyspraxia; Fawcett, Nicolson, & Dean, 1996; Rae, Harasty, Dzendrowskyj, Talcott, Simpson, Blamire, et al., 2002; Stoodley & Stein, 2011). This provides yet further indirect evidence for magnocellular involvement in dyslexic problems (Nicolson, 2001).

Functional imaging

Although there are no functional imaging studies directly examining the role of the peripheral visual m- system in dyslexia (which would be very hard to carry out and still subject to the criticism that they are not pure m-), there have been a large number whose findings are consistent with the m- hypothesis. Thus in dyslexics the visual motion area MT/V5 has been shown to be less activated than in good readers in response to moving stimuli and it is one of the areas consistently less activated in dyslexics during reading (Eden et al., 1996). Furthermore in individuals the degree of activation of V5/MT during a visual motion task correlates with that person's reading skills (Demb et al., 1998), implying a significant association between dorsal stream function and reading.

Recently a new MRI technique (diffusion tensor imaging – DTI) has been developed for tracing connections between areas in the intact human brain. This has shown that those linking the various elements of the language network in the left hemisphere are weaker in dyslexics than in good readers (Odegard, Farris, Ring, McColl, & Black, 2009). This is consistent with their being thinner (i.e., fed by smaller m- cells). Furthermore, if a dyslexic's reading is successfully improved by training these connections appear to strengthen. This is probably not associated with increased myelination of the fibres, though this is possible, but rather by reorientation of microtubules within the fibres. This may perhaps occur after they have been experiencing heavier electrical traffic leaving a prolonged trace in DTI images, following successfully learning associations between visually identified letters, eye movements, letter sounds and word meanings.

There is a general consensus that there are three main left-sided language areas that are less activated in dyslexics than in good readers when reading. The first is on the dorsal 'where' visuomotor pathway around the left occipito-parietal-temporal junction (the supramarginal and angular gyri (Shaywitz, Shaywitz, Pugh, Fulbright, Constable, Mencl, et al., 1998). The visual input to the supramarginal and angular gyri is known to be dominated by the magnocellular system, so that relative underactivity there suggests depleted m- input in dyslexics.

The second area implicated is the visual word form area (VWFA) which lies in the ventral 'what' processing stream in the anterior part of the left fusiform gyrus on the undersurface of the occipitotemporal junction. Even though this is on the ventral 'what' identification pathway, it receives about half its input from m- cells. These probably direct the VWFA to attend to visual word features. And almost all studies agree that VWFA is underactivated when dyslexics are reading compared with controls (Shaywitz, Shaywitz, Pugh, Mencl, Fulbright, Skudlarski, et al., 2002), again consistent with reduced m- input.

The third area which is underactivate in dyslexics is in the anterior part of the left inferior frontal gyrus. In addition to receiving letter sound information from the anterior part of the temporal lobe via the uncinate fasciculus, this area is a major recipient of the visual dorsal pathway projection from the posterior parietal cortex via the arcuate fasciculus. So again its underactivity is consistent with an underactive m- system.

A general magnocellular system for temporal processing?

Large nerve cells specialised for processing rapid temporal transients are found throughout the whole of the nervous system, in the auditory and cutaneous sensory systems and in memory and motor systems (Hockfield & Sur, 1990). All of these large cells are characterised by expressing common surface antigens, recognised by CAT 301, by which they recognise each other to make functional connections. Shatz and her colleagues have shown that the development of these magnocells and their connections, at least in the visual system and the hippocampus, is regulated by the major histocompatibility complex (MHC) cell recognition and immune regulation gene system (Corriveau, Huh, & Shatz, 1998). Most of the 160 MHC genes reside on the short arm of chromosome 6. When m- cells start information processing, MHC class 1 proteins begin to be expressed on their surfaces, probably to help them find other m- cells to interact with. These surface signature antigens can be labelled with antibodies such as CAT 301. This is why CAT 301 staining can be used to identify magnocellular neurones throughout the nervous system.

If neurones do not make useful connections during development they are eliminated by the process of apoptosis, summed up in the epithet 'use it or lose it'; 90 per cent of all the neurones generated in the germinal zones are eliminated in this way during the assembly of functional processing networks during development.

The surface signatures on neurones are not only important to recognise each other and make functional connections, but also to label them as 'self' so that microglia scavenging cells recognise them and do not to attempt to destroy them as foreign invaders. Magnocells seem to be particularly vulnerable to each of the three genetic, immunological and other general environmental causes of damage. They appear to be selectively impaired in prematurity, birth hypoxia, malnutrition, autoimmune diseases and in most neurodevelopmental conditions, not only dyslexia, but also dyspraxia, dysphasia, dyscalculia, ADHD and the autistic spectrum of diseases (ASD).

As we have seen, individuals' visual and auditory transient sensitivity tend to correlate with each other. This together with their common surface antigen, CAT 301, suggest that they both might be under the same genetic and other kinds of neurodevelopmental control. Therefore one can speculate that perhaps all the visual, auditory, memory and motor temporal processing impairments that are seen in dyslexics may be due to underlying weak development of this generalied, CNS-wide, pansensory, transient processing, magnocellular system (Hari & Renvall, 2001; Stein, 2001). This impairment might idiosyncratically affect different individuals more in one system than another, so that one dyslexic might suffer mainly visual problems, whereas another may have mainly auditory difficulties, and yet a third mainly motor symptoms; he would then be termed 'dyspraxic'.

One can take this idea a stage further. Ramus showed in a small group of well-compensated undergraduate dyslexics that only a few of them had demonstrable auditory, visual or motor problems, whereas despite their compensation most could still be shown to have residual phonological difficulties (Ramus et al., 2003). So he attributed the latter to a higher level developmental abnormality, perhaps in the angular gyrus (Ramus, 2004). Since the angular gyrus is an important node in the m- cell dominated dorsal visuomotor stream; clearly this impairment might also involve impaired higher level 'magnocellular' connections.

Opposition to the magnocellular theory

The great critic of the view that impaired visual magnocellular development may contribute to visual dyslexic problems is Brent Skottun. In 25 papers so far, mainly criticising others' work, he points out that it is difficult selectively to activate only visual magnocells, and that it is impossible in the cortex to record responses either psychophysiologically or physiologically that are not to some extent contaminated by parvocellular input. However parvo- influences can be made very small because dorsal 'where' pathway responses are dominated by their visual magnocellular input. Skottun claims that of the papers that use selective magnocellular stimuli to test dyslexics' m- sensitivity, there are more that fail to find such a selective deficit than to show it. Nevertheless of the experimental studies in which stimuli have been used that mainly excite m- cells, 90 per cent have shown some degree of impairment in dyslexia.

Note that even Skottun is not claiming that dyslexics do not suffer a visual deficit, but merely that it has not been clearly shown to be dependent upon impaired peripheral visual magnocellular processing. He suggests that the visual deficit can affect both parvocellular and magnocellular systems and that it may be attributed to deficiencies in visual attention. However since the evidence is now overwhelming that the magnocellular system dominates both bottom-up capture of visual attention by strong visual features and also top-down orientation of visual attention that is mediated by back projections of the dorsal stream, this still leaves the major visual deficit in dyslexia attributable to a magnocellular deficit (Vidyasagar & Pammer, 2010).

There has been little opposition to or comment on the extension of the magnocellular theory to all kinds of temporal processing that is proposed here. CAT 301-staining magno cells have been shown to permeate the whole central nervous system. They have been shown to be specialised for processing transients in real time ('temporal processing') in both the visual and auditory systems, and they certainly contribute to it in the cerebellum. There is evidence that their development is impaired in the visual and auditory systems in at least some dyslexics and in other neurodevelopmental conditions as well. Furthermore there is a gradually emerging consensus that dyslexia is indeed associated with general temporal processing deficits. Final confirmation or refutation of the general magnocellular theory will only come when the genetic mechanisms controlling the development and specialisation of magno cells are fully understood. In the meantime the evidence will remain tentative and circumstantial. In complex systems like this there is rarely one piece of evidence that is conclusive; rather observations pile on each other until finally everyone is convinced one way or the other, and then it's obvious!

Causes of m- cell impairment

Of course the really interesting question is why dyslexics may have impaired development of these magnocellular systems at all. There are three main interacting factors: genetic, immunological and nutritional. We have already considered the first two. This leaves nutrition.

Nutrition – omega 3 fish oils

Another chromosomal site that showed very strong linkage to reading difficulties in our Oxford and Colorado samples of dyslexic families was on chromosome 18 (18p11.2), very close to the melanocortin receptor 5 gene (MCR5), although this receptor is not strongly expressed in the brain. So far we do not have any direct evidence as to how this gene may be involved in dyslexia. But we do know that this gene is involved in appetite control, in particular affecting the metabolism of omega 3 essential fatty acids. The same site (18p11.2) has been implicated in bipolar depression susceptibility (Berrettini, Ferraro, Goldin, Weeks, Detera-Wadleigh, Nurnberger, et al., 1994).

The possible role of this gene in the metabolism of omega 3 long-chain poly-unsaturated fatty acids (LCPUFAs) derived from fish oils is particularly interesting because a single LCPUFA, docosahexanoic acid (DHA), makes up 20 per cent of all neuronal membranes. This 22-carbon molecule has just the right properties to contribute appropriate flexibility together with the correct membrane electrostatic profile to neuronal membranes, in order for their ionic channels, which underlie their electrical responses, to open and close rapidly. As such it has been conserved in eukaryotic membranes throughout evolution since the Cambrian explosion 600 million years ago. There are cogent reasons for believing that, evolving near water, our ready access to this molecule from eating fish, explains how our brains came to be so much larger in relation to our body size than is the case in other mammals. DHA seems to be particularly important for proper magnocellular neuronal function because it's kinky structure prevents the lipid molecules in the membrane from packing together too tightly which would make it too stiff.

But DHA is continuously leached out of the membrane by phospholipases because it also forms the basis of many prostaglandin-, leucotriene- and inter-leukin-signalling molecules. Likewise another LCPUFA, eicosapentanoic acid (EPA), is the substrate for eicosanoid-signalling molecules, such as prostaglandins, leucotrienes and resolvins. They all tend to be anti-inflammatory. Magnocells are known to be extremely vulnerable to lack of these LCPUFAs that are derived from oily fish.

Our modern Western diet is dreadful however, with too much of the 'three S's': salt, sugar and saturated fat, and far too little oily fish, fat-soluble vitamins or minerals; hence a high proportion of the population, particularly from deprived households, is dangerously deficient in these essential nutrients. In randomised controlled trials we were able to show that simply giving deprived children supplement capsules containing EPA and DHA from oily fish could improve their visual magnocellular function. Hence the children's ability to focus their attention improved and their reading benefited greatly (Richardson & Montgomery, 2005).

Conclusion

The genetic, developmental, nutritional, neuroanatomical, physiological, and psychophysiological evidence reviewed here all support the view that dyslexics' fundamental phonological reading problems may be due to mild, but pervasive, impaired development of magnocellular systems throughout the brain. However definitive proof of this will only come when we have fully worked out how genetic and environmental influences determine the development and later function of these cells.

- Currently dyslexia is viewed by the majority of researchers as due to inability to deconstruct word sounds into their constituent phonemes to match with letters, that is, as a phonological problem.
- Why dyslexics suffer these phonological problems is a far more interesting question. It can be addressed at a variety of levels: genetic, developmental, neuroanatomical, physiological, and psychophysiological.
- There is evidence at all these levels which supports the view that dyslexics' fundamental phonological reading problems may be due to mild but pervasive impaired development of magnocellular neurones throughout the brain, but particularly in the visual and auditory systems.
- The main function of magnocellular neurones is to track changes in real time, so their efficient operation is crucial for reading because they stabilise vision for identifying letter features and for sequencing the letters. They are also essential for the discrimination and accurate sequencing of speech sounds that underlies acquisition of phonological skills.

Acknowledgments

Thanks to my numerous students and colleagues who did most of the work and most of whose names are referenced here. Thanks to my funders over the years:

the MRC, the Norman Collisson, Esmee Fairbairn, Wellcome, Garfield Weston and Dyslexia Research Trusts.

References

Badcock, D. & Lovegrove, W. (1981). The effects of contrast, stimulus duration, and spatial frequency on visible persistence in normal and specifically disabled readers. *Journal of Experimental Psychology: Human Perception and Performance, 7*, 495–505.

Banai, K., Nicol, T., Zecker, S. G., & Kraus, N. (2005). Brainstem timing: Implications for cortical processing and literacy. *Journal of Neuroscience, 25*, 9850–9857.

Bednarek, D. B. & Grabowska, A. (2002). Luminance and chromatic contrast sensitivity in dyslexia: the magnocellular deficit hypothesis revisited. *Neuroreport, 13*, 2521–2525.

Ben-Yehudah, G., Sackett, E., Malchi-Ginzberg, L., & Ahissar, M. (2001). Impaired temporal contrast sensitivity in dyslexics is specific to retain-and-compare paradigms. *Brain, 124*, 1381–1395.

Berrettini, W. H., Ferraro, T. N., Goldin, L. R., Weeks, D. E., Detera-Wadleigh, S., Nurnberger, J. I., Jr., and Gershon, E. S. (1994). Chromosome 18 DNA markers and manic-depressive illness: Evidence for a susceptibility gene. *Proceedings of the National Academy of Sciences of the United States of America, 91*, 5918–5921.

Boets, B., Wouters, J., van Wieringen, A., & Ghesquiere, P. (2006). Auditory temporal information processing in preschool children at family risk for dyslexia: Relations with phonological abilities and developing literacy skills. *Brain and Language, 97*, 64–79.

Cestnick, L. & Coltheart, M. (1999). The relationship between language-processing and visual-processing deficits in developmental dyslexia. *Cognition, 71*, 231–255.

Chase, C. & Jenner, A. R. (1993). Magnocellular visual deficits affect temporal processing of dyslexics. *Annals of the New York Academy of Sciences, 682*, 326–329.

Cheng, A., Eysel, U., & Vidyasagar, T. (2004). The role of the magnocellular pathway in serial deployment of visual attention. *European Journal of Neuroscience, 20*, 2188–2192.

Chomsky, N. (1975). *Reflections on language.* New York: Pantheon.

Cohen, L. & Dehaene, S. (2004). Specialization within the ventral stream: The case for the visual word form area. *Neuroimage, 22*, 466–476.

Cornelissen, P., Richardson, A., Mason, A., Fowler, S., & Stein, J. (1995). Contrast sensitivity and coherent motion detection measured at photopic luminance levels in dyslexics and controls. *Vision Research, 35*, 1483–1494.

Corriveau, R., Huh, G., & Shatz, C. (1998). Regulation of Class 1 MHC gene expression in the developing and mature CNS by neural activity. *Neuron, 21*, 505–520.

Crawford, T. & Higham, S. (2001). Dyslexia and centre of gravity effect. *Experimental Brain Research, 137*, 122–126.

Dehaene, S. (2010). *Reading in the brain: The science and evolution of a human invention.* New York: Viking.

Demb, J. B., Boynton, G. M., Best, M., & Heeger, D. J. (1998). Psychophysical evidence for a magnocellular pathway deficit in dyslexia. *Vision Research, 38*(11), 1555–1559.

Downie, A. L., Jakobson, L. S., Frisk V., & Ushycky, I. (2003). Periventricular brain injury, visual motion processing, and reading and spelling abilities in children who were extremely low birthweight. *Journal of the International Neuropsychological Society, 9*(3), 440–449.

Eckert, M., Leonard C. M., Wilke, M., Eckert, M., Richards, T., Richards, A., & Berninger, V. (2005). Anatomical signatures of dyslexia in children: Unique information from manual and voxel based morphometry brain measures. *Cortex, 41*, 304–315.

Edwards, V. T., Giaschi, D. E., Dougherty, R. F., Edgell, D., Bjornson, B. H., Lyons, C., & Douglas, R. M. (2004). Psychophysical Indexes of Temporal Processing Abnormalities in Children With Developmental Dyslexia. *Developmental Neuropsychology, 25*(3), 321–354.

Eden, G. F., VanMeter, J. W., Rumsey, J. M., Maisog, J. M., Woods, R. P., & Zeffiro, T. A. (1996). Abnormal processing of visual motion in dyslexia revealed by functional brain imaging. *Nature, 382*(6586), 66–69.

Facoetti, A., Paganoni, P., & Lorusso, M. L. (2000). The spatial distribution of visual attention in developmental dyslexia. *Experimental Brain Research, 132*, 531–538.

Facoetti, A., Turatto, M., Lorusso, M., & Mascetti, G. (2001). Orienting visual attention in dyslexia. *Experimental Brain Research, 138*, 46–53.

Fawcett, A. J., Nicolson, R. I., & Dean, P. (1996). Impaired performance of children with dyslexia on a range of cerebellar tasks. *Annals of Dyslexia, 46*, 259–283.

Felmingham, K. L. & Jakobson, L. S. (1995). Visual and visuomotor performance in dyslexic children. *Experimental Brain Research, 106*, 467–474.

Fischer, B., Hartnegg, K., & Mokler, A. (2000). Dynamic visual perception of dyslexic children. *Perception, 29*, 523–530.

Fowler, M. S., Mason, A. J., Richardson, A., & Stein, J. F. (1991). Yellow spectacles to improve vision in children with binocular amblyopia. *Lancet, 338*, 1109–1110.

Fukushima, J., Tanaka, S., Williams, J., & Fukushima, K. (2005). Voluntary control of saccadic and smooth-pursuit eye movements in children with learning disorders. *Brain and Development, 27*, 579–588.

Galaburda, A., Sherman, G. F., Rosen, G. D., Aboitiz, F., & Geschwind, N. (1985). Developmental dyslexia: Four consecutive patients with cortical anomalies. *Annals of Neurology, 18*, 222–233.

Galaburda, A. M., Menard, M. T., & Rosen, G. D. (1994). Evidence for aberrant auditory anatomy in developmental dyslexia. *Proceedings of the National Academy of Sciences of the United States of America, 91*, 8010–8013.

Galaburda, A. M., LoTurco, J., Ramus, F., Fitch, R. H., & Rosen, G. D. (2006). From genes to behavior in developmental dyslexia. *Nature Neuroscience, 9*, 1213–1217.

Goodale, M. A. & Milner, A. D. (1992). Separate visual pathways for perception and action. *Trends in Neurosciences, 15*, 20.

Gross-Glen, K., Skottun, B. C., Glenn, W., Kushch, A., Lingua, R., Dunbar, M., Jallad, B., Lubs, H. A., Levin, B., Rabin, M., et al. (1995). Contrast sensitivity in dyslexia. *Visual Neuroscience, 12*, 153–163.

Hankins, M. W., Peirson, S. N., & Foster, R. G. (2008). Melanopsin: an exciting photopigment. *Trends in Neurosciences, 31*, 27–36.

Hari, R. & Renvall, H. (2001). Impaired processing of rapid stimulus sequences in dyslexia. *Trends in Cognitive Sciences, 5*, 525–532.

Hawelka, S. & Wimmer, H. (2005). Impaired visual processing of multi-element arrays is associated with increased number of eye movements in dyslexic reading. *Vision Research, 45*, 855–863.

Hockfield, S. & Sur, M. (1990). Monoclonal Cat-301 identifies Y cells in cat LGN. *Journal of Comparative Neurology, 300*, 320–330.

Hugdahl, K., Synnevag, B., & Satz, P. (1990). Immune and autoimmune diseases in dyslexic children. *Neuropsychologia, 28*, 673–679. [Published erratum appears in *Neuropsychologia* (1991) *29*, 211.]

Iles, J., Walsh, V., & Richardson, A. (2000). Visual search performance in dyslexia. *Dyslexia, 6*, 163–177.

Kinsey, K., Rose, M., Hansen, P., Richardson, A., & Stein, J. (2004). Magnocellular mediated visual-spatial attention and reading ability. *Neuroreport, 15*, 2215–2218.

Kuba, M., Szanyi, J., Gayer, D., Kremlacek, J., & Kubova, Z. (2001). Electrophysiological testing of dyslexia. *Acta Medica (Hradec Kralove), 44*, 131–134.

Lahita, R. G. (1988). Systemic lupus erythematosus: Learning disability in the male offspring of female patients and relationship to laterality. *Psychoneuroendocrinology, 13*, 385–396.

Livingstone, M. S., Rosen, G. D., Drislane, F. W., & Galaburda, A. M. (1991). Physiological and anatomical evidence for a magnocellular deficit in developmental dyslexia. *Proceedings of the the National Academy of Sciences of the United States of America, 88*, 7943–7947.

Lovegrove, W. J., Bowling, A., Badcock, D., & Blackwood, M. (1980). Specific reading disability: Differences in contrast sensitivity as a function of spatial frequency. *Science, 210*, 439–440.

Lurie, D. I., Pasic, T. R., Hockfield, S. J., & Rubel, E. W. (1997). Development of CAT-301 immunoreactivity in auditory brainstem nuclei of the gerbil. *Journal of Comparative Neurology, 380*, 319–334.

McAnally, K. I. & Stein, J. F. (1996). Auditory temporal coding in dyslexia. *Proceedings of the Royal Society of London Series B-Biological Sciences, 263*, 961–965.

Maddess, T., Goldberg, I., Dobinson, J., Wine, S., Welsh, A.-H., & James, A.-C. (1999). Testing for glaucoma with the spatial frequency doubling illusion. *Vision Research, 39*, 4258–4273.

Manis, F., McBride-Chang, C., Seidenberg, M., Doi, L., & Petersen, A. (1997). On the bases of two subtypes of developmental dyslexia. *Cognition, 58*, 157–195.

Martin, F. & Lovegrove, W. (1987). Flicker contrast sensitivity in normal and specifically disabled readers. *Perception, 16*(2), 215–221.

Mason, A., Cornelissen, P., Fowler, S., & Stein, J. (1993). Contrast sensitivity, ocular dominance and specific reading disability. *Clinical Vision Sciences, 8*(4), 345–353.

Maunsell, J. H. (1992). Functional visual streams. *Current Opinion in Neurobiology, 2*, 506–510.

Menell, P., McAnally, K., & Stein, J. (1999). Psychophysical and physiological responses to amplitude modulations in dyslexia. *Journal of Speech and Hearing Research, 42*, 797–803.

Merigan, W. H. & Maunsell, J. H. (1990). Macaque vision after magnocellular lateral geniculate lesions. *Visual Neuroscience, 5*, 347–352.

Murakami, I. & Cavanagh, P. (1998). A jitter after-effect reveals motion-based stabilization of vision. *Nature, 395*, 798–801.

Needleman, L. A., Liu, X.-B., El-Sabeawy, F., Jones, E. G., & McAllister, A. K. (2010). MHC class I molecules are present both pre- and postsynaptically in the visual cortex during postnatal development and in adulthood. *Proceedings of the National Academy of Sciences of the United States of America, 107*, 16999–17004.

Nicolson, R. (2001). Dyslexia, development and the cerebellum. *Trends in Neurosciences*, *24*, 515.

Odegard, T. N., Farris, E. A., Ring, J., McColl, R., & Black, J. (2009). Brain connectivity in non-reading impaired children and children diagnosed with developmental dyslexia. *Neuropsychologia*, *47*, 1972–1977.

Pammer, K. & Wheatley, C. (2001). Isolating the M(y)-cell response in dyslexia using the spatial frequency doubling illusion. *Vision Research*, *41*, 2139–2148.

Paracchini, S., Thomas, A., Castro, S., Lai, C., Paramasivam, M., Wang, Y., et al. (2006). The chromosome 6p22 haplotype associated with dyslexia reduces the expression of KIAA0319, a novel gene involved in neuronal migration. *Human Molecular Genetics*, *15*, 1659–1666.

Porteous, D. (2008). Genetic causality in schizophrenia and bipolar disorder: Out with the old and in with the new. *Current Opinion in Genetics & Development*, *18*, 229–234.

Rae, C., Harasty, J. A., Dzendrowskyj, T. E., Talcott, J. B., Simpson, J. M., Blamire, A. M., et al. (2002). Cerebellar morphology in developmental dyslexia. *Neuropsychologia*, *40*, 1285–1292.

Ramus, F. (2004). Neurobiology of dyslexia: A reinterpretation of the data. *Trends in Neurosciences*, *27*, 720.

Ramus, F., Rosen, S., Dakin, S. C., Day, B. L., Castellote, J. M., White, S., & Frith, U. (2003). Theories of developmental dyslexia: Insights from a multiple case study of dyslexic adults. *Brain*, *126*, 841–865.

Rauschecker, J. P. & Tian, B. (2000). Mechanisms and streams for processing of 'what' and 'where' in auditory cortex. *Proceedings of the National Academy of Sciences of the United States of America*, *97*, 11800–11806.

Ray, N. J., Fowler, S., & Stein, J. F. (2005). Yellow filters can improve magnocellular function: Motion sensitivity, convergence, accommodation, and reading. *Annals of the New York Academy of Sciences*, *1039*, 283–293.

Richardson, A. J. & Montgomery, P. (2005). The Oxford-Durham study: a randomized, controlled trial of dietary supplementation with fatty acids in children with developmental coordination disorder. *Pediatrics*, *115*, 1360–1366.

Robichon, F., Besson, M., & Habib, M. (2002). An electrophysiological study of dyslexic and control adults in a sentence reading task. *Biological Psychology*, *59*, 29–53.

Samar, V. J., Parasnis, I., & Berent, G. P. (2002). Deaf poor readers' pattern reversal visual evoked potentials suggest magnocellular system deficits: Implications for diagnostic neuroimaging of dyslexia in deaf individuals. *Brain and Language*, *80*(1), 21–44.

Shatz, C. J. (2009). MHC Class I: An Unexpected Role in Neuronal Plasticity. *Neuron*, *64*(1), 40–45.

Singleton, C. & Henderson, L. M. (2007). Computerized screening for visual stress in children with dyslexia. *Dyslexia*, *13*(2), 130–151.

Stein, J. F. (1986). Role of the cerebellum in the visual guidance of movement. *Nature*, *323*(6085), 217–221.

Stein, J. F. & McAnally, K. (1995). Auditory temporal processing in developmental dyslexics. *Irish Journal of Psychology*, *16*(3), 220–228.

Shaywitz, S., Shaywitz, B., Pugh, K., Fulbright, R., Constable, R., Mencl, W., et al. (1998). Functional disruption in the organization of the brain for reading in dyslexia. *Proceedings of the National Academy of Sciences of the United States of America*, *95*, 2636–2641.

Shaywitz, B. A., Shaywitz, S. E., Pugh, K. R., Mencl, W. E., Fulbright, R. K., Skudlarski, P., et al. (2002). Disruption of posterior brain systems for reading in children with developmental dyslexia. *Biological Psychiatry, 52,* 101–110.

Skottun, B. C. (1997). The magnocellular deficit theory of dyslexia. *Trends in Neurosciences, 20,* 397–398.

Skottun, B. C. (2001). On the use of the Ternus test to assess magnocellular function. *Perception, 30,* 1449–1457.

Skoyles, J. & Skottun, B. C. (2004). On the prevalence of magnocellular deficits in the visual system of non-dyslexic individuals. *Brain and Language, 88,* 79–82.

Snowling, M. (2000). *Dyslexia* (2nd Edn). Oxford: Blackwell.

Snowling, M., Goulandris, N., Bowlby, M., & Howell, P. (1986). Segmentation and speech perception in relation to reading skill: A developmental analysis. *Journal of Experimental Child Psychology, 41,* 489–507.

Sperling, A. J., Lu, Z.-L., Manis, F. R., & Seidenberg, M. S. (2005). Deficits in perceptual noise exclusion in developmental dyslexia. *Nature Neuroscience, 8,* 862–863.

Stein, J. (1992). The representation of egocentric space in the posterior parietal cortex. *Behavioral and Brain Sciences, 15,* 691–700.

Stein, J. (2001). The magnocellular theory of developmental dyslexia. *Dyslexia, 7,* 12–36.

Stein, J. F. & Fowler, S. (1981). Visual dyslexia. *Trends in Neuroscience, 4,* 77–80.

Stein, J. & Fowler, S. (1985). Effect of monocular occlusion on visuomotor perception and reading in dyslexic children. *Lancet, 2*(8446), 69–73.

Stein, J. & Fowler, S. (2005). Treatment of visual problems in children with reading difficulties. *PATOSS (Professional Association of Teachers in Special Situations) Bulletin, May,* 15–22.

Stein, J. & McAnally, K. (1996). Impaired auditory temporal processing in dyslexics. *Irish Journal of Psychology, 16,* 220–228.

Stein, J. F., Richardson, A. J., & Fowler, M. S. (2000). Monocular occlusion can improve binocular control and reading in dyslexics. *Brain, 123,* 164–170.

Stoodley, C. & Stein, J. (2011). The cerebellum and dyslexia. *Cortex, 47,* 101–116.

Stoodley, C. J., Talcott, J. B., Carter, E. L., Witton, C., & Stein, J. F. (2000). Selective deficits of vibrotactile sensitivity in dyslexic readers. *Neuroscience Letters, 295,* 13–16.

Stoodley, C. J., Hill, P. R., Stein, J. F., & Bishop, D. V. (2006). Auditory event-related potentials differ in dyslexics even when auditory psychophysical performance is normal. *Brain Research, 1121,* 190–199.

Talcott, J. B., Assoku, E., & Stein, J. (2000a). Visual motion sensitivity in dyslexia: evidence for temporal and motion energy integration deficits. *Neuropsychologia, 38,* 935–943.

Talcott, J. B., Witton, C., McLean, M. F., Hansen, P. C., Rees, A., Green, G. G., et al. (2000b). Dynamic sensory sensitivity and children's word decoding skills. *Proceedings of the National Academy of Sciences of the United States of America, 97,* 2952–2957.

Talcott, J. B., A. Gram, Van Ingelghem, M., Witton, C., Stein, J. F., & Toennessen, F. E. (2003). Impaired sensitivity to dynamic stimuli in poor readers of a regular orthography. *Brain and Language, 87*(2), 259–266.

Tallal, P. & Piercy, M. (1973). Defects of non-verbal auditory perception in children with developmental aphasia. *Nature, 241,* 468–469.

Turkeltaub, P., Flowers, D., Verbalis, A., Miranda, M., Gareau, L., & Eden, G. (2004). The neural basis of hyperlexic reading, an fMRI case study. *Neuron, 41,* 11–25.

Vidyasagar, T. R. (2004). Neural underpinnings of dyslexia as a disorder of visuo-spatial attention. *Clinical and Experimental Optometry*, *87*, 4–10.

Vidyasagar, T. R. & Pammer, K. (2010). Dyslexia: A deficit in visuo-spatial attention, not in phonological processing. *Trends in Cognitive Sciences*, *14*, 57–63.

Vincent, A., Deacon, R., Dalton, P., Salmond, C., Blamire A.M., Pendlebury, S., et al. (2002). Maternal antibody mediated dyslexia? Evidence for a pathogenic serum factor in a mother of 2 dyslexic children shown by transfer to pregnant mice shown by behavioural and MRS studies. *Journal of Neuroimmunology*, *45*, 87–89.

Wadsworth, S. J., Olson, R. K., & DeFries, J. C. (2010). Differential genetic etiology of reading difficulties as a function of IQ: an update. *Behavioral Genetics*, *40*, 751–758.

Wilkins, A. J., Evans, B. J., Brown, J. A., Busby, A. E., Wingfield, A. E., Jeanes, R. J., et al. (1994). Double-masked placebo-controlled trial of precision spectral filters in children who use coloured overlays. *Ophthalmic and Physiological Optics*, *14*, 365–370.

Williams, J. & O'Donovan, M. C. (2006). The genetics of developmental dyslexia. *European Journal of Human Genetics*, *14*, 681–689.

Williams, M. J., Stuart, G. W., Castles, A., & McAnally, K. I. (2003). Contrast sensitivity in subgroups of developmental dyslexia. *Vision Research*, *43*, 467–477.

Witton, C., Stein, J. F., Stoodley, C. J., Rosner, B. S., & Talcott, J. B. (2002). Separate influences of acoustic AM and FM sensitivity on the phonological decoding skills of impaired and normal readers. *Journal of Cognitive Neuroscience*, *14*, 866–874.

Yarbus, A. L. (1965). *Role of eye movements in the visual process*. Moscow, USSR: Nauka.

Author Index

Subject Index